Politics and Society in

Sage Politics Texts

Series Editor
IAN HOLIDAY
City University of Hong Kong

SAGE Politics Texts offer authoritative and accessible analyses of core issues in contemporary political science and international relations. Each text combines a comprehensive overview of key debates and concepts with fresh and original insights. By extending across all main areas of the discipline, SAGE Politics Texts constitute a comprehensive body of contemporary analysis. They are ideal for use on advanced courses and in research.

Politics and Society
in
South Africa

A Critical Introduction

Daryl Glaser

SAGE Publications
London • Thousand Oaks • New Delhi

First published 2001

 SAGE Publications Ltd
6 Bonhill Street
London EC2A 4PU

SAGE Publications Inc.
2455 Teller Road
Thousand Oaks, California 91320

SAGE Publications India Pvt Ltd
32, M-Block Market
Greater Kailash - I
New Delhi 110 048

British Library Cataloguing in Publication data

A catalogue record for this book is available from the British Library.

ISBN 0 7619 5016 8
ISBN 0 7619 5017 6 (pbk)

Library of Congress catalog card number available

Printed in Great Britain by Athenaeum Press, Gateshead

Summary of Contents

Contents

CONTENTS

Glossary of Acronyms

AAC	All-African Convention
ANC	African National Congress
Azapo	Azanian People's Organization
BC	Black Consciousness
Codesa	Convention for a Democratic South Africa
Cosatu	Congress of South African Trade Unions
CPSA	Communist Party of South Africa
DEIC	Dutch East India Company
DP	Democratic Party
Fosatu	Federation of South African Trade Unions
HRC	Human Rights Commission
ICU	Industrial and Commercial Workers' Union
IFP	Inkatha Freedom Party
KZN	KwaZulu-Natal
MPLA	Popular Movement for the Liberation of Angola
NEUM	Non-European Unity Movement
NIC	Natal Indian Congress
NP	National Party
NNP	New National Party
NRC	Natives' Representative Council
OFS	Orange Free State
PAC	Pan-Africanist Congress
RDP	Reconstruction and Development Programme
SACP	South African Communist Party
Sactu	South African Congress of Trade Unions
SADF	South African Defence Force
SANAC	South African Native Affairs Commission
SAR	South African Republic
SWA	South West Africa (Namibia)
Swapo	South West African People's Organization
TEC	Transitional Executive Council
TRC	Truth and Reconciliation Commission
UDF	United Democratic Front
Unita	Union for the Total Independence of Angola
UP	United Party

Chronology

Millennia BC	Hunter-gatherer ancestors of San ('Bushmen') and pastoralist ancestors of Khoi ('Hottentots') inhabit Southern Africa.
Circa 200 AD	Pastoralist-cultivators, ancestors of Bantu-speaking Africans, enter region. From around 1000 AD their economy is increasingly cattle-oriented and they practise mining and metal production.
1652-1795	Dutch East India Company presides over expanding Cape Colony.
1658-1838	Formal slavery practised at the Cape Colony. Slaves imported, mainly from Indian Ocean rim, until 1808 when British ban trade.
1659-1803	European settlers conquer Khoi and San.
From 1770s	Dutch settlers begin to practise formal racial discrimination. Indigenous peoples are increasingly subject to forms of compulsory labour.
1779-1878	Warfare on the eastern Cape frontier between Europeans and Xhosa.
Late 1700s-1830s	Period of turbulence and centralization in African societies culminating in inter-African wars between 1817 and 1828.
1806-1910	British colony at the Cape. Cape granted self-government in 1872.
1836-40	Dutch-Afrikaner mass emigration from eastern Cape leads to setting up of openly racist Boer polities in northern interior (and briefly in Natal).
1836-98	Period of intermittent British and Dutch-Afrikaner warfare against African polities of east coast and northern interior. Pedi and Zulus suffer crucial

defeats at British hands in 1879. African areas annexed in stages to Britain and its colonies.

1842-1910   British establish colony of Natal. Africans in Natal, later Zululand, subjected to indirect rule. Natal obtains self-government in 1893.

1850s-1900   Period of consolidated independent Boer states in northern interior (South African Republic and Orange Free State). Transvaal briefly annexed by Britain 1877-81.

1867, 1886   Commercial exploitation of diamonds from 1867, gold from 1886, unleashes economic revolution across region.

1870s   Constitutional black protest begins in Cape.

1899-1902   British conquer Boer states, including gold-rich Transvaal, in South African War. Conquered colonies granted self-government from 1907.

1902-22   Years of intermittent white labour unrest culminate in violent 1922 strike.

1910   Union of South Africa, drawing together four colonies, becomes autonomous dominion within Empire. Its autonomy is confirmed in 1931 by Statute of Westminster. South African entry into two World Wars on British side later proves controversial amongst Afrikaners. South Africa leaves Commonwealth, becomes a republic in 1961.

1905-48   Period of *segregation* in which white rulers confine African land ownership to reserves, give whites job protection and disenfranchise Cape Africans. Culminates in Hertzog's 1936 segregationist legislation.

1912   Formation of South African Native National Congress, known as the African National Congress or ANC from 1923, marks watershed in history of black protest.

1919-31   Period of urban and rural black unrest. ICU plays leading role.

1932-74	Decades of prolonged industrial expansion.
1948-70s	Period of *apartheid*. National Party governments enforce rigid residential, economic, sexual, educational and political segregation of races and step up efforts to limit African urbanization. A programme of 'separate development' commencing in 1959 culminates in four African ethnic 'homelands' obtaining formal independence between 1976 and 1981. NP governments also pursue sectional Afrikaner interests amongst whites.
1940s-63	Period of black radicalization and mass action. The ANC and other organizations demand universal franchise. Widespread though intermittent township, industrial and rural protest. Severe state repression and resort to armed struggle by key black groups bring above-ground protest to an end.
1970s-90	Period of *reformist neo-apartheid*. White governments hesitantly dismantle aspects of apartheid. International pressure for change grows. A new constitution adopted in 1983 enfranchises coloureds and Indians. Controls on African urbanization are largely abandoned in 1986.
1972-75	African worker unrest sets off new period of open opposition. Trade union revival culminates in formation of Cosatu in 1985.
From 1974	Economy enters prolonged (still continuing) period of slower growth.
1976-77	National black rebellion led by students and Black Consciousness organizations.
1984-87	Largest uprising in twentieth-century South African history. Affects townships, educational institutions and workplaces, all regions, urban and rural areas. Pro-ANC organizations play leading role. Mass protest met by severe repression.

1986-95	Period of intense political violence associated with ANC–Inkatha feud and 'dirty war' by elements of state security forces. Early 1990s also see terrorist actions by PAC and white far right.
1990-94	White government negotiates end of minority rule. 'Interim' democratic constitution drawn up in 1993. Transitional executive sits from late 1993 to April 1994.
1994	ANC wins first racially inclusive election and Nelson Mandela becomes president. Three-party government of national unity set up. (National Party quits cabinet in 1996.)
1994-99	ANC pursues social reforms alongside economic liberalization. Corruption, crime and HIV/Aids are rife.
1997	'Final' democratic constitution becomes operative.
1999	ANC wins second democratic election. NP vote collapses. Thabo Mbeki becomes president.

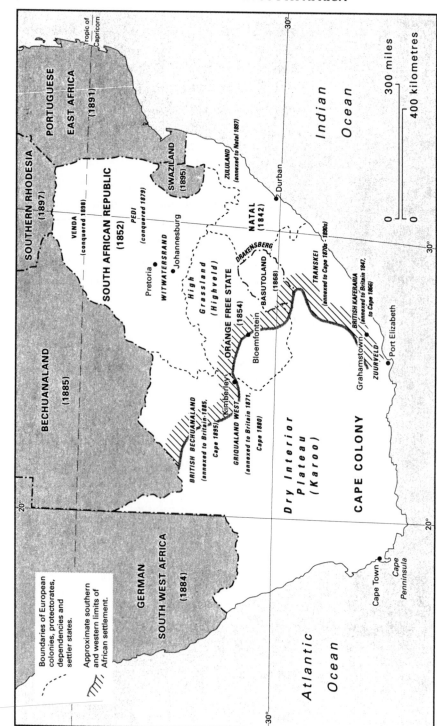

Tropic of Capricorn

PORTUGUESE EAST AFRICA (1891)

SOUTHERN RHODESIA (1897)

VENDA (conquered 1898)

SOUTH AFRICAN REPUBLIC (1852)

PEDI (conquered 1879)

SWAZILAND (1895)

ZULULAND (annexed to Natal 1897)

WITWATERSRAND

Pretoria

Johannesburg

NATAL (1842)

Durban

BECHUANALAND (1885)

High Grassland (Highveld)

DRAKENSBERG

BASUTOLAND (1868)

TRANSKEI (annexed to Cape 1870s - 1890s)

ORANGE FREE STATE (1854)

Bloemfontein

BRITISH KAFFRARIA (annexed to Britain 1847, to Cape 1866)

BRITISH BECHUANALAND (annexed to Britain 1885, Cape 1895)

Kimberley

GRIQUALAND WEST (annexed to Britain 1871, Cape 1880)

Grahamstown

ZUURVELD

Port Elizabeth

Dry Interior Plateau (Karoo)

CAPE COLONY

GERMAN SOUTH WEST AFRICA (1884)

Cape Town
Cape Penninsula

Atlantic Ocean

Indian Ocean

0   300 miles
0   400 kilometres

Boundaries of European colonies, protectorates, dependencies and settler states.

Approximate southern and western limits of African settlement.

South Africa in the late nineteenth century

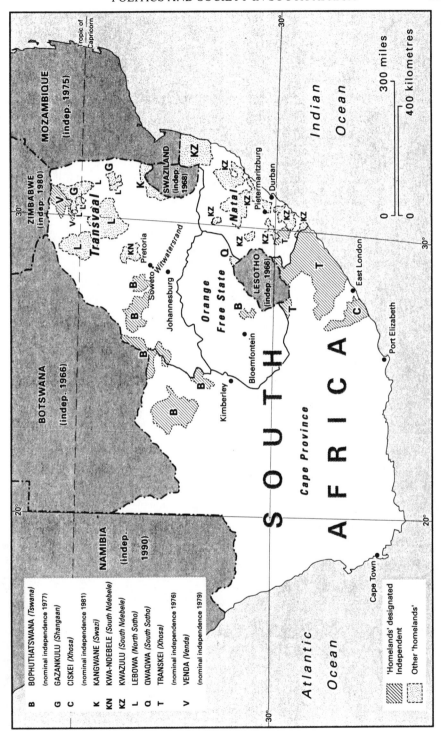

South Africa under apartheid

B   BOPHUTHATSWANA (Tswana)
     (nominal independence 1977)
G   GAZANKULU (Shangaan)
C   CISKEI (Xhosa)
     (nominal independence 1981)
K   KANGWANE (Swazi)
KN   KWA-NDEBELE (South Ndebele)
KZ   KWAZULU (South Ndebele)
L   LEBOWA (North Sotho)
Q   QWAQWA (South Sotho)
T   TRANSKEI (Xhosa)
     (nominal independence 1976)
V   VENDA (Venda)
     (nominal independence 1979)

'Homelands' designated Independent

Other 'homelands'

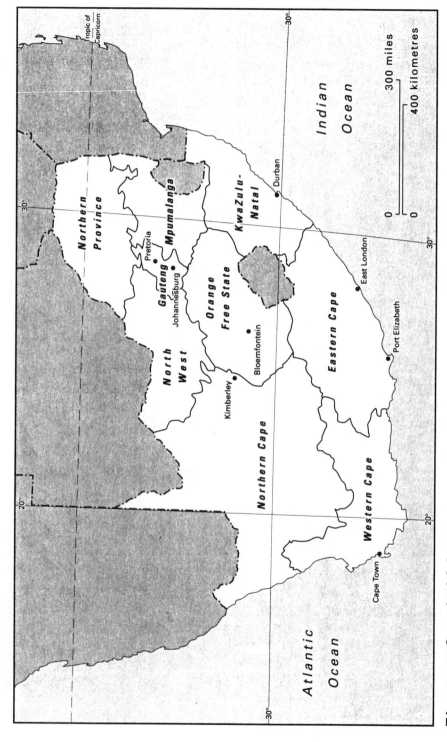

The new South Africa

Tables

The first table reveals not only the dramatic growth of South Africa's population during the twentieth century but the ongoing and expanding numerical dominance of Africans.

South African population and percentage by race

Year	Total (millions)	White (%)	Coloured (%)	Indian/ Asian (%)	African (%)
1904	5.1	21.6	8.6	2.4	67.4
1951	12.6	20.9	8.7	2.9	67.5
1996	40.5	10.9	8.9	2.6	76.7

Sources: Beinart (1994: 261), 1996 South African Census data

The second table shows how South Africa became increasingly urbanized in the twentieth century, but illustrates also how much more urbanized whites, coloureds and Indians became compared to Africans despite the numerical and economic importance of Africans in the urban areas since the 1930s.

Proportion of population in urban areas by percentage

Year	All	White	Coloured	Indian/ Asian	African
1904	23	53	49	36	10
1951	43	78	65	78	27
1991	63	91	83	96	58

Sources: Beinart (1994: 263)

This table illustrates South Africa's development as an industrial and, more recently, a service-based post-industrial society: What it does not disclose is South Africa's dependence on imported technology and the ongoing importance of the extractive sectors, especially gold mining, in earning foreign exchange.

Sectoral contribution to South African Gross Domestic Product (%)

Year	1911	1959	1999
Mining	28	13	6
Manufacturing and construction	5	22	22
Agriculture	21	19	4
Tertiary	46	46	65

Sources: Lipton (1986: 402), South African Reserve Bank

The following table illustrates the alarming extent to which South Africa's economic growth has been declining in recent decades, a trend which began around 1974 and has been accompanied by dramatically rising unemployment.

Average annual growth in South African real Gross Domestic Product

Decade	1950s	1960s	1970s	1980s	1990s
Growth rate	4.4	5.2	3.7	1.5	0.7

Sources: Gelb (1991a: 4), Black (1991: 157), Thompson (1995: 280), South African Reserve Bank

Acknowledgements

From a personal point-of-view this book represents a return to and review of a field of studies – and of a society – in which I remain heavily invested intellectually and emotionally despite having left South Africa in the late 1980s. Many thanks to Professor Bill Freund, Dr Clive Glaser, Professor Ian Holliday and Dr Jonathan Hyslop for reading and commenting on drafts of the manuscript. Thanks also to the Inter-Library Loan staff at the University of Strathclyde for making the research possible from my Glasgow outpost, to Mrs Surinder Hunjan for assistance with formatting and to Dr Owen Crankshaw and Professor Nicoli Nattrass for supplying statistical information for the tables. Konstanze's forbearance and help, offered despite her thesis-writing pressures, are lovingly acknowledged.

Introduction

South Africa is now more than a decade into a process of democratic transition that has, amongst many other things, transformed the terms in which the country's politics and society are debated. Yet this transition falls in turn against the backdrop of three decades of scholarship which themselves witnessed profound change, in this case within intellectual history. How does the intellectual transformation that began around 1970 now look, viewed now from the vantage point of a time when two social orders central to earlier debates have experienced fundamental shifts of fortune? The one social order, that of legally institutionalized racial domination, disappeared some time between 1991 and 1994. The other, capitalism, has by contrast, and during roughly the same period, seen its star rise. How relevant is the scholarship of the 1970s, which was preoccupied with the relationship between the two orders and assumed at least the possibility of a third, namely socialism? And what retrospective light is cast on those debates by recent changes? The book seeks to introduce a new generation to earlier, yet not very old, debates that continue to provide useful points of entry and comparison post-1994. It also provides an assessment of the continuing significance in the new period of issues raised in the 1970s and 1980s: issues to do with the colonial legacy, capitalism, modernity, class, ethnicity and resistance. Finally, the book discusses, in the last chapter, the specific issues thrown up by debates around South Africa's post-1990 transition to non-racial democracy.

The last third of the twentieth century saw major shifts in South African studies. To the well established canons of Afrikaner nationalist and liberal interpretation were added those of Marxist-influenced radical revisionism and, later, post-structuralism and post-modernism. This book is, at one level, an extended and critical introduction to the key issues raised at the points of contact, and often of collision, between these intellectual and political traditions. It fulfils this function by offering a wide ranging thematic survey that crosses disciplinary boundaries. On another level the book offers a series of interventions in the controversies of recent decades. It is intended not simply to register the fact of debates but, in a small way, to advance them.

While the book does not engage in continuous debate, certain arguments are picked up and developed under different headings. The first is in favour of a continued role for a roughly materialist style of theorizing. The chapters most directly pursuing this theme are 5 and 6, though the issue is touched on in most chapters. The case for it forms part of a larger attempt to vindicate, albeit only conditionally and critically, the enterprise of radical revisionism. The second argument is, up to a point, a converse of the first: it is for treating sceptically the claims of post-structuralist and post-modernist scholarship. On this theme see especially Chapters 3 to 6. The third argument is in defence of modernity against anti-modernist critics. Chapter 3 develops it explicitly. The final argument is for a kind of reconciliation of radical and liberal projects, both in their political and their intellectual aspects. While strongly supportive of the institutions and values of liberal democracy, I am suspicious of free market dogmatism and favour an egalitarian and participatory society. This value orientation is implicit in what is said especially in Chapters 2, 3, 7 and 8.

Unsurprisingly much of this book is about South Africa's racial order. For all that other kinds of social hierarchy have been posited as sources of explanation or as alternative sources of cleavage and oppression, it is race, and more widely ethnicity, which continues even now, post-apartheid, to loom largest over South Africa and its prospects. The first three chapters survey and assess three much discussed points of origin and/or sources of explanation for the (late?) racial order. Chapter 1 examines the case for the colonial origins of the racial order; Chapter 2 for its capitalist origins; Chapter 3 for its origins in the dynamics of modernity. These chapters show that generalized notions about the explanatory primacy of any of these are implausible; but that colonialism, capitalism and modernity are implicated in the racial order in particular ways. The explanation of the racial order in terms of modernity is shown to be the most problematic of the three.

Chapter 4 looks at South Africa's evolving political and state systems with, once again, shifts in policies and institutions relating to race and ethnicity constituting a central (though not exclusive) focus. Other foci include the state's developmental role and, prior to 1994, its racially exclusive democratic character. After an extensive theoretical survey some suggestions are made about the elements of a plausible theory of the state in South Africa.

Chapter 5 is about class. It considers key controversies around class in South Africa before offering a conditional defence of materialist class analysis and of the continuing social and political significance of class after apartheid.

Chapter 6 takes up in an explicit way a theme running through much of the book: ethnicity, of which race is here treated as a subset. The origins of ethnic identity are explored, as well as the reasons for both the extent of its attractions and the limit of its appeal. The chapter highlights the relatively greater resonance in South Africa of what are here called larger as opposed to smaller ethnicities.

The seventh chapter explores the long history of black resistance to white domination in South Africa. It aims to disclose the range of resistance forms and the factors behind the changing rhythms of opposition and quiescence before 1994. The chapter surveys key debates in anti-apartheid ranks and calls into question some influential resistance narratives.

Issues of post-apartheid political relevance are addressed in concluding subsections in the first seven chapters. It is the final chapter that however brings the book most clearly into the present period, discussing as it does the dynamics of political transition and democratization in South Africa in the 1990s. The chapter considers the prospects for the successful consolidation of liberal democracy in South Africa as well as the chances of creating a more deeply democratic and socially egalitarian order.

The themes of this book were chosen on the grounds that they constitute prominent sites of intellectual and political controversy in South African studies. Even on this criterion however there are problematic omissions. I decided mainly for reasons of space not to devote a separate chapter to gender, though gender-related issues are considered at various points, most notably in the chapters on ethnicity and resistance. This approach has at least the compensatory merit of not ghettoizing the subject, as well as the excuse that feminist studies in South Africa remained, until the late 1980s at least, relatively undeveloped. It is also difficult to identify a specifically *South African* gender problem, in the way that there is, for example, a specifically South African 'problem' of racial domination and ethnicity. The same might be said of class, except that it entered South African studies in part as a way of explaining race; and it entered it also in tandem with the rise of a powerful labour movement that awaits its feminist counterpart. Considerations of space entered also into the decision not to give separate attention to, for example, South African fictional writing. This particular deficit also reflects a bias in this book towards a sort of critical realism and against the reading of South African society as though it were revealed and composed in more-or-less fictional narratives. No doubt readers will find other omissions too, and important topics in South African studies which have been under-attended.

I have confronted the difficulties encountered by all writers on South Africa in making decisions about the use of terminology. I employ terms like white, coloured, Indian, African, Zulu, Xhosa etc. without inverted commas despite the fact that the definitions and boundaries of the people designated by such labels are often contested or unclear. They are, I feel, sufficiently imprinted in institutional practices, statutes, and popular consciousness to deserve the consideration of being treated as real, not least because none of them is an inherently disreputable term despite apartheid's manipulation of ethnic divisions. Since the term coloured is being proudly reclaimed by many of its referent population despite years of being scorned by radical commentators as a racist fiction, it seems improper to refer still to 'so-called coloureds'. In line with a common convention, albeit one that is certainly contestable, I use the term black as a collective label for coloureds, Indians and Africans. Whatever the wishful thinking behind its implication of unity amongst the oppressed, it is at any rate preferable to negative labels like non-white or non-European, employed here very sparingly indeed. I have been happy to use terms like reserves to indicate areas set aside for Africans, but I have balked at leaving the terms 'homelands' outside of inverted commas. I am reluctant to convey any suggestion of positive approval for these segregationist entities, even while accepting that they, too, were never simply figments of the racist imagination. Though the term 'bantustan' conveys a suitable disapproval, it is avoided here to prevent terminological multiplication.

One noteworthy aspect about the authors considered here is that they are overwhelmingly white. Despite signal contributions from a number of black writers, South African academe has yet to witness the full transformative impact of black scholarship. It is inevitable that it will do so, and that a book reviewing the next three decades of academic writing on South Africa will feature more black scholars than white. Whites were obviously the main beneficiaries of South Africa's education system before the 1990s, and in that decade the state and private sector served as powerful poles of attraction for blacks who might otherwise have achieved prominence in academic life. A combination of affirmative action and the increasing size and confidence of the black elite is sure to put this imbalance to rights in the years ahead, with consequences that can only be speculated upon.

1

Colonialism and the Racial Order

CONTENTS

Unmasking the racial order

Analysts of South Africa's racial order have always sought to unmask its real nature. They still seek to do so, though the vocabularies of unmasking have shifted with intellectual fashions and in response to changing times. The mystique of explanation lives on even in post-modern work, albeit now attaching to the deconstructive search for textual logics and silences rather than, say, to the realist exploration of underlying social and economic forces. It is unsurprising that the armouries of scholarly explanation have been directed, in the South African case, principally to one target: South Africa's racial order, unique by the late twentieth century for its institutionalized character. Those seeking explanations of this phenomenon have sought to bring South Africa under the light of comparative analysis, or to place it in the context of larger historical and systemic forces. Amongst the latter forces three have figured especially prominently: colonialism, capitalism and modernity. The location of the sources of institutionalized racial hierarchy in any one of them typically carries a political meaning, whether it lurks subtextually or is made polemically explicit. This chapter will deal with the first of the three sources, colonialism, considering both its contribution to the establishment of the post 1910-racial order and its legacy for the democratic 'new South Africa' inaugurated in 1994. The following chapters deal with capitalism and modernity in turn.

The question of colonial origins

The debate about the colonial origins of the racial order is not one about whether South Africa's Dutch and British colonial orders were based on racial domination. It is universally accepted that wherever blacks in the region were brought under white settler rule they were allocated economically and politically subordinate roles. Two amongst many issues that *are* contested about the colonial beginnings of racial hierarchy are, firstly, whether the colonial order was based on conscious and/or formalized racism and, secondly, whether the colonial pattern of racial hierarchy is continuous with, or in some sense is 'responsible' for, the conscious and formalized racism of twentieth-century South Africa. Do (in other words) the 'origins' of South Africa's racial order lie in colonial times?

There is no one set of institutions, actors or ideologies that corresponds to the term colonial. In the ordinary descriptive sense, the European colonial era in what is today South Africa began on the Cape peninsula in 1652 and concluded in 1910, eight years after the Cape, Natal, SAR and OFS came under unified British colonial control. During the intervening centuries countless actors participated in different ways in the shaping of a variegated racial order. To talk, therefore, of the colonial origins of the twentieth-century racial order is not (yet) to specify very much. A closer inspection discloses the presence of a large debate and a number of smaller debates about colonial origins.

The larger debate is essentially about whether the racial order of colonial times sprang from the metropolitan centres of the colonial order or whether it grew up on the isolated, pre-modern margins of the colonial realm, amongst those least connected culturally, economically or geographically to the metropole and its civilizing ambitions.

In twentieth-century discussion this central question is overlaid with two others of great emotional and ideological resonance. Were colonial race hierarchies developed by Afrikaners, above all by Boer 'frontiersmen', as claimed by many liberals and indeed by some Afrikaner nationalists, or were they, as radical writers have insisted, forged by the British: their colonial governments and by Anglophone merchants, missionaries, speculators and later employers? And was explicit and institutionalized colonial racism the product of pre-capitalist colonialism (as liberals and others maintain) or (as radicals prefer) of colonial-era capitalism, whether merchant or industrial?

Within the penumbra of these large debates fall many smaller debates about the role in the developing racial order of specific colonial periods, sites, people and systems – above all the pre-colonial metropole, the Western Cape slave heartland, the post-emancipation Cape, the Dutch-Afrikaner frontier, the Griqua, missionary and merchant-speculator frontiers, British Imperialism and the four republican and colonial race policies of the later nineteenth century. To which of these putative historical starting points, if any, can South Africa's twentieth-century institutionalized racial order be traced?

The European prehistory of colonial racism

A belief in the otherness and inferiority of blacks was prevalent already in Europe before Europeans first settled South Africa. Frederickson has tracked northern European racism in the sixteenth and seventeenth centuries back to three sources: a medieval belief in the existence of wild men and monsters, a post-Renaissance dichotomization of civilization and savagery and a post-Reformation marriage of Protestant Christianity and ethnic assertiveness. From these discursive structures arose negative views of non-European indigenes as heathen savages descended from the originally non-savage condition of Noah's progeny by way of the curse of Ham (Frederickson 1981: 7-13). The 'Hottentots' encountered by Europeans in Southern Africa were for many metropolitans paradigmatic of savagery and degeneracy (Elphick 1985: ch. 10). Negative images of non-European 'others' eclipsed more favourable images derived from Catholic universalism and a late sixteenth-century humanist idealization of the noble savage (Frederickson 1981: 7-13).

Given the prevalence of such negative imagery, sharpened no doubt by the contrasting appearances of dark-hued indigenes and the northern Europeans who settled the Cape, it might be considered unsurprising that racism took hold in areas of Dutch and German settlement in Southern Africa. In fact Protestant northern European perceptions of race and colour, though obviously part of the story of colonial racial hierarchy, explain too little about its unfolding. They may go a part of the way to explaining the contrast between the Dutch record of colonization in the Cape and the more racially assimilationist style of colonization practised in Latin America by darker-hued settlers from Catholic and Southern European states (Spain and Portugal). European racial understandings cast much less light on the contrast between the records of Dutch colonizers in the East Indies (characterized by relative racial tolerance and a degree of assimilation) and the Cape – even if we factor in the respect elicited from Europeans by the more complex nature of indigenous social orders in places like Java. Nor would such considerations explain why the Cape became more racially self-conscious and racial hierarchy more formalized towards the end of the eighteenth century than they were at the outset of European settlement (and in contrast to, for example, the experience of the gradually assimilated Portuguese *prazeros* of Mozambique). It is an illustration of the limits of analysis of the discursive construction of otherness that it gives insufficient weight to factors – demographic, economic, ecological, and so on – which (though themselves discursively interpreted by people affected by them) belong less straightforwardly to the realm of language or text.

One crucial factor distinguishing the Dutch colonial engagement in the Cape from the Dutch experience in Java was the European-friendly temperate climate of the coastal and near-inland Cape. Another was the relative vulnerability to conquest and occupation (mountain barriers aside) of land used by loosely organized nomadic pastoralists and hunter-gatherers, those referred to later as the 'Khoi' ('Hottentots') and 'San' ('bushmen'). Together with the smallpox, which decimated the Khoisan in 1713, these circumstances favoured the sort of colony of expansive settlement which the Dutch, for the most part founders of trading rather than settler colonies, elsewhere eschewed. Settler expansionism in turn placed a premium on secure access to land and water sources, and acquiring these meant creating a colony of conquest.

White settler expansion did more than simply displace the Khoisan indigenes. The land-extensive economy permitted a large proportion of whites to set up as landowners, even as the termination of assisted white immigration from 1717 left white settlers without sufficient labour to work their fields or tend their stock. Two solutions to labour scarcity were found whose net effect was to draw non-Europeans into subordinate positions within colonial societies. One involved the importation of non-European slaves into (mainly) the southwestern Cape of wine and wheat farms. The other, pursued later, involved the absorption of conquered Khoisan indigenes into the white pastoral economy of the Cape's moving northern and eastern frontier. These racially-based master–servant hierarchies were the first of numerous that would form a central feature of the South African social order through to the late twentieth century and likely beyond.

The Cape slave heartland

Until relatively recently slavery in South Africa was seen as a phenomenon that began with the importation into the Dutch Cape of shiploads of slaves from Angola and Dahomey in 1658, was largely confined to Cape Town and the arable southwestern Cape, and was terminated by British Imperial power in 1838. More recently historians have argued that the military capture and/or forced servitude of indigenous children and women (both Khoisan and Bantu-speaking) amounted to a form of slavery, or at least enserfment bordering on slavery (Elphick 1988: 42, 52; Eldredge and Morton 1994; Shell 1994: 26-39). Since this practice of using captive labour occurred throughout the period 1730 to 1870, was a phenomenon of the stock-keeping rather than arable frontier, and practised on the outer fringes of nineteenth-century Boer settlement, such a definition of slavery would extend its boundaries dramatically in temporal, spatial and economic terms. It would also imply (as Morton 1994a, b, c argues) a far more central role for slavery in South African history than has hitherto been assumed.

Nevertheless there is a case for considering separately the slave system in the southwestern Cape and Cape Town, partly because it was distinctive in being based on long-distance imported slaves rather than the labour of adjacent or nearby indigenes, and partly because it was formalized and open. Moreover import slavery developed partly as a result of an initial Dutch *reluctance* to indenture or enslave adjacent indigenes, a reluctance reinforced by Khoisan pastoralists' lack of experience with regular sedentary labour (Frederickson 1981: 54-6).

Slaves were imported to South Africa between the late 1650s and the British abolition of the slave trade in 1808. They were shipped in from (mainly eastern) Africa (26.4%), Madagascar (25.1%), the Indian subcontinent (25.9%), the Indonesian archipelago (22.7%) and other parts of the Indian Ocean rim. Import-based slavery was obviously enough a system of European racial domination, in that the great majority of slave owners were Europeans of various nationalities, and the slave population, though ethnically extremely heterogeneous, included no one of pure European descent. However, the racial basis of slavery was neither explicit nor clear-cut prior to the late eighteenth century. Slaves were a distinctive legal status group to which not all non-Europeans belonged: there was a small population of 'free blacks' and indeed there were African, Indonesian, Indian and mulatto slave-owners. Slave status was seen by Europeans as the result of capture of individuals in war by non-European slave-trading societies, and as justified both by the prisoner-of-war status of the slaves and by their heathenism. Slaves could be admitted into the 'free black' population through a process of manumission, and 'free blacks' enjoyed formal equality with whites until the later eighteenth century. There remains a question mark therefore over whether the beginnings of the rigidly formalized racial hierarchy marking twentieth-century South Africa can be found in the imported slave system of the Cape. Slavery's contribution to formalized racism is open to query not least because in some other countries, notably Brazil, effectively racial slave systems yielded to societies characterized by a relatively greater degree of racial assimilation, or at least to a graded or pluralistic rather than bipolar racial order (Marx 1998).

The extent to which Cape importation-based slavery contributed to the entrenchment of racial assumptions is disputed. Frederickson argued that intermarriage between European males and freed slave women was relatively common and socially acceptable in white society and that, moreover, the offspring of mixed unions encountered (at least until the later eighteenth century) less prejudice and fewer obstacles to upward mobility than their counterparts in America. Slavery thus did not, in Frederickson's view (1981: ch. 3), lead to the delineation of clear race lines extending to the 'free black' population. Ross has more recently reiterated this view (Ross 1993: ch. 3; see also Freund 1976).

In practice slavery contributed to the informal entrenchment of a racial order in a variety of ways. By freeing so many Europeans from labour (apart from family labour) slavery helped establish from an early stage a rough coincidence between being white and part of a master class. Pure Europeans were ineligible for enslavement. There were only a very small number of non-European slave owners and relatively few 'free blacks'. Labour shortages suffered by white masters and tightening Cape colonial regulations ensured a low rate of slave manumission (Elphick and Shell 1979/80: 135-45; Elphick and Giliomee 1988: 537). The simple agrarian economy with its scarcity of artisanal and other intermediate roles meant that there were limited opportunities for ex-slaves to acquire material independence, and the ruling Dutch East India Company (*Verenigde Oost-Indische Companie*) did not wish to have destitute 'free blacks' living off its coffers. The scarcity of intermediate roles also closed off routes of economic upward mobility to the freed (Elphick and Giliomee 1988: 532-6). The view that whites constituted an internally egalitarian group is now discredited, especially for the longer-settled western Cape. There is no reason however to dispute Frederickson's (1981: 69, 162-79) notion that widespread white control of land and ownership of slaves diffused social tensions in white society and infused it with a sense of shared superiority over non-Europeans.

Slaves were, it remains true, distinguishable from whites by the fact of their widespread heathenism as well as by race. Colonialists were convinced that Christian ancestry conferred a fuller entitlement to baptism than heathen ancestry (Gerstner 1997). Masters moreover feared that Christianization might result in slave freedom, especially after the Council of Indies in Batavia decreed in 1770 that Christianized slaves could not be sold or alienated. The result was a very low level of master-initiated Christianization, especially of private slaves, and even white tolerance of slave Islamization. Nevertheless there *were* baptized slaves, and from 1812 enslavement of Christians was officially sanctioned, ironically by British authorities seeking to remove obstacles to slave baptism. Most manumitted slaves were not baptized (Elphick and Shell 1979/80: 117-22; Shell 1997). The statuses of heathen and slave were thus at least partly decoupled.

More importantly, Christianization and manumission did not erase heathen and slave status: their stigma became heritable. Even miscegenation did not efface that stigma. Free Christian offspring of mixed unions were marginalized by an increasingly status-conscious white society, despite the success of some in 'passing for white' (Elphick and Shell 1979/80: 126-35; Elphick and Giliomee 1988: 537). By the mid-nineteenth century miscegenation and intermarriage in the western Cape were essentially, amongst those of pure European descent, lower class phenomena (Bickford-Smith 1989: 47-8, 61).

Clarification of racial lines was further strengthened by the trend towards a more homogeneous black population. There occurred over time a cultural deracination and creolization of the originally ethnically diverse slave population, and indeed a convergence between the status and conditions of imported slaves and enserfed Khoi. Creolization and slave-Khoi convergence helped to substitute something like race or at least slave/heathen descent for linguistic and geographical origin, legal slave status and heathenism as cultural markers of subordination.

Another issue carrying implications for future race relations was the treatment of slaves. Historians have debated the extent to which masters maintained control over slaves by coercive as opposed to hegemonic means. The thesis that Cape slavery was 'mild' is easily rebutted by evidence of disparity between criminal penalties inflicted on offending slaves and freemen, gruesome punishments visited by the Company on slaves until 1795, brutal mistreatment of slaves by private masters, and of subjection of slaves to passes, curfews and lock-ups (Armstrong and Worden 1988: 149-57). Nevertheless there was another, more complex side to master/slave relations that may tell us more about the cultural and psychological cement holding the system together. A number of factors constrained the private coercion of slaves. The company formally monopolized the right to punish slaves severely, excessively cruel masters faced ostracism in white society and following the termination of slave importation in 1808 slave owners were more careful to avoid damaging their slave property. Largely because of the Cape's dispersed, non-plantation pattern of slave ownership slaves were, as Shell shows, drawn into paternalistic and patriarchal household relationships where they shared a position of subordination and vulnerability with white children and women. Even so Shell stresses that slaves occupied the lowest rung in the household hierarchy, that they were treated as perpetual children and moreover were lower in status than white children. Such paternalism and patriarchal dominance were to form a component (alongside violence and threatened violence) of many subsequent South African systems of labour control in agriculture, domestic service and mining (Shell 1994).

It would be a mistake, all the same, to argue, as Shell does, that slavery 'shaped South Africa' (Shell 1994: 395). Slavery did not itself involve (initially at least) a formalized system of racial dominance such as appeared in South Africa in stages from the late eighteenth century. Nor does its historical presence sufficiently explain why, in its aftermath, and in notable contrast to Brazil, explicit race boundaries hardened rather than weakened (Marx 1998). And even if slavery is taken to include relations of coercive indenture that continued until 1870 in the interior, the straightforward formal deprivation of choice about enlisting for work (as opposed to breaking contracts or moving freely) has not been a characteristic mode of labour coercion in twentieth-century South Africa (convict labour apart).

The Dutch-Afrikaner frontier

If Shell can detect the origins of South Africa's racial order in the western Cape's import-based slavery, its point of origin is more often sought on the Dutch-Afrikaner frontier: on the expanding boundaries of trading, raiding, hunting, more-or-less nomadic pastoral agriculture and, later, land speculation practised by Dutch- or Afrikaans-speaking farmers (Boers) of European descent between, roughly, 1700 and the later nineteenth century. The idea that expanding frontiers of European settlement can provide an important crucible of national character was made famous for America by the work of Frederick Jackson Turner, and it has well-worn South African counterparts.

Frontiers are more than just interfaces with non-human nature, despite the occasional assumption of frontier expansionists that they are occupying near-empty lands or that indigenes they encounter are part of the natural rather than human world. A frontier is, at least for the comparative historians Lamar and Thompson, 'a territory or zone of interpenetration between two previously distinct societies' (Lamar and Thompson 1981: 7). It therefore necessarily plays an initial part in forging modes of interaction between groups whose members later go on to form, as in South Africa, members of a single polity and society. The frontier most classically considered formative in the South African case is the Dutch-Afrikaner one.

Saunders has noted, and writers like Elphick and Hall have clearly illustrated (Saunders 1981: 151; Elphick, 1985; Hall 1987), that frontier encounters between distinctive groups in southern Africa long pre-dated European intrusion. If the Dutch-Afrikaner frontier has been singled out for special attention it is because of the argument, especially dear to Anglophone liberals of a later period, that twentieth-century racial segregation represented a victory for race attitudes forged on the Dutch-Afrikaner frontier and an historic defeat for the more liberal world-view emanating from the British colonial Cape. A famous formulation of this 'frontier thesis' was supplied by MacCrone, who contrasted the Europe-influenced Christian/heathen dichotomy and relative racial fluidity of the original Dutch refreshment station at the Cape with the racial group consciousness generated (above all) on the moving frontier. MacCrone attributed frontier race consciousness to a combination of factors including the trekboers' isolation from metropolitan cultural influences and their communal self-defence against 're-barbarization' (MacCrone 1937). Proponents of the thesis have also emphasized the racially polarizing effects of frontier conflict and the influence of the Boers' seventeenth-century version of Calvinist religion (variously associated with a binary division of the world into the saved and damned and a self-image of Afrikaners as God's chosen in flight from oppression). It was this same cultural universe, proponents of the thesis argue, which framed the racial and ethnic policies of post-1910 South Africa.

The frontier argument in its many variants has been criticized in more recent decades for underestimating the formative influence on the racial order of pre-frontier European racism and western Cape slavery and/or of the later transformations wrought by commercial, mining and industrial capitalism. It has also been accused of mischaracterizing the European frontier itself. Legassick insisted that the frontier was a 'fluid zone of social transition' (1980: 247) rather than a sphere of clearly demarcated racial boundaries. It was characterized by a variety of Boer relations with 'non-Europeans' including both co-operation and conflict varying in importance according to a shifting balance of power. Legassick pointed to the dependence of the Dutch-Afrikaner commando (a crucial instrument of frontier collective action) on Bastard and Khoi fighters, the faction-ridden nature of supposedly group-conscious Boer communities and the client–patron relationships formed by initially fragile Boer societies with autonomous African societies of the interior. These latter extended sometimes, both in the eastern Cape and in the Transvaal, to seeking alliances with African chiefdoms against both British or Dutch-Afrikaner fellow whites. Frontier race relations, Legassick implied, were if anything less rigid than those of the western Cape (Legassick 1980). In a similar spirit Keegan has more recently affirmed the 'instrumentalism, pragmatism and variability' of Dutch-Afrikaner frontier relations with blacks (Keegan 1996: 32).

Another typical claim of the frontier thesis exponents, that a primitive frontier version of Calvinism fostered a white sense of racial consciousness and superiority, was contested in the 1980s by writers such as Elphick and Giliomee (1988) and Du Toit (1983, 1985). Giliomee and Du Toit argued that for much of the frontier period Calvinism was too weakly rooted to instil a widespread sense of Dutch-Afrikaners being an Elect or chosen people of divinely-ordained Old Testament destiny. Much early white frontier belief was moreover 'far removed from orthodox Calvinism', accommodating folk medicine, spiritual healing, herbal remedies and magic in ways not dissimilar to nearby non-Christian Africans (Hexham and Poewe 1997: 124).

Critics have also questioned the extent to which the Dutch-Afrikaner frontier is properly contrasted, as an outpost of supposed pre-capitalist backwardness, to the commercial modernity of the southwestern Cape. Neumark's boldly revisionist claim that trekboer expansion was prompted by a search for profitable market opportunities (Neumark 1957) has not been widely accepted. It is much more likely that whites moving onto the frontier were taking advantage of its low economic entry requirements in order to retain their independence as farmers, and that they practised a land-extensive, inefficient agriculture (Guelke 1979/80: 67-71; Keegan 1996: 251-4, 267). Nevertheless, a number of writers have shown that eastern Cape frontier trekboers were from an early stage market-dependent rather than self-sufficient, and that they were by the late eighteenth century 'being drawn, willingly, into the orbit of commerce' (Ross 1993: 37). Much of their impoverishment was due to debt rather than isolation, to an inability rather than refusal to emulate southwestern Cape standards of colonial civility (Keegan 1996: 28-9). In the later nineteenth century trekkers drew British capital after them onto the northern frontier, and, in the case of the emerging Dutch-Afrikaner gentry in the Boer republics, profited from hunting, trading, office-holding and land speculation (Beinart and Delius 1986: 22-3).

What most tells against the traditional formulation of the frontier thesis is not, however, the simple fact of commercial activity on the frontier. It is the association, noted by Keegan and Morton, between merchant capitalism, militaristic settler-colonial expansionism (Keegan 1996) and the intensification of frontier slaving (Morton 1994a: 4). This association suggests that commercialism was more important than frontier backwardness and isolation as a wellspring of heightened racial competition and conflict.

For all the exaggerations of the frontier thesis, it would be wrong to suppose that the majority of Dutch-Afrikaners on the frontier did not, in the main, preserve a degree of racial group consciousness. Guelke has helpfully distinguished 'orthodox' or stable frontier communities from an 'unorthodox' or 'pluralist' minority. The orthodox were characterized by hierarchical and brutal master–servant relationships and an exclusionist 'European' way of life marked by racial consciousness. The pluralists, many poor or unable to find white wives, mingled socially and sexually with the Khoisan and served as a warning to the more orthodox about the dangers of absorption by the savage frontier (Guelke 1988: 93-100). A single individual could however appear in different guises at different times; as Penn argues, there was nothing to stop today's 'cross-cultural robber-rapist' from becoming tomorrow's 'white-wived, prosperous farmer' (Penn 1999). The debate about the role of religion in the Colonial Cape moreover remains open, with Gerstner recently reasserting its centrality to colonists both on the frontier and in the Cape colonial core. Gerstner argues that Dutch reformed theology allowed colonists to think of themselves as redeemed by a 'thousand-generation covenant' with God that excluded slaves and indigenes (Gerstner 1997).

The fluidity of external frontier race relations had its counterpart in what were, in the early stages of the trekboer frontier of the eastern Cape, diverse racial master–servant relationships *within* areas of white control. Labour-starved trekboers of the Cape initially entered relations of 'semi-cooperative symbiosis' (Penn 1989: 2) or 'paternalism' (Elphick 1988: 31) with Khoi who supplied them with herding, hunting and other skills as well as military service. Frontier military conflict amidst intensifying competition for resources was however accompanied by a deterioration in the status of Khoi and mixed race (Khoi-slave or Khoi-white) servants. From 1775 Cape authorities legally sanctioned the forcible indenture, ostensibly of Khoi-slave offspring, but effectively of Khoi as well.

Meanwhile the Boers began, from the 1730s, supplementing their labour supply through the capture of children and women from San and African societies. Captives were acquired both through raiding and, later, purchase from African societies like the Swazi in the Transvaal. Though illegal throughout southern Africa during the British period, the practice was informally sanctioned and even joined in by state officials of the northern South African Republic (*Zuid-Afrikaanse Republiek*). Ostensibly apprenticed only until adulthood, captives were culturally deracinated and alienated from surrounding indigenous societies, acquiring skills other indigenes did not, but never granted equality in Boer society.

Giliomee famously classified the shifting complex of frontier relations under the headings of 'open' and 'closed' frontier. The opening Dutch-Afrikaner frontier, Giliomee suggested, was characterized by an essential indeterminacy fostered by land plenitude and weak state authority. It featured endemic conflict, the release of social tensions in white society through territorial expansion and political secession, diverse master–servant relationships and a European conceptualization of Africans as alien rather than inferior. The closing Afrikaner frontier, by contrast, was characterized by a greater scarcity and more intensive use of land, the assertion of state authority, increasingly repressive and codified labour relations, a crystallizing Boer group consciousness alongside deepening class tensions in white society, and the aggravation of race relations as a result of heightened economic competition and hunger for black labour. Giliomee describes a succession of opening and closing Dutch-Afrikaner frontiers in the southwestern Cape, the eastern Cape and the northern interior (Giliomee 1979/80, 1981).

The Dutch-Afrikaner frontier – or to be precise, frontiers – certainly played a part in shaping South Africa's racial order. On these frontiers whites fought and conquered African polities and devised a new variant of racist master–servant relations (above all the forcible indenture of local blacks). In the nineteenth century Dutch-Afrikaner frontiersmen transmitted labour-repression to the northern interior, where it was insulated from British colonial meliorism. Racial labour-repression was not however invented on the frontier, but in the southwestern Cape; labour relations in the frontier zones were in fact varied before the frontier began to close. African societies were conquered, but Boer–African external relations were diverse until the balance of forces shifted decisively against black societies. The frontier-based forces that sponsored racial labour-repression and military conquest were in any case not exclusively the isolated Boer subsistence farmers of legend: they included commercializing Boers as well as a range of British-linked actors, from merchants and missionaries to mine owners, not to mention British troops.

The Griqua frontier

In his critique of the notion of frontier as crucible of crystallized black–white hostility, Legassick drew attention to another phenomenon: the fact that the advance guard of Cape colonial expansion was led not by Dutch-Afrikaner whites but by mixed race people, the 'bastaards', who, after migrating to Transorangia, became known as the Griqua (Legassick 1979/80, 1988). The 'bastaards' were offspring of mainly Khoi-white, but also Khoi-slave extra-marital unions. They were Christianized, Dutch-speaking, occupied less menial economic roles (including those of overseer and small farmer), and considered themselves superior to the Khoisan, though their ranks were successfully joined by numbers of Khoisan, slaves and others. In the last quarter of the nineteenth-century bastaards and Khoi (who had long served in colonial commandos) became eligible for compulsory colonial military service in the Cape Colony while increasingly being denied civic rights (Penn 1989: 13-19). Many responded by trekking north out of the colony. Their northward trek extended the economic and, with the 1843 Cape–Griqua treaty, the political reach of the colony during the first half of the nineteenth century. Griquas engaged actively in state-building in Transorangia, guided by missionaries linked to the London Missionary Society. Like the initial state-building of the trekkers, their attempts to consolidate central state power beyond the Cape were subverted by constant factionalism and the emergence amongst them of competing statelets. As Legassick notes (1988: 405), they attempted, again like their Dutch-Afrikaner counterparts, to impose military hegemony over the 'bushmen', Kora and Sotho-Tswana of Transorangia; through the church they also sought a cultural hegemony. Unlike the Dutch-Afrikaners, however, their political dominance was not lastingly shored up by Imperial power and this mixed race colonial vanguard was soon displaced, the Griqua finding themselves subject, after 1854, to racially discriminatory legislation in the white-dominated independent Orange Free State Republic.

On the Cape northern frontier the 'bastaards'/Griqua entered into relations with indigenous peoples which included a legitimate component but also raiding for booty and 'bushman' labour. This latter activity was both lubricated by the colonial arms trade and fed captive labour into the colonial economy. Recent research suggests that Griqua and Kora slave-raiding intensified and helped prolong the wave of wars and migrations among African groups in the 1820s known as the *mfecane* (Cobbing 1988; Eldredge 1994, 1995).

The Griqua frontier is not generally seen as a source of twentieth-century South African racial order, except perhaps insofar as it helped (partially and temporarily) depopulate areas of the interior into which Europeans subsequently migrated. It did give rise to a lasting Griqua identity, resurgent in post-apartheid South Africa. But what is most important here is that, as Legassick and others argued, it contradicts the picture of the colonial frontier as one responsible for clarifying black–white enmity. On the contrary, the story of the Griquas, partly autonomous refugees from colonial discrimination, partly agents of the colony, dominators and plunderers of various indigenous groups, and finally forced down into an oppressed coloured population in the OFS, nicely illustrates the racial complexity of the early open frontier.

The missionary and merchant frontiers

In the frontier tradition of South African historiography Dutch-Afrikaners figure as the principal bearers of racial prejudice and domination. Radical writers by contrast charge forces linked to the British metropole with playing a central role in the dispossession and conquest of Africans and in the authorship of twentieth-century forms of institutionalized racial domination. Two of these forces, the missionaries and the merchants, were at the forefront of expanding frontiers of European influence and control.

Although the first European mission station amongst South Africa's indigenous people (in this case the Khoi) was established in 1737, it was not until the 1790s that missionaries began to pour into the region, inspired by the evangelical Protestant revival in Europe and the United States and facilitated by British conquest of the Cape. In contrast to the established reform church of the Dutch-Afrikaners, the new wave of missionaries zealously promoted conversion of the heathen and were committed to living and working amongst blacks, often establishing mission stations beyond colonial borders in areas of coloured or African authority. Their identification with black opposition to forced labour and dispossession placed them in many cases on a path of confrontation with Dutch-Afrikaner and, later, British settlers who coveted black land and labour. Mission stations offered economically pressured Khoi and Africans access to land and missionaries provided diplomatic, welfare and other services which won them, though often only for a while, varying degrees of African chiefly patronage. Missionaries made early and rapid progress in converting the Khoi. Although largely unsuccessful in their efforts to convert Africans until late in the nineteenth century, they did in time attract numbers of Africans to their stations. Those joining the missions were initially individuals marginal to surrounding African societies, but they formed the nuclei of relatively educated and briefly economically successful black Christian communities. In the twentieth century Christianity would spread to the majority of Africans in South Africa (Etherington 1978; Beck 1997; Elbourne and Ross 1997: 34-9; Hodgson 1997).

Though regarded contemporaneously by settler opponents and subsequently by many liberals as vigorous supporters of black causes, radical critics later cast colonial-era missionaries as 'agents of a pervasive economic and cultural imperialism' (Keegan 1996: 133) and as cheerleaders of British Imperial expansion. Guided by the middle class Christian norms they sought to instil both in Europe and in the colonies, the missionaries (with a few exceptions) harboured a deep and undifferentiating contempt for all African cultural practices, from witch persecution to polygyny and *lobola* (bride-price payments accompanying marriage). Missionary universalism took the form of a belief in the possibility of making all into good Christians rather than a commitment to accommodating diverse cultural forms. Missionaries thus demanded a 'revolutionary' reorientation of African cosmology (Elphick 1981: 282). They also believed firmly in the virtues of capitalism, campaigning against both forced black labour and the traditional African economy in favour of wage labour and market peasant production. They encouraged amongst blacks western consumption habits and technological innovation and brought Africans within the nexus of the white economy as both consumers and producers. Finally, many missionaries, not only British ones, believed, or came to believe, in the extension of British imperial control. This they judged essentially benign in its consequences for Africans, protecting the latter from the more rapacious settlers and facilitating missionary endeavour.

To the charge of intolerant assimilationism critics would add, for missionaries of a later period, that of proto-segregationist racism. Missionaries became over time increasingly pessimistic about the possibility of civilizing Africans. Many chose to swim with a late nineteenth-century tide running in Britain and the white settler Cape away from mid-Victorian liberalism towards pseudo-scientific scepticism about innate African equality with Europeans and about the possibility of successful racial integration (Hodgson 1997: 82).

The impact of missionaries on African life was undoubtedly large, whether in conveying doctrines or ways of life, and missionaries were equally certainly torch bearers of European imperialism. A number of critics of the missionaries do, however, highlight the ambiguous and double-edged character of Christianizing efforts (e.g. Elphick 1981: 278; Delius 1983: ch. 7; Comaroff and Comaroff 1991: 26, Crais 1992: 82-93, 100-4). In the first place western doctrine was often not taken up in a pure form: Christian and African religious world-views became intermeshed in the region. Already in the nineteenth century independent-minded African evangelists were recasting the Christian message. The burgeoning of indigenous African churches in the twentieth century strengthened the tendency towards an eclectic admixture of Christian and traditional African beliefs and rituals in South Africa (Elphick 1997: 4; Hexham and Poewe, 1997: 132; Hodgson 1997; Pretorius and Jafta 1997: 217).

The missionaries moreover introduced blacks to ideas of universal brotherhood, equality before God and continuous progress. In doing so they supplied standards against which educated and converted blacks could judge the failure of white power-holders to grant them equal consideration and rights. At the same time mission educators passed on to a minority of blacks an essential resource for contesting European hegemony on its own terms: literacy. Missions would remain the principal source of African schooling in South Africa until the 1950s. It was from the ranks of the mission-educated, especially those frustrated by blockages to their upward mobility, that many future leading black nationalists and dissidents would emerge. Nor would Christians prove to be exclusively a moderating force in black opposition politics, as some suppose: there were moments both in the nineteenth and twentieth centuries when Christianized or clerical black figures took militant stands against whites.

A second key frontier pioneer issuing from the British metropole was the merchant. A recent cohort of mainly radical historians has stressed the very large role of nineteenth-century merchant capitalism in promoting the conquest and dispossession of blacks and encouraging the elaboration of a racial order in colonial South Africa (Peires 1988; Ross 1993: 90-4; Keegan 1996). Keegan has indeed argued that merchant and speculator capitalists from British settler ranks played a more aggressive role in promoting the subordination of blacks on the subcontinent than the much more infamous patriarchs of the Dutch-Afrikaner frontier (or at least than those Dutch-Afrikaners who were not themselves closely connected to Cape merchant capital). His portrayal reverses a more conventional view of British settlers as, on balance, a liberalizing force promoting free labour and cross-frontier trade. The merchant-centred argument also challenges the 1970s Marxist assumption that mercantile capitalism had a much less profound impact on race relations than mining capitalism.

British merchants arriving in the wake of the British take-over of the Cape first established a foothold in Cape Town, where they formed a tightly knit expatriate elite linked economically to Britain and rose to dominance over local Dutch merchants. Of more profound impact were the 1820 British settlers in the eastern Cape. Attuned to commercial ways and backed by credit from Cape Town wholesale merchants, settlers established trade entrepôts like Graaff-Reinet or invested in woolled merino sheep. Sheep were soon at the centre of a booming wool export industry that transformed the fortunes of the (until then) relatively economically becalmed eastern Cape (Crais 1986). Traders and wool farmers in turn bought up further land, initiating a trail of speculative land grabbing that would extend deep into the interior (Peires 1988: 475-6). Eastern Cape British settlers also established extensive trade ties with the Xhosa, setting in motion a process that drew Africans over a wide area more fully into the commercial economy (Keegan 1996: 67-8, 72-4). In the process a distinctive and self-conscious settler bourgeoisie emerged centred on Grahams Town (Keegan 1996: 67-8, 72-4).

The Grahams Town elite's expansionist agitation led, according to Keegan (1996), directly or indirectly to a string of British conquests and annexations between 1842 and 1851 in Natal, the eastern Cape frontier and Transorangia.

Keegan also suggests, in his critique of the frontier thesis, that the Boers were mostly reluctant to support British military expeditions against the Xhosa in the eastern Cape and Sotho in Transorangia. On occasion, as with the *maatschappy* in Transorangia, they looked to African chiefdoms rather than the British for protection and patronage. In the case of Transorangia/OFS a rising Boer elite linked to the British pursued the more aggressive stance against the Sotho in the 1850s and 1860s than the original Dutch-Afrikaner frontier settlers of the 1820s (Keegan 1996: 215-19, 267-74). The mining revolution of the 1870s and 1880s opened new avenues of speculative investment by, amongst others, Anglophone mining and land companies and Cape merchants and traders. It also encouraged British settler pressure for fresh Imperial advance, this time in Griqualand West and the Transvaal (Shillington 1985: chs 2, 5, 6; Beinart and Delius 1986; Keegan 1986a: 38-50; Trapido 1986).

The eastern Cape settler elite played an anti-black role from the outset, campaigning for vagrancy laws to control black labour movement and for the deployment of British imperial power to dispossess Khoi and Xhosa of their land (Crais 1986). By contrast the Cape Town mercantile bourgeoisie initially forged an alliance with the humanitarians. Together with the latter they campaigned for free labour and trade and a range of political reforms including freedom of the press and representative government for the Cape. But there was, according to Keegan, a contradiction between the philanthropic and utilitarian aspects of the humanitarian–mercantile lobby. By the 1840s the utilitarian had won out as the Cape Town mercantile interests, their battle against official slavery won, identified increasingly with the white colonists in their pursuit of racially repressive laws and eastern territorial expansion (Keegan 1996: 98-106, 129). Clearly both the western and eastern Cape British settler elites played a part, whether as authors or collaborators, in the founding of a regional racial order.

The imperial factor

What has been the role of the Imperial powers in shaping South Africa's racial order? The DEIC, which presided over the first Dutch occupation of the Cape, is generally considered an ambivalent, sometimes reluctant author of the early racial order. From the outset, according to Elphick and Giliomee, the DEIC divided the colony into legal status groups that roughly coincided with racial differences and helped frame and reinforce racial hierarchy (1988: 528-9). The DEIC was initially committed to recognizing Khoi autonomy and keeping the expansionist freeburghers in check, yet lacked either the will or institutional capacity to police effectively the advancing white frontier or control the depredations visited upon indigenes by frontier settlers. It reserved for itself the right severely to punish slaves and servants, but could only monopolize punishment up to a point in a society dominated, especially on the frontier, by private patriarchal violence; and it often exercised its prerogative brutally in a system bereft of any pretence of equal treatment of all before the law. From the 1760s and 1770s it began to sanction outright racial discrimination.

What the DEIC could not do was lastingly alter the balance of power in southern Africa. It presided over the destruction of the political power of weak Khoi polities, but neither it nor its Dutch Batavian successor could inflict a decisive blow against the more numerous and organized Africans whom the Dutch settlers began to encounter and fight on the eastern Cape frontier from the 1770s.

The role of the British state is altogether more controversial. Few credit the DEIC with a progressive and racially liberalizing role. Its British Imperial successors were, by contrast, considered by many settlers to be negrophile or at least subject to the influence of humanitarians, a theme echoed by many later Afrikaner nationalist, pro-British and Anglophone-liberal historians (Smith 1988: chs 2, 4). Some of the facts adduced in support of such a view are not disputed: the British abolished the slave trade in 1808, emancipated the Khoi from compulsory apprenticeship in 1828, freed the slaves in 1838, and granted the Cape self-government on the basis of a colour-blind constitution. They also governed Natal, which the Cape annexed in 1843, on a formally non-racial basis. Britain granted recognition to trekker polities only on the condition that they renounce slavery, and to South Africa in 1910 on condition that it retain, subject to tough constitution-change provisions, the non-racial Cape franchise. More arguably, Britain's establishment of protectorates, dependencies and locations in Southern Africa may have spared Africans more complete territorial dispossession at the hands of strengthening Afrikaner and Anglophone settler power in the later nineteenth century.

In more recent decades the British record has been subject to critical examination, most enthusiastically by radical historians like Atmore, Marks, Legassick and Keegan. Two aspects of that record can be distinguished. One is Britain's part in colonial expansion and consolidation; the other is its involvement in shaping a racial order in areas under its direct and indirect control. With regard to the first, Atmore and Marks argued that whereas 'until the 1870s–80s (with the exception of the Cape), the various societies in South Africa were far more evenly balanced than is generally appreciated ... [a]fter the 1870s and 1880s, the balance of political and economic power swung rapidly in favour of white colonist societies'. In their view it was 'British imperialist intervention more than of any other single factor' which tipped the balance. Without British support, they suggested, Afrikaners might well have eventually merged with the majority population (1974: 107-10). Certainly Dutch-Afrikaners both on the eastern frontier and later in the northern Transvaal suffered serious setbacks at the hands of the *Zuurveld* Xhosa and the Pedi before these African chiefdoms were conquered by the British Imperial forces (the Xhosa most decisively in 1811–12 and the 1840s and 1850s; the Pedi in 1879). It was also the British who crushed the most powerful of African polities, the Zulu, in 1879. Though the Boers could, like many African polities in the region, also win battles and indeed wars, it was the military resources of the largest of global empires, backed by the technological dynamism of the world's first industrial revolution, which irreversibly secured white settler military advantage.

Britain's setting aside of land for Africans was furthermore not always protective of African interests. The annexation of Basutoland in 1868 may have preserved the territory from Boer capture, but it also confirmed the loss of the most fertile Sotho land to the Boers. The British were at times on the side of those grabbing land from Africans on behalf of white settlers. To be sure, the British military campaigns against the Xhosa and Sotho in the 1830s and 1840s were driven by colonial governors captive to settler interests rather than by London (which reversed the annexations). The annexations of Griqualand West in 1871 and British Bechuanaland in 1885, though impelled partly by the agitations of settler speculators, were part of British colonial policy.

Britain's role in constructing a racial order in areas under its own jurisdiction is equally ambiguous. A part of the case against Britain is that its initial reformist proclamations on black–white relations after taking power – the legislation on labour relations in 1809 and 1812 especially – were of decidedly mixed benefit for those they were ostensibly intended to benefit (Ross 1993: ch. 3, 1994). While the legislation reduced the arbitrary powers of masters over servants, it codified a system of compulsory apprenticeship for farm children up to the age of 25, restricted Khoi mobility and land-ownership and legalized the enslavement of Christians. While free-trade Britain was opposed to forced labour, it nevertheless sanctioned, however reluctantly, settler-initiated legislation restricting the mobility and bargaining power of free labourers. Though the Colonial Office disallowed some anti-labour legislation it sanctioned a Master and Servant Ordinance in 1841 criminalizing a range of employee misconduct. Master and servant legislation remained, in revised form, in operation until the end of the 1960s (Ross 1994: 163). Moreover in 1828 the British colonial government imposed on Africans entering the Cape the first pass laws applicable to non-slave Africans in what became South Africa.

The second part of the case against Britain is that in its search for local collaborating elites it was prepared to hand autonomy to white settlers, subject only to weak restrictions on how settlers could use their power against blacks (Atmore and Marks 1974: 108-11). Notwithstanding the importance of its armed campaigns and annexations in confirming white regional dominance, for most of the nineteenth century the British government was concerned to avoid expensive military expansion and direct rule over remote peoples, and sought to govern where possible through local collaborators or proxies. Collaborating elites were invariably white and rarely protective of blacks. The Sand River and Bloemfontein Conventions of 1852 and 1854, which granted political independence to the Transvaal and Transorangian polities respectively, did prohibit slavery by Boers. The treaties nevertheless contributed to the diplomatic and military isolation of African polities and were ineffectual in preventing exploitation of captive labour in the SAR. The granting to the Cape of representative government in 1853 and responsible government in 1872 left colonists there with a relatively free hand to pass legislation in 1854 criminalizing breach of contract and disobedience by (in practice mostly black) labourers, to take measures in 1887 and 1892 limiting the coloured and African franchise and to enforce increasing levels of racial segregation. In 1910 the British granted independence to a unitary South Africa on the basis of a constitution which, though preserving the Cape non-racial franchise, ensured white control of a potentially powerful new centralized state.

The third part of the case against Britain is that British colonial officials contributed to designing and entrenching new institutions of labour coercion and racial segregation in the later nineteenth century. They endórsed the policies of labour coercion to appease (mainly Anglophone) mining capitalists. British colonial authorities sanctioned the imposition of pass controls on Africans in Kimberley in 1872. From 1902 the British Milner administration enforced restrictions on African movement on the Rand more rigorously than the defeated Boer regime (Marks and Trapido 1981: 69; Worger 1987: 114-17).

British and colonial governments also helped set in place the territorially-based political segregation of races by demarcating areas for African occupation in the Cape and Natal and by placing them, in Natal, under indirect rule exercised through African chiefs (Mamdani 1996: ch. 3). Urban segregation made its first appearance in the mid- and later nineteenth-century eastern Cape, Durban and Kimberley, all in British colonies (Mabin 1986; Maylam 1995: 22-3). The South African Native Affairs Commission of 1903-5, set up by the British colonial regime after the South African War and dominated by white Anglophone experts, outlined the country's first blueprint for comprehensive territorial and political segregation (Legassick 1973b). Britain and British colonial agents initiated segregation partly to protect Africans from dispossession and the trauma of urbanization, but some of their other motives were more prosaic or protective of whites. The policy of segregated reserves and indirect rule offered colonial administrators a way of saving money on African administration and maintaining order (Welsh 1971; Shillington 1985). Colonial and municipal officials in the British colonies looked to segregation in urban areas to contain imagined hygiene dangers to white residents (Swanson 1976, 1977, 1983) and rescue 'poor whites' from racial competition. The turn to segregation also reflected a growing attachment in British and Anglophone governing circles to the view that Africans could not be assimilated successfully into a common society.

Late colonial race relations

It was during the later eighteenth and the nineteenth centuries that the South African racial order acquired a more explicit character. Writers attribute this development either to the closing of the Cape frontier (Elphick and Giliomee 1988) or to the incorporation of the Cape into the world economy (Freund 1976: 64; Ross 1993; Keegan 1996). Elphick and Giliomee argue that between 1770 and 1814 an informal taken-for-granted racial order in the Cape was challenged by new shortages of land and labour, a crisis in master–servant relationships and, from 1806, the British claim that Europeans and blacks were equal before the law. These threats to the old Cape order brought forth 'the elaboration and frequent expression of sentiments amongst Europeans, that slaves, Khoisan and Xhosa were intrinsically inferior to the colonists' (1988: 546), sentiments carried into the northern interior by the Dutch-Afrikaner emigrants of the 1830s. Those who attribute a more conscious and open racial order to the incorporation of South Africa into the world capitalist economy point to, amongst other things, the increased labour demands commercial production made upon black farm servants irrespective of their origins (Ross 1993: ch. 3), the aggressive militarism and acquisitiveness of the eastern Cape merchant elite (Keegan 1996) and the demands of mine owners for regimented and cheap African labour from the 1870s (Freund 1976; Trapido 1980a; Worger 1987; Bundy 1988: ch. 8).

The later eighteenth century saw the beginnings of statutory discrimination in the Cape. Supposedly free Khoi and mixed race 'bastaards' were subject to compulsory conscription and restrictions on their freedom of movement. This marked, in effect, the beginning of formalized racial discrimination in what is today South Africa. The British imposed a *formally* colour-blind political and legal order in the Cape. By the time the British took over however a conscious racism had taken hold amongst white Southern Africans. This the British settlers, with their strong sense of cultural superiority, if anything magnified (and joined to ethnic contempt for Dutch-Afrikaners). Effective segregation in the Cape was evident by the 1870s in the churches, nondenominational government schools, prisons and in residential housing. Under responsible government it was extended to hospitals, asylums, supreme court juries and, in 1905, further entrenched in education (Bickford-Smith 1989; Maylam 1995).

Two phenomena appeared to contradict this picture of a racist Cape. One was the relative racial fluidity of Cape Town throughout the nineteenth century. Bickford-Smith has, however, demonstrated that writers like Frederickson exaggerated the extent of this fluidity or, rather, failed to acknowledge the extent to which racial integration was increasingly confined, on the white side, to the city's less well-off (Bickford-Smith 1989, 1995). Ross has shown that despite the absence of a clear racial division of labour in Cape Town there was from early on an elaborate etiquette of race in the city (Ross 1989, 1993: ch. 4). From the 1880s and 1890s segregation began to appear in a range of Cape Town institutions, including hotels, theatres and cinemas, and around the turn of the twentieth century it was extended to the residential location of Africans. Capetonian segregationism reflected a growing concern on the part of the city elite to rescue 'poor whites' from degradation through racial mixing and competition as well as a swelling sectional consciousness and civic pride in the Anglophone upper classes (Bickford-Smith 1989, 1995).

The other was the phenomenon of 'Cape liberalism'. Throughout the nineteenth century a moderately liberal elite defended the Cape's non-racial qualified franchise, colour-blind legislation and large African reserves. Conveyed into the Cape initially by European missionaries, liberalism found supporters in the ranks of lawyers, journalists, merchants, politicians vying for African votes and Transkeian magistrates. Its adherents were mainly white Anglophones but included also Afrikaners and Africans. Historians have distinguished an administrative from a political tradition of liberalism (Lewsen 1983: 41-2) and a 'great' tradition of liberalism based in Cape Town from a 'small' tradition of constituency electoral politics in the eastern Cape (Trapido 1968, 1980a). Trapido and other radical writers argued that Cape liberalism was rooted in an alliance of merchants and black peasants which began to crumble once, in the later nineteenth century, new dominant classes (especially mine owners) came to value blacks more as labourers than as independent producers, consumers or middle class co-optees (Legassick 1973a; Trapido 1980a; Bundy 1988). Lewsen is sceptical of this material interpretation, contending that Cape liberalism was at its most extended just before being engulfed by the formation of the Union in 1910 (Lewsen 1983). What all recent academic observers agree is that Cape liberalism was generally shallow and idiosyncratic. Cape liberals sought to preserve existing black rights, rather than significantly to extend them, in the face of assaults from farming and mining interests. They were dismissive of African culture and political independence, paternalistic, protectively segregationist and steeped in class and racial consciousness (Davenport 1966; Lewsen 1983; Keegan 1996).

The Cape gave rise to a distinctive approach to administration of African areas which illustrated well the ambivalence of its liberalism. It involved the weakening of chiefs, the monopolization of authority by white magistrates (assisted by African headmen) and, from 1894, the establishment of nominated, later partially elective, advisory councils (Southall 1982: 90-5). On the one hand this system entailed the open replacement of African traditional leaders by white ones in a manner inspired by the integrationist policies of Cape Governor Sir

George Grey in Kaffraria in the 1850s. On the other hand Cape administration nurtured an occupational culture amongst white magistrates characterized by benevolent paternalism and a strong sense of vocation (Dubow 1989: 99-103).

In Natal, by contrast, there developed from 1849 the Shepstone-inspired system of indirect rule. Natal's Native Affairs Secretary Theophilus Shepstone sought to preserve African 'locations' from white settler land demands and favoured governing Africans through chiefs and African customary law rather than white magistrates and legislation. The system was later extended to Zululand, conquered in 1879. Shepstonian indirect rule was partly a way of getting around financial constraints and shortages of personnel, but it also expressed a particular theory about what was required to maintain stability in African areas. Eschewing British principles of liberal government for African areas, it drew ingeniously on African traditionalist discourses including an 'African model of domination' (Hamilton 1998: 93). Natal's white lieutenant-governor set himself up as a supreme chief with arbitrary powers, his post tailored to fit Zulu notions of centralized authority. At the same time whites reworked African traditionalism to suit their political needs. They codified African customary law in controversial ways and on occasions appointed their own African chiefs (Welsh 1971; Etherington 1978; Mamdani 1996).

Since Natal was a British colony its legislation was required to be colour-blind, but Natal's whites were deeply racist. Though lacking powers of self-government, they could get their voices heard in a Legislative Council set up in 1856. White settlers made it difficult for Christianized Africans to exempt themselves from customary law and placed numerous obstacles in the way of African enfranchisement. The result was a negligible black vote, in contrast to the Cape (Welsh 1971: ch. 4). After the granting of responsible government in 1893 white racism manifested itself also in discriminatory legislation against Indians, designed mainly to curtail the competitive threat posed by Indian merchants and traders and to encourage Indian repatriation (Brain 1989).

White Natalian racism was sharpened by the fact that a large and nearby African population commanded land and labour coveted by white speculators, merchants and planters. It was facilitated, negatively, by the absence of black voters and Natal's distance from Cape Town's relative cosmopolitanism. Natal racism was however changeable in its expression. White Natalians' greed for African land and labour and their aggressive brand of mid-Victorian cultural universalism initially placed them in conflict with Shepstonian schemes of territorial, political and legal segregation. Yet a hatred of the educated and Christianized African 'kholwa' led them by the early twentieth century to switch to supporting the segregation of Africans from whites (Welsh 1971).

The racial orders established in the northern Boer republics were based straightforwardly on white domination over Africans. The republics openly expressed a commitment to racial inequality in their laws, including their constitutions. The 1858 *Grondwet* of the SAR declared that there would be 'no equality between coloured people and the white inhabitants of the country either in Church or State' (cited Frederickson 1981: 177). Inter-racial marriage was not recognized in the Transvaal. Legislation against African squatters was passed in the SAR in 1895. Indians were banished from the Free State in the early 1890s.

Clearly Boer racism was more explicit than that of the British colonies. It is clear though that the trekker orders were not the exclusive wellspring of twentieth-century patterns of racial segregation. Natal was aggressively racist and the Cape increasingly so by the late nineteenth century despite their ostensible non-racialism. Urban and territorial segregation was developed more fully in the Cape and Natal than in the northern republics. The pass laws that the SAR imposed on Africans in 1895 were drawn up by 'uitlander' Anglophone mine owners rather than Boers. South Africa's twentieth century racial order developed against the backdrop of late colonial race policies that varied in form but were uniformly bound up with white political domination and economic advance.

Colonialism and white post-colonial domination

In formal terms South Africa's colonial order concluded when the newly unified country became an independent dominion within the British Empire in 1910. The 1931 Statute of Westminster confirmed the autonomy of the dominions. In 1961 South Africa took the further step of becoming a republic outside the Commonwealth (which it rejoined in 1994). The case has been made that European neo-colonial control continued in various guises beyond 1910 (Simson 1973). It is true that South Africa's political autonomy did not translate into economic autonomy. At the same time the neo-colonial label underestimated the dynamism of locally based political and economic institutions (see Chapter 4). Others suggested that white South Africa after 1910 became in effect a colonial power in relation to its own black subjects (the South African Communist Party line). This depiction was insensitive to the way in which a portion of the African population transmuted into a subordinate proletariat within a common economy; the colonialism metaphor successfully captured only the central state's relationship with reserve-based Africans. What was probably more true is that post-1910 South Africa assumed the role of a sub-Imperial power in black Africa (Innes 1984: conclusion). Whatever the merits of these various attempts to extend the temporal boundaries of colonialism in the region, this chapter has focused on a narrower question: to what extent can it be said that the origins of South Africa's twentieth-century racial order lie in its pre-1910 colonial past?

Colonialism-as-originator could, in principle, supply the modern racial order with precedents, designs, authors and structural legacies.

In terms of precedents, few doubt that areas of white colonial jurisdiction were characterized by white political and economic domination continuously from 1652. Nor can it be doubted that this precedent cast a long shadow over the post-colonial period. The simple fact of colonial precedent does not, however, explain the twentieth-century racial order. Firstly, the precedent was inexact: colonial racist domination did not invariably take the form of formalized racial discrimination (absent in the British colonies) or of segregation (mostly absent in the Boer republics). Yet both of these were features of twentieth-century South Africa. In the second place, precedents need not be followed. Human inertia and conservatism made it inevitable that the colonial forms and discourses would be around, at least for a while, after 1910; but colonial precedent cannot, as Cell notes (Cell 1982: 4), explain why these forms did not disappear over time or why they were developed in the particular direction that they were after 1910.

The late colonial era also generated designs. The SANAC of 1903-5 formulated influential segregationist blueprints for the post-colonial order. In doing so it built upon the distinctive race policies of the four white-run South African polities. SANAC's designs thus provided a bridge between colonial-era and post-1910 patterns of racial ordering; and the earlier post-1910 patterns in turn influenced (in various ways) what came after 1948. But by the late 1940s the colonial designs offered a rather remote reference point, and there is a chance that a break might have been made with the colonial model around mid-century, especially given the pressures of African urbanization. Although they left their traces in much of post-colonial Africa, colonial institutional designs did not elsewhere on the continent harden into something like apartheid. In South Africa by contrast colonial designs for segregationist indirect rule received their fullest elaboration only after 1948, well into the post-colonial era (Mamdani 1996). The inheritance of colonial designs cannot explain their persistent influence under changed conditions.

The colonial period additionally offered human authors of twentieth-century racial domination. There is, to be sure, little basis for the long-held Anglophone liberal belief that white racial domination was the near-exclusive invention of colonial-era Dutch-Afrikaners. Without exonerating the Boers, the chapter has surveyed a range of other colonial actors, including missionaries and British settlers and English-speaking capitalists, not to mention the Griqua, who played substantial parts in the conquest, dispossession, cultural subjugation and economic exploitation of blacks. In class terms, merchants, speculators and commercial planters were all active shapers of South African racial structures and practices. Mine owners, though late participants in the colonial elaboration of white domination, made, as Chapter 2 will show, a specific and large contribution to it.

Colonial authoring of the racial order continued until the last years of colonial rule. The final colonial decade threw up influential individuals and groups explicitly committed to formulating systems of racial governance appropriate to a post-colonial era, or at least to a self-governing South African union. They ranged from SANAC commissioners to the local white politicians to whom Britain handed increased powers from 1907. Prominent late colonial politicians continued to exercise power into the 1940s and even 1950s.

Again, however, there remains the question of why the visions and actions of colonial-era actors should have exerted influence so many decades after the end of colonialism. After all, these actors left the scene through natural attrition, and before they did so some – notably Jan Smuts – had adopted more racially reformist positions in response to the shifting imperatives of the post-colonial decades. New sets of influential class actors emerged with interest profiles distinct from those of the colonial era – most importantly manufacturers. Certainly colonial authorship cannot explain the reactionary turn of 1948.

Some structural legacies of the colonial period supplied conditions not only for post-1910 segregation but also for post-1948 apartheid. The most important were demographic. South Africa combined the large-scale white population of the US, Australia, New Zealand and Canada – countries in which indigenes were largely annihilated or reduced to insignificant minorities – with the survival intact of large non-European populations as in most of Africa and Asia. Despite South Africa's black majority and the uncertain loyalties of Afrikaner whites, it was to the leaders of the white population that Britain fatefully handed power in 1910. It did so for a range of reasons, including the Boers' demonstrated capacity for military resistance, feelings of racial solidarity with fellow whites and the then weakness of black nationalism in sub-Saharan Africa. The willingness of dominant Afrikaner elites to support the British Empire in the decade after the South African War eliminated one area where black elites, imbued with empire loyalism, might have enjoyed comparative advantage as compradors.

Once given power, the white population was numerous enough to defend its political gains by force. With privileges to protect, it had little incentive to enfranchise an African population large enough to dominate it numerically. The white oligarchy exempted South Africa from post-Second World War decolonization: it was a post-colonial ruling oligarchy already, outside British influence, numerous and resourced enough to go it alone. Unlike also-numerous Algerian settlers, white Afrikaners lacked a metropolitan hinterland to which to retreat. White political elites confronted the question of lower class incorporation from the perspective of a long-established domestic ruling class rather than that of footloose expatriates. In these circumstances there was every chance that rising black nationalism, the acceleration of black urbanization and international pressure, when their challenge came, would lead at least initially not to liberalization, nor even to more of the same, but to a reactionary elaboration of white domination. This was made more likely by the early dominance of labour-repressive sectors amongst the white employers (another colonial legacy) and by the capacity of whites, until the late 1960s, to provide a sufficiency of consumers and skilled labour for a prosperous economy. Blacks, needed mostly as unskilled labour, enjoyed little bargaining power.

Ethnic fissures amongst whites gave an additional reactionary twist to settler politics. As in Canada, the ethnic composition of the white population had been shaped by an exchange of European colonial overlord prior to decolonization. In both Canada and South Africa the conquering British acquired large numbers of white subjects who were of a different language and cultural background to themselves; in the case of South Africa these reluctant subjects constituted the majority of whites. The Afrikaner majority of whites in South Africa was antagonized by British liberalism, economically subordinate to Anglophones and disproportionately represented amongst labour-repressive farmers and insecure white workers. They had both the incentive and means to advance their own position at the expense of blacks after 1910, and with a vigour that the Anglophones, more sensitive to world opinion and economically secure, might have balked at had they been left in control of the post-colonial state.

Colonialism in post-apartheid perspective

The inauguration of Nelson Mandela as president in 1994 can be seen as marking, in a certain sense, the second of two phases of a process which European decolonization elsewhere in Africa telescoped into a single event. Whereas in the rest of sub-Saharan Africa retreating European colonialists handed political power directly to members of the indigenous African majority, in South Africa alone they granted independence to a European settler-descended minority. Whites of course acquired self-government in *non-African* former European colonies such as America, Canada and Australia, but in these cases they made up a majority of the population of the newly autonomous states. In South Africa, with its black majority, a decolonized white settler state was in the long run impossible to sustain.

The limits of white conquest in Africa are now clear at the end of the twentieth century. The old question of whether whites have a future on the African continent has been posed afresh since the early 1990s. According to the 1996 census whites constitute but 11% of South Africa's population. Their demographic presence in the rural interior is tenuous, and they have abandoned city centres to blacks. A large number of whites, faced with the encroachment of African realities, are contemplating relocating to the safety of white-majority states such as the US and Australia. Many stay in South Africa only because currency exchange rates are prohibitive or because the states they would prefer to live under are reluctant to admit them in large numbers. White political influence is much reduced and many whites, bunkered in sprawling suburbs, feel physically endangered. At the same time South Africa's whites are not 'settlers': 91% are locally born, and Afrikaners in particular have deep historical and sentimental roots in the country. While the days of continuously rising white prosperity came to an end in the 1970s, most whites remain affluent and the white minority still commands the bulk of private wealth. There is no precedent on the basis of which to assess their likely fate: post-1994 South Africa is the first black-run state to govern a large number of whites.

In capturing the central institutions of the South African state the African majority has decisively reversed one of the principal legacies of colonial-era settler conquest, and it has, in the process, won for itself the most powerful and resourceful African-controlled state in the world. Even so, the colonial legacy will not be easy to efface or overturn. White privilege is the most important but also the most obvious overhang of colonial times, reinforced after 1910 and persisting into the 'new' South Africa. Less obvious are constraints on the democratic government flowing from the limits of white conquest on the African periphery and the colonial mode of indirect rule. As Mamdani reminds us, there remain in South Africa today, notwithstanding the urbanization of so many Africans, large areas controlled by chiefs whose subjects are marginal to the new order (Mamdani 1996). Secluded by customary law from some of the rights and liberties of common citizenship they are in some cases also, as in the former KwaZulu, deeply suspicious of the new black-controlled centre.

Perhaps more importantly, South Africa's fate is linked to that of a continent which has been undergoing an extended and traumatic crisis. Africa may have expelled white colonial rulers and but it is, in the wake of its wars, famine and epidemics, under the cosh of powerful capitalist states in the north, most of whom are European and several of whom are former colonial powers. Western lending agencies have since the 1980s imposed a new informal imperium. South Africa's fate here is pivotal. Long a key player on the subcontinent, it is looked to by many after apartheid as the potential wellspring of an African renaissance (even while being feared by its neighbours as a potential sub-imperial hegemon). Yet South Africa is itself externally vulnerable in ways that place a question mark over its capacity to catalyse far-reaching changes beyond its borders. Despite national industrialization in the post-colonial era, the country never freed itself of dependence on foreign capital, technology and markets (see Chapter 4). Since the 1990s trade and currency liberalization and privatization have removed much of South Africa's insulation from the world economy. In consequence the state which blacks have inherited is, like its white-controlled predecessor but more so, exposed to the vagaries of a world economy dominated by forces from abroad. Colonialism is gone but its imprint, including on racial power relations, remains all too visible.

2

Capitalism and Racial Domination

The revisionist challenge

The extent of capitalism's responsibility for South Africa's racial order has recently been revived as a topic by the Truth and Reconciliation Commission, instituted by the post-1994 democratic government to reckon with apartheid's human rights violations. It is no small irony that the TRC, which found capitalists morally complicit in apartheid, was sitting even as the first post-apartheid government was dedicating itself firmly to a capitalist road to non-racial social justice. The TRC's deliberations on capitalism and apartheid echoed a 1970s debate known as the liberal–radical controversy. The participants in the earlier debate too considered whether capitalism was to 'blame' for the racial order, though in the very different context of trying to determine whether capitalists and capitalist growth were potential allies in the struggle against apartheid. Today the question for capitalism is different: whether it can bring racial equality, and social justice more generally, to a society of deep ethnic and class disparities. Even so, the issued raised by the debate in its previous incarnation have never gone away. They remain interesting for the light they throw both on South African history and on the entrenchment and decline of ethnic orders historically and globally. There remains further the matter of whether, and how far, the dramatic political changes of the 1990s have settled the political questions posed by the older debate.

The 1970s debate was initiated by Marxist-influenced radical critics of apartheid. The burden of their 'revisionist' case was that South Africa's racial order was an essentially modern phenomenon and that one modernizing force in particular – capitalism – authored, shaped and benefited from it. For many radicals the crucible of the modern racial order was the diamond and gold mining capitalism that got underway in the 1870s and 1880s, although other radicals traced the origins of the racial order to earlier, merchant, phases of capitalism (see Chapter 1). Radicals also argued that white agriculture, an undisputed co-author and beneficiary of racial domination, was capitalist rather than a pre-capitalist relic, or at least that its process of capitalist modernization deepened rather than ameliorated its racial oppressiveness. Still more provocatively, many radicals insisted that secondary industrial capitalism – which took off between the two world wars – was itself, contrary to the claims of liberals, compatible with or a beneficiary of the racial order.

Why (according to revisionists) did capitalism require a racial order? The answer lay in South African capitalism's need for a large, cheap and regimented labour force, and the racial order provided this above all by facilitating the coercive exploitation of black labour. The result – according to revisionists – was the compression of the bulk of the black, especially African population, into a cheap labour force, and the evisceration of independent black production and the black middle class. The racial order in turn elevated the white wage earning strata into a privileged position, dividing the working class and containing its anti-capitalist challenge.

The assumption that capitalism could very largely get the racial order it needed flowed from the Marxist understanding of South Africa's state as essentially capitalist. Its capitalist nature could (Marxists believed) be verified by reference to things it did to promote capitalist growth which all capitalist states sought to do, such as provide infrastructure, protect industries, regulate the money supply, shape cyclical demand; but also by its copious efforts to prise black labour from the land, crush the African peasantry, perpetuate oscillating labour migrancy, canalize cheap labour to needy sectors and undermine black working class bargaining power.

In arguing these points the principal adversaries of the revisionists were the largely Anglophone liberals who presumed that capitalism and the racial order were incompatible, and the optimists amongst whom believed that the rational colour-blind logic of capitalist industrialism would in time subvert the racial order. The revisionists, by contrast, argued that capitalist industrial growth would not gradually erode the racial order but at best accommodate, at worst strengthen it. The abolition of the racial order required open political struggle, and it quite possibly required the revolutionary abolition of capitalism itself.

The liberal positions which the revisionists of the 1970s were most keen to challenge were those arising from modernization theory, the dual economy thesis and so-called 'pluralist' accounts of race relations (Wolpe 1970; Legassick 1975; Johnstone 1976: introduction). Modernization theory posited a tendency for pre-modern institutions prevalent in less 'developed' societies to evolve into something approximating those found in modern societies by way of processes of economic and cultural diffusion. Transposed into the South African context it suggested that forces of modernity would gradually erode both the archaic racial prejudices of the Afrikaners in power and – here entered the dual economy thesis – transform through contact the backward economies of the African reserves. To such notions – shared it should be said by more orthodox Marxists of an earlier generation – Marxists counterposed an array of arguments derived from Lenin, dependency and underdevelopment theory, peasant studies, French structuralist anthropology, Barrington Moore's theories about differential paths to modernity and Blumer's theses about the adaptation of industrialism to race hierarchy (Johnstone 1970; Wolpe 1970; Trapido 1971; Legassick 1975; Morris 1976; Bonner 1980; Slater 1980; Delius 1983; Bundy 1988). The Marxists of the 1970s argued that capitalist industrial growth was compatible with supposedly pre-modern racial structures and consciousness; that capitalism in certain circumstances attempted to preserve and live parasitically off pre-capitalist relationships, in the process underdeveloping pre-capitalist economies (Johnstone 1970; Wolpe 1970, 1972; Legassick 1974a, 1975); and that capitalist modernity was durably shaped by the labour-repressive practices of modernizing pre-capitalist farmers and extractive mining capitalists (Trapido 1971; Morris 1976). Thus the African reserves were not undeveloped spaces awaiting the diffusion of modern techniques, but pre-capitalist modes of production whose independent peasant producers were deliberately undermined by the state and ruling classes of the dominant capitalist mode in order to obtain labour (Bundy 1988). What remained of African peasant output partially subsidized the reproduction requirements of migrant-peasant households, lowering the labour costs of male household members working for mining and urban capitalists. In time the underdevelopment process so eroded the rural productive base that it eliminated this hidden subsidy, leaving urbanizing workers stranded without rural means of support and generating a crisis of urban social control to which post-1948 apartheid provided a solution (Wolpe 1972).

The other object of radical critique was Furnivallian pluralist theories of race relations which took racial differences as given and immutable, as points of departure for explanations of other phenomena (for example of how ethnically divided societies cohere, or for that matter apartheid) rather than as requiring explanation themselves. The origins of racial and ethnic mobilization could only be exposed, Marxists thought, through an exploration of the material interests that such superstructural phenomena served. These might be the material interests of either working or dominant classes, though revisionists tended to allocate primary responsibility for fostering racial divisions to the dominant.

The revisionist wave here described was mainly a phenomenon of the early to middle 1970s, and was superseded by later Marxist-influenced scholarship in two senses. Firstly, the later 1970s and 1980s saw the consolidation of new trends, above all slower economic growth and the reformist restructuring of apartheid, which challenged some revisionist assumptions (such as that apartheid generated sustainable economic prosperity) and demanded a reworking of revisionist claims. Secondly, Marxist approaches to South African political economy and history became internally differentiated as the Marxist-influenced scholarly cadre expanded. Radical social historians in particular distanced themselves from what they perceived to be the functionalism of 1970s Marxism. Nevertheless important revisionist theoretical and political claims about the positive relationship between apartheid and capitalism survived relatively intact Marxism's transition from radical upstart status to semi-hegemonic orthodoxy.

This book will explore many of the revisionist as well as later Marxist claims, for example about the nature of the state (Chapter 4) and the interaction of race, ethnicity and class and the utility of materialist explanation (Chapters 5 and 6). In this chapter the concern will be primarily with one facet of the revisionist thesis: the argument that capitalism required, benefited from or readily accommodated a racial order in South Africa.

Arguments about the importance for capitalist development of racial domination turn out, on inspection, to be about a range of quite distinguishable propositions. These propositions could be (and many were) debated separately, and the assumption (on the part of either radicals or liberals) that they were either identical in meaning or always linked probably did a great deal to confuse issues and inhibit effective understanding of opposing positions. What follows is an exploration of the range of potential meanings of capitalism and the pre-1990s racial order as they figured in these debates, and of the range of claims that might be made about their relationship.

The terms of debate

Capitalism itself is not always understood to mean the same thing by radicals and liberals. For radicals capitalism is a social order that includes political and ideological as well as economic relationships. The state and its activity may thus be capitalist; and the economy, though in part self-reproducing and governed by internal laws, is in part also a product of extra-economic actions, and has extra-economic conditions of existence. Liberals, by contrast, tended in the post-war period to adopt (as Nattrass shows) the marginalist premise that the term capitalism referred to a (neo-classically conceived) market economy; they saw political power as external to it, and very likely to complicate its proper functioning unless kept at bay (Nattrass 1991: 662-4). Whereas radicals emphasized an intrinsic connection between capitalist economic relations and the political realm, for liberals the two were often definitionally distinctive.

Connected to this was a subterranean disagreement about whether South Africa was fully capitalist. For Marxists the indices of the capitalist nature of the South African economy, or at least the dominance of the capitalist mode within it (Wolpe 1972: 295; Legassick 1974a: 255-9), lay in (variously) the large scale of private ownership, the extent of capitalist concentration and centralization, the commodification of means of production and labour and the apparent operation of capitalist laws of motion (Wolpe 1972: 293-4). For liberals the capitalist nature of the South African economic system was called into question by the extent of the state's bureaucratic growth and interference in private production. There was a capitalist sector in the South African economy, but for liberals it was a moot point whether the South African economy taken as a whole was capitalist, and certainly doubtful that the state was pro-capitalist let alone essentially capitalist. For some liberals, indeed, apartheid represented a kind of 'socialist regime' (Mann 1988: 59). The problem with these liberal arguments were that they were disconnected from the world of power relations and potentially disqualified the capitalist credentials of all economies and the pro-capitalist credentials of all states. After all, the South African state sector was not that large in comparative terms (Yudelman 1987: 257; MERG 1993: 49; Seegers 1994: 75-6). On the other hand radicals were vulnerable to the charge that they treated all the operations of state power, whether ostensibly pro- or anti-capitalist, as expressions of deep capitalist imperatives – a stance that was both reductionist and non-falsifiable.

Beyond these different understandings of capitalism there are other questions, for both liberal and radical participants in the debate, about which aspects of capitalism they were referring to in making claims about its relationship to the racial order. There is a distinction to be made between capitalism as a system or social order and capitalists as owners of means of production and hirers of wage labour (Nattrass 1991: 659). The former, as a system, operates at least in part behind the backs of its participants: it is a structural force without a necessary conscious command centre. Capitalists are human beings who are also more than just capitalists: they may be (for example) Afrikaners or Anglophones, black or white, Christian or Jewish, prejudiced or enlightened. Straddling these two terms is the notion of *capital*: the capitalists qua bearers of the structural imperatives of the system of which they form part. The differences between these terms matter greatly for a discussion of the relationship between capitalism and the racial order.

Firstly, capitalism and capitalists can 'behave' differently, or have different 'needs'. Capitalists may behave in ways that maximize advantage to themselves, but harm capitalism as a system (say by refusing to subsidize worker training or by behaving monopolistically); or thrive on state policies which benefit themselves but endanger long-term systemic health (say seek state handouts or trade protection). Conversely what is good for capitalism is not necessarily good for particular capitalists, or sought by them (for example anti-inflationary policies, or a culling of inefficient firms in a recession). The express preferences of individual capitalists are (moreover) easier to verify than the true requirements of capitalism as a socio-economic system.

Secondly, it is clear that capital and the capitalist class are internally differentiated. There is a distinction to be made between the interests of particular capitalists and capitalists as a class, as well as between aggregates of capital located in different sectors or regions, based on different levels of capital or labour-intensity, oriented to different markets, and so on. It may be possible also to distinguish between sectors or firms at the leading edge of capital, which represent as it were capitalism's future, and those that are backward, representing its past. Moreover capitals may be interpenetrated through ownership, elite social networks, agreements, and so on; holding companies may be more or less loosely centralized. Common interests of firms and sectors may manifest at some levels, their competing interests at others.

Finally, there are distinctions to be made within the organizational world of capital, both intra- and inter-firm, which matter in particular circumstances. Owners, managers and expert advisers may proffer divergent perspectives, rooted in different perceived interests or constructions of the world originating in turn in distinctive forms of socialization, training or peer pressure. The complex structures of mining houses provide notable examples of organizational heterogeneity. There is a disagreement relevant here between a Weberian understanding of firms as bureaucracies run by managers or technocrats and a Marxist view of firms as ultimately accountable to the interests of owners or driven by the external imperatives of capitalist competition. Marxists probably more correctly grasp the bottom-line pressures impelling firm behaviour. Even so, there might be room in a firm for distinctive tactical and strategic readings of the interests of its owners in changing markets. Conflicts may also occur between a firm's interests and those of its managers. Firms do not always act in their own best interests; some go under.

Outside the individual firm, the voluntary organizations to which firms subscribe, like the Federated Chamber of Industries or South African Chamber of Business before the 1990s, may be more or less representative of their members, or more representative of some members than others. When non-representative, they may nevertheless serve as the long-term and globally strategizing brain of a capitalist class whose individual members perceive only narrow or short-term interests. Employer associations can become theatres for ideological and partisan struggles not directly connected to economics. Some capitalist firms have direct lines of communication with, for example, government, behaving as interest groups in their own right and bypassing collective associations.

If these are the complexities of defining the 'capitalism' part of the capitalism/racial order relationship, there are equivalent complications attending the question of which aspect of the racial order is at stake in a given debate about its significance for capitalism. At least three of many possible distinctions are worth highlighting. One is between the looser system of racial domination known as segregation and the more rigid system of apartheid. The second is between the political aspect of the racial order (white control of the state) and the economic aspects (such as job colour bars). A third is between legally institutionalized racism and informal, culturally embedded racism, the second of which continues under democratic majority rule. Capitalism may in some instances challenge institutionalized racism but tend to exploit or bolster informal racial hierarchies.

What of the types of relationship between capitalism and the racial order? At least six broad kinds of non-hostile relationship can be distinguished amongst those advanced by radicals and contested by liberals: co-existential, opportunist, supportive, authorial, dependent and historical. Each carried or carries quite distinctive moral, strategic and explanatory significance.

It is possible firstly for capitalism to *co-exist* with a racial order. Capitalists may survive or thrive alongside the racial order unaffected by it (perhaps exempted from its provisions) or build the racial order into their mode of functioning without harmful results for their businesses.

Secondly, capitalism could have an *opportunistic* relationship with the racial order. A weak form of such a relationship would obtain where, say, capitalists take advantage of the stable investment environment created by a repressive state crackdown. A stronger form would exist where, for example, capitalists oppose a particular kind of repressive labour regime but take advantage of it while it is there to boost their profits.

A third type of relationship is *supportive.* In the case of subjective support, capitalists approve or defend an aspect of the racial order. A second subtype, collaboration, includes everything from capitalists supplying willing support or co-operation to those running the racial order through to their lacking the moral courage to take a stand against it. Subjective support and collaboration are about the moral failings of capitalists rather than the requirements of capital or capitalism. The third subtype, objective support, is less obvious in its moral implications. It refers to a situation where, say, a flourishing private sector economy generates the tax revenue needed to finance apartheid. This example ironically reverses the causation normally debated: here capitalism is functional to the racial order, rather than vice versa.

A fourth type of relationship is *authorial*. Capitalists as individuals or groups may seek, initiate, design or help, non-melioratively, to shape particular racial policies.

It is only with the fifth type of relationship, *dependent*, that functionality of the racial order enters the picture. It may be that capitalism or capitalists functionally depend on aspects of the racial order either for their survival or for their prosperity.

The final type of relationship is *historical*. Capitalism and the racial order may be joined simply as matters of fact, even contingent historical fact. Two subtypes of such connection are existential–contingent and objective–causal. We may say, as an example of the first, that capitalism in South Africa took a racial form. This does not entail the further proposition that capitalism could not have survived or flourished in the absence of a racial order. It might however (as it did for some, we now know mistaken, Marxist analysts like Slovo and Magubane) imply a degree of mutual intertwining such that apartheid could not be abolished except by the simultaneous abolition of capitalism (Slovo 1976; Magubane 1979).

An example of an objective–causal proposition is one holding that particular racial policies were instituted by dominant groups in response to capitalism and its effects, without necessarily being either sought by capitalists or required by capitalism. Here capitalism provides the environment to which political actors react.

Not all of these relationships involve capitalism or capitalists benefiting from the racial order, but the notion of functional dependence does, and was a central stake in liberal–radical debates of the 1970s. Moreover, capitalists may have collaborated with, taken advantage of or helped design the racial order because they anticipated benefits from it, even if these were not received. But what form might benefits to capitalism take, and how could these be measured?

An elementary distinction should be made between original existence/survival measures and measures of flourishing. It could logically be argued that capitalism in South Africa would not have come into *existence* without a racial order. This is however historically improbable: it is surely the case that in the absence of a racial order, even of white colonization, some form of capitalism would have made an appearance in South Africa by the end of the twentieth century as it has done in all other countries (though deep-level gold mining may well not have done).

It could be argued that the *survival* of capitalism either depended on the racial order, or that capitalists perceived it to do so. Many whites in South Africa, including capitalists, assumed (and acted on the assumption) that the survival of capitalism in the country depended on white political supremacy. It may conceivably have done so at times given the anti-capitalist radicalization of black nationalism during the Cold War.

The criteria of capitalist *flourishing* are more complex and varied. The fact that a social system is an unconscious entity unable to articulate its own purpose naturally makes it impossible to determine objectively whether it is 'succeeding'. The revisionists assumed that the racial state guaranteed not only the political reproduction of capitalism, but that it enabled capitalism to flourish, and they understood flourishing economically. But even in respect of economics participants in the liberal–radical controversies debated different measures of flourishing at different times. Criteria have included, for example, both rates of growth and rates of profit, with profit rates in turn devolving into a range of different technical measures. Thus the claim of Legassick that apartheid South Africa generated unusually high rates of economic growth until the 1970s has been challenged by writers like Moll (1990, 1991) while Nattrass has challenged the assumption that it generated high rates of profit (1990).

It is debatable whether or not some criteria constitute plausible measures of capitalist flourishing. Legassick argued that apartheid was conducive to a particular form of capital-intensive industrialization, and seemed to assume that capital-intensity, because it augmented labour productivity, perhaps because it developed society's productive forces, was a yardstick of capitalist dynamism (Legassick 1974b: 14-18, 23-9; Crankshaw 1997: 43-8). Others however have argued that South African capitalism was driven by apartheid-induced artificial labour shortages to a greater capital intensity than was warranted on economic grounds given South Africa's labour surplus, capital scarcity and the costs of imported capital goods. Excessive capital intensity may thus have limited the country's longer-term economic growth potential (Gelb 1991a; Kahn 1991; O'Meara 1996: 173-6).

For any given criterion there is (further) the question of an appropriate comparative yardstick for assessing success or failure. Should South Africa's economy be compared with other comparable economies, in which case which? Other present or former white settler dominions? Middle income countries? African countries? World averages? Comparison with which country offers a sense of how the economy might have fared in the absence of racial policies? The issue is additionally complicated by difficulties in determining whether given levels of success or failure are attributable to racial policies as opposed to 'a-racial' trade, monetary and fiscal policies and 'a-racial' factors such as market structures, managerial styles, international alliances, levels of human capital investment, distribution of wealth, cultural orientations, social cohesion, population size, resource endowments, climate and geographical location (not to mention luck).

Another factor affecting adjudication of debates about the relationship between capitalist success and the racial order is time frame. Following the economic slowdown beginning in the mid-1970s a number of radicals developed the argument that while apartheid had been largely functional to capitalist success before the 1970s, it ceased to be so thereafter. The apartheid-linked regime of economic growth had, writers like Gelb argued, reached limits or generated contradictions which required that the racial order be modified (or more) in order to restore capitalist growth and profitability. This was a far from implausible argument in Marxist terms; it would have been much odder if Marxists had ever argued, or meant, that capitalist prosperity in apartheid South Africa would continue for ever in a contradiction-free way (in any social order racial or otherwise). Marxists (Saul and Gelb 1981: 16-18; O'Meara 1996: 81-2, 171-8) in the 1980s provided a definitely class-analytic and materialist account of 'reform' or 'restructuring' (see Chapter 4). And the long boom of the apartheid economy was no passing affair: it spanned, albeit not uninterruptedly, more than two decades. It is thus not easy to dismiss the argument that revisionists correctly identified some of the dynamics of the apartheid–capitalism relationship in the post-war decades.

Nevertheless this line of argument raises complex questions for radical analysis and especially for the revisionist thesis of the 1970s. It smacked of a non-falsifiable argument. When evidence appeared of apartheid harming economic growth, Marxists chose to treat this not as a refutation of their earlier argument but as evidence that a new period had arrived. If evidence of conflict between apartheid and capitalism did not falsify the earlier Marxist position, then no possible outcome could (Lipton 1979: 72; Nattrass 1991: 668-9). (Marxists could of course still be shown to be wrong about the earlier period, as Moll and Nattrass argue that they were.) The 1980s radical position assumes also that the revisionist thesis of the earlier 1970s, though correct for the time, was not intended for extrapolation into the future. If its exponents did not intend it to be so extrapolated, they did not indicate as much, nor anticipate the dynamics that would lead to a collision of interests between capital and the apartheid state, an economic slowdown or state restructuring.

Finally, we should consider the often contextual or situational character of any judgement about the functionality of particular racial policies for capitalism. In the context of a racial order in which white mine labour enjoyed the political bargaining power needed to maintain its expensiveness, the recruitment of cheap and regimented African mine labour offered mine owners a solution to the problem of labour costs. One aspect of the racial order (the exclusive enfranchisement of whites) contributed to the problem to which another aspect of the racial order (racial labour-repression) offered a solution. Similarly, state controls over the influx of Africans into urban areas – a feature of the racial order which increased the cost and fussiness of urban African labourers – generated a problem to which the hiring of illegal migrants represented, for manufacturers of an earlier period, at least a partial solution. It may be that mine owners would have preferred cheaper white labour, or manufacturers a flooding of urban areas with rural workseekers, but the racial order, having shut off these first-best scenarios, offered second-best solutions for capital.

The key capitalist sectors

One way to exhibit these complexities is by focusing on the economic sectors most commonly debated in relation to the racial order. A sector-by-sector examination is not without its limitations given the South African economy's intersectoral connections (which grew over time) and the potential divergence between sectoral imperatives and those of capital, or capitalism, as a whole. A sectoral breakdown of this sort nevertheless provides one useful platform for illustrating the different kinds of relationship that joined capitalism to the pre-1994 racial order.

Mining

The mining industry irrevocably shaped South Africa's politics, economics and social geography. Not surprisingly, it also affected South Africa's racial order in vital ways. The industry presided over the creation of a new racial division of labour and a vast, regimented, rightless African labour force.

Diamonds were discovered in commercial quantities in 1867. The emerging industry drew tens of thousands of Africans, a fair number initially as independent diggers, but mainly, and eventually exclusively, as migrant labourers. Migrants came uncoerced by capital or the state, attracted by the relatively high wages they could command, their bargaining power strengthened by their access to alternative means of livelihood in semi-independent agricultural production. In time, however, the discretionary element of migrancy weakened as peasant independence declined (Worger 1987: ch. 2) and the concentration and centralization of diamond mining companies strengthened the owners' hand relative to that of employees. Mine owners forged a labour-repressive order in Griqualand west with state co-operation. By the mid-1880s the African labour force, already mostly excluded from independent diamond digging (since 1871), was subject to pass laws (introduced on the diamond fields in 1872, strengthened in 1879), victimized by repressive policing (especially from 1876), made to undergo intrusive body searches (1883) and allocated to segregated locations (from 1879). African labourers were later confined to closed compounds inspired by convict camps (from 1885). De Beers, the principal diamond mining company, employed convict labour from 1884, a practice which continued in mining until 1932 (Turrell 1987: 156-8). As companies displaced small diggers from the mines, former white share-workers were able to secure jobs as waged overseers, while African upward mobility was blocked. White workers, exploiting their political power and employers' feelings of racial solidarity, secured the exclusion of Africans from certain jobs, such as blasters (1885) and team leaders (1889) (Turrell 1987: 87-9; Harries 1994: 71).

Despite a wage cut forced on African workers in 1890-91, the regimentation of African workers was not driven primarily by a need for cheap labour. Diamond mine wages continued to compare favourably to those on less regimented gold mines. Diamond companies could contain costs by means other than radical wage reduction, including (once a degree of inter-company co-operation had been achieved) by reducing production and thus raising diamond prices. What mattered to diamond producers above all was their ability to manipulate diamond prices, and diggers and mine owners considered themselves vulnerable for this reason to illegal buying and selling of diamonds. Searches and compounds had a general value in disciplining African workers (Turrell 1987: ch. 8), but their principal role was undoubtedly to prevent theft of diamonds from the diggings. African workers were perceived by whites as the most likely thieves, and white workers anyway had sufficient clout, whatever their own degree of complicity in illicit diamond trading, to evade the most onerous forms of surveillance and coercion instituted in response to it. The white perception of the African as criminal was both a product and reinforcer of white racism.

The compounds enjoyed, in the minds of mine owners, another non-economic justification, that of protecting African rural migrants from proletarian degeneration. The compound served as a 'fictive chiefdom' (Harries 1994: 73) offering the alienated worker detached from his rural setting a source of authoritarian social cohesion and discipline, as well as exposure to mission work. According to Harries, 'the industrialist, like the missionary, believed he had a civilizing mission, that of elevating blacks from barbarousness and savagery through the discipline of labour' (Harries 1994: 72). This discourse of 'industrial paternalism' was accompanied, during the 1890s, by real improvements in (initially awful) compound conditions, or in what Harries calls 'the social sector of the wage' (71), to offset a reduced monetary wage (Harries 1994: 71- 80).

The diamond mines provide clear instances of capitalists (together with the colonial state) actively authoring important institutions of the racial order; and a *possible* case of their depending on some of its provisions for their profits. The picture of capitalist complicity in the racial order is however complicated by three factors: the active role of white labour in imparting a racially discriminatory character to mine owners' impositions, the opposition of sections of capital (mainly smaller local merchants and traders) to closed compounding in Kimberley (Worger 1987: 5) and the likelihood that mine owners' racism reflected that of the wider white society. Some of the labour-repressive legislation for which diamond magnates pressed extended existing Cape master–servant legislation whose origins were mainly agrarian. Nor, as subjects of the colonial Cape, were mine owners able to secure explicitly racist laws in the manner of South Africa after 1910. In the twentieth century, as in the late nineteenth, diamond mines would prove on the whole less oppressive of African labour than gold mines. For all this, Worger's observation – that diamond mine owners helped create 'the most basic institutions that were to shape the lives of black workers in South African cities' – is difficult to contest (Worger 1987: 111).

Gold mining capitalists borrowed some of the diamond industry's ideas about labour control. But gold mining added elements of its own to the armoury of labour-repression, and its subsequent economic centrality to South Africa ensured for it a more crucial role in shaping and sustaining the modern racial order.

The case for ascribing to gold mining *capitalists* an authorial role in shaping the twentieth century racial order is unquestionably strong. So is the case for considering gold mining *capital*, perhaps uniquely amongst South African economic sectors, functionally dependent on racial labour-repression for its very existence (Crush et al. 1991: 1). Gold mining capital needed cheap African labour on a vast scale to extract gold profitably. With the international gold price fixed (unlike that of diamonds), it had an incentive to maximize output; and because it could not pass production costs onto consumers its profits depended on cost control. Certain elements of gold mining cost were, however, unavoidably high due to the depth and low average grade of ore. Mining capitalists had little choice but to seek to minimize labour costs. In South African circumstances the burden of labour cheapening fell inevitably on African labour (Johnstone 1976).

The market for produce generated by gold (as for diamonds) in the interior briefly bolstered a commercial African peasantry, and for a while mining capitalists in the role of rentiers provided land on which African peasants could produce marketable surpluses (Trapido 1986). But (as again with diamond mining) the gold mine owners were mainly interested in the region's African population as labourers rather than as independent producers or consumers. They consequently pushed for tax measures (such as the 1894 Glen Grey Act in the Cape) that were intended to force African peasants in South Africa onto the labour market (Crush et al. 1991). Migrants' access to the rural household economy did for a while strengthen their bargaining power, enabling them to withdraw their labour. However as alternatives to waged work diminished, their access to the supplementary means of subsistence and social security advantaged mining capital, enabling the industry to reproduce its African labour force more cheaply than that of fully proletarianized whites (Wolpe 1972). It furthermore helped to sustain ethnic and regional attachments amongst mineworkers that hindered trans-ethnic proletarian unity against capital.

Mine owners sought to cheapen African labour in a variety of ways. One of their principal concerns was to limit competition between mines for African labour. They struggled over a long period to agree maximum average wages for African workers – the labour buyers' monopsony – and to cut out independent labour touts who encouraged competitive company recruiting. In these endeavours mining houses began to succeed from around 1912. Mine owners also wanted state help in reducing the ability of Africans to move freely between mines in search of higher wages. A result of this pressure was the Law no. 23 of 1895, drafted by the mining industry, imposing passes on Africans on the gold fields. Mining capital also benefited from the extension to African mineworkers of legislation that criminalized breach of contract. In addition the state helped to forge a far-flung labour recruitment 'empire' extending to the tropics of Africa and briefly to China (Richardson 1982), reducing worker bargaining power by expanding the pool of recruits. Thanks to these measures, and their refusal to recognize black trade unions, mine owners were able to establish wage levels after the South African War that did not rise in real terms until the 1970s.

Gold mining houses emulated the diamond industry's idea of compounding African workers. In the case of gold mining, which did not need to worry about theft, the compounds were open, though in other respects the conditions in them were worse for longer than on the diamond mines. Their principal function for the gold mining industry was to provide a cheap way of housing male migrant labourers. The need for cheap mining accommodation arose from the reluctance of governments to subsidize permanent housing for those employed in limited-life enterprises. The compound regime also helpfully served to divide workers along ethnic lines and subjected them to a system of authoritarian control via African 'indunas'.

Liberals faced with this catalogue of evidence about gold mining's part in maintaining and extending the racial order do offer some lines of defence which merit attention. They point out, first, that mine owners did not support one of the most glaringly racist institutions associated with their industry: the racial job colour bar reserving certain mining jobs for white workers. The South African Republic (*Zuid-Afrikaanse Republiek*) government began reserving certain mining jobs for whites in 1893 and a series of racially discriminatory measures thereafter culminated in the 1911 Mines and Works Act and the 1926 Mines and Works Amendment Act. The latter was the first and only overtly racist job reservation legislation prior to apartheid. Mine owners around 1908 successfully promoted at least one racial job exclusion of their own. To the chagrin of those seeking a white labour policy on the mines, they successfully fought to exclude relatively expensive white labour from unskilled jobs (Davies 1979: 52–65). Mine owners were also sufficiently given to feelings of racial solidarity and respect for the co-ordinating skills and 'assumed authority' of whites to support their retention in supervisory positions (Davies 1979: 66–7). It was, however, only reluctantly that they went along with the reservation of skilled and semi-skilled production jobs for whites.

The responsibility or otherwise of mine owners for job reservations is a basic point of disagreement between liberal interpreters like Lipton (1986: ch. 5) and radicals like Johnstone and Davies. Liberals are keen to stress the active agency of white labour (whether motivated by racial prejudice or self-interest) in fighting for a colour bar to protect white workers from African advancement. They argue that the electoral victory of the white Labour Party, in alliance with the Afrikaner nationalists, enabled them to secure the 1926 job reservation legislation over the heads of a protesting industry. With whites' wage bill almost equaling that of Africans despite small white numbers, mine owners had no choice but to save costs by imposing low wages and harsh conditions on the more rightless African labour force. Radicals like Johnstone and Davies reverse the order of causation and hence responsibility. White mineworkers, they argue, struggled for job protection in response to the efforts of mine owners to replace them with cheap African labour. The prospect of replacement threatened especially the less skilled Afrikaners who increasingly predominated in the white mine labour force of the early twentieth century – the more so as less expensive African labourers acquired experience and skill. A key reason for the inexpensiveness of African labour was its 'ultra-exploitation' by mine owners, which paradoxically placed the less skilled white workers in a position of 'extreme structural insecurity' (Johnstone 1976: 64). In fact there is no way of determining a prime mover within a chain of causality that can equally be seen as beginning with the capitalist drive for profits or white workers' economic insecurity and political and organizational power. (Chapter 5 offers a fuller treatment of the racial strategies of white labour.) And whoever was responsible for job reservation, there is no doubt that capital did derive some benefits from having a co-opted white labour force.

A second line of defence for liberals is to argue that mining has become more racially liberal since the 1970s. This is certainly so. The uncapping of the gold price early in that decade provided mines with the means to offer large wage increases to Africans. Mining houses boosted African wages also in response to international pressure and unrest on the mines. A computerized recruiting system facilitated the repeated reengagement of, and acquisition of experience by, African migrants. Higher wages allowed mines to attract more of South Africa's less docile, more educated workers following political turbulence in labour supply areas beyond South Africa's borders. This more South African and stabilized labour force in turn proved readier than previous cohorts to overcome ethnic divisions and challenge mining bosses. The industry, led by Anglo-American, began to accept black unionization. The growing weight of the black National Union of Mineworkers, and the declining influence of the white Mine Workers Union, facilitated the abolition of job reservation by 1987. Meanwhile other factors worked to liberalize the racist and authoritarian culture of the mining houses. These included the diversification of the mining industry into sectors with less interest in labour repression, the overseas investment aspirations of the larger mining houses and the industry's employment of more enlightened industrial relations professionals (Lipton 1986: ch. 5).

Such evidence certainly supports the liberal argument that by the 1970s capitalists were a force corrosive of the racial order. However, gold mining's reformism was late in developing and (dramatic wage increases apart) much of it was grudging. Its labour-repressive regime saw hardly any alteration before 1970. In the 1970s and 1980s the industry lagged behind manufacturing in declaring support for African unions; it moved tardily on job reservation and until the 1990s remained opposed to significant provision of family housing for its workforce. Lipton attributes the weakness of gold mining's reformism to the consensual decision-making style of the Chamber of Mines, which allowed more reactionary mining houses to veto change, and the conservatism of mining's middle-level bureaucracy (Lipton 1986: ch. 5).

Gold mining's latter day meliorism also does not weaken the argument that the industry played an authorial role in relation to the modern racial order and was functionally dependent upon racial labour-repression for its existence and, for many decades, profitability. The industry's racism was of a more than localized significance. Gold mining made possible South Africa's industrialization through its attraction of foreign capital, diversification into industry, provision of tax revenue for state economic investment and its role in earning the foreign exchange needed to import capital goods for manufacturing. In a sense then the larger South African capitalist economy owes its scale and character to the surpluses generated by an industry deeply rooted in the racial order. What is less certain is whether in the long run the central role of this primary extractive sector in determining South Africa's path of industrial development was a boon or bane. It arguably made possible the sheltering of an uncompetitive manufacturing industry and has left the economy vulnerable to commodity price fluctuations. It is to that extent conceivable, though entirely unprovable, that South African capitalism might have flourished more fully in the long run without the opportunities offered by racial labour-repression for the establishment of deep-level mining.

Agriculture

Mining and agriculture are widely agreed to be partners in elaborating racial labour-repression in South Africa, whether it be the 'alliance of diamonds, wine, and wool' in the later nineteenth century Cape (Beinart 1994: 27) or the 'alliance of gold and maize' (Trapido 1971: 311) in the trekker republics, reconstruction states and early Union. What they shared in common (despite important differences) was an interest in cheap black labour, in agriculture's case for reasons including the labour-intensive nature of many farming operations, market instability and the cost constraints arising from ecologically difficult farming conditions, undercapitalization and debt. The low wages agriculture and mining offered rendered them uncompetitive in the labour market compared to better paying urban industrial employers. Both sought labour from beyond South Africa's borders (imported slaves in the western Cape, indentured Indian labour in the sugar industry, migrants from southern Africa) and both looked to the state for help in recruiting and canalizing labour supplies (Morris 1977; Greenberg 1980: 87-9; Bradford 1993).

Agriculture's authorial role with respect to the labour order is little disputed; its functional dependence or not on that order depends on whether it might have been possible for agriculture to develop as profitably and productively on the basis of better paid labour or family farming: another imponderable. Agriculture's role in forging a racial order long pre-dates that of mining. It goes back, as we saw in Chapter 1, to the 1650s. By the later nineteenth century agricultural labour repression was legally embodied in coercive master–servant legislation. For a century after 1870 farmers (especially in the Transvaal) were involved in elaborating controls to prevent Africans leaving 'white' farmland for emerging, more remunerative centres of employment. The 1911 Native Labour Regulation Act limited recruitment of African farm labour by mines. The departure of African workers for urban centres was blocked most notoriously by the Native Laws Amendment Act of 1952. Other measures were taken to strengthen the hand of farmers in controlling tenants and redistributing squatters from larger to smaller farms. They included anti-squatter laws in the Transvaal in 1895 and 1908, and in the Union (though mainly affecting Free State sharecroppers) the notorious 1913 Natives Land Act. Farmers made extensive use of convict labour well into the 1980s. Many Africans were arrested under influx control provisions specifically to augment farm labour supplies (Cooper 1988: 56; Bradford 1993).

White farmers acquired a reputation for brutality in treatment of their black employees, who were denied union rights, and persisted in paying them very low wages until the late 1960s. Brutality could be accompanied by a degree of paternalism (including provision of farm schools) and 'cultural osmosis' between the African and white worlds but in the context of clearly understood racial hierarchies (Van Onselen 1990; Shell 1994). White farmers generally favoured restricting African reserve land, though their positions and interests with respect to this issue were in practice quite diverse or ambivalent (Beinart 1986: 293-6; Beinart and Delius 1986: 41-2; Dubow 1989: 60-6; Murray 1992: 127). They enthusiastically supported the racially discriminatory policies of successive Afrikaner nationalist governments although, in a striking assertion of material self-interest over ethnic or racial solidarity, they (like the mines) succeeded in exempting themselves from the obligation to employ unskilled white labour.

The vital role of farmers in seeking and initiating policies central to the racial order is widely acknowledged by liberals and radicals alike, but it is variously interpreted. Two possibilities complicate the marshalling of evidence from agriculture to back the case that capitalists, or capitalism, created the racial order. The first arises from the fact that most white farmers were Dutch or (later) Afrikaans-speakers, raising the possibility that in pursuing racial labour-repression they were acting as Afrikaners, indeed as descendants of the isolated and prejudiced Boers upon which the frontier thesis alighted, rather than as employers or capitalists. The second possibility is that they were not capitalists at all, at any rate before the 1970s, but masters dependent on a range of non-capitalist relationships, from slavery through to various forms of 'quasi-feudal' surplus extraction, such as sharecropping and labour tenancy.

Afrikaner numerical dominance in agriculture is not in dispute, and claims by the radical scholar Morris that South African agriculture was uniformly capitalist by the 1920s have been largely discredited (see Chapter 5). Even so, radical historians have shown that the commercialization process itself frequently gave rise to the relationships described as quasi-feudal and caused these quasi-feudal labour relations to become increasingly repressive over time (Keegan 1986a: 166-73; Bradford 1990: 75-9). Furthermore, many of the most commercially progressive farmers in the twentieth century were Cape and Natal Anglophones and Eastern European immigrants who bought land from creditors and speculators (Beinart and Delius 1986: 28-30; Keegan 1986a: 196-201). At least some of these non-Afrikaner incomers were amongst the most viciously repressive of their African labourers (Morrell 1986; Bradford 1993).

Like mining, agriculture began slowly and unevenly to move in a racially reformist direction from the later 1960s. By the 1970s white farmers, who had for decades complained of labour shortage, found themselves confronted by a surplus, especially of unskilled labour, thanks to mechanization of large grain farms and later to slowing growth in the wider economy. Whereas for long farmers had sought measures to hold African labour down on the *platteland*, they now increasingly evicted labour tenants. At the same time agriculture was confronted, from the late 1960s, by a shortage of the more skilled male labour needed in mechanized production. This shortage was aggravated by the loss of increasingly skilled farm operatives to industrial jobs and a generally tight labour market at the tail end of the 1960s boom. For a while farmers were actually obliged to increase the wages of their (reduced) permanent labour force before further mechanization and economic slowdown restored the employers' advantage and renewed wage stagnation (Hofmeyr 1994: 93-100). At the same time farmers began increasingly to value black purchasing power. Some farmers, notably the Natal sugar miller-planters, began to sponsor limited political reform and to promote black farmers (Lipton 1986: ch. 4; De Klerk 1991: 223). The expansion of a big business sector in farming, much of it backed by large banking and industrial capital, probably strengthened reformist tendencies, not least because agribusiness tended to offer higher wages (Cooper 1988: 51).

Declining white farmer interest in controls over African movement should not be interpreted as a sign of generalized liberalization, however. While shedding of labour is a typical accompaniment to urbanization, and happened much earlier to white farm tenants, evicted blacks in the 1960s and 1970s were forcibly deflected by the state away from 'white' urban areas to impoverished resettlement camps in African reserves. Against this process farmers raised little protest, not least because the landless unemployed accumulating in the reserves offered a continuing source of seasonal casual labour (Cooper 1988: 57-8). White farmers continued to oppose moves to open white farming areas to mine recruiters. While unconcerned about eviction of Africans from 'black spots' of African-owned land outside the reserves, they continued to be wary of attempts to consolidate African reserves in the 1970s. In the 1980s many farmers in less productive areas of the Transvaal and Orange Free State, suffering from debt and drought, abandoned the neo-apartheid National Party for the extreme right-wing Conservative Party (Cooper 1988: 49). Smaller and poorer farmers in particular were aggrieved by NP policies which from the early 1970s favoured a minority of more productive and mechanized large farmers. In the 1990s many white farmers emerged as fierce opponents of land reform, and evicted tenants in anticipation of legislation giving them rights to white farmland. This continuing racial conservatism may have something to do with the murder of hundreds of white farmers since 1994, though a causal link has never been definitely shown.

Secondary industry

If liberals and radicals concurred for the most part about the racially conservative character of the primary sectors, the sharpest debate developed around the role of secondary or manufacturing industry. The importance of secondary industry is underlined by its emergence as the largest sector in the economy during the Second World War and, since the 1930s, its function as a magnet drawing Africans from reserves and white farming areas to expanding towns and cities.

For the liberals, the defence of the progressive character of South African capitalism turned on the fact that secondary industry increasingly depended, from the later 1960s, on Africans as skilled workers and as consumers. In its first labour-intensive decades, manufacturing relied largely on skilled artisan labour, supplied by whites and coloureds, and unskilled labour, provided at first mainly by urbanizing Afrikaner women and juveniles, later by migrant or newly urbanized Africans. Manufacturing's requirements for a market could be satisfied by an increasingly affluent white population, its access to which was protected, from the mid-1920s, by tariff barriers. Its economic needs at the time were not, in other words, a reason to challenge the priorities of the racial order, except, importantly, insofar as manufacturers favoured freer African access to urban labour markets. From the 1960s, however, an increasingly mechanized and capital-intensive industrial sector demanded more semi-skilled operatives and skilled workers than could be supplied by the white minority alone. Likewise, manufacturing's requirement of an expanded market to permit economies of scale in the employment of expensive machinery heightened the importance of blacks as consumers, as well as the need for a more skilled labour force to achieve international competitiveness. These requirements generated, as liberals emphasized, structural tensions between manufacturing capital and an apartheid government that was committed to educating Africans exclusively for manual labour, maintaining racial job reservations, restricting African access to urban areas and inhibiting the sort of workforce stabilization that could justify investment in job training. The state, liberals reasoned, was confronted by a choice between the crippling of South Africa's leading economic sector by the racial *status quo* and the dynamic manufacturing economy that would be made possible by deracialization. That manufacturers understood this was, liberals argued, reflected in their overt and behind-the-scenes opposition to apartheid labour market policies (Lipton 1986: ch. 6).

Revisionists in the 1970s took issue with the claim that apartheid was dysfunctional to capitalist growth in general and to the secondary industrial sector in particular. They pursued their argument down two potentially (though not necessarily) contradictory paths. A 'weak' revisionist position held that apartheid restrictions on employer freedom of action did not in practice have much impact; even that much of the apartheid programme was an ideological façade behind which the state did whatever was necessary to facilitate white economic prosperity (Johnstone 1970: 125-7). Radicals pointed especially to the phenomenon of 'floating colour bars' which, from the late 1960s, enabled Africans to be trained for more skilled roles as whites moved upwards to supervisory jobs (Legassick 1974b). Though the argument that apartheid did no harm to capitalist interests was contested by liberals, the 'weak' revisionist line was ironically compatible with a liberal modernizationist view that capitalism was eroding apartheid by forcing pragmatic adjustments of racial dogma.

A second, 'strong' revisionist position held that apartheid was functional to secondary industrial capitalism. There are two versions of this argument. One is that apartheid facilitated industrial prosperity by cheapening African labour and limiting the welfare, housing and other costs of reproducing the urban African workforce. It did this principally through political repression, the forcible containment of African urbanization and the shoring up of African links with tribal reserves. That political repression could facilitate industrial capitalist prosperity was, for revisionists writing in the early 1970s, evidenced by the boom that followed the Verwoerdian crackdown of the 1960s.

This repressionist/cheap labour argument had its vulnerable points. It underestimated the extent to which the state accepted a degree of African urbanization and invested in the reproduction of an urban African workforce, providing housing on a massive scale in the 1950s and introducing elements of universal state education for Africans (Wilkinson 1983; Hindson 1987; Posel 1991; Hyslop 1993). It did not take sufficient account of the economic costs to manufacturers of the low productivity of migrant labour and a constricted urban market, or of alternative means by which the costs of African urbanization could have been reduced (for example by saturating urban areas with cheap labour and leaving the newly urbanized to build informal housing). Nor, finally, did it consider the implications of the fact that apartheid itself generated the political instability which repression successfully stilled in the 1960s.

These objections do not entirely cancel the repressionist/cheap labour case. Apartheid governments did seek to offload social security and policing costs on to the 'homelands'. The resistance which apartheid suppressed was a response to white rule (which manufacturers backed) as well as to economic apartheid. And revisionists had anyway not, in general, maintained that the apartheid model was the only conceivable one for securing cheap and docile African labour or for maintaining capitalism. They usually argued that it was one possible option for doing so which won out in a political class struggle in the 1940s, and agreed that it was not the option manufacturers preferred (Wolpe 1972: 309; Saul and Gelb 1981: 14).

A second version of the 'strong' argument proposed that apartheid was conducive to a particular, namely capital-intensive, kind of industrial capitalism. In contrast to the exemptionist and cheap labour theses, this position appeared to accept that in the largest urban centres apartheid raised manufacturing labour costs, albeit not immoderately or dogmatically (the argument still allowed for exemptionist claims). In so doing it encouraged capital-intensive industrialization, which reduced relative labour costs by boosting productivity (Legassick 1974b: 14-18; Crankshaw 1997: 43-8). At the same time apartheid helped more inherently labour-intensive firms to find cheap labour outside the major urban areas, in decentralization growth points located in or adjacent to African reserves (though capital-intensive firms followed there too) (Legassick 1974b: 14-18). It was indeed suggested by some that decentralization policy battened on to and encouraged spontaneous tendencies for industry to suburbanize and decentralize. Industries wished to decentralize not only to avoid apartheid-inflated urban labour costs but also to escape diseconomies of agglomeration and, from the 1970s, growing black trade union power (Bell 1987; Glaser 1988: 203-7).

The counterargument here, as we have noted, is that capital-intensification was not necessarily good for the South African economy. Furthermore, state decentralization policies that assisted what capitalists were doing anyway seem hardly rational either for the state or capital, unless they were to be counted as necessary facilitation measures. While the facilitation argument may hold true for those growth points manufacturers would have liked to move to anyway but could not do so without state assistance, there were other areas and instances where manufacturers relocated exclusively to claim government decentralization subsidies.

If so far the issue has been the objective needs of industrial *capital*, a parallel debate has focused on the political behaviour of industrial *capitalists*. Where liberals presented evidence that manufacturing industry leaders were critical of apartheid labour policies (Lipton 1986: ch. 6), radicals emphasized the narrow limits and inconsistency of manufacturers' reformism and the large extent of industry–government collaboration in various areas of racial policy. Firstly, radical critics pointed out, organized capital preferred where possible to adopt a low profile in its dealings with the state. It criticized the government openly only during periods of political crisis, and quickly fell back into quietude when crises receded. Industrialists mostly respected the NP government demand that they confine their agitation to economic rather than overtly political issues (Mann 1988: 64-5; Pretorius 1994). Secondly, organized capital, including industry, directly participated in negotiating details of government policy through forums like the Economic Advisory Council established in 1960, the Wiehahn Commission in the 1970s and Regional Development Advisory Committees in the 1980s (Glaser 1988: 197-9; Pretorius 1994: 226-9). Thirdly, organized industry was often seriously divided in its opposition to state racial policies with, for example, the Border Chamber of Industries enthusiastically backing the industrial decentralization policies opposed by the Federated Chamber of Industries (Glaser 1988: 207-21). Fourthly, there was often a gap between the words of organized industry and the actions of individual industrialists. While organized industry opposed influx control, individual employers often opportunistically preferred cheap unskilled migrants and vulnerable illegal labourers to established urban residents (Posel 1991: 13-15); whereas organized industry criticized industrial decentralization incentives as wasteful, individual industrialists often accepted them gladly (Glaser 1988: 195). Finally, organized capital, including industry, generally supported white minority rule or offered no criticism of it until, and then only for a while, the insurrectionary emergency of the mid-1980s. Its opposition was to economic rather than political apartheid, and in its majority tacitly supported some government political crackdowns (Lipton 1986: ch. 6, epilogue).

Liberals (e.g. Lipton 1986: ch. 6) could respond to these arguments in turn by defending organized capital's low political profile as tactically necessary in dealing with a government hypersensitive to public criticism. They could also argue that the impact of industry's participation in government policy-making was meliorative, on the whole softening its oppressiveness towards blacks. Thirdly, liberals could argue that support within industrial capital for government racial policies was the exception that proved the rule, especially since the consistently most pro-government manufacturers were Afrikaners who benefited from government patronage and privileged lobbying access, and were anyway moved by sentimental ethnic loyalties. Within the spectrum of Afrikaner nationalism the Afrikaner *Handelsinstituut* represented a pragmatic influence. Fourthly, in supporting white minority rule manufacturers were behaving no differently from most whites, and thus quite possibly as whites rather than as capitalists specifically. Their interests as capitalists on the whole increasingly drew them away from rather than towards racist behaviour and attitudes. Finally, liberal economists could distinguish between individual capitalist behaviour and what was good for capitalism: capitalists as rational self-maximizers would engage where they could in rent-seeking behaviour which contradicted the collective interests of capital and confounded the rationality of capitalism. It was not, therefore, surprising that businessmen as individuals gratefully received industrial decentralization handouts; the problem lay in governments offering them.

These rebuttals should be sufficient to persuade all but the most determined radical critics that manufacturing, unlike agriculture and mining, was not a significant co-author of the racial order. There is also no convincing evidence that secondary industry was functionally dependent upon legalized racism for its existence, survival or long-term prosperity (except indirectly insofar as it was dependent on a kick-start from gold mining). This was so even if, for several decades, manufacturing prospered alongside and (in certain respects) benefited from that order. Yet it is also certain that the manufacturers were neither vigorous nor courageous in their criticism of apartheid and that their opposition to it was rarely wide in scope or sustained. The picture of their behaviour is, overall, closer to the accommodationism depicted by Greenberg than the opposition celebrated by Lipton (Greenberg 1980: 26-8, 129-43, 398-403; Lipton 1986: ch. 6).

The preceding survey of capitalist sectors is not exhaustive. It leaves out, for example, the financial services sector, the relatively liberal employment policies of which Crankshaw has recently highlighted (Crankshaw 1997). It has been sufficient, however, to demonstrate that capitalism and the racial order were indeed joined by every one of the non-hostile relationships specified in the earlier typology but that there were also many points of genuine opposition and conflict between capitalism/capitalists and the racial order. The discussion underlines the importance of precision in specifying the type of relationship being hypothesized or debated on a given occasion. It is not simply a matter of (say) apartheid being both good and bad for capitalism, or of being initially good then later bad for it, or of there being a dialectical relationship between the racial and economic orders. What we have instead is evidence of a range of connections, conceptually distinguishable, between a range of entities situated at different points in time. This does not point to the impossibility of clear answers; only to the need clearly to specify the questions.

Capitalist economic growth and racial domination

One key question for the participants of the liberal–radical controversy was whether capitalist industrialization and urbanization were forces eroding the racial order. Liberals were not all convinced that they were. Modernization theorists like O'Dowd were sure economic growth would engender the same liberalization that it had done in the advanced capitalist world. Other liberals were pessimistic enough to fear that racial and ethnic sentiment would prevail over economic rationality, and that ruling Afrikaner nationalists would choose power maintenance over economic growth (see Lipton 1986: 3-4; Nattrass 1991: 661-2). Radicals shifted ground on the issue. In the interwar years they hewed to the orthodox Marxist assumption that capitalism would impose a logic of economic class over archaic and ascriptive loyalties of race and ethnicity. In the 1970s they emphasized (as we have seen) the capacity of capitalism to coexist with or batten on to a racial order, and the role of capitalist prosperity in strengthening the apartheid state. In the 1980s radicals concluded that capitalism in its new circumstances required a dilution of formalized racism (though not necessarily racial inequality).

In addressing the growth/racial domination conundrum, arguments about the functional needs of capitalism, and the political behaviour of capitalists, need to be distinguished from those about the objective-historical effects of capitalist growth. A number of writers have interpreted interwar segregationist and later apartheid policies as the response of white political elites to urbanization: or more specifically, to the way in which urbanization, with industrialization as its engine, brought blacks and whites into new forms of contact (Wolpe 1972: 303-8; Marks 1986: 38; Dubow 1989: 1-3). From this contact, and its associated dangers of racial competition and assimilation, segregation and apartheid were intended to insulate whites. If this depiction of the state's response is right – and I think it is – it demonstrates that capitalist industrialization can go along with, even (inadvertently) foster, racial repression, at least initially. It does not show that industrial capitalism authored or 'required' racial repression, or that it was inevitable that the state would respond to capitalist industrialization and urbanization in the way that it did. Furthermore, if it was urbanization that worried the state, this could be considered as a product of any form of industrialization and not only capitalist.

By the later 1960s industrialization and urbanization were eliciting contradictory responses from the state. The regime remained determined to halt black movement into 'white' South Africa, but gave up on trying to stop urbanization in 'homeland' areas abutting 'white' urban centres. By the early 1970s it was making pragmatic adjustments to labour market policy in response to the demands of industrialists. At the same time, though, industrial growth buttressed the apartheid state, providing revenue for social engineering and the expansion of the defence force. Private industry became a willing participant in a burgeoning military–industrial complex in the 1970s. Capitalist growth provided objective and subjective support for the apartheid state in some areas even while putting pressure on apartheid in other areas. Its impact on change was thus mixed.

The course of events in the 1980s and 1990s left the debate about the effects of growth undecidable. It seems certain that capitalist growth contributed to the dismantling of apartheid, primarily by generating an Afrikaner middle class and a need for black skills and spending power – developments which influenced the state in a reformist direction (see Chapter 4). Yet liberals had to contend with the weight of militant mass action and external economic sanctions in securing the end of apartheid, factors which most of them sought to exclude from their script of *how* capitalism would bring about change (on this see Lipton 1986: 355-64, epilogue; Kane-Berman 1991). Ethnocentric pluralists in their ranks were left to explain the dissolution of ethnically based alliances in white society they had earlier (Giliomee 1989a; Giliomee and Schlemmer 1989: chs 5, 7) depicted as immutable. If the influence of mass struggle and the assertion of class interests supported a radical analysis, revisionists had to reckon with evidence of conflicts between capitalist and racist imperatives in a range of economic areas. They also had to confront the capacity of capitalism to slough off and outlive apartheid (O'Meara 1996: 425). Both liberals and radicals had to adjust to the evaporation of the post-Second World War global capitalist expansion whose continuation neither side in the earlier 1970s seriously doubted. The meaning of the slowdown was unclear. Did economic stagnation prove that capitalism had been damaged by apartheid, or was it part of a global capitalist downturn? Was reform a response to economic growth or to its absence? History did not offer clear answers.

Capitalism and the racial order after apartheid

The capitalism–apartheid relationship did not cease to matter in 1994. As noted in the introduction, it was one focus of the deliberations of the Truth and

Reconciliation Commission, set up by the government of the African National Congress in 1995. The TRC set about examining both the moral choices of capitalists in collaborating with apartheid or supplying goods to the apartheid regime, and the extent to which capitalists benefited from an immoral system. For the first time the capitalists themselves felt compelled to join a previously academic debate. The commission concluded that capitalists benefited from apartheid and ought to pay a wealth tax in recompense (Nattrass 1999). This was a sort of vindication of the revisionist line. It is interesting however that the 1990s debate should have been conducted in moral terms, rather than the more ostensibly 'scientific' terms of the scholarly encounters of earlier decades. The earlier debate was driven by strategic and forward-looking questions; the 1990s deliberations of the TRC are retrospective and judgemental. More importantly, perhaps, the 1970s debate was about the systemic implications of capitalism, with a subtextual question about whether it should be overthrown. In the 1990s, with capitalism now apparently triumphant, the focus is on what individuals and firms could have done differently and on how capitalists, transformed into heroes of the new order, can clear their moral debts.

The role of capital and capitalists in generating and sustaining South Africa's formal racial order remains important also for the comparative historical study of race relations. The more recent tendency of race relations scholars is to divert attention from class and economic imperatives to those issuing from culture, identity and the institutional character of the state. This chapter has not attempted to calculate the relative weight of narrowly economic and other factors in the formation, maintenance and erosion of the racial order. It *has* confirmed that capitalists and capitalism were linked to the racial order in multiple and significant ways. This is of more than academic importance, for both capitalism and a (kind of) racial order are still with us.

Indeed, what must now be theorized in a South African context is the relationship between capitalism and those features of the racial order which have outlived apartheid, including racism, race consciousness and racial inequality. These remain hugely prominent features of life in the 'new' South Africa, and their material basis remains a matter of great moment, one from which culturalist analyses should not prematurely deflect attention. The 1996 census confirms that in South Africa whites are still disproportionately located in the business and professional classes, Africans in the ranks of working and poor people; coloureds are better off than Africans, Indians than coloureds. If we take the 'national' question to be about more than the end of formal apartheid, and to embrace a concern with racial equality more broadly, then that question remains unresolved and the further question of whether capitalism can contribute to its resolution still unanswered.

If capitalism is incapable of resolving it, there are a variety of reasons why this might be so. Capitalists are suspicious of labour and equality legislation which threaten to raise the costs of labour – legislation which might nevertheless be necessary to tackle inherited racial inequalities. Organized business is currently placing substantial pressure on the ANC government to water down its pro-labour legislation. If under apartheid business abhorred labour market measures which artificially protected white workers, they now view suspiciously labour market interventions that favour black workers (or women). Perhaps more importantly, capitalism has a tendency to preserve and sometimes extend existing inequalities: those who are outside of the dominant market positions find it difficult to break into the domains occupied by those who got there first. The South African economy is dominated by a small number of giant concerns owned overwhelmingly by whites, and white workers bring skill advantages to the labour market. Blacks are for historical reasons skill-poor, and struggle to assemble capital. The state can attempt to address these imbalances, but in doing so is constrained, more so than ever in an age of 'globalization', by the scepticism and hostility of private economic power.

At the same time there can be no doubt that many capitalists would welcome more effective deracialization of the economy and an expanded black middle class, provided capitalists could secure this desideratum without much sacrifice. Structurally there are capitalist sectors that need and are ready to absorb skilled blacks. Blacks have made substantial advances into supervisory and professional strata in recent decades and they are also making it into the bourgeoisie, assisted now by a majority-ruled state and a business class happy to appease the spirit of the 'new' South Africa when this can be done relatively painlessly. Though whites remain on top, the income gap between blacks and whites has diminished. The problem is that, given the size of the economy, its capital intensity and its oligopolostic character, and black educational disadvantage, there are only so many blacks who can get ahead, and indeed only so many who can gain employment in the formal economy at all. The result is deepening differentiation in the black population, between middle class and proletariat, skilled and unskilled, employed and unemployed and the fully, partly and non-urbanized (Whiteford and Van Seventer 1999). A class or social question has thus opened up within the black population itself, quite transfiguring the 'national' question and arguably overtaking it in importance. As it begins the twenty-first century therefore South African society confronts a residual 'national' and growing social question simultaneously. There is, on the one hand, the old question of whether capitalism can erode racial hierarchy; on the other, that of whether it can prevent an ever deepening polarization between those who, whatever their race or ethnicity, are economic insiders, and those who are shut out. There remain legitimate reasons to question the capacity of capitalism to do either.

3

Modernity and Racial Oppression

The question of South Africa's 'modernity'

A creeping disillusionment with materialist accounts and socialist diagnoses had by the middle to later 1980s opened the way to a new kind of analysis of South Africa's racial order, one issuing not from Marxism but from post-structuralism and post-modernism. According to these newer perspectives – which have, like Marxism before them, gained ground in tandem with fashion shifts in Europe and America – the South African racial order is one instance of a larger phenomenon: modernity. Post-modernists and post-structuralists understand capitalism, socialism and the South African racial order alike as products of a modernist western historical culture characterized by a belief in science, reason and human progress. They view modernity as an essentially cultural artefact. It is modernist culture – interpreted as a particular system of language through which reality is comprehended and articulated – which both produces the South African racial order and which should therefore be the real object of critique for those fighting it. Since socialism and liberalism like capitalism are part of the modernity that produces oppressive systems like apartheid, neither can offer an emancipatory alternative to it.

There is an *older* tradition of theorization about modernity which is essentially optimistic, and which has its South African counterparts. Liberal modernization theory treats liberal capitalist democracy as the paradigm of modernity and looks forward to other societies participating in its benefits, which it will be increasingly possible for them to do as a result of economic exchange and cultural diffusion. Orthodox Marxism too assumed that Western capitalism would reshape the world in its own image, but believed that it would in turn, its historical mission exhausted, be replaced by socialism. A conflictual conception of social change was more central to the Marxist than the liberal position. But both approaches saw value in science and technology, appropriately applied to human problems; both valued progress, and considered the expansion of economic productivity through human mastery of nature to be a part of it. Neo-Marxist dependency and underdevelopment theory called into question the capacity of western capitalism to modernize its global periphery (including South Africa or at least its underdeveloped areas) along similar lines to the metropolitan core. It did not, with some partial 'Maoist' exceptions perhaps, attach itself to a critique of modernity in any deeper sense. The liberal–radical controversy in South Africa was in part about whether capitalism could deliver modernity or deliver it in a desirable form, or whether, for example because of its historical entanglement with institutionalized racism, it needed to be replaced by socialism, conceived as a superior model of modernity.

There is a second way of viewing modernity that, though not uniformly hostile to it, considers it more inherently problematic. Writers like Weber, members of the Frankfurt School and more recent post-structuralists and post-modernists comprehend modernization as a process whereby a technocratic logic is imposed on human reasoning and organization. This logic compels a search for objective knowledge of and technical control over inner (human) and outer (non-human) nature. It is animated by an instrumental rationality that treats people and nature as means to higher ends. Its custodian is the expert and the bureaucrat and it justifies itself to the world through stories or narratives about inexorable human progress. Those adopting such a perspective have not been uniformly anti-modernist. Weber believed bureaucracy and legal-rational legitimacy would generate efficiency and, though they were irreversibly established and threatened to impose conformity, could be kept in check by democratic politicians. Habermas championed a modernity in which instrumental rationality was kept within proper bounds, human life-worlds re-established and genuinely non-instrumental rational communication made possible (1984, 1987). For the more pessimistic anti-modernists, influenced by Adorno and Horkheimer (1972), Foucault (1977) and 'post-colonialism' theorists (Moore-Gilbert 1997), modernity is irrevocably committed to developing technologies of classification, surveillance and control, enacting dangerous projects of social engineering, erasing cultural difference in the name of universal western values (or squashing it under a commodifying consumerism), and silencing the understandings and voices of those who do not conform to its model of the rational citizen. For commentators surveying the modernization process through this lens, South

Africa's racial order could be seen as a logical product of modernity rather than (as for many liberals) a challenge to it or (as for Marxists) the misbegotten progeny of a specifically capitalist modernity. The post-war South African state's passion for bureaucratic regulation of markets and spaces, its elaborate apparatus of surveillance and its arcane systems of racial classification are, for them, the typical features of modernity.

Modernity in South African history

Tracing the history in South Africa of the relationship between modernity and the racial order is complicated by an uncertainty which may be said to afflict critical accounts of modernity more generally: determining its beginning. The most commonly cited founding event of modernity, more especially when seen as a cultural form, is the eighteenth-century Enlightenment, but other contenders both pre-date it (ancient Greece and Rome, the Renaissance, the Reformation) and post-date it (Victorian scientific optimism and humanitarianism, the industrial revolution, twentieth-century movements in planning and architecture). These rival candidates suggest different possible ways of dating the advent of modernity in South Africa.

The European force usually credited with bringing modernity to South Africa is nineteenth-century Britain, together with British bureaucrats, missionaries, merchants and journalists in the colonies and republics. However, the colonial officials who presided over the first and long Dutch occupation of the Cape issued from a country already affected by modernizing episodes such as the Renaissance, Reformation and mercantilism. In the Cape the Dutch East India Company (*Verenigde Oost-Indische Companie*) ruled through forms of bureaucracy and written law. At the same time it was essentially a company state, part public and part private, inherently authoritarian and lacking separation of powers, suffused with personalized power and corruption. Company law distinguished classes of subjects that largely corresponded in practice to distinct racial groups. The DEIC lacked the resources to police an advancing frontier, thus leaving much of the regulation of race contact – whether trade with indigenes or control of servants – to the sphere of private violence, whether of the freebooter or patriarch. Calvinism at the Cape was pastoral and ethnically particularistic rather than universalistic. Settlers in the Dutch period exhibited only a faint acquaintance with Enlightenment precepts.

The coming of the British marked an important departure that Crais has attempted to comprehend in Foucauldian terms. British commodities, liberal ideas and colonists disrupted the hegemony of the frontier patriarch. The British set about dismantling a system in which power over servants 'radiated from the body of the master' in the form of physical violence. They put in its place where power rested on the accumulation of knowledge about the dominated (Crais 1992: 87) and in which punishment was 'interiorized' through the transformation of inner characters (via jails, mental asylums and surveillance) (127). The rule of law expressed the dual nature of British liberal humanitarianism, for it simultaneously reproduced the system of racial labour-repression while restraining the dominators (60). It represented, in other words, the 'more diffuse but potentially more invidious forms of control' characteristic of modernity (87). The self-conscious modernity of the British settlers was reflected in their construction of the indigenous 'other' as barbaric and their conviction that the Dutch-Afrikaner frontier settler was reverting to barbarism (ch. 3). What is distinctive in this account is not the claim that the British period entailed the maintenance or elaboration of racial domination – that is for example argued by Ross – but the implication that the new, more subtle forms of oppression were products of modernity understood as a cultural or discursive order.

A similar sense is conveyed by the Comaroffs in their account of nineteenth-century colonial evangelism, which they consider 'the progeny of modernism' (Comaroff and Comaroff 1991:15), tasked with subduing the 'forces of savagery, otherness, and unreason' at work in Africa (11). European colonization of Africa was for them 'often less a directly coercive conquest than a persuasive attempt to colonize consciousness, to remake people by redefining the taken-for-granted surfaces of their everyday worlds' (313). Modernist hegemony was conveyed through 'the silent power of the sign' and the 'unspoken authority of habit' (22) as much as through outright violence, and in this hegemonic project missionaries played a signal role.

Post-structuralist writers have deployed a similar vocabulary to interpret the twentieth-century racial order. Ashforth (1990), who is concerned to uncover the 'discourses' (12) and 'symbolic rituals' (7) which underpin modern state power, turns his attention to South Africa's 'Grand Tradition' of commissions of inquiry on the 'native question'. These he sees as interesting for the way they helped to fashion 'knowledge, strategies, policies, and justifications' of domination (1). Commissions of enquiry reduced Africans to depoliticized objects of technical administration, denying them the right to speak for themselves, providing for their representation instead through 'experts' who purported to understand their true natures. At the same time commissions of inquiry advertised the state's supposed commitment to seeking out 'the common good' (1, 7, 97, 253). Ashforth is clear that they are associated with a wider Western, European, modern tradition enshrining 'values and techniques of mastery' over nature and the social world (Ashforth 1990: 5).

Other writers less committed to overthrowing materialist analysis have also joined in the study of the 'discourses' through which the ruling groups constructed knowledge about the racial other or subjected them to surveillance. Dubow (1995) has argued that race, 'considered as a social and intellectual construct, has had a real and enduring existence' for much of the twentieth century (1995: 5), and explores the systematization of ethnological and anthropological knowledge within South Africa's expanding university system. These developing disciplines could supply the sorts of 'experts' whose authority satisfied the longing for a scientifically positivist justification of segregation and apartheid (Chapter 1). Posel (1996) has provided a Foucault-influenced account on the apartheid state's modernist preoccupation with gathering vast amounts of statistical knowledge about the African population, arguing for an intimate connection between 'capacities to count and control in South Africa' (1996: 3). She has also explored the role of technocratic language in legitimating a reformist neo-apartheid state in the 1980s, in this case in opposition to the sort of Verwoerdian racism previously justified by pro-apartheid anthropologists (Posel 1987).

Urban studies have proved a fertile field for demonstrating the influence of modernist impulses in the making of South Africa's racial order, primarily because of the preoccupation of urban planners in South Africa with spatial planning approaches popular in post-Second World War Europe and America. Modernist thinking about urban planning and architecture, brought into South Africa by a range of practitioners, scholars and students, 'lent itself to apartheid' (Parnell and Mabin 1995: 55). It shared with exponents of the latter an interest in large-scale spatial engineering to manage problems of urban economic and population growth and especially in slum clearance and the creation of coherent communities separated by green belts. These shared priorities allowed planning professionals to join in the designing of the 'racially distinct, well-separated zones' characteristic of urban segregation (Mabin 1992: 415). Robinson's Foucauldian analysis (1992) also emphasizes the link between planning discourses, the commitment of the modern state to achieving order and surveillance and the construction of twentieth-century urban racial orders in South Africa. Technocratic planning connected up with apartheid spatial engineering also at the level of macro-spatial 'regional planning', as this author has shown in his account of the history of industrial decentralization policies from the 1940s (Glaser 1988).

A critique

How useful is this attempt to understand South Africa's racial order through the prism of modernity? One undoubted benefit of exposing the presence of modern discourses and institutions in South Africa is that it helps to illustrate some of the ways in which that country's experiences and challenges are shared with other countries and societies. It provides useful comparative reference points and challenges the parochialism of South Africa's scholarly community. It also serves as a reminder that the roots of South Africa's oppressions lie not only in irrational racial prejudice but also in, for example, the hegemony of technocratic values which are authoritarian, depoliticizing and place undue authority in the laps of unaccountable and far from neutral 'experts'. The concept of capitalism previously highlighted by radicals served broadly similar intellectual and political functions. It allowed scholars to place South Africa in a comparative context and to draw attention to the deeper and more universal oppression of class underlying race oppression. However, the critique of modernity suggests, rightly, that some of the challenges and oppressions afflicting South Africa belong to a wider field of phenomena than capitalism itself, and perhaps to all modern or industrial societies – as for example radical Weberians have long argued or implied. It offers an additional vantage point for healthy scrutiny of the modernizing and universalizing ambitions of South Africa's post-liberation elite, and a warning about how modernist principles can be used to entrench state power or efface difference (Robinson 1992: 300-2; Norval 1996, ch. 6, conclusion).

There are, nevertheless, serious problems associated with the recourse to the concept of modernity as an explanatory key for understanding South Africa's racial order or challenging its oppressions. The first of these problems arises from the lack of specificity attaching to modernity. The concept can be stretched to cover a very wide range of historical phenomena, assumptions and propositions. Expansive usages of the notion of modernity exaggerate the significance of commonalities and underplay the importance of distinctions between competing modernities and modernist discourses. Societies conceived as modern vary greatly in form from, say, Anglo-American liberalism to Soviet-style totalitarianism. There are certainly important features these societies shared, such as the presence of large organizations, the granting of prestige to science and the preoccupation with economic growth. Two strategies for linking such apparently diverse societies must however be rejected. One treats the most oppressive industrial societies as the highest expressions of modernist rationality, perhaps as representing the future for all modern societies. Arguments of this sort have been made about Nazi Germany and the East Bloc: social orders characterized by industrialized extermination and/or faith in the possibility or comprehensive planning of human affairs. In South Africa apartheid could be seen as another modernist apotheosis. The notion that such societies represent the culmination of modernity seems wildly misplaced at the end of the twentieth century. A second strategy could argue that these different kinds of society are essentially similar, perhaps converging in fundamental respects, despite superficial differences. A 'convergence thesis' has certainly been canvassed from time to time in post-war political sociology; its principal effect is to obscure differences – crucial both normatively and in terms of understanding for example economic dynamics – between (say) liberal democracy and single-party bureaucratic dictatorship.

The elasticity of notions of modernity and Enlightenment is well illustrated in respect of race and ethnic relations. For some, the Enlightenment is associated with a spirit of tolerance, a commitment to equality of political and legal rights and a belief in the possibility that all can enjoy the benefits of civilization. To others it connotes colonialism, the suppression of non-Western cultures and the beginning of a process of subjecting human beings to pseudo-scientific race classification. It is true that the dominant discourses of political and scientific communities since (say) the eighteenth century have been diverse enough to include both pluralistic and repressive tendencies, and also that, on occasion, apparently 'enlightened' doctrines can have a repressive side – as in the case of liberal assimilationism. What is unhelpful is any implication that these diverse tendencies are all essentially alike and all essentially racially and ethnically repressive. Such a characterization fails to comprehend the intense historical rivalry between modernist political and intellectual traditions, or important differences between the types of policies and governments these traditions have justified. It absorbs the textured complexity of the 'modern' centuries into the kind of undifferentiating grand narrative, in this case of a singular and oppressive modernity, that post-modernists claim to eschew.

Employment of the concept of modernity is further complicated by difficulties in judging which phenomena are properly classified as modern. Nationalism, for example, is considered by some to be a primordial force, by others to be an invention of modern industrial society or even print-capitalism. Some have emphasized the relative modernity of Afrikaner nationalism, dating it as a movement of politicized ethnic mobilization no further back than the 1870s, and some indeed dating its apartheid-era form back no further than the 1930s (see Chapter 6). It certainly partook of a wider nineteenth-century nationalism associated with the rise of modern nation-states in Europe and the Americas, albeit that it embodied a spirit more of German-style ethnic than of Western European or American civic nationalism. Afrikaner nationalism in power could be a secularizing force despite its 'Christian-national' goals. It determinedly appropriated the task of African education from Christian missions and placed it in the hands of a bureaucratic state. Yet at the same time its discourse even in the middle to late twentieth-century was anti-urban and amounted to a 'comprehensive indictment of modernity' (Elphick 1997: 9). Can modernity be ascribed both to a particularistic ethnic nationalism like that of Afrikaners and to the universalizing British imperial and Anglophone forces it was ranged against? If indeed Afrikaner nationalism was in some sense modern, then the need is underlined always to specify which modernity is being discussed and to differentiate the manifestations of it.

A similar point can be made about racial policies. Both assimilationist liberalism and segregationist policies designed to separate races can be credibly interpreted as springing from modern impulses: the former from Enlightenment-inspired universalism and evolutionism, the latter from, amongst other 'modern' phenomena, scientific racism, university-based cultural anthropology and spatial planning. The modern aspects of both sets of phenomena are not uninteresting, even if they are sometimes exaggerated. What is clear is that the fact of their modernity on its own gives us relatively little explanatory purchase when it comes to the issue of why this rather than that modern path was followed in particular societies at given times.

There are, secondly, difficulties associated with attempts to distinguish a modern character or essence from modern trappings and tools. Modernity may simply be a *mask* for anti-modern interests and purposes. The prestige accorded science places a premium on scientific authority and technocratic legitimacy; very different ruling orders lay claim to it. Nor is it always easy to tell whether scientific impulses are driving politics or supplying *post hoc* justifications and superficial veneers. In South Africa it is highly likely that racism and ethnocentrism fostered racist and ethnocentric science, rather than the other way around. Modernity can also serve as an *instrument,* in the sense of a technology, resource or institutional capacity. The propagation of Islamic medievalism by tape cassettes and the Nazi use of gas chambers to systematize a process that began with massacres are both instances of modernity as technique or means rather than of modernity as a project or goal. Apartheid too could be modernized in this technical and organizational sense, as Heribert Adam long ago recognized (Adam 1971). For example, National Party governments appropriated the resources of 1960s industrial growth to build a military-industrial complex and, later, sustain a siege economy. The distinction between a regime and its technical armoury may not seem important to those who reduce modern forms of power to technologies of domination: but it does or should matter which social forces wield modern technologies and to what end.

The conflation of a regime of domination with its (modern) techniques has the effect also of reducing a very wide range of scientific and intellectual activity to its oppressive and political content. This reductionism is evident in (for example) discussions about the production of knowledge by whites about blacks. 'Post-colonialist' radical writers abroad tend to consider representations of the colonized 'other' in 'modern' or 'western' discourse to be essentially fictive constructions designed to bolster the power of the colonizer. Critics of western modernity argue that in South Africa this process of 'othering' proceeded as much in the work of official 'scientific' commissions on race policy as it did in, say, the novelist H. Rider Haggard's imaginative depictions of Zulus. The claim that knowledge about blacks generated by whites in South Africa is essentially a medium of domination is clearly evident in Ashforth's writing but is detectable also, at least up to a point, in the work of Dubow and Posel. The possibility that 'western' knowledge of the other is at least in part shaped by the discourses of the colonized, or that it might bear sufficient traces of the world-view of the colonized to tell us something useful about them, is rarely considered in such accounts. It is precisely these latter possibilities that Hamilton invites us to consider in her recent work on the evolution of discourses about the Zulu king Shaka (Hamilton 1998). She shows that colonial officials sometimes drew on an intimate knowledge of African ways. The officials used this knowledge to strengthen white rule, but they did not in so doing void it of any connection with the real world of the colonized. Equally the work of commissioners and anthropologists and official collectors of statistics is not so inherently tainted by its connection to power that it cannot ever supply valuable historical insights or information of use to progressive policy-makers. If different modernist phenomena need to be sharply distinguished, so do we need a more complex and differentiated way of thinking about 'modernist' intellectual and technological instruments.

Modernity and reconstruction

A final objection to the anti-modernist critique of the racial order concerns its implications for an emancipatory politics. Two salutary political cautions issue from the post-modernists and other critics of modernity. One is against projects of utopian social engineering driven by encompassing metanarratives of progress and implemented by impersonal and centralized bureaucratic machines. The other is against the project of building a homogeneously conceived national unity that effaces cultural diversity. Pitched at this level of generality either of these cautions could, of course, have issued from the proponents of conventional forms of liberalism and social democracy; but they are no less important for that. It is in one way South Africa's good fortune to have been emancipated from apartheid into an age of post-modern scepticism about totalizing ideologies and projects. The rhetoric in favour of an autonomous civil society and bottom-up development which has flowed through post-apartheid politics owes something to post-modern doubt as well as to an international convergence around liberal-democratic norms. So too does the democratic state's rhetorical deference to the country's linguistic diversity and culturally plural character. South Africa's newly governing African elite has not, for example, attempted to abolish ethnic identities and institutions in the name of nation-building.

At the same time it is worrying that anti-modernist critique often fails to distinguish modernity's good, bad and indifferent features. It is an indiscriminateness which opens the way to a delegitimation of aspects of modernity that are deeply necessary to any good society or polity. It is common for critics of modernity to accuse it of forms of oppression which, because they are subtle or insidious, are in some ways worse, and certainly no better than forms that are more openly violent. The rule of law is associated in such writing above all with surveillance, interiorization of punishment and institutions of incarceration; its role in containing arbitrariness and atrocity is devalued. It is never made clear what might replace it. Again, liberalism is condemned, not for the insufficiency and hypocrisy of its actual practice, but for its modernity, without any serious effort to identify those features of it which are crucial to any democratic and pluralistic civil society.

As we have seen, the critics of modernity also appear to consider some of the essential techniques of modern social regulation, such as gathering statistics, to be inherently productive of domination, and certainly incapable of providing valuable information about an external world. They thus cast doubt on whether these techniques ought to have any place in the armoury of governments and other political actors fighting for social welfare, popular empowerment or equality. Anti-modern critique makes it more difficult to understand what better kind of order might replace racial domination precisely because its practitioners mis-identify what is wrong with the present order. The objectionable features of the pre-1994 racial order were not lawfulness, planning, bureaucratic regulation or the professionalization of knowledge, but the institutionalization of a racial hierarchy of wealth, status and power, enforced by repressive, often arbitrary state authority, assisted by bad laws. The order needed to replace it requires more and better law, effectively enforced, and more 'scientific' information about the condition of the people, not less of these 'modern' goods. It may also require an active and sophisticated state, one that observes liberal self-limitation but deploys the organizational machinery of 'modernity' to give effect to 'modern' ideals like social justice.

There is little, either concrete or specific, that anti-modernists can add to the repertoire of reconstruction strategies. Post-modern politics appears to have something to do with struggling for local autonomies and deepening respect for cultural difference. These are worthy ideals to which most liberals and socialists would subscribe. Taken to some of its more radical conclusions anti-modern political thinking can, however, become quite alarming in its prescriptions. There are, after all, two 'others' to the modern. One is the pre-modern, sometimes favourably invoked on the deep-green wing of anti-modernism as well as by some Africanists who would romanticize pre-colonial African communality. Whatever the genuine merits of consultative decision-making in pre-modern African societies, it is clear both that they bore the imprint of a variety of oppressions, notably of women by men, of young by elders and of all by nature. They are anyway inaccessible to, and rarely genuinely sought by, those who have grown up with modernity. The other 'other' to modernity is a kind of carnival of 'difference' in which universal rules and rights – the hallmarks of Western liberal universalism – give way to informal conversations between proliferating cultural fragments. Whatever one may think of cultural pluralization, there is certainly a right to cultural identity and separatenesss, one that is for the most part given sufficient due by liberal freedoms of association and expression. What would be problematic is a disavowal of the project of seeking universally agreed rules for mediating antagonisms between cultural communities, or a relativism which sanctions the repression of internal dissidents and minorities by cultural leaders. Yet indefinite conflict and the subordination of individuals to cultural collectives is precisely what would follow from the victory of a politics of 'difference' that is not anchored in liberal universalism.

What should matter to progressives is not whether post-apartheid South Africa is modern, but whether it is liberal, democratic, egalitarian and provides economic and social security to its citizens. These goals are for the most part 'modern' ones, but that is not the point; there are less worthy modern goals too. The rhetoric of 'modernization' is often employed by those seeking to defend privilege against 'old-fashioned' ideas like socialism. The point is rather that the dichotomization of modernity and its 'others' gives us too little guidance in distinguishing good courses of action from bad ones. Its deficiencies are both analytic and programmatic.

4

South African States

```
┌─────────────────────────────────────────────────────────────┐
│                                                               │
│                         CONTENTS                              │
│                                                               │
│                 Delimiting the state   70                     │
│            State formation in Southern Africa   71            │
│             The South African state 1910-89  75              │
│               The state in transition    108                  │
│                                                               │
└─────────────────────────────────────────────────────────────┘
```

Delimiting the state

In the 1970s radical scholars began to discuss and debate the South African 'state'. The concept of state was meant to bring into focus something larger than the dynamics of government or administration, understood descriptively: it cast a searchlight on the mechanisms whereby social domination was 'reproduced' or, alternatively, challenged; and in particular those mechanisms associated with public power. Marxist-influenced radical scholars were particularly concerned to understand the role of the South African state in maintaining or bolstering capitalism. In searching for an account of the state they drew on a contemporaneous revival in so-called 'state theory' amongst European Marxists dissatisfied with the simplistic nostrums of inherited Leninist state theory according to which the state was a coercive instrument of capital. The South African state was clearly not an instrument of capital; it was, on the contrary, in the hands of Afrikaner farmers and bureaucrats, and Marxist theory (they realized) would need to be sophisticated to explain how such a state could serve capital. At the same time Marxists were concerned to challenge liberal accounts of the South African political system that treated the state as an instrument of the 'common good' temporarily being misused by dogmatic Afrikaner nationalists. For Marxists the state was an ensemble of institutions suffused with relations of unequal power requiring revolutionary overthrow. This chapter is in the first instance about the radical theories of the state and the controversies provoked by them both within Marxist ranks and amongst liberals and a range of eclectic non-Marxist radicals. But it is more generally about the origins and nature of the state and political power in South Africa.

The state referred to by writers surveyed here is variously defined and understood by them. All societies are governed in some fashion but not all can be said to have states. The state discussed in this chapter refers to that institution which exercises supreme decision-making power in a territorial political unit and whose functions are performed by specialized personnel belonging to recognizably 'public' organizations. The chapter begins by addressing the historical–sociological question of how states of this kind arose in Southern Africa.

State formation in Southern Africa

A centralized state encompassing what is today South Africa came into being in 1910. Until that time a range of political systems, more or less state-like, jostled for territory, resources and jurisdiction across shifting and ill-defined frontiers. Both white settlers and indigenous peoples in Southern Africa created states or state-like bodies, and for both the nineteenth century was a key period of state formation.

White settler states in the region were in many ways outposts of European state formation, initially that of the United Netherlands, later that of industrializing Britain. African states by contrast developed out of the region's indigenous modes of political authority. Kingdoms crystallized in the nineteenth century amongst certain groups of pastoralist-cultivators that centralized the powers previously held in small, fissiparous chiefdoms. The reasons centralized polities emerged are widely debated, the principal candidates being resource conflicts associated with ecological pressures and struggles to control the prestige goods brought via trade networks radiating from the east coast of Southern Africa (Guy 1980, Bonner 1983, Hall 1987). Shaka's militaristic and expansionist Zulu state was for long seen as the prime mover of the *mfecane*, the destructive wars that brought African state-formation to a head in the 1820s (Omer-Cooper 1966/78). It is now seen as one player amongst others in a protracted process of political centralization dating back to the mid-eighteenth century. The *mfecane* itself had as one of its stimulants Griqua slave-raiding on behalf of white colonists, though it was primarily a product of dynamics in African societies (Cobbing 1988; Hamilton 1995; Manson 1995; Parsons 1995).

What seems clear is that decades of tensions, wars and migrations led to a situation where some chiefly lineages were able to impose their authority on others, whether by aggression (as in the Zulu and Swazi states) or by offering armed protection to displaced groups (as with the Basotho). New ruling aristocracies were able to extract from previously decentralized homestead economies the labour and other resources necessary to sustain relatively centralized polities. This development marked, in Marxist-structuralist terms, the replacement of a 'lineage mode of production' with a 'tributary mode' (Bonner 1980).

Early state formation did not invariably bring forth specialized political and administrative strata on a substantial scale. Bureaucratization developed further and faster in white than African polities, stimulated, *inter alia*, by traditions of legalism and literacy inherited from Europe. Though centralized and officious the Dutch East India Company (*Verenigde Oost-Indische Companie*) lacked the impersonality of ideal-typical bureaucracy. Top officials used the state as a vehicle of private accumulation through 'profiteering, nepotism and bribery' (Scutte 1979/80: 204) while distinct branches of authority were united in the persons of single individuals. Post-DEIC Dutch governors managed only hesitant reforms during their brief tenure between 1803 and 1806 (Freund 1979/80). The nineteenth-century Boer states were also slow to impose bureaucratic order: the Transvaal state was debilitated in its early decades by corruption and inefficient tax collection.

The British by contrast were bureaucratizers, imposing a more definite rule of law and a range of modernizing administrative reforms, both in the Cape Colony and in the Transvaal (Peires 1988). By the late nineteenth century there had emerged in the Cape a clearly discernible administrative stratum with its own occupational culture. By professionalizing administration the British partly disentangled the official caste from the locally dominant landowning classes, and thus political from economic power. However landowners, and later mine owners, retained a significant presence in the state and could anyway exercise substantial political influence from a position external to it (Denoon 1980; Trapido 1980b; Lewsen 1983; Jeeves 1985, ch. 1; Beinart and Delius 1986; Dubow 1989: 99-103; Giliomee 1989b).

African states departed only imperfectly from traditional pre-bureaucratic form of authority, and some have questioned whether they were markedly more state-like than chiefdoms (which also satisfied some criteria of statehood) (Maylam 1986: 64-5). There were administrative officials of various kinds in the emerging states, but there were no large functionally specialized administrative organizations. While indigenous African polities varied in character (Mamdani 1996: 40-8), positions of political leadership in emerging states of Southern Africa fell largely to members of dominant lineages, as in earlier European dynasties, and polities were bound by customary rules rather than the codified sort favoured by Europeans. On conquered African states too the British imposed a form of legal-rational bureaucratic authority, whether by replacing chiefs with magistrates, administratively controlling chiefly appointments, recruiting chiefs and headmen as paid state officials, or codifying customary law.

New white and African states were not able to impose a uniform writ over clearly defined territories. They attempted to monopolize the legitimate use of violence, whether by prohibiting certain forms of private violence (such as that of settlers against slaves), disarming subjects (notably the Basotho by the Cape in 1880-81) or mobilizing male labour for military purposes (imposing conscription in the Cape or mobilizing age-regiments in Shaka's Zulu state). At the boundaries of both kind of state, however, were to be found groups, ranging in size from patriarchal homesteads to small polities, which exercised considerable autonomy. In both kinds of state, too, powers and functions were delegated, whether to landed notables in the Cape or to senior members of African royal lineages. The closing of the frontier in the later nineteenth century was in part the story of the incorporation of autonomous groups, both black and white, into more efficient frameworks of (white) central governance.

Regional state formation was for long constricted by a limited base of revenue. Dutch and British imperial governments sought to spend as little as possible on their colonies, tax demands were few or (in the Transvaal) evaded, and the local economies were, prior to the 1870s, agrarian and fairly small. The British presided over a more interventionist colonial state at the Cape than had the Dutch, and a greater degree of settler self-government in the 1850s brought with it increased spending on roads, hospitals, schools, prisons and other infrastructure (Davenport 1969). The wealth generated by diamond and gold mining transformed the revenue-generating potential of regional states, stimulating state-led railway provision in the Cape and Transvaal and paving the way for the much more extensive and interventionist state of twentieth-century South Africa.

African kings and chiefs appropriated labour and various forms of fines and tribute from their subject communities. In the nineteenth century trade, peasant agriculture and migrant labour provided new sources of revenue for chiefs. But the African states never acquired the resources to become major providers of infrastructure, and their principal economic responsibility was to maintain a broadly redistributive social system, for example by regulating access to land and loaning cattle to impoverished communities, as well as by providing armed protection for their subjects. Later traditional leaders were drawn into the bureaucratic and interventionist systems of conquering white states, and they were required to assist in, for example, tax collection, agricultural rationalization and labour recruitment.

The power of state-like rulers was constrained also by the need to legitimize their rule. In a few instances, such as perhaps Shaka's Zulu polity, state authority could be maintained principally by force and terror, but for the most part both white and black states were expected to deliver certain goods and observe certain rules in order to secure popular respect and compliance. African chiefs were invested with a wide range of theoretical powers and functions, but were also expected to discharge a range of social duties and to govern consultatively. There was a premium on accumulating and retaining followers, who added to a chiefdom's productive powers and military strength but who until the closure of the frontiers enjoyed an option of exit from one chiefdom to form another. The conquest-based African states of the nineteenth century centralized powers to varying degrees, though in many cases their authority remained circumscribed by that of subordinate clan and lineage leaders. White conquerors in erecting systems of indirect rule built on the most authoritarian traditions of the African conquest states while removing many of the checks on state power which operated in a traditional setting. Granted near-absolute powers by white authorities, and with their subjects' exit option foreclosed by land loss, chiefs under white colonial rule exploited their subjects more aggressively even as their capacity to perform their traditional social roles or defend their subjects from external impositions diminished (Eldredge 1993; Mamdani 1996). The result was the creation, in rural areas of African communal-tenure occupation, of systems of 'decentralized despotism' (Mamdani 1996: ch. 2). Unsurprisingly the legitimacy of traditional rulers frequently declined in the decades following white conquest.

White states too were expected to deliver goods and observe rules as a condition of their legitimacy. The DEIC government suffered a legitimacy deficit because of its corruption and its attempts to regulate settler–Khoisan interaction, a deficit deepened in the final years of Company rule by economic and frontier crises. The DEIC regime survived in part because settlers were relatively few in number, economically dependent, and untouched for the most part by Enlightenment ideas about the rights of individuals (despite their invocation in the 1778-87 Patriot Rebellion). While the DEIC delivered little by way of economic and administrative progress, it also made few demands on its subjects. The DEIC's authority was nevertheless definitely eroding towards the end of its period of government at the Cape (Schutte 1979/80).

The British delivered more by way of economic prosperity and administrative competence, but they also presided over the arrival in the Cape of settlers convinced of their entitlement to traditional English liberties and political rights. Western Cape Anglophones, together with some members of the Dutch middle classes, chafed under the autocratic governors who presided over the first decades of British rule and fought successfully for a free press, parliamentary representation (on the basis of a class-qualified male franchise) and greater self-government (Davenport 1969).

Other colonists who resented the whole direction of the reforms introduced by the British from the 1820s could exercise a different option: that of exit, as in the case of the Boer emigration to the interior in the 1830s. The Boers in Natal, the

Transvaal and Transorangia experimented with a variety of forms of government, from populist to military, but their fractious polities struggled to establish a stable legitimacy before the later nineteenth century. A combination of British-induced modernization and charismatic presidential leadership finally enabled them to consolidate. It was however the British model of parliamentary government and rule of law which, more or less, prevailed over the whole of (white) South Africa following the 1899-1902 British conquest of the Boer states.

The South African state 1910-89

The state in outline

The twentieth-century South African state is, like modern states generally, vastly larger than its nineteenth century precursors. In 1980 it employed 1.6 million people in 39 departments and 952 semi-government bodies, up from 150,718 employees in 22 departments and 106 semi-government bodies in 1920 (Seegers 1994: 40). Its rapid expansion in South Africa's case derived from its actively developmentalist role in a late industrializing society, its commitment to maintaining a racial order and its more conventional modern welfare functions as provider of state educational and health services. Over much of the century state expansion chimed with the global twentieth-century fashion for interventionism that was well established by the 1930s and exhausted itself in the 1970s.

In constitutional terms the post-1910 central state began life as a British style parliamentary system of government. The electorate was confined to whites (who won full universal franchise in 1931) except in the Cape where (qualified) Africans retained the vote until 1936 and coloureds until 1956. The constitution that came into effect in 1984 replaced the Westminster with a more presidential mixed form of government and added coloured and Indian elected chambers to form a 'tricameral' parliament.

The state was established in 1910 on a unitary rather than federal basis, though with functions devolved to four white provincial assemblies (reconstituted on an appointive basis in 1986) and an array of local government bodies. The predominant tendency in the white-dominated core over the century state (as in many modern states) was towards the concentration of power in the central executive at the expense of both parliament and local government.

For most of the century final control of African affairs rested firmly with white-controlled departmental bureaucracies at the centre. At the same time the state was 'bifurcated' (Mamdani 1996). From the 1920s reserve-based Africans were placed under the authority of state-backed traditional leaders, and from the

1960s a range of powers and functions were devolved to African ethnic 'homelands' and later to (formally independent) 'national states'. In the 1970s the state became more segmented as functions and later powers were devolved also to African, coloured and Indian municipal bodies.

The nature of the state in the African-controlled reserves has been the subject of considerable scholarly attention concerning, amongst other things, its role in sustaining South Africa's wider political economy, its effects on private and bureaucratic class formation amongst Africans and its resemblance or otherwise to other neo-colonial peripheral states (Molteno 1977; Southall 1982; Maré and Hamilton 1987; de V. Graaff 1990; Mamdani 1996). It is however the white controlled core state apparatus that has been the main object of debates within state theory since the 1970s and which will claim most attention here. These debates have been concerned to identify the changing social and political forces controlling the state, the state's role in economic development, its instruments and languages of domination and the extent and sources of its uniqueness or 'specificity'. Only relatively recently has a new issue intruded, the gendered character of the state.

Theoretical approaches to the state

Marxist state theory Who ran the South African state before 1994 and whose interests did it serve? Radical writers in the 1970s and early 1980s typically posited a South African state that was either controlled by the capitalist class or that objectively served capitalism. The state defended capitalism as a social order and/or helped satisfy capitalists' drive for profits ('accumulation'). However, the capitalist character of the South African state before 1989 was rarely self-evident. The one section of the employer class that was undoubtedly influential in the South African state over much of the period between 1910 and 1989 was also the least straightforwardly capitalist: the white farmers. Moreover, the Afrikaner nationalists who ran the state over much of the twentieth century were at times given to anti-capitalist rhetoric, the hated foreign, Jewish and English-speaking businessman symbolized for them by the satirical figure of 'Hoggenheimer'. Afrikaner nationalists in power presided over a large expansion of state bureaucracy and restricted urban capitalists' access to African labour. Liberals had much apparent reason for considering the Afrikaner nationalist state hostile to capitalism.

Marxists by contrast presented a state geared to meeting capitalist needs. It helped transform a black peasantry into a labour force (Bundy 1988) and canalize cheap labour to capitalist sectors experiencing labour shortages (Johnstone 1976; Morris 1977; Lacey 1981). It suppressed black labour organization and militancy and helped to keep the working class divided on racial lines (Legassick 1974a: 265-6; Davies 1979). State expansion and interventionism has been typical of twentieth-century capitalist states, and in South Africa it was dedicated to boosting capitalist growth by providing trade protection, infrastructure and cheap credit (Wolpe 1972: 293-4; Legassick 1975: 252-6; Christie 1984, 1991; Martin 1990, 1991). The state did engage in direct economic production over a wide area, but often in partnership with big capital (Clark 1987, 1993, 1994), and it left the bulk of the economy in private hands. It was obliged to exempt capital from the effects of racial policies which posed an urgent threat to capitalists' profitability or willingness to invest, or at least to tailor its own priorities to take account of capitalist needs (Legassick 1975: 262-3; Glaser 1988). Afrikaner anti-capitalist rhetoric was a cover for an Afrikaner elite determined to win a place for itself and its constituents in the capitalist sun, and in power that elite dedicated itself, with brilliant success, to building an Afrikaner bourgeoisie and professional middle class (O'Meara 1983). And in practice Afrikaner nationalist governments presided over rapid growth in the capitalist economy, at least until the mid-1970s (Johnstone 1970; Legassick 1974b).

Radical positions on the state were neither uniform nor unchanging, even in their heyday. Marxist state theory as it developed in Europe and North America from the later 1960s was marked by tensions between what can loosely be classified as instrumentalist, structuralist and derivationist accounts, and these tensions had their counterpart in South African debates, which followed metropolitan fashions closely.

Marxist instrumentalists, like non-Marxist radical elite theorists, viewed the state as a tool of capital. South African radical writers never explicitly developed an instrumentalist account. This was probably largely because the Anglophone capitalist class was so obviously out of the loop of political power at least after 1948, and in part because other theoretical approaches were more fashionable by the 1970s. Instrumentalist assumptions could however be detected in a fair amount of Marxist writing before and during the 1970s.

It was structuralists influenced by the theorist Nicos Poulantzas (1978, 1980) who first established the political as a specific object of investigation in South Africa. They conceptualized the state in South Africa as bourgeois-democratic, albeit on a racially exclusive basis. While the state served capital in various ways, *inter alia* by disorganizing the working class, it enjoyed relative autonomy from the capitalist class. Poulantzians insisted South Africa's dominant classes were uniformly capitalist, but criticized earlier Marxist writers (for example theorists of an 'alliance of gold and maize') for overestimating the unity of capital, a product, they believed, of focusing exclusively on capitalists' shared labour needs and ignoring their rivalry over intersectoral distributional questions. The Poulantzians presented a picture of 'fractions' of capital competing for political hegemony and 'periodized' the South African state in terms of the shifting fortunes of 'national' and 'imperial', later 'monopoly' capital (Davies et al. 1976; Kaplan 1980).

The Poulantzians were vulnerable to the charge that they treated political parties as either instruments of class fractions or as expressions of class essences, thus denying the autonomous dynamics of the political or the distinctive interests and concerns of state managers. At the same time they (if anything) overestimated the autonomy of the state from the economy, analysing the inter-capitalist balance of power as though it were determined exclusively on the parliamentary and interest-group terrain, and underestimating limits imposed on state action by the accumulation process (Clarke 1978: 55; Innes and Plaut 1978; Yudelman 1984: 22-8, ch. 7). The Poulantzians were also vulnerable to the more general charge against structuralism, that they could not specify the mechanisms which ensured that the state served capitalist interests.

Both instrumentalist and structuralist approaches were attacked in South Africa, as in British and German debates, by a current of 'derivationist' writers. These rejected the Poulantzian notion of a relatively autonomous political realm, arguing instead for a holistic treatment of capitalism as both an economic and political system using the deductive method of the mature Marx and of the Russian writer Pashukanis. Derivationists logically 'derived' the forms and functions of the state from an elemental feature of capitalism, such as the class struggle (Innes and Plaut 1978) or the requirements of 'capital-in-general' (Clarke 1978: 55). Thus Innes and Plaut objected to the way fractionalists explained the South African state's economic and social policy in terms of intra-capitalist struggles within the state rather than the primary class struggle between capital and labour. Clarke objected to the account of a state driven by parliamentary/interest group politics to support the interests of one fraction over another, and which ignored (as he saw it) the role of the state as economic manager defending the interests of capital-in-general through, for example, monetary policy. Derivationists could not, however, offer convincing reasons for disregarding the partly autonomous dynamics of the political or for accepting that the operation of the state could be explained simply by extrapolation from the economic or political needs of capital or capitalism. Their understanding of the state was either essentialist (insofar as the state depicted by derivationists was the expression of an elemental social fact or dynamic) or functionalist (insofar as it appeared to be summoned forth by capitalist requirements). Derivationism was also guilty of a kind of rationalist idealism, conflating processes of theoretical deduction with real social processes.

Bringing the state back in In the 1980s a number of radical and radical–liberal writers began to argue for bringing the state back in. Along with 'statist' thinkers abroad (Block 1980; Nordlinger 1981; Skocpol 1985), and drawing on the insights of Max Weber and the later Poulantzas (1980), they stressed the state's autonomy and the need to take seriously its internal structure and operation.

'Statist' theorists firstly launched a critique of the tendency to treat the state as an expression or instrument of external social forces. They argued that society-centred approaches neglected the concrete organizational forms of the state (Wolpe 1980, 1988: ch. 2; Mamdani 1996: chs 1, 2) and the capacity of 'state managers' to pursue their own interests (Block 1980; Greenberg 1980: 26-8, 388-90; Yudelman 1984: 30-3; Lipton 1986: 318, 323-5; Hyslop 1989a; Posel 1991: 18-22). They secondly argued that the 'black box' of the state had to be opened up to allow investigation of its competing bureaucratic bases, the motivations and actions of its rival personnel and the operation of its decision-making mechanisms (Greenberg 1987a, 1987b: xvii; Hyslop 1989a; Posel 1991: 18-22). 'Statists' shared with the later Poulantzas a concern to understand the state as internally contested rather than singular or unitary, but rejected the notion that its conflicting actors necessarily represented external classes. They shared with conventional political science an interest in concrete institutional forms. At the same time they kept in view themes of class and political economy and rejected liberal notions of the state as a neutral servant of the common good or pluralist depictions of it as a mere cipher of, or broker between, societal interest groups. The state and its component elites and organizations were active historical agents.

It did not follow, however, that the state enjoyed the power imputed to it by many Marxists to shape events on the ground. State effectiveness could be undermined by internal divisions in the state or by the evasion and resistance of people who were the intended objects of state policy, as was the case with influx control policy (Greenberg 1987b: xviii, 18-23, 31-3; Posel 1991). State intervention to undermine sharecroppers or promote secondary industry, though ultimately very important, did not necessarily produce the immediately dramatic effects sometimes assumed (Keegan 1982, 1986a: 182-95; Freund 1989: 95-101).

The statists did not discount the class power of capital: capitalist control of the economy put it in a position to frustrate the designs of state economic planning and exercise leverage over government policy-making. However, relations between capital and the state had to be understood as a relationship between distinctive sets of actors and interests in which the superordinacy of capital could not be assumed in advance and capital did not necessarily prevail in practice (Greenberg 1980; Glaser 1988; Posel 1991).

Writers in this broad *oeuvre* rightly rejected the assumption that bureaucratic groups or elite political organizations represented only self-interested economic or class concerns. They could be motivated by 'paternalism' (Dubow 1989: ch. 4; Duncan 1995: 27-8), 'visionary' utopianism (Lazar 1993) or by sectional (bureaucratic or ideological) allegiances which placed them in conflict with external social classes. Their priorities and concerns were as much artefacts of culture, including internal departmental cultures of public service or non-partisan professionalism, as of external material imperatives (Frankel 1984: 13-28; Dubow 1989: ch. 4; Ashforth 1990; Duncan 1995: 28-9).

A salutary product of the new paradigm has been much closer scrutiny of inter-departmental conflicts and power balances within the 1910-94 state. Thus Dubow (1989: ch. 3) and Duncan (1995) have illuminated some of the contours of inter-departmental politics, especially over administration of Africans, during the interwar 'segregationist' years. Posel and Lazar have exposed internal machinations of the state and the Afrikaner nationalist political movement during the period from the 1940s through to the 1960s (Posel 1991: 49-75; Lazar 1993). In the 1980s radical writers (Cock and Nathan 1989; Swilling and Phillips 1989a) joined liberal institutionalists (Frankel 1984; Grundy 1986; Alden 1996) in charting the rise of a 'security state'. Radical writers also explored the varied, part-conflictual, part-cooperative relations between the local state and central government, above all over the initiation or implementation of urban segregation (Adler 1987; Todes et al. 1989: 195-6; Posel 1991: 190-1, 211-21, 246-8; Maharaj 1992; van Tonder 1993). Conflicts and tensions in particular policy areas, such as industrial decentralization (Glaser 1988) and influx control (Bekker and Humphries 1985; Greenberg 1987b; Posel 1991), have been traced through time. The role of influential personalities in the state has been highlighted (Sapire 1987: 383-4, 1993: 260; Chaskalson 1988; Gelb, 1989: 58-62; Christie 1991: 603-6; Clark 1994).

This literature has certainly cast a useful light into areas of political and institutional life which radicals had tended to consign to a secondary or 'superstructural' realm. It has properly avoided the earlier revisionist propensity to search for class essences or manipulations in all political processes and structures. 'Statist' writing nevertheless produced a mixed yield. While usually enlarging empirical knowledge, its more narrowly focused contributions provided little more than descriptions of political intrigues, organizational mechanisms and state ideologies and strategies. Its richest work explored the sociology of organizations, the cultural worlds of actors and the pressures and constraints issuing from the state's location in a larger political economy and society.

The turn to discourse A second (and overlapping) product of the radicals' turn away from the material and economic determinants of politics is a new fascination with what Ashforth has termed 'discourses of ruling' (Ashforth 1990: 12). A number of writers have since the later 1980s directed attention to the languages of political actors – their explicit doctrines, unspoken suppositions and verbal and non-verbal rituals. The starting point for many of these writers is that the languages of the powerful are not mediations or expressions of material forces, but powerful shaping forces in their own right. While some interested in discourses of power continue to locate these in a wider economic and social context, for others languages *are* the context – and indeed the contextualized. They not only constitute the way in which actors comprehend reality (and thus the way they act in the world) but constitute subjectivity itself: that is to say, shape the identities and personalities of those doing the comprehending. Languages (for the post-structuralists) confer meaning and supply criteria of truth: they cannot themselves be judged true or false from a vantage point outside language. The concern with myth and worldview echoes more conventional histories of ideas, for example those exploring the ideational world of Afrikaner nationalism (MacCrone 1937; Moodie 1975; Hexham 1981; Thompson 1985). Unlike some other analysts of ideas in history, however, post-structuralists posit no distinction between idea and reality or between text and author: the discourse constitutes reality and operates independently of its author. The post-structuralists moreover employ a more theoretically sophisticated (and abstruse) analytical apparatus to delve into the inner structures – including the silences and subtexts – of language.

Some writers have given attention to the discourses of the political life without travelling the full post-structuralist mile. They include Dubow (in his studies of segregationism and scientific racism), Lazar (in his account of Afrikaner nationalism in the early years of apartheid) and Posel (in her work on Afrikaner nationalist politics and languages of state legitimation) (Posel 1987, 1989; Dubow 1989, 1995; Lazar 1993). The seminal full-length post-structuralist analyses of the discursive worlds of twentieth century ruling groups are those of Ashforth (in his account of the role of commissions of inquiry) (1990) and Norval (in her exploration of the discursive logics of segregation and apartheid) (1996). The former attempts to show how commissions provided 'terms of reference' (Ashforth 1990: 4) for understanding social reality and explores the relationship between expert 'knowledge' and political power. Norval, influenced by the writing of Laclau and Mouffe, explicates the inner logics of apartheid as a body of discourse. She sees it as capable of expanding to constitute an 'imaginary horizon' (Norval 1996: 27) for reading all social divisions (as in the transition from segregation to apartheid) but as vulnerable to unravelling in the face of internal logical gaps or areas of 'undecidability' (for example in terms of how to explain the position of coloureds and urban blacks) (Norval 1996: 9).

The turn to discourse has illuminated new fields of social reality previously closed to radical analysis, and its advocates are certainly right to argue that languages and ideas matter in ways that materialists failed to appreciate. Human beings are not bearers of objective interests that translate into world-views in a predetermined way; people construe their worlds discursively and act within the terms of their understandings. They moreover make choices, including moral ones, which affect historical outcomes. Nevertheless the most ambitious of the discourse-theoretic and post-structuralist writers propose an approach which they cannot themselves sustain when they turn to the task of concrete analysis. In the first place, their work treats discourses as realities that can be described and explicated from positions outside of them, despite disclaimers. It seems to assume that true or at least academically serious statements can be made about discourses (like apartheid) but not about the external realities that discourses supposedly construct (such as material inequalities). This exemption of discourse from the unknowability of external reality is not explained. In the second place, discourse analysis cannot in practice provide an intelligible narrative without making repeated reference to phenomena outside a given discourse that shape or constrain it. Thus Ashforth concedes that in South Africa official accounts of reality lose their legitimatory usefulness once they 'fail to correspond meaningfully with that reality as it is lived' (Ashforth 1990: 9). Norval presents apartheid as a 'response' to various social upheavals in the 1930s and 1940s, albeit not the only possible one (Norval 1996: 5); as rooted in them (169); as giving 'precise' articulation to experiences of social change (12); as only explicable in terms of its 'context' (25) and so on. It is never explained why if 'discourses instituted imaginary horizons which structured *all* social relations' (Norval 1996: 27 – emphasis in original) they also corresponded to, were rooted in, precisely articulated, or had as their context realities (or experiences of realities). Conceding these intrusions of 'reality' amounts to an admission that extra-discursive circumstances condition the construction of, and popular receptiveness to, discursive interpretations. Discourse-theoretic approaches offer many important insights about the construction (and unravelling) of 'discourses of ruling', but they offer no realized or productive alternative to the longstanding concern of academic observers to 'understand' the real world beyond language.

State and society: a conclusion Some may consider the tendency to construct state theories around the question of the state's autonomy from capital to be dated, a relic of a time when the overthrow of capitalism itself seemed possible and (to those on the left) desirable. The end of such radical optimism certainly casts earlier state debates in a different light, as does the rise of newer forms of emancipatory politics concerned with, for example, gender oppression and the state's role in generating and reproducing it. The consistently patriarchal character of the state is bound to find its place in future state research alongside its class and ethnic character (Manicom 1992). Nevertheless, the tension between political sovereignty and private economic power is as important an issue today as ever. It continues to be very necessary, for this and other reasons, to explore the nature and implications of the structural constraints placed upon the state by capitalism as well as the empirical connections, in a given period, between economic-class and state power.

It is generally agreed in the literature that the South African state was not run by capitalists, and certainly not by capitalists from the dominant economic sectors. At the same time it has (even after apartheid) preserved a capitalist social order. Is this a contingent fact, or is there something about the state that predisposes it to defend capitalism?

Any answer to this question must proceed from a recognition that state administrators and politicians are individuals with (perceived) interests and (often strongly held) opinions, and that they are first of all concerned to express and realize these, and not to do the bidding of social forces outside the state. Secondly, the state manager/capitalism dichotomy cannot be considered to coincide in a simple way with that of structure/agency. State actors operate in the context of structures constituted at the level of the state, including organizations with histories and well-entrenched constitutional and legal rituals, and these constrain state actors to varying degrees. Finally, much goes on in the state in relation to which capital is not so much powerless as indifferent.

Capitalists can exercise direct leverage over politics: money can buy political influence, and capitalists and politicians often mix in similar circles. However, this factor was until recently of secondary importance in South Africa, a country in which the state was run between 1907 and 1994 by Afrikaner elites and the economy by Anglophone ones. Indeed, the economic dominance of capital, and the dominance of Anglophones amongst capitalists, underlay a history of state–capitalist tension.

Yet a state is an organization whose employees live off politics (Jessop 1982:104). To retain their jobs (sources in turn of money, status and authority) they need to secure both popular legitimacy and revenue. Capitalists enjoy disproportionate power in the subsystem that determines patterns of individual access to social wealth (via the wage system) as well as the extent of revenue available for the state. This ensures for them important leverage where they choose to exercise it (as they often do in respect of economic policy). The state, a conservative institution loath to disrupt revenue sources or contemplate a legitimacy-threatening economic crisis, is in turn reluctant to interfere with capitalist dominance in the economic subsystem. It cannot both ignore the capitalist class and leave it in charge economically: the most pressing and persistent capitalist demands (whether racially reactionary or meliorative) must ultimately be accommodated or else capital must be deposed. This self-imposed economic constraint on the political is operative in South Africa as in other capitalist societies.

Questions about the South African state

The issue of uniqueness The South African state possessed from the late 1940s until 1994 at least one certainly unique feature. It – alone or at least more comprehensively than any other state – was structured on the basis of a formalized system of racial difference and hierarchy. Scholars searching for ways to understand its exceptionalism have tried to place it in the context of world history, searching for historical factors and episodes explaining its deviance from the course followed by other countries or seeking out analogies and similarities between the South African and other states. Many liberals explained South Africa's uniqueness in terms of the factors cutting Afrikaners off from metropolitan enlightenment, though optimists amongst them, like O'Dowd, believed that under the pressure of industrial modernization the country would be induced to rejoin the path of 'normal' (European liberal capitalist) history (O'Dowd 1978). In positing Afrikaners as a source of uniqueness they of course echoed the more affirmative Afrikaner nationalist version of the same thesis.

Radicals by contrast tended to treat South Africa as an instance of a wider capitalist phenomenon. At the same time they disputed amongst themselves the extent to which South African capitalism was tending in character towards a 'classic' system of bourgeois rule or belonged to a specific subcategory of capitalist societies marked out by the exceptional violence and/or sectional ethnic capture of the state. Thus the South African state has been presented as typical of both fascist (see below) and colonial forms of state (as in the thesis of internal colonialism).

A more recent tendency in radical writing has highlighted the extent to which South Africa's is a typical 'modern' state. It has faced like others this century the challenge of promoting accumulation while incorporating the organized working class (Yudelman 1984). It has employed like other states technologies of surveillance and control and schemes of large-scale social engineering (Robinson 1992; Parnell and Mabin 1995). Those writing in this vein usually play down the uniqueness of South Africa and its race obsession. Others see the South African state as typical only of certain *kinds* of modern state: those, like the United States, presiding over the urbanization and industrialization in a context of race competition (Cell 1982).

Another recent strand of literature has drawn attention to the way in which South African state forms both emulated and inspired models implemented elsewhere. Mamdani's work on the colonial model of indirect rule, partly pioneered in Natal and later reappropriated by twentieth-century South African rulers from elsewhere in British colonial Africa, offers the most notable example (Mamdani 1996). Earlier Cell (1982) drew attention to the links between segregationist thinking in South Africa and the United States.

It is certainly wrong to assume that the South African state 1910-89 was so essentially singular that everything it did could be attributed to its character as an institutionally racist state, or that its racial forms were unparalleled elsewhere. It was a state located in a capitalist society concerned, as were other such states, with promoting growth in a largely private economy and containing social conflict; it was a modern state, anxious to modernize society and responsive to global fashions for state expansion and contraction; and it was a welfare state of sorts. It learnt from other states and offered them lessons. Yet the South African state was also distinctive in important ways, notably in the longevity and timing of its pursuit of institutionalized race discrimination, its juxtaposing of conventional British-style democracy, semi-totalitarian dictatorship and colonial-style indirect rule and its extended effort to halt, postpone or displace urbanization even while building a modern economy. To overplay South Africa's uniqueness is to deny the problems and challenges it shares with others (for example other semi-peripheral, middle income, urbanizing, deeply unequal capitalist societies) and to forgo the valuable insights of comparative analysis. At the same time to deny its uniqueness is to consign its many empirically distinctive features to the realm of 'mere' appearance, ignoring the power of their presence in people's lives even to the present.

Democracy and authoritarianism The South African state 1910-89 combined features of both a liberal-democratic and an authoritarian (even totalitarian) state. Was the democratic component a sham or real? And why did South Africa exhibit this combination?

The strongest expressions of scepticism about the pre-1994 South African state's democratic credentials (at least regarding the post-1948 apartheid period) issued from those, mainly Communists and Trotskyists influenced by events in Europe, who portrayed it as fascist or Nazi (Bunting 1964; Simson 1973). The most visible evidence for its fascism was the fact that the Afrikaner nationalist movement in the 1930s and 1940s resembled European fascist and Nazi movements. It was anti-black and often anti-Semitic, rhetorically hostile to international and large-scale capitalism as well as to the emerging organizations of the (black) working class, bitterly opposed to liberal individualism and materialist rationalism, harboured visions of an organic ethnic Christian state transcending class divisions, and contemplated replacing the liberal-democratic constitution with a Mussolini-style corporatist one. Key intellectuals in the movement who had studied abroad were at least touched by German romantic nationalism (Furlong 1991: 87-96; cf Norval 1996: ch. 2). In addition Afrikaner nationalists sympathized with Germany during the Second World War (a few acting treasonably on its behalf) and during the 1930s and 1940s their movement acquired a coat-tail of semi-fascist paramilitary organizations, most importantly the *Ossewa Brandwag* (Furlong 1991: chs 5, 6). Some orthodox Marxists tried to read Afrikaner nationalism onto a Marxist–Leninist template of European fascism. According to Simson, the white working class base of Afrikaner nationalism was in fact an exploiting petit-bourgeoisie and Afrikaner nationalism was handed power by metropolitan monopolists and their South African compradors in order to contain the growing challenge of the black working class (Simson 1973, 1974). 'Fascism' theorists argued that white liberal democracy in the post-war decades was either a 'sham' (Simson 1973: 445) or a form of 'Herrenvolk democracy' reserved for a minority (Lewis 1987: 208-9, 215).

While there were undoubtedly fascist-like elements to Afrikaner nationalism, this analysis captured neither the subtlety of Afrikaner nationalist discourse and politics nor the complexity of South Africa's combination of liberal democracy and authoritarianism. The Afrikaner nationalist National Party included a 'bourgeois' Cape wing suspicious of radical politics as well as strong organizational partisans in the north who strenuously opposed the challenge from extraparliamentary movements during the war. The NP, despite an initial opportunistic dalliance with the radical right, acted from late 1941 to marginalize them politically (although of course the NP's claim that it alone embodied the people had its own totalitarian ring) (Furlong 1991). The corporatist-organic *volkstaat* envisaged by many in the nationalist movement was never fully fascist. The NP leadership anyway disowned it in 1942. There were traditionalist Afrikaners suspicious of foreign doctrines like fascism, and many (as in some other anti-colonial movements of the time) sympathized with Germany mainly for anti-British reasons.

Afrikaner nationalist ranks included followers of biological theories of race hierarchy (notably Geoff Cronjé) and all Nationalists execrated race mixing. Even so, the dominant current in Afrikaner nationalism, especially in the post-1948 era, favoured a culturally essentialist conception of ethnic uniqueness and difference – albeit one that often masked a more straightforward racism (Dubow 1995: ch. 7; Norval 1996: ch. 2). Africans figured in the Afrikaner imagination either as child-like objects of white authority or as a patchwork of peoples entitled to achieve their adulthood in separate ethnic states. In either event Africans were essentially 'good-natured' as long as they could be separated from urban influences and communist agitators (Adam et al. 1997: 39). Blacks were economic competitors to Afrikaner workers, but essential labour to more powerful Afrikaner farmers. They were thus never marked out for elimination. Anti-Semitism for its part was quietly dropped after the war, despite the Afrikaners' mental association of Jews with Anglophone financial power and agitational mischief-making amongst blacks.

In power after 1948 Afrikaner nationalists preserved white parliamentary democracy and a quasi-independent judiciary (despite some brazen constitutional gerrymandering in the 1950s). White democracy assumed a one-party aspect, but this was due to the quirks of the voting system and, later, whites rallying behind the NP, rather than open suppression of party pluralism. Though parliamentary control of the executive, never impressive, weakened over time, this was attributable (in part) to the longevity of Nationalist electoral dominance and the subservience of NP membership in the country, and was anyway not dramatically out of line with trends in many other liberal democracies. While the freedoms of autonomous civil institutions were subjected to repeated challenge and abridgement, much to justified liberal outrage, they were far from eliminated. Even if this was a 'Herrenvolk' democracy, its field of operation could not be entirely contained within white society. Blacks found sympathetic voices in parliament, the press and white pressure groups. They in principle enjoyed the protection of the law and a range of political and civil liberties that, though periodically subject to massive attack, offered spaces for black protest (Wolpe 1988: 40-7). While security laws grew increasingly repressive, defining wide areas of executive discretion outside legal or judicial control, the state's outright resort to 'dirty war' tactics was a feature largely of the last and dying decade of apartheid. The NP always ran a brutal regime, presenting a dictatorial face to the majority of its subjects and evincing a totalitarian aspiration to control African movement and settlement, but fascism is not a useful category for comprehending its combination of features.

How is the presence and persistence of white parliamentary democracy to be explained? The Poulantzians offered a Marxist account that attributed South Africa's racially exclusive bourgeois democracy to three factors. Firstly, the universally capitalist character of its ruling class (Morris 1976) meant it shared enough by way of common interests to permit the containment and mediation of its internal differences within a framework of peaceful parliamentary competition. Secondly, white workers, being fully proletarianized, and enjoying in some cases a history of self-organization inherited from Europe, could only be incorporated by conventional 'bourgeois-democratic' methods that supplied them with a sense of full membership of the 'people-nation'. Thirdly, Africans, being only partly proletarianized and still linked in many cases to a communal subsistence economy, could be maintained and incorporated largely through propped-up 'tribal' forms of economy and polity. When in the 1970s African proletarianization and popular militancy reached the point where the state felt compelled to incorporate blacks, it simultaneously moved away from parliamentary to a more executive-dominated but racially inclusive form of government. Only in this way could reformers hope to overcome democratically expressed white racist opposition to black incorporation and placate an African working class that it could not afford to incorporate on bourgeois-democratic terms (Kaplan 1980; Morris and Padayachee 1989: 71, 93).

A number of objections could be raised to the Poulantzians' elegant but stark account. The capitalist character claimed for white agriculture from the 1920s has been disputed. The account glides too easily over the question of coloureds and Indians and their much earlier proletarianization. So too does it fail to address the urbanization of Africans from the 1930s, or the efforts of successive governments from the 1940s onwards partially to incorporate a minority of fully proletarianized Africans into the urban economy (but not polity). Nevertheless the fractionalists did offer a convincing account of some of the underlying material and demographic forces sustaining (and then demanding changes in) 'racially exclusive bourgeois democracy'.

What is more profoundly problematic about the Poulantzian account is its reductionist understanding of 'bourgeois democracy'. In the Marxist manner of the time, it reduced institutions in general to their class function or essence. More particularly, it comprehended parliamentary or representative democracy as essentially bourgeois, in the sense of either masking or expressing bourgeois domination. This analysis seriously underestimated the democratic value of representative democracy, even in its racially exclusive form, in providing spaces for popular protest and inculcating a cultural and technical familiarity with democratic ways. This familiarity has, at least arguably, helped to sustain the racially inclusive form of representative democracy inaugurated in 1994.

More seriously for its historical explanation, the Poulantzian account dismisses too easily the importance of British colonialism as a cultural transmission system for British parliamentary and civic norms. Some of these (such as rule of law) were transmitted from on high by British colonial governments; others (such as press freedom) had to be won by British settlers (Davenport 1969). Britain as a colonial power was quicker to concede parliamentary government to white than black colonists, and to better-off than poorer whites. Even so, the transmission of parliamentary norms was not entirely dependent on the local ethnic and class structure. A number of British colonies with varying ethnic and social profiles established post-colonial representative democracies of sorts, including India and several Afro-Caribbean states.

The obverse of white democracy in South Africa, the subjection of rural Africans to a system of indirect rule based on chiefs and customary law, was also a British colonial innovation. Tried first in India, it was transplanted to Africa in Natal, then later generalized through a range of British African colonies before reaching its apogee under apartheid in post-colonial South Africa (Mamdani 1996: chs 1, 2).

The political traditions and instrumental calculations of Afrikanerdom also count for something in explaining the persistence of white democracy. The historical relationship between Afrikaners and democracy is mixed. The Dutch-Afrikaner frontier was largely impervious to Enlightenment ideas and the Afrikaner household was an authoritarian patriarchy; but the frontier also nurtured a fierce quasi-anarchistic individualism. When the Boers established polities of their own, they experimented with constitutional forms ranging from populist parliamentary democracy (in Natalia) to presidential constitutionalism (in the Free state) to military government (under Potgieter). It took the Transvaal state a long time to establish its authority, but in the later nineteenth century strong Boer leaders stabilized both Boer states. Afrikaner political culture was in many respects anti-modern and illiberal, but it also harboured elements of legalism and a religiously-based belief in the sovereignty of God, separation of spheres (alongside and in counterposition to organicist ideas) and a distrust of state worship (Furlong 1991: 92).

Perhaps more importantly for the twentieth-century persistence of parliamentary democracy, the model served Afrikaner elites well because Afrikaners constituted a majority of the white population and because the voting system established in 1910 favoured the Afrikaner-dominated countryside. Afrikaners led all governing parties and coalitions between 1910 and 1994, and much of South African politics was a contest between Afrikaner elites committed to alliances with Anglophones and those committed to a more ethnically exclusive course. The Afrikaner armed rebellion of 1914 was led by marginal elements in Afrikanerdom, and its failure taught lessons about the greater tactical wisdom of constitutional politics (Garson 1962: 140). The NP preferred to concentrate on building an effective vote-gathering machinery. Afrikaner leaders had little reason to follow the *Ossewa Brandwag* or Greyshirts down an anti-parliamentary route in the 1940s.

At the same time neither Afrikaners nor Anglophones had an interest in a racially *inclusive* parliamentary democracy. Where elements of one already existed, as in the Cape, it provided an incentive for both English and Afrikaner parties to compete for black votes, and they did so in the late nineteenth-century Cape and in South Africa until the end of the 1920s. But by the 1930s the black vote was negligible as a proportion of the total, thanks mainly to an enfranchisement of female voters that mimicked voting reforms in Europe and Australasia but in South Africa excluded black women. Although Afrikaners competed with moderate success for African and coloured electoral allegiance, they feared that black enfranchisement would benefit mainly Anglophone politicians. Moreover, the 'black danger' was a good election-winning slogan. English speakers had, conversely, some incentive to retain a black franchise as an electoral resource, but little incentive to extend it to the point where it would threaten the white supremacy in which they partook. Both Anglophones and Afrikaners were, in any case, given to feelings of racial solidarity, especially in the face of threats from black or foreign 'others'.

White democracy can be seen more generally as the 'achievement' of a racial minority sufficiently rooted in the country to want to govern itself, sufficiently large and (in the case of Afrikaners) aggressive to fight effectively for self-government, and sufficiently bound by a sense of equality amongst its members to expect that self-government should be based on universal white political rights. At the same time it was the product of the juxtaposition of this minority to a black population too large to be safely politically incorporated. Unlike Irish Protestants or Israeli Jews, South African whites could not engineer an artificial electoral majority by partition or expulsion of the colonized. The attempt to do so through ethnic partition and influx control never came close to being viable given, *inter alia*, that South African whites, unlike Irish Protestants and Zionist Jews, hungered for the *in situ* labour of the colonized. If South African whites wanted democratic self-government it could only be on a racially discriminatory basis.

The survival of democracy in white South Africa was not inevitable. The black majority posed a standing threat to white rule, and the state faced the temptation, which it did not always resist, to attack the legal spaces which blacks and sympathetic whites used to propagate their cause. There were deeply illiberal elements in white society which, placed under sufficient stress, might well have sought outrightly authoritarian solutions. Though white democracy made it to 1994, it did so in pretty battered shape.

Neo-colonialism and national capitalism It is a common observation that formal political independence does not automatically translate into economic independence. This was obviously true of South Africa: in 1910 it lacked an industrial base, its mines were foreign-owned and it was dependent on primary product exports. And yet, or so it seemed to Marxist writers who read the underdevelopment literature of the 1960s and 1970s, South Africa was by the later twentieth century rare amongst former colonies and 'Third World' countries for having broken out of a condition of dependence. It had industrialized, and its capitalist class had acquired a national rather than comprador character. The developed character of the dominant capitalist economy (if indeed developed it was) required explanation. For some Marxists, notably the Poulantzian fractionalists, the key lay with the developmental role of the state and, more particularly, the success of national-capitalist forces in establishing a relatively early hegemony within the political system.

Until 1924, the fractionalists argued (Davies et al. 1976), hegemony rested with an 'imperial' fraction of capital, the main component of which was foreign-owned mining capital. Mining capital opposed a policy of industrial protection because it would raise the cost of its inputs, whereas a 'national' capitalist fraction, consisting of agriculture and a nascent manufacturing sector, favoured protection. National capital achieved hegemony in 1924, when the NP (supported by agriculture and increasingly by manufacturing) won a general election in alliance with the South African Labour Party (representing wage-earning and petit bourgeois white strata outside the power bloc). After coming to power in 1924 the 'Pact' government proceeded to support the development of industry through tariff measures and the establishment of state capitalist enterprises like Iscor in 1928 as well as to give stepped-up aid to agriculture.

State intervention laid the basis for South Africa's industrial take-off. National capital (in whole or part) remained more or less hegemonic until the 1960s, when hegemony fell to a newly emergent 'monopoly' capitalist fraction growing from the interpenetration of previously Imperial and national fractions.

This argument faced criticism from several directions. Some argued that the foundations of industrial development were laid already under the 'imperialist' governments of Louis Botha and Jan Smuts, especially through their provision of electricity and railway infrastructure (Christie 1984, 1991). Others insisted that industrial take-off occurred only around 1933, as a result less of tariff policy designed to promote national capital than of the boom that followed the government's reluctant departure from the gold standard in December 1932 (Clarke 1978; Freund 1989). Bozzoli and Morrell agreed with the fractionalists that national capital established its hegemony, but they saw it doing so only in the 1930s. For Bozzoli, its victory was a result of national capital's extended ideological struggle in state and civil society. According to Morrell, it followed upon the disintegration of the old 'alliance of gold and maize'. For neither Bozzoli nor Morrell could national capitalist hegemony be conceived exclusively in the sorts of electoral terms that led the fractionalists to pinpoint the 1924 election as a turning point (Bozzoli 1978; 1981; Morrell 1988). Yudelman for his part denied that mining capital *ever* lost its position of dominance economically or politically. He argued that manufacturing rather than mining bore the main costs of the Pact's civilized labour policies and that the mining sector was not heavily taxed until 1933 when because of the boom it could well afford to pay higher taxes (Clarke 1978; Yudelman 1984: chs 1, 7). Simon Clarke insisted that the state served capital-in-general, not one or another fraction (Clarke 1978: 55).

More recently writers have criticized earlier ways of pigeon-holing 'imperial' and 'national' capitals. It has been pointed out that neither Imperial Britain nor mining were hostile to indigenous industrial development, the former agreeing to support a national reserve bank (Gelb 1989) and the latter diversifying extensively into manufacturing and itself becoming increasingly national in character (Yudelman 1984; Innes 1984: 79-80, 119-20, 124; Gelb 1989: 52). Nancy Clark has argued that the state capitalist 'parastatals', far from representing the forces of national ranged against imperial capital, developed in partnership with mining and foreign capital (Clark 1987, 1994). Fine and Rustomjee detect the early development in South Africa of a dominant 'minerals–energy complex' embracing mining capital, the state and forms of heavy industry devoted to servicing mineral and energy production (Fine and Rustomjee 1996). In the case of diamonds the 'national' state treated this 'imperialist' industry with suspicion already before 1924; tensions escalated during the Pact period but the state entered into a cartel with the mining industry in the 1930s (Newbury 1989).

The balance of evidence suggests that the fractionalist account was far too schematic and simplified. It unreasonably neglected the impact of economic and political developments outside the electoral process, was too quick to allocate fractional labels and overstated the singularity of 1924 as a turning point in the fortunes of a South African manufacturing sector which experienced several sources and moments of acceleration. Nevertheless it would be to place South Africa outside of the comparative history of the twentieth century not to note that it did, from the mid-1920s, join other late industrial developers pursuing tariff-based import-substitution industrialization (Martin 1990, 1991). This strategy as it was developed over time profoundly shaped the pattern of economic development in South Africa. It is equally clear that from the mid-1920s the South African state was in the hands of forces more committed than their predecessors to seizing, within constraints imposed by the concerns of the crucial mining sector, opportunities to develop South African industry both to extend national autonomy and provide employment for poor whites.

There are certainly grounds to question a key premiss of much of the debate: that South Africa found a unique, or at least unusual, path out of underdevelopment. South Africa by the end of the 1980s was marked by dependence on foreign technology and imported capital goods, paid for by foreign exchange earned by primary product exports. South Africa, it turns out, did not experience an unusually high rate of growth for middle-income countries in the post-war period (Moll 1991) and in the 1970s and 1980s it fell far behind the rapidly advancing economies of Asia. South Africa's manufacturing sector, long sheltered by import-substitution policies, is inefficient and uncompetitive. The removal of tariff protection in the 1990s threatens to blow much of it away.

Twentieth-century racial regimes

The South African state 1910-89 was not only a racial state. It embodied forms of power other than racial, including that of men and the socially better-off and it was interested in matters other than dominating blacks including, amongst many other things, expanding the economy. It can thus be periodized in different ways depending on the focus of analysis. It nevertheless certainly *was* a racial order, and this dimension of its existence was both especially notorious and at the centre of scholarly attention. Three predominant regimes of racial domination have commonly been identified: segregation, apartheid and (neo-apartheid) 'reform'.

In each case writers have debated the extent of continuity and discontinuity with preceding periods. Some tended to portray the South African racial order 1910-89 as essentially seamless, implying that changes only belonged to the realm of appearance, or that changes of opposition tactics and strategies were unnecessary. Others emphasized important shifts in its mode of operation, implying a need to review tactics and strategies of opposition (Wolpe 1988: 8-9, 61).

There are other controversies surrounding shifts in the mode of rule: were they products of ideological and institutional change, or of underlying social and economic forces? Did party politics matter, or was it secondary to the machinations of capitalists, bureaucrats or military men? Which social constituencies supported, which opposed major changes? Whereas radicals in the 1970s tended to focus very largely on the class bases of these modes of domination, more recent writers have highlighted conflicts in the state and discourses of power.

Segregation In the early twentieth century the South African state committed itself to 'segregation': the institutional separation of races. The 1913 and 1936 Land Acts entrenched macro-territorial racial segregation and legislation in 1923 attempted to systematize urban segregation. Measures were introduced, notably in 1937, to tighten rural efflux and urban influx controls on Africans. Africans in the reserves were subject to reconstituted tribal forms of administration from 1927, and Africans were removed from the Cape common franchise in 1936. Extended debates have developed around the origins of segregationism and the forces driving its implementation up to 1948, when the NP victory heralded its replacement by 'apartheid'.

Segregationism is commonly associated with Afrikaners, most famously General J. B. Hertzog who promoted the 1913 Land Act (the first key piece of territorial segregationist legislation) and under whose premiership it reached its apogee in the mid-1930s. However, Afrikaner leaders until the early twentieth century preferred direct domination of Africans to setting aside reserves for their separate development (Cell 1982: 47-51). Boer states were also slow to develop policies of urban segregation. The thrust of much recent literature, mostly from radical writers, has been to stress the originally British colonial origins of segregation (see Chapter 1). Early twentieth century Anglophones like J. Howard Pim, Maurice Evans and Charles Loram played a formative role in developing segregationist theory. For them segregation offered a middle way between assimilation of the Cape type (which many liberals had ceased to trust) and the racially repressive policies of the Boer republics. While Hertzog appropriated the segregationist plank from the British and English-speakers, Anglophones of more conservative bent, especially from Natal (like Charles Stallard and George Heaton Nicholls), continued to play a role in shaping segregationist policy well beyond the point of its appropriation by Afrikaner leaders (Legassick 1973a; Rich 1979: 85-106, 1984; Dubow 1989: ch. 1).

While by the later 1920s liberals were disillusioned by the repressive consequences of segregation, radical critics claim that the more mainstream interwar liberals continued to argue within the broad terms of segregationism. Radicals also charge liberals with dampening militant black opposition to segregation in a period when African elites valued liberal traditions and ties with white intermediaries (Rich 1984, 1996; Dubow 1989: ch. 6). At the same time, however, radical writers have demonstrated ambiguities in the black stance towards segregation. The urban African working class was still relatively small in the interwar period and sections of the African population (notably in Natal) remained committed to the preservation of reserves and quasi-traditional polities. Some Africans objected less to segregation than to the inadequate amounts of land allocated to Africans. Indian and coloured politicians were for their part far from certain that they wished to live alongside Africans (see Chapter 6). Segregation was thus a programme flexible enough to appeal to disparate audiences, and this helps to explain limits to resistance against it (Marks 1986; Beinart and Bundy 1987: 36-8; Dubow 1989: ch. 6; Rich 1996: ch. 5).

Whereas some emphasize the pre-industrial colonial origins of segregation (Welsh 1971; Mamdani 1996) others locate it in a context of industrial capitalism (Cell 1982: 3-13). Amongst those positing the modernity of segregation are writers who relate it to employer labour requirements. Wolpe attributed the maintenance of separate African reserves (and a redistributive African economy within them) to the demands of a mining industry keen to benefit from the cheapening of labour costs made possible by the pre-capitalist economy's supplementary provision of subsistence goods for migrant households (Wolpe 1972). Greenberg and Lacey traced some of the roots of urban influx controls to farmers' demands for tied labour. Lacey however warned against viewing the cheap labour demands of 'gold' and 'maize' as identical or readily compatible. She argued that there was a tension between the South African Party's support for reserves as bases of migrant labour (in keeping with the Cape tradition and backed by mining interests) and the Hertzogite NP's concern to limit their size and thus capacity to bottle up labour (continuing in this case a Free state tradition of breaking up black reserves). She judged segregation as it crystallized after 1932 to be the outcome of a compromise between the two which involved, amongst other things, retention and conservation of reserves (Greenberg 1980; Lacey 1981).

Others, more sceptical of this 'cheap labour thesis', prefer to emphasize the general anxieties of white society and its political elites about the consequences of industrialization and black urbanization. White rulers (they argue) feared that black advance into 'white' urban society would aggravate labour unrest (of which there was a considerable amount in the twelve years or so after the First World War) and accelerate the economic and cultural degradation of poor whites faced by competition from cheaper black labour (Cell 1982; Dubow 1989: chs 1, 2). In addition Rich has pointed to the narrowly political advantages for Hertzog in adopting a segregationist programme (Rich 1979: 89-106).

The ideological and discursive dimension of segregation has long fascinated radical analysts (Legassick 1973a, 1973b), but it has in recent years been granted an autonomous importance denied it by an earlier generation of radical writers. Segregationist ideologues tended to construct Africans as internally homogeneous yet essentially different to whites, thus rationalizing their separate treatment. The role in this process of 'experts', many drawn from academic disciplines in the expanding university system, has come under scrutiny (Ashforth 1990; Dubow 1995). This depiction was accompanied by a public discourse of 'South Africanism' that emphasized a common white loyalty to South Africa. Some radicals offered a materialist analysis of South Africanism as a hegemonic ideology of national as opposed to imperial capital (Bozzoli 1981), or as expressing a closing of white ranks in the 1930s around the need to exploit cheap black labour (Lacey 1981; cf Dubow 1989: ch. 5). Marx has recently suggested that South Africa's sharp race lines were the obverse of a process of state and nation building pursued by dominant elites to cement a white population divided on sectional lines (Marx 1998).

In contrast to accounts depicting segregation as a product of societal demands, writers like Dubow, Duncan and Rich have revealed the strength of the interwar state's own institutional traditions and internal divisions. Officials in some departments continuing an earlier tradition of paternalistic trusteeship (rooted for example in magisterial rule in Transkei) competed with other sections of the state committed to a more repressive segregation. The Department of Native Affairs (like much of the interwar civil service still an Anglophone preserve) was for example reluctant to implement legislation to pin African labourers down on white farm land, arguing that farmers should attract labour rather by offering better wages. The segregationist state was not only divided but fairly fluid: the fortunes of departments fluctuated, while at the top Hertzog (Prime Minister 1924-39) pursued segregation more systematically than Smuts (1919-24, 1939-48) (Dubow 1989; Duncan 1995; Rich 1996). Internal divisions, the slow crystallization of the segregation programme, scarce state resources and evasion by elements of both black and white society meant that implementation of legislation was often limited or halting.

Apartheid The Reunited (or *Herenigde*) National Party came to power in 1948 on a programme of racial apartheid and Afrikaner nationalism. During the years between then and the 1970s the ruling NP formalized and extended racial segregation in sexual, occupational, educational, residential and territorial spheres, earning global notoriety in the process. Yet a good deal of debate centres on whether apartheid represented a radical break from interwar segregation or largely built upon it.

Liberals interpreted the 1948 victory of the Afrikaner nationalist Reunited NP as the beginning of a huge lurch towards a more rigid system of racial discrimination. They pointed out that the last pre-apartheid government, that of Smuts, made tentative moves in a more racially inclusive direction, questioning segregation as a concept, laying some basic struts of a welfare state for Africans, contemplating recognition of African unions and preparing to accept the inevitability of African urbanization. Legassick by contrast insisted that apartheid represented essentially a tightening up of segregationist labour controls rather than a departure from them. He suggested that the future envisaged by the Smuts-initiated Fagan Commission of 1946-48 was not radically divergent from the actual outcome which resulted from the NP's implementation of its 1947 Sauer Report (Legassick 1974b). Some subsequent research has underlined marked continuities between segregation and apartheid in terms of the development of policies for urban segregation (Mabin 1992; Maharaj 1992; Van Tonder 1993) and securing cheap coerced labour for white agriculture (Bradford 1993).

Not all radicals adopted a 'continuity' position, though the sources and areas of rupture have been identified variously. Earlier revisionists analysed the discontinuity at the level of systems of production and class alliances. Wolpe (1972) argued that apartheid was instituted as a response to the erosion of the system pre-capitalist reserve agriculture that had sustained the segregationist political economy. Confronted by the accelerated settlement of impoverished Africans in the towns and cities of 'white' South Africa and associated political conflict, large-scale English capital argued for permitting more African urbanization. A class alliance of Afrikaner farmers and workers, Cape Afrikaner financiers and a northern Afrikaner petit bourgeoisie favoured instead coercive measures to secure African labour for agriculture, blunt black economic competition and reassert white political control. The latter option won out in 1948. The idea that the NP's ascendancy resulted from a 'crisis' in the pre-1940s mode of class rule, one which imposed on the dominant classes and elites the need to choose a new strategy, is implicit or explicit in much radical writing (see e.g. Saul and Gelb 1981: ch. 1).

A second and more recent radical approach focuses on alterations in rulers' discursive constructions of the world. The transition to apartheid marked for Ashforth and Norval an important shift from a dominant construction of whites and Africans as internally homogeneous to the dominance of a new conception of each as composed of irreducibly distinctive cultures (Ashforth 1990; Norval 1996).

A third, more institutional radical approach highlights changes in patterns of governance over Africans. Thus for Rich the 1940s marked a transition from a situation where a loosely clientilistic state engaged with an elitist black opposition to one where a bureaucratic state confronted black mass mobilization (Rich 1996).

Still others have adopted intermediate positions, recognizing both continuities and discontinuities between segregation and apartheid (Dubow 1989: conclusion; Beinart 1994: 137).

The debate about continuity and discontinuity is complicated by two considerations. Firstly, the Smuts administration itself shifted from a policy of loosening up on segregation in the early years of the Second World War (when there was a premium on African co-operation) to more repressive policies beginning in 1943. From around that year Smuts began adopting a more reactionary approach to union recognition and influx control and a more disdainful approach to African participation in politics (Fine and Davis 1990: 18-26; Rich 1996: 152).

Secondly, and as both Posel and Lazar have clearly shown, the NP did not come to power with a blueprint for apartheid. Apartheid policies were refined and altered in the course of struggles within the radical wing of Afrikaner nationalism that pre-dated the 1948 victory and continued into the 1960s (Lazar 1987; Posel 1987, 1991: 49-75). Thus in the 1950s, as both Hindson and Posel note, the state did not opt for an immediate expulsion of Africans from cities or remigrantization of all urban Africans: it made a distinction between established urban insiders and Africans originating in the reserves or 'white' countryside. On the former it conferred preferential treatment in the labour market (Hindson 1987: ch. 4; Posel 1991: 78-90). To stabilize and reproduce this insider group dependent upon wages for its existence the state intervened to provide housing and education on a large scale (Legassick 1974b: 18-21; Wilkinson 1983; Hyslop 1993). Only in the 1960s did the state embark upon a path of reducing and reversing urbanization in 'white' South Africa, mainly by displacing African urbanization behind 'homeland' boundaries and encouraging cross-border commuting (Hindson 1987: ch. 5; Posel 1991: ch. 9).

Again, apartheid rulers were not in the 1950s enamoured with ambitious schemes for establishing economically viable self-governing African reserves. Verwoerd fought bitterly with the apartheid 'idealists' of the Tomlinson Commission and South African Bureau of Racial Affairs over the issue before himself abruptly opting for 'separate development' in 1959 (Posel 1991: 235-48; Lazar 1993; O'Meara 1996: 70-4). In 1968 the government of B. J. Vorster acceded to another Tomlinson Commission recommendation when it decided to permit white capital into the African reserves, having earlier (in 1960) settled on a more limited 'border industry' policy (Glaser 1988).

A third significant shift, from the policy of 'Afrikaners first' propelling the nationalist project of the 1930s and 1940s to something more like the once-despised notion of a common white South Africanism, accompanied the NP campaign for Anglophone support in the 1960 referendum over establishing a republic. It was a new course pursued still more vigorously by Verwoerd's successors Vorster and P. W. Botha. An imaginary homogeneity of interest was thus restored to 'white' South Africa even as the policy of ethnically parcellizing Africans was taking off.

As should be clear, the debate over continuity/discontinuity is bound up with controversies about whether the victory of the NP and its apartheid programme in 1948 was explicable primarily in material or ideological terms. The lines of division are not clear-cut. While Marxists in general emphasized the economic and class forces underlying the advent and unfolding of apartheid, some amongst them warned against simple economic and class reductionism (Saul and Gelb 1981: 11-13). Though they give little attention to the nuances of political struggle, Marxists tended to present the ascendancy of apartheid as the product of a combination of structural pressures and political class struggles rather than as the only possible course of development open to capitalism (Wolpe 1972; Davies et al. 1976). Liberals and Afrikaner nationalists (by contrast with Marxists) on the whole stressed the importance of political and ideological motivations propelling the Afrikaner nationalist movement and attracting supporters to it, as well as external factors feeding nationalist sentiment such as South Africa's entry into the Second World War (Stultz 1974). But liberals were not unanimous in this approach. Lipton explained the hardening of racial domination in 1948 in terms of the economic interests ascendant in an earlier phase of capitalist industrialism which were hostile to reform, resulting in an argument actually more deterministic than many Marxist ones (Lipton 1986: 274-81).

What were the institutional forms of the apartheid state? Despite its flirtation in opposition with a corporatist Christian-national state, in power the NP maintained the existing Westminster parliamentary system until 1983-84. It did, however, proceed to Afrikanerize the civil service, army and state corporations and to give Afrikaner firms privileged access to state patronage. Successive NP governments tightened central control over the African administration and spatial planning functions of (often Anglophone dominated) metropolitan municipalities. They presided over a continuing expansion of state employment and, in the 1960s and 1970s in the wake of the Sharpeville emergency and funded by the proceeds of rapid growth, built up the military and other security forces, providing the basis for an impressive military–industrial complex.

Three power centres of the apartheid state merit special mention. One was the Department of Native/Bantu affairs, built up by Verwoerd as Minister of Native Affairs and then (from 1958) as Prime Minister into a formidable state-within-a-state as well as ideological vanguard of apartheid policy that lasted until the early 1980s (Welsh 1994: 136, 164; O'Meara 1996: 64-70, 326-8). The second was the Afrikaner Broederbond, the secret sect set up in 1918 by the Afrikaans-speaking petit bourgeoisie in the northern provinces to co-ordinate the Afrikaner cultural and economic advance. Widely viewed by liberals as the covert powerhouse behind Nationalist governments after 1948, its fortunes in fact fluctuated. Prime Minister Strijdom was determined to keep it at a distance. It reached the height of its influence under Verwoerd after 1959, when the AB established a tight grip on the executive and a range of Afrikaner organizations (Lazar 1987: 66, 75, 78; Posel 1993: 241-4). From the late 1960s it was gradually reduced to a sounding board for the party leadership, an ideological think-tank and a communication channel between the party leadership and Afrikaner elite (Giliomee 1980a: 37-42,1994a: 124; O'Meara 1996: 43-8).

The third was the NP itself. The party was built up into an impressive and disciplined electoral machine under the centralized control of the *Hoofleier*, but was marked by perennial and often bitter competition for positions and influence between the Cape provincial party (which was somewhat more bourgeois and pragmatic) and the Transvaal party (whose ascendancy under Premiers Strijdom and Verwoerd between 1954 and 1966 marked the apogee of hard-line apartheid). Rivalry between provincial NPs was accompanied by conflict between Afrikanerdom's Cape and Transvaal business and press establishments. However, during the NP's long hegemony party leaders were able to establish separate bases in the state apparatus, winning by the late 1960s substantial independence of action from the party in the country (Giliomee 1980, 1989d, 1994a; O'Meara 1996: 48-57).

White Anglophones and capitalists were largely excluded from this new political establishment before the 1970s. The United Party, which had ruled between 1934 and 1948, housed after its defeat a broad church of oppositional political elites, but it was subject to fragmentation under the triple pressures of increasing NP success in winning over Anglophone voters from the 1960s, internal ideological incoherence and desertion by reform-minded politicians. The UP finally disintegrated in 1977, leaving behind a patchwork of smaller opposition parties.

While businessmen of the *Afrikaner Handelsinstituut* enjoyed some influence as a pragmatic force in the Nationalist camp, the more economically powerful Anglophone businessmen were largely outside the portals of political power, despite the formalized access granted them through the Economic Advisory Council in 1960 (Pretorius 1994). Nevertheless their ascendant position in the economy (demonstrated in the 1968 capital strike which greeted the Physical Planning Act of 1967) meant that NP governments had little choice but to proceed cautiously in implementing aspects of apartheid disliked by business. Business anyway prospered during most of the 1960s and, with the exception of the Sharpeville crisis interlude, kept a low political profile. It was this prosperity amidst apartheid that impressed the radical revisionists and led them to consider apartheid functional to capitalism. It was a conclusion which, whatever its merits as an account of the relationship between capital and racial domination in that period, failed to observe a build-up of contradictions in the system of 'racial capitalism' (Saul and Gelb 1981: ch. 1; Bloch 1984: 17-20).

Apartheid in the 1960s reached the apotheosis of its repressiveness (reflected in stepped-up urban influx controls, forced resettlement and police repression) and its self-confidence as a system of power (helped by the cowing of mass-based opposition after 1963, an unprecedented economic boom and widening white support for the NP). But the decade also witnessed the first signs of policy retreat, opening spats in what would become a long-running battle between reformers and hard-liners in the NP.

Reformist neo-apartheid It is not possible to identify the moment when 'reform' got underway. Different areas of policy-making proceeded by their own partly separate rhythms. Controls over African labour movement and capital location were intensifying even as the government in the late 1960s took its first hesitant steps towards multiracial sport and détente with African states. It can be difficult to distinguish a reform of apartheid from an enactment taking it to its logical conclusion (the tricameral parliament is a case in point). Some policies that became visible under the reformist Botha were actually initiated by his predecessor Vorster. Giliomee (1994a: 120) claims to detect a continuity of reluctant reformism over the whole period of the premierships of Vorster and Botha (1966-89) but such a dating conveys little information about the uneven, differentiated nature and competing logics of reform over this period. There is no single direction of policy-making or evidence of long-term or single-minded reform planning.

The Vorster premiership, inaugurated after the 1966 assassination of Verwoerd and ending in scandal in 1978, saw several reform processes set in motion. In the later 1960s and early 1970s there were moves towards gradual sport integration and more flexible application of job colour bars. Capital location controls were first intensified (in 1967) then eased. The appointment of the Theron commission in 1973 marked a serious attempt to grapple with the long-running debate in the party, instigated by its Cape wing, about how to fit coloureds into the scheme of separate development.

Until 1975 the reforms amounted to little more than adjustments. From 1975, however, the government began showing signs of contemplating something more remarkable, at least compared to the apartheid of Verwoerd: recognizing the permanence of urban Africans in 'white' South Africa. Urban Africans were granted urban leasehold rights and freed of certain urban trading restrictions in 1975 and conceded a limited form of municipal self-government in 1977. The latter year also saw the establishment of the Wiehahn and Riekert Commissions to examine labour reforms. However, the government remained determined to confine African national political expression to ethnic 'homelands', which the government was then seeking to consolidate territorially and set on the road to independence (Transkei in 1976 was the first to gain formal independence). In 1977 the NP caucus accepted a constitutional model incorporating coloureds and

Indians into parliament, but on the basis of segregated legislatures and ethnically segmented self-government.

What drove this early reform process? A key factor was Vorster's pragmatism on racial policy. Lacking ideological zeal, Vorster sought a free hand to deal with economic bottlenecks, arrest the gathering isolation of South Africa and, in the case of coloureds, tie up an ideological loose end. In the middle of the 1970s, however, four 'shocks' (Price 1991: 71-3) drastically altered the environment of state decision-making. The first was the beginning, around 1974, of a significant slowdown in economic growth, part of a global downturn but attributed by domestic commentators in important measure to apartheid-induced economic distortions. The second was the military coup against the Salazar dictatorship in 1974, precipitating Portugal's withdrawal from its African colonies. Mozambique and Angola gained independence the following year under Marxist–Leninist Soviet-backed governments. They abutted South Africa and South West Africa respectively and would later provide rear bases for the armed wing of the African National Congress. The third was the upsurge, after a long quietude, of labour unrest (beginning in Durban in1972-73) and, in 1976-77, the nation-wide township youth rebellion beginning in Soweto. Pretoria's brutal suppression of the township uprisings and subsequent crackdown on black political activity in turn precipitated the fourth 'shock', an arms embargo and other diplomatic moves ratcheting up South Africa's international isolation. Despite the government's repressive reflex response to the challenge from below, and its continued solid support from the white electorate, these developments cumulatively generated powerful pressures to step beyond desultory tinkering with apartheid.

Vorster, however, made only very hesitant and small steps during his years in power. If he was not an apartheid ideologue, nor was he a reformist one. He was moreover, as is oft remarked, a 'chairman of the board' type prime minister rather than a strong leader. Chosen because his record as a tough Minister of Police endeared him to the right and his personal links to Cape politicians made him acceptable to the left, he presided over a party increasingly split between hard-line *verkramptes* and more pragmatic *verligtes*. A rightist opposition had begun to appear in the early 1960s already under Verwoerd, opposing conciliatory moves towards Anglophones, suggestions of accommodating coloureds and even, in some cases, doubtful about giving Africans independent 'homelands'. Vorster's early signals of a readiness to row back from apartheid rectitude excited the verkramptes into open opposition, but Vorster successfully marginalized them, suborning the Broederbond and deliberately precipitating the departure from the NP in 1969 of rightists (whose *Herstigte Nasionale Party* the NP proceeded to obliterate in elections in 1970). Vorster, lacking a strong provincial party base, established a political base in the Bureau of State Security. Though the party leader's own position was thus secured, and he was able to hold the NP together, Vorster could not offer the clear leadership given by his predecessor. He was unable, for this reason as well as because of his cautious instincts, to move with bold steps down a reformist road.

The years in power of P. W. Botha were quite different in character. The new *Hoofleier* was honed (as provincial leader) in the organizational life of the pragmatic Cape NP and (as Minister of Defence) in a military apparatus steeped in the reading of French and American counterinsurgency manuals. The product of this background was a man of action determined to initiate and control a programme of reform from above. Botha called his programme a 'total strategy'. The key motif of Botha's premiership, later presidency, was the twinning of repressive action against radical opponents (including the destabilization of neighbouring countries offering rear bases to ANC guerrillas) with a range of racially reformist moves designed to weaken black popular support for radical politics. To accomplish the latter, Botha drew coloureds and Indians into a tricameral parliament (set up in 1984) while trying to co-opt Africans through a variable mixture of local political accommodation, improved material living standards and freedom from a range of apartheid controls. The government's public discourse combined survivalist, technocratic and free market elements (Adam and Giliomee 1979: ch. 5; Greenberg 1987a; Posel 1987; Mann 1988: 65-73). These were allied to tentative moves to reduce the state's economic role and devolve functions to appointive, technical or locally elected bodies. Botha sought to accomplish these changes through a more executive-oriented and streamlined state apparatus drawing on the advice of the military as well as outside experts and the private sector. The presidential system of government inaugurated by the 1983 constitution was well suited to this purpose.

Price (1991: 99) argues that during his period in office Botha set out to realize in fairly consistent fashion a 'grand design' spelt out in a 1979 'twelve point plan'. Its clearest expression was found in the incorporation or attempted incorporation of coloureds, Indians and (later) Africans into governing bodies at various tiers on the basis of ethnic self-government over 'own affairs' and cross-racial involvement in deliberation on 'general affairs', subject to overall white control. The implementation of this 'design' had, Price notes, the unforeseen consequence of generating intense resistance. Pass law, constitutional and municipal reforms precipitated the formation of two broad opposition alliances in 1983 and triggered the massive national uprising of 1984-86. The latter rebellion destroyed much of the African local government system. At the same time Botha's halting style of reform in the face of increasingly urgent demands from below, and the repression unleashed against township rebels under the cover of two States of Emergency, elicited an unprecedented degree of hostile international pressure. Foreign governments, private firms and banks stepped up economic sanctions and capital disinvestment. By the end of the decade, the reformist state had reached an impasse, restabilizing society but unable to win popular legitimacy or renew economic growth.

Others have argued more convincingly that the Botha years in power were punctuated by discontinuities both in policy and the balance of power in the state apparatus (Cobbett et al. 1988; Morris and Padayachee 1989: 73-80; Swilling and Phillips 1989b; Morris 1991). Guided by the Riekert and Wiehahn Commission proposals, the government initially favoured a strategy of co-opting urban African 'insiders' with a range of concessions (extended labour mobility, union rights and municipal self-government) while reinforcing the exclusion of homeland 'outsiders' from the 'white' urban domain. Under this strategy 'homeland'-based 'outsiders' were to be palliated with an ambitiously escalated policy of decentralized regional development. There was from the outset a marked inconsistency between policies to firm up the insider/outsider divide and a regional development initiative premissed on the reincorporation of non-viable ethnic 'homelands' into common South African functional spaces (Cobbett et al. 1988). Faced with domestic and overseas opposition to exclusion of the 'outsiders', the government shifted ground, incorporating rural migrants first into a reformed industrial relations apparatus (already by 1981) and then, in 1986, after years of confusion over policy (Greenberg 1987b: chs 3, 4), abandoning coercive urban influx controls altogether. The original insider/outsider strategy, never effectively implemented, was quietly dropped.

There were also shifts in the balance of power within the state during the Botha years. Botha elevated two kinds of reforming technocrat: the constitutional engineer and the counterinsurgency strategist. The former devised grand schemes of constitutional reorganization and development planning to co-opt the disaffected. The latter – the 'securocrat' – placed the emphasis on physically crushing radical opposition while winning black hearts and minds through practical service delivery targeted locally at militant townships. Between 1982 and 1984 Botha systematically dismantled the empire of the apartheid-rooted Department of Co-operation and Development (the successor to the the the Native/Bantu Affairs Department). In its place he built up the empire of the constitutional engineers and development technocrats, gathered under the rubric of a Department of Constitutional Development and Planning. The 1984-86 uprising had, however, the effect of discrediting these reformers, and of activating a shadow 'security state', the National Security Management System, under the control of a State Security Council and the Office of the State President (Swilling and Phillips 1989a, 1989b). However, contrary to the implication of much writing of the time stressing the militarization of the state, the security establishment had not so ensconced itself in power that it could insulate itself from the effects of changes in party-political leadership. President F. W. De Klerk suddenly terminated the ascendancy of the securocrats in 1989.

(On the limits of the militarization thesis, see Giliomee and Schlemmer 1989: 133-5; Hyslop 1989a: 5-6; Morris 1991: 55; O'Meara 1996: 427-8.)

Is it possible to detect, behind this drama of personalities and events, a series of underlying economic and sociological changes that made possible the gear-change from a state of high apartheid in the 1960s to the reformist neo-apartheid state of the 1980s? The argument that there were was advanced both by some modernizationist liberals (like Adam) but more systematically by Marxist-influenced radicals in the 1980s and 1990s (Adam and Giliomee 1979: ch. 7; Moss 1980; Saul and Gelb 1981; O'Meara 1982, 1996; Charney 1984; Morris and Padayachee 1989). Radicals proposed that a series of alterations in the economy, class structure and political balance of forces came to a head in the 'organic crisis' (Saul and Gelb 1981: ch. 1) of the 1970s and 1980s, generating powerful pressures for economic and political 'restructuring'.

In respect of the class structure, a key development was growing social differentiation in Afrikaner society. The 1960s witnessed an accelerated expansion of the Afrikaner bourgeoisie. Afrikaner capitalists increasingly linked up with Anglophone capital through cross-ownership and came to share with it a common class perspective in favour of initiating reforms which might save the capitalist system by jettisoning its unnecessary racist accompaniments. The development of Afrikaner capital, and also of an Afrikaner urban professional class with a more liberal and cosmopolitan outlook, sundered the Afrikaner class alliance which had come to power in 1948. In the 1970s and 1980s the residual Afrikaner working class and poorer farmers found themselves increasingly marginalized from centres of political influence.

The interlinking of Afrikaner and Anglophone capital was part of a larger 'interpenetration' of private, state and foreign capital, as well as of cross-sectoral diversification, that produced in the 1960s a new constellation of concentrated economic power. This emergent 'monopoly capital' (Innes 1984: introduction, ch. 8) invested heavily in capital-intensive forms of production which required increasing amounts of trained semi-skilled African labour as well as enlarged markets to secure economies of scale. These the white labour and consumer pools were no longer sufficiently large to supply. There thus came to an end the long-successful 'racial Fordist social structure of accumulation' based on mass production of goods by white skilled and black unskilled workers for an expanding market of white consumers (Morris and Padayachee 1989; Gelb 1991a). Business began to demand the removal of fetters which apartheid placed on the stabilization, training and free movement of African labour. At the same time it set up the Urban Foundation in 1977 to seek practical ways of improving the lot of urban Africans in the hope of winning their support for capitalism.

Business began to be heard in the counsels of state in the 1970s (Glaser 1988: 197-9; Pretorius 1994: 226-9) but remained frustrated by the tardiness of the Vorster regime in prosecuting political and economic change, especially in the wake of the 1976-77 uprising. According to O'Meara and others, the 'Muldergate' affair of 1978-79 provided an opportunity for an axis of reformist forces finally to stage a 'virtual putsch' (O'Meara 1996: 313). 'Muldergate' is conventionally interpreted by liberals as a scandal about misuse of state funds, exposed by a courageous English press, which resulted fortuitously in the discrediting of the right-wing contender for NP leadership succession, Connie Mulder. Radicals interpreted it as the partly orchestrated effort of reformers based in the Cape Party and military, linked to 'monopoly' capital via the military–industrial complex, to put their man, Botha, in charge (O'Meara 1982, 1996: 224-49). The open warmth displayed by Prime Minister Botha towards big capital, consulted in high profile conferences, was read as confirmation of the emergence of this new alliance. It was only the trauma of the 1984-86 township revolt, and the ineffectiveness of the government's response to it, which triggered the later breach between Botha and the capitalist class and persuaded capital's liberal vanguard to explore new political alliances (such as with the ANC). Important sections of capital subsequently rallied around the state's crackdown on popular dissent, but business's early enthusiasm for Botha did not return. Meanwhile the breakdown of the old apartheid class alliance found expression in the right-wing split from the NP in 1982, though continued Afrikaner business dependence on government patronage limited criticism of the government from the left (Charney 1984: 280).

This sort of economic and class analysis of the state's reformist turn has been criticized by writers who, to varying extents, have sought to reassert the importance of the symbolic or discursive dimension of politics. Giliomee pointed to survey evidence questioning the correlation between the socio-economic positions of Afrikaners and their support for the NP as opposed to breakaway right-wing parties. He also argued that Anglophone capital, as an interest group, remained without political influence in the state until the end of the 1980s. The NP remained an essentially Afrikaner nationalist rather than becoming a bourgeois party (Giliomee 1992: 348-56). Giliomee's survey results certainly require explanation by those committed to the strong version of the class-analytic account. They weaken that account even if we factor in the determination of the right-wing Conservative Party not to become identified, as the rightist Reconstituted (or *Herstigte*) National Party was, with marginalized social forces in Afrikanerdom. Nevertheless, there is no doubt that organized white labour, especially its Afrikaner leaders and members, adopted right-wing stands on a range of issues from the late 1970s, yet increasingly found themselves unable to influence events. White workers harboured more reactionary attitudes generally (Giliomee 1989d: 118-21). It is also clear that debt-ridden farmers in the Transvaal expressed a resentment of marginalization in the form of a protest vote for the far right. Still more certain is that Afrikaner capitalists like Sanlam's Andries Wassenaar were in the vanguard of demands for a more colour-blind free enterprise, and that in the 1990s the Afrikaner political elite was willing to ditch apartheid and white rule in order to save capitalism.

A more far-reaching critique of the materalists is implicit in the work of Norval (1996: chs 4, 5). She traces the unravelling of apartheid in substantial measure to the inability of apartheid discourse to accommodate coloureds and urban Africans within its internal logic. Such a proposition deserves serious consideration because, as writers like Lazar have shown, the logical and moral plausibility of ideas mattered to important sections of Afrikanerdom, especially the 'idealists' (Lazar 1987). There were Afrikaners who believed in the claims made for apartheid as a guarantor of the self-determination of all groups, and they would have been troubled by the incongruous position of coloureds (and perhaps urban Africans) in a scheme of territorial separation. Politicians more widely are bearers of opinions and values as well as interests or, put differently, invest themselves in intellectual and symbolic as well as material 'capital'. Yet it would be a mistake to assume that ideas, or at any rate finer philosophical details, were matters of overriding concern to all or most Afrikaner elites. In any case sincerely held ideas flourish most readily when they coincide with material self-interest, least well when they conflict with it. The claim can be sustained that the changing class and economic map of South Africa since the 1960s generated conditions in which Afrikaner self-doubt could readily take root and spread.

Regimes of racial domination: concluding remarks   Throughout the 1910-89 period the South African state was in the hands of white elites whose perceived self-interest lay in maintaining white supremacy. It does not follow that the period represented an unbroken continuity of forms of racial domination. Discontinuities occurred in four main areas: electoral coalition-building, elite projects, means of ensuring economic growth and strategies of state stabilization. Out of differing configurations of these four elements arose the regimes of segregation, apartheid and reform.

The rules of the parliamentary political game agreed in 1909 permitted a voter-arbitrated circulation of party-political elites, and in order to win and keep power under those rules politicians had to mobilize *constituencies of white popular support*. To do this they had to make appeals to both the material and psychological concerns of voters, knitting together shifting alliances of white social groups. Segregation appealed to a cross-class, bi-ethnic coalition of whites committed to political autonomy and industrial development for South Africa and to white unity. Apartheid mobilized an ethnically sectional cross-class coalition concerned with Afrikaner embourgeoisement, satisfying farmers' labour needs, protecting white workers from black competition and, more intangibly, with enhancing Afrikaner status and power. The reformism of the

1980s made its most effective appeal to professionals, managers, capitalists and other better-off whites, both English and Afrikaner, who considered statutory racism an impediment to economic growth and political stability and felt they did not need its protection. Political coalitions shifted in response to signal political events like the 1922 strike, the 1932 Gold Standard crisis, the Second World War and the political and economic shocks of the 1970s. The shape of potential coalitions was also influenced by more glacial changes in white social structure.

Regimes of racial dominance arose also out of the *ideological preoccupations* of politicians and bureaucrats. State managers were impelled by more than naked self-interest. Many invested themselves existentially in what might be called moral projects, or visions of social uplift. These they aimed most immediately at their electoral constituents and imagined ethnic kin (with whom their empathy was also greatest) but they sought to realize moral projects on terms that they could believe were compatible with the common good. Many whites persuaded themselves that segregation and apartheid promoted black as well as white economic progress and political self-determination. Supporters of 1980s reformism were convinced of the universal benefits of the free market and technocratic thrust of the Botha regime. Changes in the dominant vision were determined in part by which parties and coalitions held power, but also by developments in international opinion, for example in favour of economic planning (in the 1940s), decolonization (in the 1950s) and free markets (from the 1970s).

Further, politicians had to pursue their visions on the basis of an understanding that while voters had votes, controllers of *private economic power* possessed other crucial resources. These the politicians had to respect if they wished to ensure revenue for the state and employment and improving wages for voters. Segregation and apartheid were not designed to meet the needs of capitalists (apart from farmers), but they had to be rendered compatible with capitalist growth (through flexible application of laws or labour market reforms) or to supply capitalists with spin-off benefits like cheap labour, political stability and relocation incentives. Capital had to be bought off, and during the segregation and apartheid periods they could be relatively easily appeased. Neo-apartheid reformism signalled in part the declining viability of earlier trade-offs and the need for new forms of accommodation with capital.

Finally state managers sought to maintain *order*. In the first decades of the twentieth century the threat to state stability came mainly from Afrikaner nationalists and white labour, but by the 1940s the principal threat emanated from the black majority. Social stability from then onwards depended on crushing black opposition and/or winning black acquiescence if not support. Segregation, apartheid and reform represented distinctive strategies for managing black opposition. All however combined repression with efforts to win black hearts and minds.

From the struggle by state managers to satisfy political constituencies, moral-existential concerns, economic power-holders and stability requirements arose regimes of racial rule distinguishable in important ways: in the trade-offs they imposed on different sections of the privileged and powerful but above all in their implications for the dominated.

The state in transition

At one level the negotiated transition to an inclusive democracy in the 1990s marked a crucial break with earlier dynamics. By the end of the 1980s top NP leaders had concluded that white minority rule was incompatible with the continued stability and long-run effectiveness of the state. They also decided that minority rule was inessential to the material well-being of whites. The ruling party's sense of ideological purpose was by then anyway largely depleted. NP reformers gambled on forging a cross-racial elite agreement outside the existing electoral process, unleashing (in part inadvertently) a transition to majority rule described in Chapter 8. Its outcome was the most wide-ranging restructuring of South Africa's political system since 1910.

In what ways is the post-1994 state different from the 1910-89 state? There are of course sharp discontinuities. Some are in the form of the state, others in the character and orientation of its personnel. The new state in formal terms is a representative democracy like its predecessor, but is racially inclusive in its citizenship base and more clearly constrained by liberal-type constitutional limitations on its authority. The universalization of the franchise has ensured that the key personnel in the state are now mainly black, and that the current state is more geared than the pre-1994 state to meeting black needs. The constitutional founders and rulers of the new order have attempted to knit together elements of the old state apparatus separated out through ethnic duplication. Consolidated provinces now encompass the former 'homelands' and consolidated municipalities link ethnically distinct localities. The resulting centralizing and homogenizing tendency is only partly offset by a delegation of functions and limited powers to elected provincial governments, and by the recognition of traditional forms of local authority in many former 'homeland' areas.

Despite these changes, there are striking continuities with the past. Most immediately, the transformation of the state has been constrained by employment guarantees given to personnel of the old order, by the dependence of new rulers on technical skills accumulated by whites over previous decades and by the desire of the new elites to maintain political stability. Males have not lost their grip on the state, despite an influx of women into parliament.

In addition to this, the hegemony of the ANC bears a close resemblance to that of the NP. Both involve a party achieving a lock on formal political power with the help of an ethnically-defined electoral majority. And in both cases one has a ruling party using its leverage to staff the state machine with supporters, dispense patronage to ethnic allies outside the state and concentrate power in the executive branch – even, up to a point, to fuse party and state.

Furthermore, the ANC is constrained by the demands and requirements of external private power-holders, the capitalists, in much the same fashion as the NP. Both ruling parties, indeed, confronted/confront a business world dominated by Anglophone-dominated capital. In some ways the ANC has ceded more power to business than did the NP, being readier to privatize state assets and free up the movement of capital and goods. Like its predecessor the ANC-dominated state is dependent on foreign capital and technology, but in an age where planning and protection are out and markets are in, the post-1994 state is, if anything, more vulnerable to the pressures of international competition and the decisions of international investors. Like the Nationalists of the 1920s, the ANC has allies in organized labour suspicious of capitalism, but black labour's effective political influence is tending to diminish as the ruling party consolidates its power, much the fate that befell white labour from the later 1920s.

Similarities between the old and new state should not divert attention from the fact that the arrival of democratic majority rule represents immense progress across a range of axes. It permits the state to govern with wider consent; it requires the state to attend to an electorate that has been extended to encompass not only more people but also the poorest and most historically oppressed South Africans. If it succeeded in advancing the interests of Africans as effectively as the NP did those of Afrikaners its achievements would be everywhere hailed. It is not certain however that it can do so: the Afrikaner–African analogy breaks down not least because Africans are more numerous and most are materially worse-off than were Afrikaners in, say, 1948. Capitalism worked for the Afrikaners; it has yet to be established that it can deliver the goods for black working and poor people. The state's efforts to harness and humanize capitalism in the interests of the majority ensure that the nexus between public and private power will be an object of interest for a long time to come.

5

The Continuing Significance of Class

The appearance of class

Marxists did not introduce the concept of class into South African scholarship, but they gave it a particular prominence. Some non-Marxists recognized class as one useful category amongst others in explaining human action. Prior to the Marxists, however, class as an explanatory category lay in the shadow of the more visible categories of race and ethnicity. Class was obscured from view either by class-transcending ethnic solidarities or by coincidences of 'race', ethnicity and class, both of which militated against class consciousness and action.

To the South African Marxists who came to scholarly prominence in the 1970s the concept of class seemed important both to analysing societies and to changing them in desired directions. Many proceeded from the loosely 'realist' assumption that the appearance of things concealed subterranean realities, and in particular hidden wellsprings of human motivation; and that these were best excavated by the theoretical spadework of class (and more generally materialist) analysis (Bozzoli and Delius 1990: 21). Race and ethnicity should not (Marxists in the 1970s argued) be treated as starting points for explanation of South African politics but needed themselves to be explained. Interests arising from economic class positions and antagonisms were key factors influencing the formation and dissolution of ethnic solidarities. They were therefore crucial also to explaining the origins and forms of race domination in South Africa. Politically, class analysis could identify agents and enemies of the struggle for a non-racial, and eventually classless, society which radicals wanted to see in South Africa.

The main adversaries of Marxists as class analysts, at least during the 1970s and earlier 1980s, were liberals. Marxists berated non-radical sociologists and political scientists for treating racial and ethnic attitudes as unproblematically given rather than exploring the economic and power relationships which formed their context (Wolpe 1970; Johnstone 1976: introduction). Liberal writers in turn criticized Marxists for underestimating the importance of ideas and psychological motivations in general and the autonomous importance of ethnic symbols and solidarities in particular (Giliomee 1983: 91-6, 1989a, 1992; Giliomee and Schlemmer 1989: 162-70). These lines of disagreement could blur, however. The liberal Lipton shared, albeit with qualification, the Marxist emphasis on class and material interests, disagreeing with Marxists rather over which classes supported the racial order and which did not (Lipton 1986: 10-11). Some liberals critical of Marxism's class preoccupations built a sense of the importance of class and material interests into their own analyses (Adam and Giliomee 1979: chs 6, 7; Giliomee 1989b, 1989d: 118-25). There were of course traditions of class analysis other than Marxist they could draw upon, above all the Weberian.

Marxists and Marxist-influenced writers on South Africa themselves adopted a variety of approaches to class. In an echo of European debates, radical social historians in the 1980s rejected the earlier (1970s) functionalist understanding of class as an objective entity that could be apprehended only through abstract theory. They insisted that ideological and cultural forces had their own histories and regularities ignored by instrumentalist or functionalist class analysis (Marks and Rathbone 1982: 5). The forging of class had to be explained with reference to its cultural environment, as well as non-class social categories such as gender, ethnicity and age (Bozzoli 1987 22-5, 36-9; Bozzoli and Delius 1990: 30-4). Moreover classes were not simply bearers of objective forces but historical agents acting consciously on the world around them. Social historians offered a history 'from below' to bring to light and celebrate the previously 'hidden struggles' of subaltern classes, whether for survival against the odds or for political change (Bozzoli 1983a: 3-4, 6, 28-34, 1987; Bozzoli and Delius 1990: 27-35).

In the 1980s the left in South Africa, as in much of North America and Europe, retreated from class. A range of radical writers reasserted the importance of categories like gender and ethnicity, denying that class enjoyed causal or explanatory priority over them (Greenstein 1993: 2-4). Others questioned the materialist premises of class analysis, insisting on the independent, even overwhelming importance of culture and language as determinants of consciousness and action (Ashforth 1990; Norval 1996). While the social historians too foregrounded culture, their residual attention to inner-Marxist debates and their concern with class and class struggle came to seem quaint by the assertively anti-materialist standards of some later post-modernist and post-structuralist writers (Harries 1994 xvii-xix).

Against this backdrop it is pertinent to ask whether the focus on class and the enterprise of class analysis are plausible and whether they remain relevant in the 1990s and post-apartheid South Africa. This chapter will provide a survey of the radical engagement with class in South Africa before offering a conditional defence of class and materialist analysis.

Approaching class

Radical studies of class in South Africa generally followed one of two broad intellectual strategies corresponding, but only up to a point, with the divide between structuralist class analysis and social history. One strategy focused on class *interests:* above all on how the material requirements of this or that class (or class fraction) shaped the social and political world. An abstractly functionalist version assumed that institutions and policies existed to satisfy class interests; its practitioners did not always explain how class interests were able to summon those institutions and policies into being. Another variant supplied the agents of important historical changes, explaining their behaviour in class terms. Interest-based class analyses of class behaviour assumed that classes existed independently of class consciousness, and that objective class interests influenced, though did not necessarily predetermine, subjective perceptions and actions (Krikler 1993: 2-3).

A second strategy involved building up class *histories.* Its practitioners recorded and analysed the historical formation of classes. This could involve charting their emergence as discernible economic and demographic categories, but also the subjective experiences of class actors (as revealed for example in oral testimony) and the development of class cultures and consciousness. This was the preoccupation above all of the social historians.

Analysts of class interests and historians of class shared a conviction that social classes were significant intellectually and politically, and that their historical role needed to be brought to light whether as sources of inspiration, objects of critique or as dynamic historical forces. The themes that concerned South African radicals included patterns of social differentiation in the countryside and town, the dynamics of proletarianization, urbanization and industrialization and the political interests, identities and alignments of classes.

Social differentiation

A key concern of South African radical writers has been to expose class differentials and tensions in societies and groups widely considered to be relatively egalitarian. Radicals thus looked critically at romantic nationalist myths of homogeneous peoples. At the same time they identified the presence of forces limiting social differentiation. They looked to patterns of differentiation for clues about class interests and alliances, both past and prospective.

Class differentiation in the countryside

Radical writers revealed underexplored landscapes of class differentiation in both country and town, and amongst both blacks and whites. Much of their work focused on the impact of market processes in dissolving and reordering class structures. This survey of their findings begins with the rural domain.

Radical historians have done much to illuminate shifting class divisions in pre-colonial African societies. They challenged social-anthropological depictions of African societies as becalmed and tradition-bound while critically probing the interests behind the African state formation celebrated by liberal 'Africanist' historians in the late 1960s. For centuries before the colonial era Africans were organized in small chiefdoms where they were subject to the authority of male homestead heads and chiefs. Bonner and others showed how dominant lineages imposed their authority on smaller chiefdoms from the mid-eighteenth century (Bonner 1983). Both chiefs and ruling aristocracies extracted resources from their subjects, but carried out redistributive functions which contained social differentiation. A chiefly elite remained at the apex of the African rural hierarchy into the twentieth century, first attacked, later sustained by the white-run state (see Chapter 4).

Although the theme was anticipated by amongst others the liberal anthropologist Monica Wilson (1971), Colin Bundy was the first of a number of radical historians to draw attention to the rise of a commercially successful class of African agricultural producers during the middle to later nineteenth century. Historians revealed a 'progressive' African peasantry drawn disproportionately from the ranks of Christian converts and refugees and concentrated in areas close to white settler economic centres in the eastern Cape, Natal, on the Orange Free State and Transvaal Highveld. They showed African peasants cultivating crops (especially grains) on a range of locales, including mission stations, African-controlled communal-tenure areas, land privately owned by white farmers or companies and (in a few cases) on African-owned land. African cultivators appeared in the personae variously of communal-tenure peasants, cash or labour tenants, sharecroppers and (more rarely) private landowners. Peasants initiated or stepped up commercial production in response to internal markets that were greatly augmented by large-scale diamond and gold mining from the 1870s and 1880s. Expanding markets generated demand for African produce and offered Africans desired manufactured goods that they could buy with the proceeds of sales. African commercial cultivation of crops was also prompted by the erosion of alternative livelihoods due to the depletion of commercial game and timber resources and the undermining of the extensive pastoral economy by land shortage. Later on peasant production was stimulated also by the need to find cash to pay colonial taxes (Trapido 1978, 1986; Slater 1980; Beinart 1982, 1994: chs 1, 2; Etherington 1985; Shillington 1985: chs 3, 4; Keegan 1986a; Bundy 1988; Murray 1992; Eldredge 1993).

Radicals shared the liberal Africanist concern to show that Africans were commercially initiating and capable of technological innovation. Africans, they argued, adapted traditional farming methods and even their domestic social order in order to produce for expanding markets. In some cases African producers were crucial sources of food supply for whites. In addition, claims Keegan, African sharecroppers made an important contribution to the capitalization of white farming (Keegan 1986a: 86).

In the long run neither a substantial black landowning bourgeoisie nor a durably prosperous African middle peasantry developed in South Africa. Radicals resisted the conventional argument that African peasant decline was largely due to inappropriate farming techniques, cattle diseases and droughts. They listed as additional causes of decline (varying in incidence and importance) loss of African-held land due to white conquest and expropriation, eviction of tenants from white owned farms, the exclusion of Africans from land purchase outside reserves (from 1913), confiscation of African cattle on grounds of trespass, restrictions on African cattle movement, the draining of able-bodied males from agriculture by labour migrancy and relative government neglect of African compared to white rural infrastructure needs. Radical writers suggested that these impositions on the peasantry were a response largely to the demands of white settlers for land, later for tighter control of tenant labour, and the demands of mining capital for migrant workers; and their neglect a product of the state's favouritism towards politically powerful white farmers. From the late nineteenth century the labour demands of mine owners trumped the earlier concern of merchants and missionaries to foster an African peasantry (Trapido

1971, 1980a; Bundy 1988: conclusion) while capitalization of land enabled white farmers to displace independent tenants and move directly into production on their own account (Keegan 1986a).

Radical writers have not, however, presented a simple or agreed picture of a peasantry suddenly appearing in response to external market opportunities and subsequently crushed by the state and capital. Eldredge has shown that African surplus production and agricultural trade in certain cases long preceded the arrival of the colonial economy (Eldredge 1994: 6-7). Others have emphasized that the peasantry continued to exist in various reduced forms into the later twentieth century both in the reserves and on white-owned land, kept going by a determination to cling to rural resources (Van Onselen 1996). African systems of communal tenure and cultures of 'community obligation', it has been noted, preserved African access to land but inhibited a transition to capitalist agriculture (Murray 1992: 118). At the same time African landowners lost land through market as well as political pressures, and sometimes by the two combined (Murray 1992: 43-8, 136-44). Wage labour migrancy, considered by some earlier radicals a product of state coercion, was revealed by later radical historians to be initially discretionary rather than coerced, in some cases continuing a longer pre-colonial history of migration by Africans in search of economic opportunities. Judged by many radicals an engine of rural underdevelopment, oscillating migrancy could also provide resources for investment in agriculture and stimulate commercial activity in labour export areas (Beinart 1982: 68, 100-1; Kimble 1982; Delius 1983: ch. 3; Eldredge 1994: ch. 13; Harries 1994: 16-17, 229). And while state intervention in rural relationships was in the long run crucial, the impact of state legislation aimed against African tenants was not always immediately felt, and much of it was evaded by farmers in collusion with tenants (Keegan 1986a: 182-95).

What is clear, though, is that during the twentieth century a majority of African tenants on white farms were pushed down into the ranks of labour tenants and wage labourers, while households in the reserves experienced a growing impoverishment and wage dependence. A large number of Africans deserted the white countryside for urban centres, their efflux accelerated from the 1960s by mechanization and forced removals. Many Africans permanently abandoned the reserves too, though a remarkable proportion retained a rural connection. Some were inspired to hold on to rural resources by their traditionalist values, others were immobilized by restrictions on urbanization. Economically non-viable rural households were sustained by migrant remittances. Nevertheless landless strata did develop in the reserves, augmented by agricultural rationalization policies and from the 1960s by the forced resettlement of evicted Africans from outside the reserves.

The reserves meanwhile became sites of new forms of differentiation. Migrant workers brought prized income into the reserves which elders sought to appropriate through brideprice demands. Chiefs exploited their state-conferred powers to tax and fine their subjects. With the determined state-promoted retribalization of reserve administration from 1951 and the granting of autonomy to 'homelands' in stages after 1959, chiefly and commoner elites could use the emerging African ethnic statelets as vehicles of personal wealth and status accumulation. Apartheid rulers designated the reserves as the appropriate places to build up the African elites suppressed in 'white' South Africa, and some Africans indeed developed a stake in the building of the ethno-national 'homelands' that were central pillars of territorial and political apartheid (Southall 1982; Murray 1992; Beinart 1994).

In the case of white rural society, Ross, Crais and Trapido demonstrated the presence of class inequalities in Dutch-Afrikaner agrarian societies of the eighteenth and nineteenth centuries, casting doubt on notions of an egalitarian 'Herrenvolk democracy' of white masters (Trapido 1978, 1980b; Guelke and Shell 1983; Ross 1993: ch. 2). Inequalities and class tensions in white society intensified wherever frontiers closed and unclaimed land grew scarce. By the late nineteenth century the deteriorating conditions of many poorer farmers and tenants in the Transvaal had generated bitter divisions in Afrikaner agrarian society and set the stage for a large-scale Afrikaner flight to the cities.

Radical historians have revealed how during the early and middle twentieth century a small vanguard of white 'progressive' farmers, some relatively late arrivals from outside the Afrikaner *platteland*, led the way in capitalizing agriculture. The latter part of the century saw an accelerating concentration of white land ownership. From the 1970s state assistance became heavily skewed towards better-off producers (Morrell 1986, 1988; Cooper 1988: 48-54; Bradford 1993).

Class differentiation in towns and cities

Radicals also highlighted inequalities internal to white and black societies in urban and industrial contexts. It has always been common cause that in the period following the mining revolution English-speakers dominated urban economic life, predominating in the capitalist class and skilled working class occupations and leaving urban Afrikaners economically marginalized at least until the 1950s. Radical writers however emphasized that class hierarchies marked both Anglophone and Afrikaner urban worlds. These were pronounced from the outset in an English-speaking population that included the wealthiest businessmen as well as an imported European working class, and which never, partly for this reason, forged a common identity. Though pronounced in rural settings, inequalities developed more slowly amongst urban Afrikaners in the northern provinces especially, mainly because Afrikaners took a while to get a foothold in the state and economy. Though there was a petit bourgeois elite of mainly teachers and clerics to be found in both rural and urban areas, many of these were materially humble enough to identify downwards with less affluent Afrikaners. In the decades after 1948, however, a significant number of Afrikaners advanced into the industrial and commercial bourgeoisie and the managerial and professional strata and still more into the ranks of skilled, white-collar and supervisory workers. They shared in an overall advance in white living standards prior to the 1970s, albeit one accompanied by deepening Afrikaner social differentiation (Adam and Giliomee 1979: ch. 6; Davies 1979: ch. 8; Giliomee and Schlemmer 1989: 120; O'Meara 1996: 136-41).

Africans, coloureds and Indians occupied different positions in the black urban job hierarchy, with Indians at the top (and therefore the most likely to fill white-collar positions), coloureds below them (well represented in artisan trades) and Africans (for most of the century mainly unskilled at least by classification) at the bottom. After 1948 urban Africans in particular were subject to the persistent efforts of the state to limit the development amongst them of a middle and capitalist class. However, as Crankshaw has shown, the African working class became sharply internally differentiated from the late 1960s as more of its members moved into semi-skilled, skilled, white-collar and (within segregated structures) supervisory positions (Crankshaw 1997). Increasingly freed from restrictions from the mid-1970s and given new forms of access to municipal patronage in townships, a black middle class also began to develop. The rise of an African stratum with a stake in the existing order called into question the assumption that Africans, and blacks more widely, shared a cross-class interest in national liberation and progressive social change (Wolpe 1977; Hudson and Sarakinsky 1986; Nzimande 1986, 1990; Sarakinsky 1987; Charney 1988).

The makings of an urban working class

Those charting 'history from below' unsurprisingly placed the working class centre-stage. They gave special attention to the African working class, but the histories of white, coloured and Indian working classes also attracted interest (Bundy 1986; van Duin 1989; Beall 1990; Morrell 1992; Freund 1995). The terms on which producers were proletarianized – separated from the means and instruments of production – and their bitter struggles to avoid proletarianization (say by operating as agricultural tenants or petty traders) were key themes in this writing (Van Onselen 1982a, b, 1996; Bozzoli 1983b; Keegan 1986a; Bradford 1987a). The process of urbanization was another. Social historians addressed the evolving consciousness of urbanizers, and showed how it could be torn between that of the peasant and wage labourer (Bradford 1987a). They also showed how rural commitments and ethnic allegiances, reinterpreted in a compound or township context, shaped the world-views of migrants and the recently urbanized, such as shack dwellers (Beinart 1987; Freund 1989: 86; Bonner 1990a: 108, 1993; Sapire 1992; Delius 1993; Harries 1994; Moodie 1994). Urban culture more generally – from marabi music and coon carnivals to gangsterism – was documented (Van Onselen 1982a, b; Koch 1983; Pinnock 1987; Bonner 1993; Glaser 1993). Social historians showed that class consciousness was more rare, and the consciousness of classes more complicated, than some Marxists had imagined.

Social historians also brought out the gender dimension of proletarianization and urbanization. They documented the gender-differentiated patterns of migration to towns and cities and of incorporation into urban labour markets, the survival strategies of urban women and their complex, often conflictual relations with men and the state (Van Onselen 1982a: Sec 3, 1982b: chs 1, 2; Bozzoli 1983b; Wells 1983; Bradford 1987b; Brink 1987; Bonner 1990b, 1993; Berger 1992).

The bulk of urban social history was devoted to the sphere of reproduction or collective consumption – the urban residential space, where blacks of different classes were thrown together (Bozzoli 1987). A distinctive if smaller tradition in the historiography of the urban working class took as its object the capitalist labour process, exploring the sphere of production. Writers like Webster and Lewis highlighted struggles between capital and labour to control the division of labour, organization of work and technological change in the 'hidden abode' of production. They also traced connections between workplace conflicts and the evolution of racial attitudes and divisions within the working class (Lewis 1984; Webster 1985). A few historians studied the lives of groups of workers both in work and outside of it (Witz 1987; Berger 1992; Harries 1994).

The dominant classes in history

The history of the dominant classes has received less attention from radicals, partly because it necessarily entailed elements of the sort of magisterial 'history from above' that some social historians eschewed. Radical intellectuals moreover lacked the organic connections to capitalist companies that they enjoyed with unionized workers and others amongst the racially oppressed. They wrote about capital in a way that reflected their sympathies with those employed by it. Their contributions to economic history were distinguished also by a less descriptive and institutionalist approach than was common in most conventional company and sectoral histories, of which there are several (Coleman 1983; Jones 1992; Jones and Müller 1992), and by a greater concern with capital's labour regimes, political connections and internal conflicts.

Bozzoli uniquely provided a cultural history of the South African bourgeoisie, especially its 'national' wing, during the earlier twentieth century (Bozzoli 1981). More commonly radicals offered histories of companies and company formation in the mining sector, with special emphasis on the formation of production and selling monopolies and labour-recruiting monopsonies (Innes 1984; Turrell 1987; Worger 1987; Newbury 1989). More recently they have provided histories of state industries and economic agencies (Christie 1984; Freund 1989; Gelb 1989; Kaplan 1990; Clark 1994). There have also been attempts to chart the historical development of whole economic sectors, like mining and manufacturing, and of sub-sectors like the metal and engineering industries (Webster 1985; Freund 1989; Crush et al. 1991; James 1992). Radicals drew attention to divisions and alliances within capital, with the rather schematic 1970s fractionalist account of rivalry between 'imperial' and 'national' capital giving way increasingly in the 1980s and 1990s to efforts to comprehend the evolving system of intersectoral connections between state, foreign and domestic capital (Seidman and Seidman 1978; Innes 1984; Fine and Rustomjee 1996). It should be noted here also that in the 1980s radical work on capitalism and the racial order began to pay closer attention to what capitalists said and did (Greenberg 1980; Lipton 1986; Glaser 1988; Posel 1991) compared to earlier preoccupations with an abstractly conceived capital and its purported objective 'needs'.

Bourgeoisie and proletariat?

The proper specification of classes was unsurprisingly a matter of importance for class analysts, even if attempts to provide it generated debates that outside observers considered arcane. Its significance flowed above all from the Marxist assumption that objective economic locations shaped or strongly influenced the political posture of social groups.

One key issue in the mapping of classes was determining which mode of production they fell into. Were particular sets of masters capitalists or not (perhaps semi-feudal or slave owning)? Were particular groups of labourers proletarian or composed, say, of slaves, serfs or peasants?

In South Africa these questions mainly revolved around agriculture, because the capitalist character of large-scale mining, secondary industry and a range of other sectors employing wage labour was never in doubt. In agricultural development however there was a tremendous unevenness in time and space, with wage labour employment developing in, say, the Natal sugar industry in some cases a century or more before it did so on the maize growing Highveld. If the advent of capitalism in agriculture involves the commoditization of agricultural produce, means of production and labour-power, then quite clearly these criteria were satisfied at different times in different sectors and regions. On the basis of a criterion of commercial production, much of South African agriculture was capitalist by the 1860s, especially but not only in the Cape and Natal. Judged by the wage-labour criterion there were areas of agriculture in at least three of four provinces which were not fully capitalist until the 1970s, and in a few cases beyond (Beinart and Delius 1986; Ross 1986; Bradford 1990)

This might have been simply a matter of taxonomic pedantry, except that a range of writers required the capitalist or non-capitalist character of the countryside to carry an explanatory burden. For Morris, famously, it was central to his thesis of Prussian-style capitalist modernization from above, upon which rested in turn Kaplan's concept of racially exclusive bourgeois democracy and arguably a good part of the 'fractionalist' edifice (see Chapter 4). The question of whether or not the *labouring* class on the land was proletarian mattered for discussions of the tactics and strategies of rural-based movements. It most notably influenced the debate about whether the Industrial and Commercial Workers' Union should have mobilized rural workers in the 1920s on a proletarian or cross-class populist basis (Bradford 1987a). The class structure of the countryside also had a bearing on the political strategies of urban-centred movements (Bundy 1987a). The continued access of many urban wage labourers to rural means of production raised difficult questions about the class and political allegiances of oscillating migrants (Delius 1993; Bonner 1993; Moodie 1994).

Class boundaries/boundary classes

Another problem for the mapping of classes was identifying properly the boundaries between them, the better to navigate a path through a range of explanatory and strategic tasks.

One key class boundary question confronting South African Marxists was posed by the petit bourgeoisie. This intermediate grouping occupies a peculiar position in Marxist class theory, at once marginal and highly significant. It is marginal because it is not one of the two classes which dominate the Marxist bipolar class scheme. The 'traditional' petit bourgeoisie of traders and small business people was scheduled by Marxist class theory to disappear with the expansion of the other classes. The future expansion of other parts of the petit bourgeoisie was barely glimpsed, as in the case of the 'new' petit bourgeoisie of supervisory and white-collar workers employed in corporate and state bureaucracies and service sector industries. At the same time the class is significant in Marxist theory because the petit bourgeoisie's usually small numbers give it an incentive to latch onto other classes in order to secure its own position politically and economically. The ideological productivity of the intelligentsia moreover often places the petit bourgeoisie at the head of populist and nationalist mobilizations. The petit bourgeoisie thus occupies a position characterized by 'dependency' on other social forces, whether above or below it. Its position is characterized also by 'ambiguity', because the petit bourgeoisie retains its own interests distinct from those of the masses it mobilizes, and because it aspires to upward mobility – often identifying downwards only where its advance is blocked by dominant classes (Marks 1986).

The two most discussed petit bourgeoisies in the South African case are the Afrikaner and African. Both found their upward mobility barred by dominant economic and political groups: by the English-speaking establishment in the case of Afrikaners, and by the white state in the case of Africans. Both identified themselves with the causes of their fellow-oppressed, seeking to mobilize their constituencies on a cross-class basis against a common foe. In both cases cultural brokers like teachers, journalists and clerics – in the case of Africans also clerks, messengers and interpreters – gave a political lead (O'Meara 1983). Afrikaner and African petit bourgeoisies both found themselves torn between left-populist and right-nationalist ideologies, and once in power both used political office to promote their embourgeoisement as a class. There were disanalogies. Afrikaner nationalism was less dependent on petit bourgeois leadership, because it enjoyed a bourgeois connection in the Cape; and because whites were enfranchised, the Afrikaner nationalist leadership had little reason to mobilize the Afrikaner masses on an extraparliamentary basis. The African petit bourgeoisie was much more fully marginalized from political and economic power than the Afrikaner; but having been imbued with missionary education and steeped in Cape liberalism, it was nevertheless reluctant, for a long time, to take on the state in a confrontational way. The African petit bourgeoisie radicalized from the 1940s, but the whole of its twentieth century record is dogged by controversy in Marxist-influenced circles. Some writers insisted that blacks in South Africa shared interests and concerns that cut across class boundaries (Nolutshungu 1983), in Magubane's case even denying that black society was composed of distinctive classes (Magubane 1979). Others queried the extent to which the petit bourgeoisie genuinely identified with the interests of its mass constituency as opposed to being concerned to promote or protect its own interests in (for example) winning white establishment respectability, ingratiating itself with traditional leaders or accumulating capital (Etherington 1978; Bonner 1982; Bradford 1986; Marks 1986; La Hausse 1993).

The strength of class analyses of the petit bourgeoisie is that they exposed the differential interests concealed by homogenizing populist ideologies, and revealed some of the self-interested calculations behind the actions of nationalist leaders. They also provided a materialist basis for understanding cross-class solidarities. Nevertheless some more harshly economic-materialist accounts invited an underestimation of the extent of the petit bourgeoisie's investment in its own ideology; of its moral sincerity, its preoccupation with ideas and its capacity for genuine empathy with its constituents (Lazar 1987). They tended also, perhaps rather too easily, to explain petit bourgeois political strategy by reference to class interests and too little by reference to the objective possibilities, constraints and pressures confronting petit bourgeois leaders.

Class solidarities/divided classes

One of the key puzzles of South African history, from a Marxist point of view, was the failure in several cases of classes to engage in collective action across boundaries of race. It was this failure which appeared to liberals to underline the ethnic rather than class nature of conflict in South Africa. Liberals could explain this lack of class solidarity either in terms of the power of ethnic ideological appeals or, as in the more sophisticated account of Lipton, the coincidence of material and cultural-symbolic needs to which ethnic nationalism appealed (Lipton 1986: chs 1, 7). For Marxists by contrast the non-appearance of class unity was an intellectual problem for three reasons: Marxists questioned the autonomous power of ethnicity, they considered that members of classes shared common interests and their historicist teleology led them to expect that the working class would ultimately achieve a class consciousness.

It was the racial fragmentation of the working class that Marxists found most troubling, since that class was the assumed bearer of socialist politics and because its disunity posed immediate dilemmas for labour organizers (to organize the white working class or not?). Marxists found a part of the explanation for the divided working class in the interests and actions of non-working class strata: the petit bourgeoisie and the capitalist class.

Marxists suggested that petit bourgeois politicians, lacking a political base of substantial size in their own class, wanted the working class (or at least sections of it) to themselves. One way to win a proletarian base was by exploiting the grievances of rank-and-file workers against ethnically 'different' labour leaders. Thus petit bourgeois Afrikaner nationalists struggled with eventual success to sever Afrikaner workers from Anglophone-dominated labour organizations and to rally them behind an ethnic rather than class banner (O'Meara 1983: ch. 6). Coloured petit bourgeois leaders of the African People's Organization fought in the early decades of the twentieth century to extract coloured artisans from alliances with white workers (Lewis 1987: 46, 54-5, ch. 4; Van Duin 1989: 98-110).

The capitalist class for its part had (radicals argued) an interest in preventing the working class from uniting, or its ethnic components fighting simultaneously, against capital and capitalism. The racially differentiated incorporation of the working class enabled white labour (and up to a point coloured and Indian labour) to be won over to the capitalist industrial and political order. At the same time racism legitimated (in white eyes) the harsh exploitation of African labour. Racial divisions amongst workers also allowed capitalists to employ whites (and sometimes coloureds and Indians) as agents of control over African workers (see Chapter 2).

Other Marxist accounts placed more emphasis on the active agency of the working class in forging an ethnically divided proletariat. In doing this they partly echoed liberals (e.g. Lipton 1986) who stressed the role of organized white labour both in securing racial job reservation and, through its political arm the South African Labour Party, in promoting segregationism. Marxists downplayed the relative importance of white labour as an author of segregation. They emphasized the constraints, imposed by capital and capitalism, within which white workers operated, and they took issue with those liberals who considered white working class behaviour irrational. Nevertheless there were Marxist accounts in which the choices made by white labour were considered blameworthy, especially when they were made by leaders rather than led.

One such account emphasized the choices of strategy open to skilled and semi-skilled white trade unionists in responding to capitalist efforts to reorganize or mechanize the labour process in order to displace them by cheaper black labour. They could, in the case of artisans (some of whom were coloured or Indian), seek to place ostensibly non-racial barriers in the way of those (whether black or white) seeking to join their trade, and resist efforts to deskill artisanal labour. In this way they could preserve the scarcity and higher cost of their labour. Such a strategy did not depend upon racially exclusive unionism or colour bars. Secondly, they could appeal to the state to bar Africans from jobs, either by statutory job reservation or by securing Industrial Council agreements reserving jobs for members of unions open only to whites. Finally, they could take the initiative to organize black workers to secure a 'rate for the job' for all workers and thus head off racial labour market competition. This was especially an option for less skilled white workers in mass production secondary industries.

Organized white workers and their leaders tried all three approaches. White mineworkers resorted from early on to explicit racial exclusion, seeking statutory job reservation and securing it in 1911. Sections of the predominantly white artisan unions employed restrictive craft practices that were not openly racist. As they lost their hold over the work process some, for example in the metal and engineering industries, rejected African union membership and turned to the state to shore up white workers through political measures (Webster 1985). This right-wing turn led to the break-up of the artisan-dominated Trades and Labour Council and eventually to the formation of the pro-apartheid South African Confederation of Labour (Lewis 1984). A portion of white artisans and skilled workers continued to oppose racist state intervention, the majority amongst this section (organized mainly in the Trade Union Council of South Africa) preferring traditional restrictive craft practices to open industrial unionism. There were also, finally, instances of non-racial open industrial unionism from the 1920s in light manufacturing industry and commerce, especially in the garment and food processing sectors where keeping Africans out was never an option, but they were of marginal long-term significance (Greenberg 1980: chs 12-14; Lipton 1986 ch. 7; Berger 1992). In practice, then, white labour mostly opted for strategies of 'exclusion' rather than 'incorporation' (Lipton 1986: ch. 7). Radicals portrayed this choice as partly self-interestedly rational, but partly also as avoidable and misguided.

Another radical approach emphasizing working class agency focused on the political choices of the labour movement and/or of the leadership of 'left' parties and movements. A wide range of leaders has been accused of betraying the working class and the cause of non-racial, cross-ethnic class solidarity. They include Communists who from the 1950s abandoned efforts to organize white workers, Indian Communists who after the Second World War chose passive resistance in defence of Indian traders over the pursuit of cross-racial working-class unionism and corrupt and reformist Anglophone labour leaders who forfeited Afrikaner working class support in the 1940s (Davies 1979; O'Meara 1983: ch. 6; Padayachee et al. 1985; Fine and Davis 1990: 80-94).

Radical arguments which attributed workers' ethnocentrism to their material interests or leadership betrayal, though not inherently implausible, carried a theoretical cost for Marxists, forcing them to concede either that agency (leadership choices) readily overrode structural tendencies towards class solidarity, or else that no such solidaristic tendencies existed. The first concession weakened materialism as such, the second the assumption that classes were defined by a shared material interest.

There were three implicit Marxist strategies for containing this theoretical damage. One involved solving the problem by redefining the large and growing proportion of white wage-earners in technical and supervisory jobs as 'new petit bourgeois'. This was the explanatory strategy adopted by Simson (1974) and, more influentially, Davies (1979).

A second was to suggest that in opting for ethnic solidarity the working class, though acting rationally, was pursuing its short- rather than long-term interests. This possibility was suggested by the way Afrikaner workers were ejected from the ethnic class coalition they had previously supported once, in the 1970s, the Afrikaner middle class and bourgeoisie no longer needed them.

A third possible answer was to insist on the presence of a counter-pull towards class solidarity of considerable significance even if it was too weak to gain the upper hand. For this proposition there is considerable evidence. White-dominated artisan and industrial unions did explore inclusionist options. Ethnic coalitions did not form spontaneously; the active political efforts of the bourgeoisie and petit bourgeoisie were necessary to break up class-based

THE CONTINUING SIGNIFICANCE OF CLASS?

movements and suppress cross-class militancy, outbreaks of which nevertheless occurred episodically in South African history. Perhaps as importantly, the tug of class solidarity did not disappear once ethnic coalitions were formed but manifested itself in intra-ethnic class tensions and conflicts, as in the case of South African Afrikaners (O'Meara 1983, 1996). If class analysis could appear to rest on an impermissible class teleology, the service it provided was to encourage a closer exploration of the class tensions and allegiances which challenged ethnic mobilization, in the process illuminating important dynamics of South African history.

Class and Marxist materialism

Materialist premises

How plausible was the South African Marxist exercise in class analysis? Those engaging in it rarely examined its premises. Of these two were implicit. The first was that class had a fundamental quality because it was rooted in the elementary necessity to produce material life. Human beings entered social relationships in order to produce goods; under conditions of scarcity some sought to appropriate the surplus labour of others. In struggles for control of the conditions and products of labour, human beings had differing interests depending on where they stood in the economic hierarchy. These interests shaped the ideas they generated or adopted, the allies they sought and the policies they demanded of the state (itself above all a product of class antagonism). The second, more humanist, premiss was that creative appropriation of external nature was central to the realization of human nature or 'species-being'. Humans had an inner need to escape the alienation attendant upon heteronomous control of labour and to regain control of both the conception and execution of creative tasks. The development of productive forces played two positive roles in the Marxist scheme. It allowed human beings to escape scarcity-driven competitive struggles over surpluses. It also offered a way of lifting humans out of the realm of necessity, in which labour appeared an arduous and mechanical task, into a realm of freedom where work could regain its convivial and creative possibilities.

South African Marxists in the 1970s avoided exploring these premises partly because most were attracted to the structuralist view that human agents were bearers of objective social relations and that their subjective natures were either of secondary causal significance or else constituted by structures themselves. They thus preferred to deal in categories like 'mode of production' and 'social formation'. Nevertheless the priority accorded by structuralists to economic categories and 'levels' and their tributes to the central role of class struggle would have been largely unintelligible were they not rooted in notions about the priority accorded by human beings to the production of material life.

Radical social historians could sidestep examination of materialist premisses for different reasons: because they disavowed economic determinism and/or were atheoretical. Materialist political economy nevertheless more often than not framed the questions they asked and shaped their literary style, at least prior to the post-structuralist turn. The defensibility or otherwise of materialist suppositions is thus relevant also to the social history project.

As represented here these suppositions are problematic. They involve, for one thing, a rather narrow conception of the material. Even if it is proper to dismiss the metaphysical claims made for the ideational and to seek its material substructure, it does not follow that producing and obtaining material goods is the sole materially rooted activity. The brain itself is a material entity. While it may have evolved to enable us to act in the world to satisfy urgent material needs there is no reason to assume that it did not, either as an evolutionary adaptation or as a by-product of its evolution, equip us to attach priority to goods other than material ones. These non-material goods sought by our material brains, or our 'psychology', might include (for examples) companionship, social esteem and existential explanation (see Chapter 6).

The Marxist premisses involve, secondly, a narrow conception of the range of the cultural – meaning, in this context, patterns of human interaction which are variable rather than universal, built up through meaningful interaction between people in space and across generations. The ways we interpret the world, and the meanings with which we invest material objects, are themselves in part cultural in this sense. The accumulation of cattle by Bantu-speaking mixed farmers served a cultural purpose surplus to any basic material needs it satisfied. African groups controlling trade in beads and cloth could attract followers because people invested such goods with prestige (Hall 1987: 89-90). Production for the market may impose a coercive logic of its own once embarked upon, but the decision to produce for it may be propelled as much by culturally 'new needs' (introduced say by missionaries or traders) as by any necessity to (say) avoid starvation. What constitutes an acceptable material living standard is a matter of cultural expectation. It is with reference to points such as these that many post-structuralists reject Marxist materialism. For them the shared languages structuring our subjectivity enjoy a position of priority in the explanation of what people want and fight and die for. There are, for them, no unmediated material needs at all.

There remain nevertheless good reasons for taking economic class seriously and for doing class analysis. The argument that we have psychological needs for non-material goods still allows for the possibility that humans attach psychological importance to satisfying material needs and obtaining economic security, and it is doubtful that human beings would have survived to the present if they did not. The motivational force arising from material need will presumably be greatest when basic biological survival is threatened. But even when it is not, it may not be so easily 'switched off' when necessities once scarce become plentiful. Equally important, the attainment of non-material goods is not so easily disconnected from the attainment of material ones. The need for status illustrates the point. Status can be boosted by the acquisition of material goods valued by society. There is a tendency in complex economies to 'cash in' or 'store' status materially, by using it to acquire material goods. Status may itself be valued in part because it enables us to acquire material goods more readily. The circumstances in which goods are produced and surpluses appropriated are thus of direct interest to the status seeker.

The argument from cultural relativism is, in its strongest form, unanswerable: everything we perceive and do is filtered through cultural interpretation; there is nothing outside of it by definition. This kind of formulation is, however, so encompassing that it authorizes discussion of nothing apart from the workings of language; and it is a truism, just like the claim that, say, all thoughts are biochemical. It moreover encounters the performative contradiction inherent in making transculturally 'true' claims about cultural relativity. Any less grandiose and reductionist definition of culture, one that accepts that it might be a moment within the human world rather than compose it, would allow that cultures form and change in complex patterns of interaction with material forces and social relations. Thus cultures may prosper and propagate because they encourage a material productivity that is envied and imitated by others (as with market culture, with its powerful culturally solvent effects in Southern Africa and elsewhere). Conversely all cultures express themselves aesthetically in material objects which may be more or less scarce. There may be situations where an apparently cultural shift – for example in Basutos' choice of clothing – is influenced by economic calculations (Eldredge 1993: 93-100). Moreover, there will likely be situations where the material trumps the cultural – most obviously in situations of dire scarcity (as when South African whites averse to manual labour perform it when they have no alternative).

Neither of these defences of the importance of material-economic can be said to establish its primacy over the psychological and cultural, except in fairly unusual situations. The connections described between the material-economic on one side and the psychological and cultural on the other cut both ways. The Comaroffs are not mistaken in their claim that 'the primary processes involved in the production of the everyday world are inseparably material and meaningful' (Comaroff and Comaroff 1991: 8). Nor can there be iron laws about when one or the other term of the relation triumphs. Even physical starvation will be contemplated with greater equanimity by people in some cultures than others, as the cases of the Irish hunger strikers and, more disputably, anorexics and bulimics illustrate. War martyrs and suicides remind us that physical survival is not always an overriding imperative for all individuals.

A reasonable materialist analysis will, however, depend on neither fixed causal hierarchies nor iron laws. For materialist class analysis to work it must be reasonable to suppose the following: that economic-material interests show up in, or influence, a range of behaviours, that they will on occasion do so unconsciously and will not necessarily engender class consciousness, that they can help explain the existence and persistence of non-class collectivities, and that collectivities formed on the basis of material interests will challenge the formation and maintenance of other kinds of collectivity. The contention here is that all of these suppositions *are* reasonable.

The question of interests

Is it possible, however, to identify objective interests which arise from a person's position in the economic or class hierarchy, and which are independent of their consciousness? The notion that agents can have interests independent of their awareness of them is problematic. Interest has an irreducibly subjective side: we have an interest in achieving only that which we value positively. We can talk, more plausibly, about whether a course of action chosen by an actor constitutes an instrumentally rational way of realizing that actor's desired ends. However, interest might be difficult to gauge even in this restricted sense, given that the appropriateness of means chosen can often only be judged retrospectively, and that actions carry consequences unintended and unforeseen either by the observer or the observed. It is difficult, given advance ignorance, to see how the objective interest an actor has in choosing appropriate means could influence their behaviour.

One solution might be to refer only to *perceived* interests. On its own, however, such a suggestion would cancel out the utility of focusing on objective class location, and by focusing on the perceptual leave room only for culturalist analysis. There are ways, though, of drawing a notion of perceived interest into class analysis. At a minimum, we can explore the effects of classes pursuing their perceived interests. An analyst could try to gauge whether the Afrikaner petit bourgeoisie pursued a perceived self-interest, and record the consequences of its doing so. We can go further and couple a notion of perceived interest to a minimalistic and heuristic notion of objective interest. We could thus hypothesize, in an informed way, about what perception of their interests particular actors in particular situations might be expected to form, and proceed to search for evidence that they have such perceptions, evidence which might be found in their actions or their words. In constructing such hypotheses we can use information about actors' objective location in economic hierarchies and proceed from the hunch that economic location and material concerns influence human action in significant ways. These hypotheses would always have to be tested to see whether they are useful in explaining actual political behaviour. They often turn out to be.

Interests and ends

The application of materialist class analysis will not necessarily confirm Marxist historical teleologies. The classic Marxist belief that objective proletarian material interests would find expression in the forging of an ethnically inclusive working class committed to socialism cannot be considered as anything more than one hypothesis amongst others which class analysts might explore. This particular hypothesis is borne out neither by historical events so far nor required by the theoretical logic of class analysis. A given stratum of the working class can plausibly be shown not to have an objective interest in creating an inclusive socialist society. This was, as we have seen, true of the white working class in South Africa, which had every reason to demarcate itself racially from the black majority, the better to take advantage of white racial solidarity and secure a disproportionate claim on scarce national resources. The analysis of class interests is thus separable in principle from the Marxist theory of history. It can, as Lipton (1986) showed, be pursued by pro-capitalist liberals too, though it poses a direct challenge to liberals who assume that ethnic consciousness is primary and immutable. If class analysis cannot be tied in advance to the Marxist theory of history, it *is* connected to the historical expectation that class-driven action will repeatedly intrude upon the surface of events, making and unmaking other kinds of collectivity.

The continuing significance of class?

The retreat from class was sounded, in South Africa as elsewhere, in response to a variety of circumstances in the academic and political worlds. Scepticism about materialist or economic explanations of reality, initially about their range and power, later about the very possibility of providing them, was a part of the story. Another part of it lay in the competitive claims which gender and, later, ethnicity mounted against class – claims which the very radicals who had earlier championed class now felt obliged, in a consistent spirit of emancipatory egalitarianism, to acknowledge and respect.

Perhaps the largest part of the explanation was to be found in the decline of socialist possibilities that was in evidence long before the unravelling of the East

Bloc regimes in 1989 and 1991. If the first two raised questions about the priority accorded class, or in some cases about the possibility of materialist explanation, the last posed the question of whether there was still any *point* in class analysis. Class and the material may possess explanatory importance, but if the analysis of them is divorced from real-world political significance, and above all from a concern to identify the forces making for progressive social transformation, is its significance reduced to a purely scholastic one?

The political import of class was always grounded in the conviction that the working class would play a central role in bringing about a socialist society. It was therefore necessary to identify the boundaries of the working class, and to determine which other classes were its friends and opponents. It was also necessary to locate within the narrative of the struggle for socialism the fight against racial domination, and to understand the relationships between capitalism and the racial order, and between class and race. Were these inextricably intertwined? Was a post-apartheid capitalism possible? Should apartheid and capitalism be fought together, or should priority be given to the struggle against one of them or the other? There was a shared sense on the radical side that class *mattered*.

The current South African conjuncture is a curious one for class analysis. The 1990s have, from one point of view, offered a profound confirmation of the importance of class. We have seen the leading politicians and dominant capitalists of the *ancien régime* throw overboard their loyalty to white power and, still more spectacularly in the case of the Afrikaners, to their ethno-linguistic compatriots, in order to secure a deal that preserved capitalism and their own private property, jobs and pensions. Amongst Africans we have seen, under the guise of 'black empowerment', a burgeoning of the black bourgeoisie and professional elite, accompanied by a shamelessly individualistic jettisoning of solidarity with the black oppressed (Adam et al. 1997). This has occurred against the backdrop of a longer-standing deepening of inequality within the black and African populations – between labour market insiders and outsiders, between the unskilled and skilled – since the later 1970s (Crankshaw 1997; Whiteford and Van Seventer 1999). These developments disconfirmed one particular radical theory about race and class oppression: that (popular in the South African Communist Party) which held them to be inseparably entangled. But they have underlined the importance of class differentiation within national or ethnic groups; and they have fully vindicated the warnings, issuing from a certain kind of 'left' class analyst, that a two-stage, first national-democratic then socialist, struggle would yield no more than post-apartheid capitalist domination.

And yet, from the standpoint of the radical class analyst, this proof of the centrality of class proves a strangely hollow triumph. However vulnerable the 'new South Africa' to a class critique, the fact is that left class analysts are labouring under the burden of a failure, until this point, to demonstrate that a more socially egalitarian (let alone classless) social order is feasible or even definitely desirable. In the age of globalization, what is the political purchase of a critique of the new African bourgeoisie? If socialism is not possible, is capitalism under a racially mixed bourgeoisie not at least better than a capitalism dominated by white capitalists? Working class organization has not suffered the wholesale retreat in South Africa that it has in many parts of the world, and a socialist discourse lives on in parts of the labour movement. But the labour movement is far from having a plausible alternative programme, and parts of it are now being drawn into a process of capitalist class-building (through union investment in capitalist enterprises). Under a capitalist social order there is moreover the danger that the unionized black working class will come to represent a sectional interest group – and a relatively privileged one at that, in a country with massive unemployment – rather than a vehicle of universal liberation. Class analysis, and class politics more generally, thus finds itself in deep crisis even as a newly consolidating class order would appear to demand its critical scrutiny. Whether the South Africa of the future will be a decently egalitarian and civil order will depend on the capacity of the class-conscious left in the decades ahead to follow through the vindication of class analysis with an effectively egalitarian project able to lend their intellectual victory a more than Pyrrhic value.

6

South African Ethnicities

The significance of ethnicity as a topic

Notions of 'race' and 'ethnicity' have long been central to the way the people of Southern Africa have ordered their social world. While South Africa is far from being alone in exhibiting ethnic consciousness, inequalities and conflicts, South Africa was virtually unique in the post-Second World War decades, right up until 1994, in lending legal and constitutional force to ethnic difference and racial hierarchy. Moreover, ethnic differences in the country largely coincide with vast disparities of wealth and power, and they have formed focal points of violent conflict. Understanding ethnicity is thus crucial to resolving questions about how to secure social cohesion, achieve distributive justice and accommodate cultural pluralism in a democratic society such as South Africa is building. This chapter discusses the sources of ethnicity in the country, the extent of its significance and the problems of accommodating it in the post-apartheid political order.

Ethnic discourse in South Africa

That South Africa is a country where racial and other forms of ethnic talk figure prominently is unsurprising given the country's eleven widely spoken languages and diversity of African, European and Asian ancestries. This talk is not however simply about 'difference'; the hierarchical ranking of the ethnically 'different' ensures that it is also about the rationalization and criticism of power. Before 1994 South Africa was dominated by a white racial oligarchy; and until the present there is a wealth and income hierarchy which has Anglophone whites at the top and below them, in descending order, Afrikaners, Indians, coloureds and, at the bottom, Africans. Before 1994 these ethnic hierarchies were sustained in part by force, but in important measure also by ideologies of ethnicity.

From the outset of colonization in the 1650s Europeans controlled political power and disproportionate wealth in areas under their jurisdiction and felt themselves both different and superior to non-Europeans. Their dominance was not initially understood by them in purely racial terms: in the early Cape status depended in considerable measure on whether one was slave or free, heathen or Christian, 'civilized' or 'barbarous'. In time however racial categories superseded these others. Non-Europeans were increasingly marginalized in colonial society even when they were freed from slavery, Christianized or educated (see Chapter 1). Race superimposed itself also on other ethnic divisions: Europeans made common cause against blacks despite their own internal linguistic differences; Africans too came to recognize a common identity across language lines, as did coloureds and Indians.

Despite this developing 'race' consciousness, and the influence of social Darwinism from the later nineteenth century, the white effort to legitimate racial domination in South Africa rarely depended upon a clearly articulated theory of biological race hierarchy. While a majority of whites from early on considered blacks inferior, they did not always provide explicit doctrinal justification of their attitude; and such doctrines as were around included religious and culturally nationalist ones. Assorted forms of biological race thinking found expression in twentieth-century political and intellectual discourse, for example in the developing university discipline of physical anthropology and in the criminology of Geoff Cronjé, influential in Afrikaner nationalist circles in the 1930s and 1940s (Dubow 1995). However during the twentieth century Anglophone, African traditionalist and, later, Afrikaner elites mostly came to articulate (for their separate reasons) versions of a culturally essentialist rather than openly racist position (Dubow 1995: 246). Emphasizing differences of language, belief and way of life rather than biological distinctions between people, they drew on the authority especially of cultural anthropologists to rationalize racial segregation and later apartheid. Both whites and many Africans justified pre-1948 segregation as (*inter alia*) an alternative to the destructive clash of cultures in urban areas. Its proponents rejected teleologies that implied that Africans were fated either for permanent subjection or else to disappear through cultural assimilation or physical decline. Rather Africans were (as they saw it) associated with a distinctive culture which needed space to develop separately, albeit under white guardianship (Dubow 1989: ch. 1). Radical Afrikaner nationalist thinking from the 1930s ran with this idea, partly under the influence of European, especially German, romantic nationalist thought. It pictured Africans not as a homogeneous race or as an amalgam of primitive 'tribes' but as made up of distinctive and primordial 'ethnic' groups each destined, like the Afrikaners themselves, for nationhood and eventual statehood. Afrikaner nationalists thus projected their self-understanding onto others (Dubow 1995: ch. 7; Norval 1996: ch. 3).

In practice 'ethnicity' often came to serve in white discourse as a proxy for biological race rather than as a definitive alternative to it. The fact that under apartheid whites were assigned a single state, despite their diversity of language, religious denomination and national origin, belied the notion that Nationalists gave priority to cultural ethnicity over race, as did the fact that they focused their alarm on miscegenation between racial rather than, say, linguistic groups. The National Party in power was notorious for its efforts to codify racial (along with certain other ethnic) boundaries in law. The doctrine of a non-hierarchical ethnic pluralism, though sincerely believed in by some Afrikaner intellectuals and politicians, was used to justify white power and privilege before audiences of blacks, foreign critics and whites themselves. It 'explained', above all, the confinement of African national political rights to ethnic 'homelands'.

The transparently rationalizing or 'ideological' function of the doctrine of 'separate development', and its attempt to divide Africans into irreducibly different sub-African ethnicities, thoroughly discredited ethnic talk in the eyes of much of the black opposition camp in the post-Second World War years. The most militant and popular currents countered visions of multiple ethnic fragmentation with more inclusive discourses of African, black or non-racial unity. Nevertheless blacks in South Africa did not invariably refuse racial and ethnic categorization or acknowledge it only pragmatically. The divisions between coloured, Indian and African were internalized to varying degrees by designated (or self-designated) members of these groups, both leader and led, throughout the twentieth century. They remain widely accepted now. Discourses of sub-African ethnicity too have enjoyed a resonance amongst Africans, especially amongst rural traditionalists, migrants and the newly urbanized. To some extent, indeed, ethnic identities were forged or negotiated from within (by ethnic mobilizers) and from below (by people in everyday interaction). This popular authoring and internalization of ethnic boundaries contributed to the stabilization of white rule by dividing blacks and legitimating some of the white state's ethnocentric talk. At the same time, the unifying power of ethnicity could, where directed vertically against the dominant rather than horizontally at ethnically different fellow subordinates, provide a resource of opposition to white power, or at least to its capricious exercise. This was certainly true of larger and more inclusive (racial) ethnicities like black or African, but held for sub-African ethnicity too; most obviously true of modernist ethnic politics but true also of its traditionalist counterparts (Beinart 1987; Beinart and Bundy 1987; Delius 1993; Moodie 1994; Harries 1994). In the late nineteenth and early twentieth century the simple fact of sub-African ethnic identification constituted a form of defiance in the face of white efforts to dispossess and disperse African chiefdoms (Keegan 1986b: 239-49; Delius 1989).

Defining race and ethnicity

What is a race group, what an ethnic? The two terms are sometimes treated as though the former was simply an example of the latter, at other times as though they refer to different phenomena. When considered as different, members of a 'race' are typically assumed to share biological characteristics, whereas members of an 'ethnic group' are assumed to share non-biological attributes such as language, religion and aesthetic culture. Thus in South Africa whites, Africans and coloureds, perhaps Indians, are thought of as 'races' because of their distinctive physical features whereas Zulus, Xhosas, Sotho, Tswana and Afrikaners are considered ethnic groups because they are demarcated by shared languages and histories.

Despite the prevalence in popular consciousness of notions of race, it is not possible to find satisfactory biological definitions of racially labelled groups. Earlier efforts to distinguish races in Africa and trace their movements through time by way of a variety of disciplines from linguistics to craniology eventually ran aground (Dubow 1995: chs 2, 3). The evidence of contemporary genetics suggests that groups referred to as 'races' are both formed and their boundaries in turn blurred by complex patterns of genetic mixing over time, facilitated by cultural and economic contact as well as conquest. There are no pure or bounded races. In South Africa 'passing for white' by coloureds has, for example, ensured that there is a component of non-European genes in the white Afrikaner population (Giliomee 1989c: 22). In centuries past Bantu-speaking mixed farmers genetically assimilated Khoisan (Hall 1987: ch. 5; Crais 1992: 14-18). The coloured category itself is far too ancestrally diverse to constitute a coherent biological race group by any yardstick, and is in effect a catch-all category.

If races do not exist as clearly recognizable *biological* entities, the effort to define them *legally* has proved no less fraught. The Population Registration Act of 1950, which provided the racial classification system used in the apartheid era, was forced to rely on openly subjective criteria (such as 'generally accepted as' and 'obviously is') to define whites and blacks/Africans (and coloureds, by a process of exclusion). Its system of classification was complicated by provisions for the subdivision of blacks and coloureds into 'ethnic or other groups', 'classes' and 'tribes' determined in similar ways to races. The Act was amended numerous times to accommodate definitional anomalies and sanctioned a process whereby a Race Classification Board annually reclassified hundreds of applicants from one group to another. The apartheid government was moreover forced to use a different system of racial classification for purposes of enforcing its principal instrument of urban segregation, the Group Areas Act of 1950, mainly because its framers wished to impose a common racial definition on mixed couples who had been living together prior to the passage of the Mixed Marriages and Immorality Acts of 1949 and 1950. It thus became possible to be a member of more than one statutory race simultaneously. To add to this confusion, legislation permitted the State President to create new 'ethnic, linguistic, cultural or other' groups by proclamation (West 1988).

From the famous absurdity of all this it should not be deduced that racial labels are simple fictions without reference points in the real world. There are patterns of genetic lineage more likely to predominate in some racially labelled groups than in others. Coloureds, for example, have proportionately far more Khoisan and ex-slave genes than individuals assigned to other apartheid-designated ethnic groups; similarly whites have far more European genes. There are aggregate differences of physical appearance between 'races' which an ethnocentric culture trains South Africans to spot. Certain heritable diseases afflict some 'races' more than others.

Race is, however, a social construction in at least two crucial senses. Firstly, the allocation of people to race groups is decided in difficult cases through the subjective recognition of individuals as belonging to one or another group, and the markers that trigger recognition are not always physical ones. Secondly, and perhaps more importantly, societies confer significance on some physical traits rather than others. In South African history the distinction between European descendants and others was developed because it served a variety of ends, both material and psychological (see below). It did so above all for the white population which had the power to impress its racial definitions on the real world through law and violence.

Because of the social and subjective dimension of race, a question arises as to whether it is distinguishable from ethnicity. In many circumstances race and ethnicity are interchangeably used terms or refer to overlapping phenomena. The term 'ethnic group' typically indicates a population that shares not only cultural forms – few for example would refer to the world's Christians as an ethnic group – but also a common historical origin, traceable, say, to a particular region or state. This sense of shared ancestry, and the fact that members of ethnically-labelled groups not uncommonly discourage converts or 'marrying out', aligns the cultural concept of ethnicity more closely with race, without however rendering them identical. South Africa's Afrikaners illustrate well the fuzziness that can mark the ethnicity/race boundary as conventionally rendered. The predominant tendency amongst Afrikaner intellectuals has been to emphasize Afrikaner cultural rather than biological identity, and Afrikaner nationalist governments classified Afrikaners with other whites in a single statutory race group. Yet understood as an historical culture – one marked by a shared Afrikaans language and affiliation to reformed churches – Afrikaners are difficult to distinguish from a majority of coloureds. That Afrikaners (uneasily) exclude coloureds from their ranks suggests that they consider themselves a race or at least descent group of sorts, with an ancestry traceable to the Dutch, German and Huguenot settlers who arrived under Dutch colonial rule. The similarity of many coloureds to Afrikaners culturally, and the admixture of coloured genes in the Afrikaner population, made coloureds seem more rather than less threatening to some Afrikaners. Post-1948 legislation banning inter-racial miscegenation and marriage was framed above all with the clearer racial demarcation of whites and coloureds in mind.

The option preferred here is to understand race as a form of ethnicity (as also do Bekker 1993: 18; Bickford-Smith 1995: 3-4), and the term ethnicity will be used generically to encompass both racial and cultural ethnicity. The distinction between racial and other kinds of ethnicity is nevertheless an important one in South African history and politics. As writers like Ashforth and Norval have shown, it mattered whether ruling groups conceived of whites and Africans as homogeneous or composed of distinctive sub-racial ethnicities. It also mattered whether anti-apartheid oppositionists understood their constituency as Zulu, African, 'black' (in the sense of encompassing African, coloureds and Indians) or South African.

A distinction is made in this and other chapters between relatively more encompassing and relatively more particularistic ethnicities: between *large* and *small* ethnicities. The racial ethnicities will usually be found amongst the large ethnicities, and they are often considered unifying compared to smaller ethnicities. Post-1948 apartheid ideologues were dedicated to unscrambling the larger ethnicities of black and African but were inconsistent on the question of whether whites too were divided into (two or more) smaller ethnicities. By contrast black opponents of apartheid struggled to forge larger ethnicities, the largest of them all being the non-racial one of 'South African'. Ethnic categories within racial ones – Afrikaner, Jewish, Malay, Griqua, Hindu, Xhosa, Zulu, Sotho and Tswana – constitute small ethnicities, though they may be large relative to still smaller units based, say, on clan or chiefdom, like Pondo. The spatial metaphor of small and large captures well the relational character of ethnicity (see below).

The formation of ethnicities

Where do racial and other ethnic identities come from? Is ethnic-national identification essentially a modern product – elicited perhaps by the industrial-era demand for unified labour and product markets, the spread of literacy and printed matter, or universalistic notions about the 'rights of men' to national self-determination (Anderson 1983; Gellner 1983)? Or is it a residue of primordial religious, linguistic and territorial affinities (Smith 1986)? Those in the large literature on the subject who adopt the first stance tend to stress the malleable, situational and political character of ethnicity, whereas the primordialists stress its antiquity and durability. Adherents of both positions might recognize that the nationalist movements of the nineteenth century and subsequently represented a new kind of phenomenon associated with the rise of the nation-state. They are liable to disagree over whether modern nationalism involved the creation of a new high culture that suppressed a range of particularisms or whether it simply brought longstanding ethnic affiliations to a modern fruition. In South Africa a range of liberals and, unsurprisingly, ethnic nationalists tended towards a primordial account of Afrikaner nationalism and a timeless and static view of African cultures. Others, liberal as well as radical, have attempted to demonstrate the relatively late crystallization of Afrikaner, African and coloured identification and political mobilization.

From one point of view it is obvious that many of South Africa's ethnic identities could only be 'modern'. White settlers of the Company period mostly lost their sentimental ties to the much older European societies from which they sprang, and Afrikaner nationalism could not have pre-dated the arrival of the British 'other' in 1795. Indians only began *arriving* in the 1860s. Coloured identity could only become widespread once more primordial Khoi, San and slave cultures had very largely disappeared. Even the central conflict between Europeans and blacks of various categories goes back no further than the later seventeenth century (in the case of the Khoisan) or later eighteenth century (in the case of the Bantu-speaking mixed farmers). The only surviving ethnic identities that might potentially have stretched back unbrokenly into a very distant past *within* the region are those associated with sub-African ethnicity: that is, the various regional, linguistic and customary subdivisions of the Bantu-speaking peoples.

Yet even leaving aside sub-African ethnicity, there are some debates to be had around the issue of primordial versus invented. Primordiality is relative. The Afrikaner nationalist version of primordialism traced the development of an Afrikaner identity to events as distant as the Slachters Nek Rebellion of 1815 or, more typically, the 'Great Trek' of the 1830s. Some, both Afrikaner and Anglophone writers, have taken the story back even further, to the emergence on the isolated South African frontier of the eighteenth century of a primitive form of Calvinism from which Afrikaners were to derive a sense of being a 'chosen people'. More recent research has shown, however, that the forms of Calvinism associated with later Afrikaner nationalism were products of the later nineteenth century (Du Toit 1983, 1985). Afrikaans only displaced Dutch as a language of 'high culture' amongst Dutch-Afrikaners as a result of protracted struggles by a language movement which stretched into the early twentieth century (Hofmeyr 1987). Until the late nineteenth century Dutch-Afrikaners were moreover divided between those remaining in the Cape and those linked to various waves of emigrants to the interior. Amongst Cape-based Dutch-Afrikaners some were keener than others to hold on to the colony's British connections.

Even after it had clearly emerged, Afrikaner nationalism had to be sustained against pressures of fragmentation. Nationalists in the Transvaal struggled to overcome bitter class divisions especially in the countryside, and Afrikaners fought on opposite sides in the South African War and 1914 rebellion. Afrikaner nationalism was divided in the twentieth century, as in the late nineteenth century Cape, between currents committed to white unity (dominant between 1907 and 1934) and to Afrikaner particularism (ascendant between 1948 and 1960). O'Meara may be wrong to locate the origins of contemporary Afrikaner nationalism in the 1930s, but the movement did experience, from around the middle of that decade, a renewed radicalization. There can be no doubt that a widely-felt Afrikaner group consciousness was achieved and endured over much of the twentieth century, bolstered by a shared language and conservative religion, a fear of black advance, feelings of political and economic grievance against the English and (not least) a passion for rugby. Even so, the primordial view exaggerates the earliness of the Afrikaner ethno-national phenomenon as well as its pervasiveness and stability over time.

Ethnic identification amongst non-Afrikaner whites (those of British, Portuguese, Greek, Italian, Jewish etc. ancestry) is at one level more 'primordial' than that of Afrikaners in that it remains tied, sometimes with considerable passion, to older European nationalities and cultures. However it tended to be correspondingly looser, less politicized, and in public life at least often subsumed by Anglophone or, more typically, white European identity.

Though there was a strong strain of British imperial identification until relatively recently, British South Africanism never formed the basis of a coherent and sustained ethnicity or powerful autonomous political force. It was nourished by pride in empire, status-consciousness, resentment of Afrikaner political power and by English-language institutions. Nevertheless it was fractured from early on in the Transvaal by class divisions between mine owners and immigrant skilled workers during the period from the 1890s through the first couple of decades of the twentieth century. Only in the pro-British redoubt of Natal did there develop something like a threateningly militant British patriotism, funnelled through organizations that campaigned in the 1920s and

1930s for Natal's autonomy and even secession and expressed in a strong anti-republic vote in 1960. British cultural influence in South African life persists to the present in the ethos of state English-medium white schools, support for British sports like cricket and rugby (though the latter was appropriated by Afrikaners), even in the legal requirement to drive on the left side of the road. The royal family retains a following in the country, as does British domestic soccer (by contrast the South African domestic soccer game has long been African-dominated). On the other hand British-style currency disappeared in the 1960s, imperial measures in the 1970s. Today American cultural influences are stronger than British ones amongst Anglophone whites. The loyalty to Britain of ancestrally-British whites always came under strain when the mother country showed consideration for South Africa's blacks. It grew increasingly dilute once Britain began to decolonize and the Commonwealth began to emerge as a forum numerically dominated by independent ex-colonies hostile to apartheid.

Apart from British South Africans, the white predominantly Anglophone population originated in a spread of Eastern and Southern European countries. They established in South Africa a patchwork of ethnic enclaves that shifted from the inner cities into the suburbs with gradual bourgeoisification. Though they maintained distinctive communal organizations and links with their countries and cultures of origin, they have always kept a low profile, often, as in the case of Jews, self-protectively.

Coloured identity, like that of Afrikaners, crystallized in the course of the later nineteenth century, though its emergence was only made possible by earlier processes. The key cultural preconditions for the emergence of a coloured people were the demise of indigenous Khoisan and slave cultures, sexual intermixing of Khoi, slaves and whites, the conversion of ex-slaves to Islam, early Khoi and later coloured conversion to Christianity, and the adoption of Afrikaans (which slave and Khoisan labourers helped to forge). Socio-economically the crucial formative fact was the emancipation first of Khoi indentured labour, then slaves, into shared circumstances of coercive 'free' labour and poverty between 1828 and 1838. White economic dominance, status consciousness and later government-imposed racial discrimination contributed to a sense amongst Cape blacks of shared exclusion from white society. Increasing contact with people of darker hue, occupying different labour market positions and speaking different languages, contributed in the later nineteenth century also to a sense of the distinctiveness of 'Cape coloureds' from Africans. Though there has been some disagreement about when the term coloured began to be used separately from that of African and when coloureds developed a strong sense of sectional identity, there is little doubting the modernity of coloured origins (Goldin 1987: xxvi; Bickford-Smith 1995: 31).

While Indians only arrived in South Africa from 1860 there is the question in their case of whether they brought with them and retained linguistic and regional affiliations deriving from the Indian subcontinent, or more generally identified with India (or its post-independence offshoots). The Indians were from the beginning socially, regionally and linguistically divided between the mass of mainly Hindu indentured labourers, two thirds of whom were Tamil and Telegu speakers from southern India, and the Gujerati, predominantly Muslim merchants who arrived later as voluntary 'passengers'. Though these differences expressed themselves in distinctive political styles there were relatively few manifestations of explicitly Hindu mobilization against Indian Muslims (Swan 1985: ch. 5). Aspects of Indian subcontinental culture endured in Hindu and Muslim worship and an emphasis on extended families. Awareness of caste lingered in social interaction. However a more encompassing 'Indian' or 'Asian' identity was much more likely to be mobilized politically, spearheaded by organizations like the Natal Indian Congress.

While bodies like the NIC were typically led by elites whose religious, caste and regional background differed from that of the mass of Indians, their mobilizing discourses stressed Indian unity. While racist policies impacted on them differentially, Indians shared a degree of oppression in common. All Indians were denied the vote until 1984. Until about 1960 most white governments treated Indians as an alien rather than indigenous element whose fate was properly one of repatriation. The Indians themselves retained a degree of identification with India, the colonial-era politicians and post-independence governments of which came to their defence in diplomatic arenas. Indians continue to enjoy Indian film and music (Freund 1995). They were therefore never deracinated in the fashion of the slave and aboriginal predecessors of the coloureds. They did however absorb selective elements of the dominant culture: the Indians of South Africa stand out for the quite remarkable degree of Anglicization they underwent during the twentieth century. If South African Indian culture has ancient roots, its contemporary expression is closely shaped by South African conditions.

The strongest case for primordialism in South Africa is the one that can be made for the sub-African ethnic groups. These speak different Bantu languages with roots traceable back many hundreds of years, and they are associated with distinctive marriage rules, settlement patterns, aesthetic cultures, diets and more (Maylam 1986: chs 2, 3; Hall 1987). Certainly many both amongst white observers and Africans are inclined to think of African ethnic groups as discrete 'tribes' inheriting long established and relatively changeless traditions deeply inscribed still in the African mentality (providing ready-made explanations for 'faction fights' on the mines, or for violent battles between supporters of the African National Congress and Inkatha). It is now convincingly argued that the boundaries between African linguistic and cultural groups were far more graded and moveable than a picture of immutable and bounded ethnicities suggests. African societies sought and absorbed followers from other groups. The southern

Sotho under Moshoeshoe in the nineteenth century generated a composite nation from ethnically disparate refugees (Eldredge 1993: 196), while the Zulus brought in others by conquest. The nineteenth-century Ndundza Ndebele chiefdom was an amalgam of Sotho and Nguni elements (Delius 1989: 229-30).

Sub-African ethnicity as it has come down to us is the product of both 'primordial' and relatively modern developments. Contemporary sub-African ethnicity bears a substantial impress of a number of modern processes, from nineteenth-century African state formation to white conquest and indirect rule. Some of the boundaries between ethnic groups familiar today were fixed by missionaries, transcribers, ethnologists and administrators issuing from white society (Vail 1989: 11-14; Beck 1997: 117, 120). Others were generated and deepened in the course of resistance to whites (Keegan 1986b: 239-49; Delius 1989). Segregation and apartheid policy-makers reworked sub-African ethnic cultures to suit the purposes of white conquerors (Welsh 1971: 171; Dubow 1989: 111-19; Mamdani 1996: ch. 2). White state efforts to fix the boundaries and subjects of ethnic 'homelands' provided occasions for the revival and refashioning of ethnic identities (Streek 1984; Harries 1989; Murray 1992: 157; Bank 1995). At the same time the inventors of modern sub-African ethnicity, whether white or black, tapped into pre-existing beliefs, practices and institutions which were not limitlessly malleable and conditioned the reception of later ethnic talk. The 'homelands' established by apartheid policy-makers enjoyed a definite territorial and institutional continuity with pre-conquest African chiefdoms, and white ideologues and planners drew upon existing African models of government and law in devising methods of rule in the reserves (Beinart 1994; Hamilton 1998). Whites did not invent African ethnicity out of thin air, and nor indeed did late twentieth-century African ethnic mobilizers like Mangosuthu Buthelezi.

There is evidence that ethnic identity is situational. Ethnic groups should be viewed not only as collectives but as aggregations of individuals who each are at the intersection of, and draw upon, a repertoire of identities of which ethnic identity is but one. Individuals are inclined to highlight the identities appropriate to the situations in which they find themselves – as workers, businessmen, men, women, villagers, urbanites or whatever. In the bulk of cases non-ethnic identities do not challenge the ethnic one but are, say, contained within or irrelevant to it. There are however occasions when ethnic and non-ethnic identity needs clash, and in some such instances the ethnic identity either gives way or expediently mutates. The African women of the Khosi Bay area identify themselves as Tsonga because Tsonga tradition accords women higher status than the Zulu tradition adopted by their Zulu speaking migrant worker husbands (Webster 1991). African men in Grahamstown invoke the old Xhosa customs of polygyny and non-intimacy between spouses to justify their very contemporary urban predilection for philandering, whereas their wives argue instead for a modern concept of affective monogamous marriage (Van der Vliet 1991). In the former QwaQwa 'homeland' ruling groups shifted between an inclusive South Sotho identity and a narrower Bakwena clan identity depending on which suited their political purposes (Bank 1995).

A particular feature of South Africa is the presence of competing concentric circles of ethno-national identification – the rivalry between small and large ethnicities. If the small ethnicities tend to be associated with commonalities of language, custom and aesthetic culture, the larger tend to be associated with what in South African terms are racial identities as well as with a kind of inclusive proto-South African civic nationalism. This distinction coincides in South Africa, though particularly amongst Africans, with that between relatively more primordial and recently invented ethnicities. It is a telling indication of the limits of primordialism in South Africa that, in the case of blacks at least, the smaller and more primordial ethnicities – Zulu, Xhosa, Sotho and so on – have conceded considerable ground over the decades to the larger and more modern ones – African, black, South African. In the case of whites the trend is more complicated, since inclusive white identification had to see off Afrikaner and Anglophone sectionalism not once but twice – first under the later Hertzog regime and the United Party, and then, from 1960, as the Afrikaner NP began connecting to a wider white constituency. By the 1980s 'tribal' voting amongst whites had substantially broken down.

The pull of ethnicity

Ethnic identity in South Africa may not be static or in any simple sense primordial, but it is certainly widely and deeply embedded in the consciousness of South Africans and a basis for their collective allegiance and action. How do we account for its attraction? One popular answer to this question in the South African case is materialist (in the narrowly economic sense). Radical writers in the 1970s and early 1980s argued that ethnic mobilization succeeded (where it did) above all because it served the material or economic interests of ethnic leaders and their constituents. Radicals tried to show that where it did not do so ethnic solidarity could fail to develop or would be liable to break down. There is certainly a powerful case to be made for the economic-material basis of ethnic consciousness in South Africa.

On the whole it made economic sense for less well-off whites in South African history to identify with better-off whites and to distinguish themselves from blacks; and it mostly made sense for better-off whites to reciprocate this racial solidarity. The white settlers who first arrived in the Cape aspired to become independent farmers, and by identifying with those phenotypically and culturally similar to themselves against those different they attained several ends. Firstly, they avoided a Hobbesian war of all against all by establishing a coherent (white) civil society capable of maintaining order and engaging in collective action, such as fighting for access to land and water against external others. Secondly, by drawing a boundary around a small (white) section of the population, they could limit the number of people with whom they would have to share scarce land and water resources while simultaneously maximizing the numbers of those (the black outsiders) who could be defined as their labourers. Thirdly, by appealing to an us/them distinction they could dehumanize and demonize the 'other' sufficiently to justify to themselves treating them oppressively. Finally, by identifying with those enjoying recourse to European imperial power they could place themselves on the winning side in battles for land and labour.

When South Africa developed an urban industrial economy and a section of the white population was forced into the working class, it equally made sense for white workers to show solidarity with their racial own. By doing so they could hope to create a self-contained labour market insulated from the competition of cheap labour and demarcate a collectivity sufficiently small for its privileges to be affordable to employers and the state. For white owners this protection of white workers imposed an economic cost but it helped stabilize capitalist society and secure agents of control in the working class. It was anyway the by-product of a political institution which underwrote the privilege of all whites and which owners (like state managers) had no wish to overturn: a franchise largely or entirely confined to whites (see Chapters 2 and 5).

Material-economic interests can reasonably be imputed to others seeking to demarcate themselves ethnically. When 'Cape coloureds' found their fate linked to that of other blacks after the South African War, they had strong material reasons to reassert their separateness from Africans in particular. Africans were from the beginning of a unified South Africa subject to greater state oppression. White political elites promised coloureds, indeed delivered, preferential treatment compared to Africans (Goldin 1987). Cheap African labour undercut coloured labour (Lewis 1987: 161, 171), and from African competition the state offered coloured workers some protection. It treated coloureds ostensibly as 'civilized labour' in the interwar years and, from 1955 until 1984, attempted to limit African employment in the western Cape, where coloureds were concentrated (Goldin 1987: chs 5, 7, 10; Humphries 1989). The oppressions heaped on coloureds (especially by post-1948 NP governments) provided an incentive for coloureds to identify downward with Africans, and some did especially amongst the frustrated middle classes. However, the coloured working class arguably had more to lose than gain from African political and economic advance. The NP presided over a substantial improvement in coloured living standards in the 1970s and 1980s (Giliomee 1994b: 51-2; Mattes et al. 1996: 110-13). The tricameral political system, which gave coloureds access to new forms of patronage from 1984, probably strengthened their sense of relative advantage over Africans. By contrast African-dominated government in the 1990s clearly threatened it.

The state did not grant Indians the same degree of protection from African competition that coloureds were given. Indians nevertheless acquired a position of relative economic advantage over Africans. They did so thanks initially to skills and connections brought over from India and commercial opportunities afforded by Natal's Indian immigrant and African markets (Bhana 1985: 245-6, 252). Indians entering the urban labour market from the interwar period onwards derived an advantage over Africans from their relatively rapid urbanization and Anglicization. Indians received a further boost from the 1960s by way of state-provided mass secondary and technical education (Freund 1995: 78, 84, 90). Africans and Indians were in many instances economic competitors and antagonists. Cheap African labour threatened to undercut Indian industrial workers in the 1930s and 1940s, while Africans encountered Indians as landlords, traders and better-off workers (Freund 1995: 38, 41, ch. 6). Resentments arising from these differentials fuelled incidents of Indian–African intercommunal violence in 1949 and 1985. From an early stage Indian economic advance also elicited the hostility of competing white traders (Bhana 1985) and workers (Freund 1995: 47-8). Material factors – Indian economic competitiveness and more especially the hostility it earned – thus underpinned Indians' sense of exclusion from white society and their fear of and sense of superiority over Africans. From 1984 the incorporation of Indians into the tricameral parliament and segmentary self-government opened up new avenues for Indians (as for coloureds) to seek patronage and advantage from a set-up that excluded Africans.

Sub-African ethnic identity could also service a variety of material needs. For traditional elites, actively maintaining it was a precondition of preserving their control of land and access to wealth in the reserves (McAllister 1991). State support for the 'homeland' system gave a material stake in the ethnic order to reserve-based African bureaucratic elites, both traditional and otherwise (Murray 1992: 156-7). More westernized elites could find advantage in allying with those traditional rulers who enjoyed popular legitimacy. Thus the conservative Zulu middle class found in the Zulu monarchy a source of patronage, political leverage and a bulwark against a radicalizing proletariat (Marks 1986; Keegan 1986b: 239-49; Cope 1993, ch. 8). Aspirant peasants could use real or imagined ethnic connections to procure land, for example identifying with chiefs pursuing territorial claims or making land purchases on behalf of 'their' people (Keegan 1986b: 239-49; Bank 1995). Male migrant workers could see in the system of traditional rule in the reserves a mechanism for securing and maintaining access to rural resources and for controlling their women (Vail 1989: 14-15), while ethnic support and information networks helped them to navigate through urban labour markets (Delius 1993: 126-40).

Sub-African ethnicity also served white material interests. Mine owners valued chiefs' co-operation in labour recruitment, the role of traditional authorities in maintaining compound discipline and the informal subsidy to their workers' wage, housing and social security costs that followed from migrants' continued attachment to ethnic reserves. Urban employers of less skilled labour generally preferred the disciplined 'tribal' African to more discriminating and assertive urban African youth (Posel 1991: 158-64).

Afrikaner ethnic identity has received close attention from materialist analysts keen to refute the arguments of those, both insiders and critics, who considered it to possess a largely spiritual or metaphysical basis. O'Meara famously subjected to materialist scrutiny the radical Afrikaner nationalism that achieved political consummation with the electoral victory of the NP in 1948. He showed it to have as one of its driving forces a northern Afrikaner petit bourgeoisie frustrated by its marginal position in the Anglophone-dominated state bureaucracy and urban economy and keen to build a base of political and economic power. This stratum was uneasily allied to the more bourgeois Afrikaner nationalism of the western Cape agricultural, financial and press establishment. These twin core social groups of Afrikaner nationalism secured the support of the mass of Afrikaner workers and Afrikaner maize farmers principally (and only after sustained struggle) by appealing to their material-economic interests, promising improved African labour supplies and other support to farmers and greater economic protection to unskilled white workers. In power, O'Meara noted, the Afrikaner nationalists built up a northern Afrikaner bourgeoisie and greatly expanded the proportion of Afrikaners in professional, white-collar and supervisory jobs. By the late 1960s better-off Afrikaners had come to see an enlightened self-interest in political reform away from apartheid, the protection of which they no longer needed; and increasingly they marginalized from the Afrikaner ruling coalition the rump Afrikaner working class and poorer farmers dependent on state subsidies. This class differentiation helped, O'Meara, Charney and others argued, to shatter Afrikaner unity (O'Meara 1983, 1996; Charney 1984, 1987) (see Chapter 4).

O'Meara's account has been criticized for economic and class reductionism, and some of its details have been questioned. Critics have cast doubt on the centrality of the economic movement to northern Afrikaner nationalism and of Afrikaner finance to the Cape party and questioned whether class rivalries in the Nationalist coalition could explain key controversies and fissures. They have also emphasized continuities between the Afrikaner nationalism of the 1930s and that of earlier periods forged in different material conditions (Giliomee 1983, 1992; Lazar 1987) and cast doubt on materialist explanations of Afrikaner disunity in the 1980s (Giliomee 1992).

Interestingly, however, Giliomee, who has been one of the more relentless critics of O'Meara's reductionism, has himself given a lead in highlighting material forces at work in the birth of the first phase of Afrikaner nationalism. Giliomee argued that Afrikaner national consciousness in the western Cape grew in the 1870s and 1880s in part out of the material grievances of Dutch-Afrikaner commercial farmers who failed to obtain economic protection and repressive labour legislation from a state dominated by Anglophone politicians and merchants. It grew also out of antagonisms between British banks and poorer Dutch-Afrikaner farmers, and the efforts of Dutch-Afrikaner financial and legal middlemen to mobilize the savings of Afrikaners in support of local banking institutions. Anglophone-Afrikaner tensions were heightened during periods of economic difficulty in the farming sector. The exclusivist Afrikaner nationalism that gathered momentum in the Cape from 1915 thus mobilized a consciousness initially forged to an 'important extent' (Giliomee 1989b: 79) by material considerations (Giliomee 1989b,c).

The movement of Afrikaner linguistic revival in the later colonial Cape and early twentieth-century South Africa was itself impelled in part by material concerns. Its leaders were Afrikaner school teachers, church ministers, journalists and writers who feared that they would lose their pupils, congregations and readers, and hence their material livelihoods and social status, if Anglicization and the cultural degeneration of poor Afrikaners continued unchecked (Hofmeyr 1987; Giliomee 1989c: 48).

The attraction of the material-economic explanation of ethnic identity and conflict in South Africa is obvious: its ethnic groups are not only economically 'ranked' but the dominant groups have exploited the subordinate groups as a (mainly cheap) labour force. In many other countries, however, ethnic conflicts have little to do with either labour exploitation by the dominant ethnic group (Israel and Northern Ireland for example) or deep inequalities (Belgium, Quebec, the Basque country, Catalonia). The comparative evidence thus invites a degree of caution about the sufficiency of economic explanation (Connor 1994: ch. 6); it may indeed be that the very plausibility of material-economic explanation in South Africa masks other factors contributing to ethnic identification and conflict in the country.

A second reason for caution about material-economic accounts is that they do not seem sufficient to explain the intensities of feeling associated with ethnic mobilization. A much cited example of this is the outpouring of emotion surrounding the Afrikaner *eufees* of 1938 organized to mark the centenary of the Great Trek (Moodie 1975: ch. 9). Wars are another kind of event that could bring ethno-communal emotions to a high pitch, as they did for Dutch-Afrikaners in the 1870s, during the South African War and two World Wars. Rather than flowing from material sentiments, emotions on such occasions could rise above the mundane plane on which material considerations operate. Again, the heartfelt way in which Afrikaner intellectuals debated finer philosophical points and moral questions from the 1930s suggests an importance for ideas and idealism not readily assimilable to strictly material-economic concerns (Lazar 1987). O'Meara may be right to suggest that these debates were of little interest to workers and farmers, but he still needs to explain their relevance to a petit bourgeoisie to whom he mistakenly attributed almost exclusively material-economic motivations. The willingness of human beings to sacrifice life and liberty for ethno-national causes – as in the South African War or the Inkatha-ANC feud – is another phenomenon not readily illuminated by a model of individuals as rationally self-interested. (The ranks of self-sacrificers are not after all confined to those who have nothing to lose materially.) It may be that materialist behaviour operates at the level of aggregates (like classes) rather than individuals, but this then leaves to be addressed the relationship between collective action and its microfoundations in individual behaviour.

Some of those who reject economic-materialist explanations have in recent times preferred to understand ethnicity as a discourse bearing its own internal logic and shaping the social world rather than being influenced or determined by external forces. This is, like the materialist, a constructionist argument but one that focuses on the shaping powers of language rather than on the economic. It is in these terms that Kinghorn speaks of the centrality of the Tower of Babel story to Afrikaner thinking about ethnic mixing and Norval elaborates a 'discourse' of ethnicity associated with Afrikaner nationalism (Kinghorn 1994; Norval 1996). From such work there springs no general theory of the resonance of ethnicity, though there do issue useful reminders of the importance of the stories, or narratives, which ethnic politicians and actors tell about themselves and their 'people'. In practice those writing in this tradition are unable to avoid invoking the force of events that impinge on discourse from the outside, such as urbanization and war. Ethnicity, and race, are interpretative acts: they are never simply caused or sufficiently explained by forces 'out there'. All the same if ethnic discourse is to achieve acceptance as a basis for collective identity and action it must speak to worlds of experience fashioned by forces – economic, demographic, and so on – which challenge some interpretations and lend plausibility to others. It must also speak to human needs that may be transcultural.

An alternative critique of material-economic explanations, and the one preferred here, proceeds from an insistence on the importance of the psychological or 'human nature'. From this standpoint the problem with the Marxist and other material-economic accounts of ethnicity flows not from the limitations of material explanation as such but from the limits of a conception of the material that extends only to the economic. There is non-economic material in the world too, none more important to whom we are than our historically evolved brain. The brain we now know to be malleable, and in constant interaction with its social environment, but it, and aspects of our psychology, can also be considered the products of more glacial processes of environmental adaptation not subject to radical reordering on a short time-scale. Can we generalize about some of the more 'transcultural' and durable psychological needs which ethnic identity addresses?

One is likely to be a need for human interaction. As social creatures humans seek group association partly for material-economic support, but also for companionship. The desire for companionship may *itself* be functional to the satisfaction of material requirements, but to reduce it to its material functionality is to impose a hidden purpose on a desire which is exclusively for its own object. It is also fallaciously to derive a materially useful purpose from a materially useful effect.

Ethnic association recommends itself to people seeking both practical and affective group interaction. A common language allows undemanding conversation and co-ordination of tasks. Common values minimize emotionally hurtful challenges and misunderstandings. Shared histories multiply common points of reference, facilitating gossip, humour and reminiscence. In the course of interaction there are likely to develop feelings of mutual loyalty and obligation. These commonalities are liable to become more important to people in the course of their encounters with strangers and with processes that threaten to dissolve established bonds. Encounters with both are likely to occur in the context of urbanization which inspired, amongst both urbanizing Africans and Afrikaners, efforts to recreate, in the urban (and compound) setting, bonds associated with more familiar or remembered rural places. As elsewhere in the world, a part of the ethnic segregation of South African towns, cities and labour markets was voluntary, a result of ethnic 'kin' gathering together and drawing on shared information and support networks.

In the rural village or on the farm bonds between the culturally similar are often direct and intimate. Ethnicity in an urban context may preserve or regenerate intimate bonds (as with African youth associations), but in addition it builds on 'imagined' bonds between larger numbers of individuals who are strangers but now 'recognize' their commonality for the first time as they interact and compete with others. South Africa's systems of enforced ethnic segregation would undoubtedly have made these bonds seem more tangible, and, since proximity aids intimacy, it would have strengthened the tendency to seek conviviality amongst those ethnically alike. Ethnically segmented urban labour markets also added to the temptation to seek material support and intimacy among ethnic fellows.

Secondly, humans seek existential explanation. The adaptive mechanism of a large brain denies us, almost certainly more than it does any other animal, a capacity to live simply as things, or just for the moment. It allows us an awareness of past and future, birth and death, and induces a need to understand the 'purpose' of lives that are in reality mere accidents. Humans yearn to locate themselves within stories that begin before birth and continue beyond death (Anderson 1983). Religion offers stories conferring mystique on the earthly historical narratives of peoples such as Afrikaners, while nationalism supplies a shared past and future and a sense of collective significance. As the cases of Afrikaners and Zulus illustrate, ethnic nationalist stories work especially well where they can draw upon collective 'memories' of heroic leaders, battles and martyrs (Thompson 1985: chs 4, 5; Maré 1993: ch. 4; Hamilton 1998: introduction, ch. 1).

A third need satisfied by ethnic identity is for external affirmation or status. Individuals can seek status directly for themselves but also through identification with a group that carries high status (either in its own eyes or those of others). The value of status may lie in its capacity to bring sexual reproductive success, secure the service or loyalty of others and win advantaged positions in 'pecking orders' amongst those making claims on scarce resources. The according of status to others to whom one is linked in some fashion for its part allows the weak to identify vicariously with the strong and benefit from their leadership and patronage.

Whatever its origin or function, the evidence of status consciousness in South Africa is not hard to find. In relation to blacks, whites historically enjoyed the status that came attached to wealth, power and technical mastery over nature. White disgust at racial miscegenation, contempt for educated blacks, or hostility to 'kaffir work', are indications of the kinds of things whites feared would degrade their status. That the status of whites is not simply self-conferred is evidenced by coloureds' attempts to 'pass for white', the higher status enjoyed amongst coloureds by those lighter-skinned, and the use of skin-lightening creams by African women. The Africanists of the 1950s excoriated African radicals who appeared seduced by the white social circuit. The Black Consciousness movement, with its emphasis on psychological liberation, was an attempt amongst other things to free blacks of their sense of inferiority and to confer a status on blackness sufficiently magnetic to draw in the coloured and Indian intelligentsias. While downward identification with Africans did occur amongst politicized middle-class coloureds and Africans, the evidence is that the upward pull of white status was in the end more powerful amongst the masses of coloureds even after whites lost power in 1994. The majority of whites, coloureds and Indians continue to affirm their sense of superiority over Africans by construing crime and corruption in post-apartheid South Africa as evidence that, as they always warned, Africans are not able to run a country.

Ethnicity, class, gender

Ethnic groups are not the only ones that can provide friendship, mutual support, existential justification and status. Aristocratic blood amongst Africans, superior castes amongst Asians, gang membership in coloured townships, education: all these offer comparable attractions though they typically do not contradict, and they sometimes reinforce ethnic identity.

Two non-ethnic bases of identity isolated for special attention by radical writers are those of class and gender. These have been singled out because radicals believed them to provide keys for explaining ethnicity; but also because radicals consider the subjective self-identification and collective action of workers and women to facilitate challenges to globally pervasive systems of oppression (capitalism and patriarchy). There certainly have been numerous instances of class mobilization in South African history and noteworthy instances of gender militancy (see Chapter 7), but politicized class and gender movements have, from the radical standpoint, disappointingly often failed to surmount ethnic divides or compete with ethnic movements in winning political influence. Calculations of material-economic interest aside, class has specific disadvantages compared to ethnicity as a basis for political mobilization. Its mystique is limited by its association with the instrumental character of work, especially in societies of deskilled and alienated labour. Labour provides a basis for livelihood, but it cannot explain the purpose of life. In some cases, as with Afrikaner female garment workers before the 1950s, workers can bracket their working lives to one side, organizing economistically across ethnic lines in the workplace while identifying 'ethnically' with their families and neighbours in electoral politics (Witz 1987). Ethnicity also benefits from a special association with biological family – whole families typically though not invariably belong to the same ethnic group – and, even if only perceptually, with kinship. Though work relations matter in people's lives, relations of kin are commonly felt to be more lasting and unconditionally supportive than those amongst workmates.

In any case class identification does not necessarily challenge ethnic identification. In South Africa migrant workers associate primarily with ethnically similar migrants at work. The ethnic segregation of workplaces and segmentation of labour markets made it less likely that class intimacies would cross ethnic boundaries. At the same time the oppression of people on racial grounds in South Africa lent plausibility to the argument that opposition to class oppression was best organized on racial lines.

Gender too suffers disadvantages relative to ethnicity as a basis of politicized identity. A sectional gender politics would cut across the intimate bonds of family about which women tend to feel more strongly than men (Van der Vliet 1991). Moreover, ethnicity resonates with women in a special way. Men have commonly sought to defend ethnic cultures that accorded men higher status, but male leaders have often found in women enthusiastic recruits to the ethnic cause or been joined by women in actively propagating it. One reason is that, in the metaphorically extended family of the ethnic group, the woman is granted a special status as 'volksmoeder' raising the next generation and thus enabling the group to survive (Brink 1990). This role may be a decidedly subordinate one, but it carries a certain prestige which women, denied a wider public role, may seek to maximize.

The contemporary importance of ethnicity

How important is the ethnic factor in South African politics after apartheid? A number of liberal writers (Giliomee 1989a; Giliomee and Schlemmer 1989: ch. 7; Horowitz 1991: chs 1, 2) in the 1980s and 1990s joined Afrikaner nationalists in insisting that the conflict in South Africa is essentially ethnic, racial or communal, and that a recognition and accommodation of this fact must be a starting point for a viable long-term political solution for the country. Their analysis challenged that of the Marxist left which insisted on the explanatory centrality of class and, at the level of political mobilization, on the potential unity of democrats across ethnic lines. It challenged also the assumptions of both radicals and liberals committed to the kind of non-racial democratic constitutions which, in the end, South Africa adopted in 1994 and 1996.

In dealing with this issue two separate types of claims must be separated out. The first, extrapolated from the experience of ethnic mobilization elsewhere in post-colonial Africa, is for the importance of *sub-African* ethnicity as a factor in black politics. This is associated with notions that African societies and states are prone to 'tribal' divisions which invariably manifest themselves in the vacuum left behind by departing white rulers, challenging the aspiration to black unity and to inclusive nation-building. The second is the claim that South Africa's conflict is an essentially racial one, pitting whites against blacks, or perhaps against Africans, with coloureds and Indians choosing one or the other side. This latter position is not incompatible with the notion that Africans might unite across their own internal ethnic lines.

Backers of the first claim, that post-apartheid South Africa is no less vulnerable than others in Africa to sub-African ethnic division and conflict, can point to several items of historical precedent as well as to a few worrying portents. There is no doubt that on many occasions during the period between the mid-eighteenth century and the 1830s African societies and polities not yet conquered by whites were pitted against each other in often ruthless wars. African elite attempts to forge pan-tribal unity in the twentieth century were frustrated by the counter-pull of ethnic sectionalism, especially in Natal (Marks 1986). At the popular level ethnic conflicts have broken out amongst mineworkers (increasingly violently in the 1970s), between township-based ethnic gangs (Bonner 1993; Moodie 1994) and between Zulu migrants and non-Zulu urban residents (Sapire 1992; Mamdani 1996). Some have pursued the claim for the importance of sub-African ethnicity still further, arguing that the ANC was, and is, a Xhosa party. The ANC-Inkatha conflict is construed, in these terms, as a Xhosa-Zulu one.

Radicals who once dismissed the salience of sub-African ethnicity have had, in the last ten years and more, to retreat from their earlier sanguine views about its near irrelevance (Maré 1993). The resurgence of ethnic conflict globally, and the ANC-Inkatha war on the Rand in 1990-91, caused some radicals to doubt the thesis of South African exceptionalism according to which a relatively advanced level of industrialization compared to the rest of sub-Saharan Africa would spare South Africa tribal disorder. The work of radical historians in uncovering the importance of ethnic identity amongst urbanizing Africans has reinforced a tendency to reassessment.

The fact is that, nevertheless, sub-African ethnicity has so far been relatively mute in post-1990 South African politics, especially compared to much of sub-Saharan Africa. It has not been entirely silent. Apart from the challenge of Buthelezi in KwaZulu-Natal, the ANC faces competition from pockets of sub-African ethnic regionalism based on the followings of Lucas Mangope in the former Bophutatswana and (more recently) Bantu Holomisa in the former Transkei. The redrawing of provincial boundaries in the 1990s triggered a range of territorial claims by ethnic leaders (Humphries et al. 1994; Jones 1999) as well as ethnicity-influenced border disputes (notably Bushbuckridge's violent resistance to incorporation into Northern Province). So far, however, border disputes have been localized. Of the ethnoregional challenges, only Buthelezi's has been large enough to deprive the ANC of overwhelming dominance in any African-majority province. The earlier ANC-Inkatha wars on the Rand were undoubtedly associated with Zulu-Xhosa ethnic fissures, but the worst of these wars, those located in Natal (now KwaZulu-Natal), were between rival groups of Zulus. These were wars about (in part) the place of ethnicity, but not between ethnic groups. Despite a leadership drawn disproportionately from the Xhosa of the eastern Cape, the ANC won massive support across sub-African ethnic lines in the open national elections of 1994 and 1999. (To be sure, the ANC in power has not been ethnicity-blind; in selecting its leaders, including cabinet ministers, it has had to bear in mind the need to keep diverse sub-African ethnic constituents on board.) Urban manifestations of sub-African ethnic allegiance and conflict have been strongest amongst those with links to rural areas or the recently urbanized (Sapire 1992). The evidence is that most longer-established urban Africans do not identify themselves with the ethnic labels and 'homelands' that the post-1948 apartheid government enthusiastically promoted as part of its policy of dividing and ruling Africans (Horowitz 1991: 51). It continues to be the relative weakness of sub-African ethnic politics in South Africa, rather than its strength, which needs explaining. The cumulative operation of three factors seems central to any explanation. The first is urbanization.

Urbanization need not dissolve ethnicity. As we have seen, the urban may provide the setting in which people of differing regional, linguistic and cultural backgrounds recognize themselves as distinctive, joining with their ethnic kin for mutual support and refuge and in order to compete for urban resources (like women and jobs). In South Africa urban sub-African ethnicity has been reinforced by oscillating migrancy and enforced segregation in townships and compounds. Even now new cohorts of urbanizers help to keep urban ethnicity alive. Nevertheless the urbanization process has *over the long run* done more to dissolve than reinforce sub-African ethnicity. Where urban African populations are ethnically homogeneous (as in Natal where they are mostly Zulu), the urbanized have more readily identified with a larger pan-African or pan-black nationalism than their rural counterparts still under the sway of traditional leaders and ideologies. In the Pretoria-Witwatersrand Vereeniging complex, where Africans of diverse ethnic backgrounds mixed, there developed a distinctive, partly Americanized, African urban culture (visible for example in music and dress) as well as hybrid urban dialects, forged initially by urban youth gangs. The apartheid state half-heartedly tried to segregate African townships on ethnic lines, but it made no real attempt to incorporate or exclude urbanized Africans in an ethnically ranked fashion: urban Africans were seen as a common threat, and in 'white' South Africa the state attached greater significance to racial than to sub-racial ethnic hierarchies.

A second crucial factor containing internal African ethnicities before 1994 was the rival magnetic pull of the large ethnicities: of African, black and non-racial identities. Africans shared a common oppression across ethnic boundaries. Perhaps more importantly, their numerical preponderance in South Africa gave them reason to believe that they could win the whole of the country as their 'political kingdom'. They could do so only through cross-ethnic organization, and as Africans or blacks. Moreover the presence of a large and privileged white minority and other relatively advantaged race groups means that, even after winning political power, Africans continue to have reasons to band together to fight for collective advancement. Africans are not yet in a position to refocus entirely on fighting over the spoils of their victory over whites, for that victory is still incomplete.

Thirdly, South Africa is (despite its problems) a going economic entity. The evidence is that ethnically divided but economically viable states, like Canada, Belgium or Britain, are more likely to hold together than states which, like the former Soviet Union and Yugoslavia, are both poor overall and economically unevenly developed, and where regional economic disparities coincide in part with ethnic ones. South Africa is, if only in African terms, a wealthy country: it attracts people to itself from elsewhere in Africa, and those who are part of South Africa have little reason, economically, to break from it in pursuit of a small ethnic claim. The country is severely economically unevenly developed, but for three reasons this discouraged rather than promoted sub-African ethnic identity in South Africa's case.

Firstly, the metropolitan heartlands are fabulously wealthy compared to the rural periphery. Since most of the rural periphery was inside former ethnic 'homelands', the latter were unattractive as bases of ethnic regionalism. While some 'homelands' abutted major urban areas, the prosperous cores of the urban complexes fell outside 'homeland' boundaries and 'homeland' capitals were backwaters rather than vibrant centres of a potential ethnic resurgence.

Secondly, the pattern of uneven development was not such as to cause massive differences between sub-African ethnic groups in terms of levels of economic incorporation. While African-held areas were drawn into migrant labour and underdevelopment at different paces, none escaped these processes; the principal economic divides have occurred along the rural–urban axis rather than an ethnic or regional one, and they have tended to fall within, rather than between, sub-African ethnic groups.

Thirdly, none of South Africa's regions, whether it be the wealthiest or the poorest, has grounds to believe it could be economically better off alone. The Gauteng industrial hub is landlocked, as are the key sites of mining wealth; the port areas are dependent on interior traffic and are vulnerable to circumvention; the poorest areas have no obvious massive reserves of unexploited wealth or pecunious external patrons. South Africa has no Katanga or Cabinda or Ogoniland.

If these factors have kept sub-African ethnicity in check, a more serious case can be made for the continuing political centrality of *racial* identities in South Africa. Their centrality is not self-evident. The long struggle against white minority rule did not invariably rest upon racial mobilization and consciousness. For many activists the struggle was for a non-racial democracy, and blacks could be found on the sides of the oppressors, whites on the side of the oppressed. There was indeed no unanimity in opposition movements about which groups composed the racially oppressed. The post-apartheid relevance of race thus cannot be taken for granted. Exhibit A for those insisting on its continued importance is the April 1994 open election and its June 1999 successor.

In both elections the ANC scooped up a huge proportion of the African vote but only a minority of coloured and Indian votes and very few white ones. In the 1994 poll clear majorities of coloureds, Indians and whites voted for the former (if reinvented) apartheid ruling party, the NP (later the New National Party). In 1999 whites diverted a large portion of their votes to another *de facto* white party, the Democratic Party. The 1994 vote shattered illusions, nurtured in the ranks of the radicalized middle-class coloureds and Indians, of black or non-racial unity (barring a few collaborators) behind the anti-apartheid liberation struggle. It would be wrong however to interpret the 1994 and 1999 results as straightforward evidence of racial voting. Firstly, in both cases citizens voted in significant numbers for parties primarily identified with ethnic groups other than their own, or with more than one ethnic group. The ANC won substantial numbers of votes amongst coloureds and Indians, especially from their middle classes but also from amongst the poorest coloureds (Mattes et al. 1996: 148). In 1994 the NP won majorities of three race groups and a respectable number of votes even amongst Africans. Coloureds and Indians did not support communal parties but in both elections split their votes between predominantly white and African parties.

Secondly, voting along roughly racial lines did not necessarily indicate ethnic consciousness in any active or conscious sense. It could reflect rather the conflicting interest perceptions of those located at different positions in the hierarchy of wealth and power. Blacks identify with the ANC as a party of political liberation and wealth redistribution. Whites, coloureds and Indians identify with parties like the NP/NNP and Democratic Party because they view them as bastions of minority rights and privilege. The evidence of a post-1994 election survey was that 'the vast majority of South African voters do not recognize race or ethnicity as a primary reason for their party support' (cited in Adam et al. 1997: 77).

Still, it can hardly be gainsaid that South Africa is a racially if not, at this point, a seriously sub-African ethnically divided country. What are the future prospects for both kind of division? While the fate of particular political parties may differ – with the NP/NNP seemingly in decline now – there is little to suggest that the racial voting pattern will shift qualitatively in the near future. It is unlikely that coloureds and Indians will vote in their majority for largely African parties. Nor are very large numbers of whites or Africans about to start voting for parties that are not identified principally with their 'own'. Controversies over language policy, education, provincial resource distribution and affirmative action seem likely to strengthen inter-racial suspicion, despite former President Nelson Mandela's determined rhetoric of reconciliation.

Perhaps the more important question for South Africa's future national coherence is whether the potential giant of mobilized sub-African ethnicity will continue to sleep. The intra-Zulu conflict between the ANC and Inkatha is currently being managed at a relatively low level of violence; its future containment will depend in part on the outcome of efforts to ally or merge the ANC and Inkatha Freedom Party. A new round of municipal demarcation threatens to activate tensions between Transkeian clans and between traditional ethnic leaders and the central state. Disillusionment with the ANC's economic and social welfare policies could strengthen centrifugal forces; signs of regionalist strength in the former Transkei and Bophutatswana during the 1999 general election might be the harbinger of such a trend. The cementing of identification with the new provinces, some of which are dominated by particular sub-African ethnic groups, and contain more viable economies and impressive urban centres than the old ethnic 'homelands', could crystallize ethnic allegiances. The access of African elites to levers of power, and the corruption accompanying their rise, could see the emergence of patterns of ethnic patronage and exclusion in some places, as well as of ethnic scapegoating. It is even conceivable that an economy like Botswana's could become sufficiently substantial to revive ideas, floated for a while by Mangope, about pan-Tswana unification across South Africa/Botswana boundaries.

To these possibilities, however, must be counterposed the continuation of white economic dominance as a unifying force amongst Africans; the racial and ethnic heterogeneity of all provinces; the hold of hybrid and cosmopolitan urban cultures; the sheer strength and discipline of the ANC and the extent of prestige it enjoys as a party of liberation; and the likely continued weakness of economic incentives for secession. It would be wrong to proffer a glib optimism about nation-building in a country containing so many potential lines of sub-African ethnic fissure. A reasonable observer would however have to agree that, so far, sub-African inter-ethnic conflict has not played a major role in South African politics, and does not appear likely to do so in the near future.

Accommodating ethnicity

The apartheid experience thoroughly discredited, amongst the African majority in particular, the idea that race or cultural ethnicity should form the basis of constitutional units or be given institutional recognition. The South African constitutions of 1994 and 1996 opted for an essentially liberal-democratic principle of free association according to which citizens exercise their rights, including rights of ethnic association, as individuals. They nevertheless grant recognition to eleven official languages and allow a place for traditional sub-African ethnic institutions. The question of how far ethnicity should be constitutionally acknowledged was a major issue of contention during the earlier 1990s, and the debate around it is not yet spent.

The anti-ethnicist, universalist impulse in South African opposition politics prior to 1994 was not only a negative reaction to imposed racial and ethnic segregation. It sprung also from a widespread tendency amongst non-traditionalist African elites, evident already by the later nineteenth century, to favour cultural and economic modernization and the incorporation of blacks into a common society. Initially promoted by pro-assimilationist missionaries and liberals in the Cape, the modernist orientation was carried forward in the twentieth century by – in addition to some strands of liberalism – Marxist-influenced intellectuals and leaders. It attracted also a range of coloured and Indian leaders. The modernist position was in some instances inimical to all ethnic sectionalism; in other cases it favoured larger and more inclusive ethnicities (such as African and black) over more parochial ethnicities and explored grounds for multi-racial or non-racial co-operation between progressive elites of the different race groups.

The circumstances accompanying the dismantling of apartheid and the negotiation of a new constitutional order produced a reassessment of the place of ethnicity in a future South Africa by the ANC and its allies. The most important of these were the Zulu ethnic/Natal regionalist challenge from Inkatha and the ANC's own efforts to win over sympathetic 'homeland' leaders and traditional chiefs (who were to form the Congress of Traditional Leaders of South Africa). While the 'new South Africa' is liberal-democratic rather than communalist in its constitutional form, its founders made a number of concessions to ethnicity and ethno-regionalism. They agreed to a constitutional monarchy in KwaZulu-Natal, advisory Houses of Traditional Leaders in six provinces, a national Council of Traditional Leaders (still to be set up), state payment of chiefs, recognition of traditional local authorities in former 'homeland' areas, a continuing role for customary law, eleven official languages and a limited degree of provincial devolution.

How should these sorts of concessions be assessed? Two ethnicity-related issues need separating: that of ethnicity as a basis of identity and difference, and that of ethnic traditionalism as a source of pre- or non-democratic norms. Ethnic identity is not inherently reactionary or undemocratic, since ethnic groups do not necessarily relate to each other in a hierarchical fashion or in ways that are mutually hostile. Insofar as ethnicity provides the basis for a non-hierarchical and non-coercive form of 'difference' it can contribute to the variety and richness of larger national cultures while satisfying a range of individual psychological needs.

At the same time there is an inherently problematic side to ethnicity. It does posit a divide between the collective 'own' and 'other' and presume a hierarchy of regard for fellow human beings depending on their ethnic allegiance; and it is not usually a strictly voluntary association, least of all where it assumes a racial form. People tend to get born into ethnic groups. In situations where resources are scarce, the temptation to compete for them through collective ethnic organization is strong. The ethnic patterning of political life in other parts of Africa has not only generated violent conflicts but prevented the normalization of democratic politics around competing programmes and ideas. Ethnic politics implies a permanent dominance of numerically preponderant ethnic groups, violating the democratic principle that political majorities, pluralities and minorities should vary in their composition over time. Politics reduced to competition between rival ethnic champions moreover blurs class and other divisions within ethnic groups to the advantage of political and economic elites who can use the ethnic card to escape genuine democratic scrutiny while pursuing their sectional advantage at the expense of their constituents.

There may be circumstances where Phillips's 'politics of presence' has merit, and in particular there is a case to be made for representative bodies that proportionately reflect the gender, class, ethnic, and so on, make-up of society (Phillips 1995). The proportional representation of ethnic and other groups symbolically affirms the right and capacity of people from all backgrounds to participate in political life, is arguably more distributively just, and may at least in some cases improve the quality of the representation of minority or oppressed groups. This is the defensible kernel of proposals for affirmative action politics to improve representation of under-represented groups, for example through parties instituting minimum quotas of women candidates or ethnically balancing electoral lists.

What would always have been more dubious is a constitution based on group representation rather than representation of individuals – the sorts of ethnic consociational schemes proffered during the 1980s and which the NP initially wanted to secure, in a subtly disguised form, in the early 1990s. In their explicitly ethnic form such proposals raised complicated questions about which sorts of groups were to be represented in what proportions, and by what sorts of mechanisms, as well as about how to accommodate group non-identifiers. In South Africa these problems, endemic to ethnic consociational schemes, were made more complicated by the country's particular historical inheritance of white minority domination and privilege – a legacy which entrenched minority powers might have prevented from being reversed. Even where consociational schemes eschewed explicit references to ethnicity but sought, for example, a rotation of power between major parties, they threatened, in the South African context, to frustrate the realization of the democratic will of the underprivileged majority while further advantaging an already materially advantaged minority.

Democratically speaking it is more appropriate to seek forms of representation framed in terms of individual citizenship, one-person, one-vote and rights of voluntary association but which, nevertheless, are conducive to microcosmically proportional representation of the various elements of a country's population. South Africa's system of proportional representation is finely calibrated to achieve just the combination of delegative and microscosmic representation needed to secure this balance. It allows parties to stand on the basis of programmes framed in non-ethnic ideological terms while providing ethnic, gender and regional proportionality on their candidate lists. While justified criticism can be levelled at the particular form of pure list-based proportional representation operating in South Africa, democrats should ensure that any future electoral game rules chosen retain the strongly proportional thrust of the existing system.

The constitution provides for a limited amount of territorial devolution. In practice this grants ethnic groups and ethnic coalitions potential bases in provincial legislatures, but without conceding the principle of ethnic regions. There would be real democratic advantages in strengthening regional devolution, but any gains would have to be weighed against possible risks to the construction of an inclusively multi-ethnic state. Although provinces are ethnically mixed, the overwhelming preponderance of particular groups in some of them could, in future, encourage ethnic populism in provincial politics. Territorially concentrated groups are certainly morally entitled to demand greater autonomy and (on certain conditions) even secession, but there is little point in having the central state actually sponsor or encourage ethnoregionalist aspirations not currently present to any high degree.

The 1994 constitution prescribed an interim government of national unity. Though this involved a disguised consociational element of grand ethnic coalition, it was not of such a form as to impede majority rule. Compulsory power sharing is anyway done away with, on the whole justifiably, in the final constitution. South Africa's constitutional designers have thus got much right, despite the fact that elements of the design undoubtedly need reworking.

Concessions to the non-democratic and non-egalitarian forms associated with ethnic traditionalism – in particular to an advisory role for chiefs at provincial and national levels, and to traditional local authorities and customary law – are more difficult to justify on democratic grounds. Those agreeing to a constitution that is in some ways the most progressive in the world also provided space for elements of monarchy, male-only hereditary peerage and deeply patriarchal land-control rules, much to the justified outrage of the women's movement. These concessions preserve the 'bifurcated state' which Mamdani plausibly views as a serious obstacle to the inclusion of rural Africans in full citizenship (Mamdani 1996). It remains to be seen, though, whether concessions to chiefly authority will prove more than tokenistic. Certainly many chiefs have complained that this is all that they are, which is why some previously sympathetic to the ANC have grown increasingly disaffected with the ruling party. There is something to be said, on pragmatic grounds, for progressive and culturally liberal urban elites moving cautiously in imposing their values on a countryside where conservative values and traditional leaders command widespread support, including amongst women. The struggle for an egalitarian social order in areas subject to traditionalist authority is best waged through protracted efforts of persuasion and education, even as the state intervenes to contain traditionalist excesses and protect the constitutional rights of individuals. It is important, though, to make sure that universalistic, egalitarian and liberal aspirations are not sacrificed in the name of a relativistic celebration of cultural 'difference'.

7

Narratives of Resistance

Ways of seeing 'the struggle'

It is possible to read the 1994 election victory of the African National Congress as the culmination of more than three hundred years of black resistance to white domination in South Africa. The 27 April poll was the moment when, at last, the black majority entered the 'political kingdom'. It is possible, also, to locate the centuries of resistance within a narrative that appears rational, inexorable, coherent, heroic and, in its impact on South African history, central. Rational, in that resistance politics followed seemingly logically sequential steps through primary resistance, constitutional protest, armed struggle, mass uprising; inexorable in that victory for the black opposition was probably inevitable, given the demographics of the subcontinent; coherent in that the many strands of opposition to the system cumulatively subverted white rule; heroic because the black majority was, in South Africa's circumstances, the bearer of democracy and non-racialism; and all-important because so much of South Africa's history was shaped by black struggle – if not the fact then the anticipation and fear of it on the part of whites. These readings are possible because they build upon certain essential truths about Southern African history.

Yet endorsed without serious qualification they conceal as much as they reveal. The 'stages' of the struggle were outcomes of debatable tactical and strategic choices rather than the realization in history of an underlying rationality. The timing and advent of black victory was in many ways a product of circumstances other than domestic black resistance. A good deal of what is pictured as black resistance consisted in local or individual struggles for survival or adaptation, bereft of conscious political purpose. The black population and oppositional elites were rarely united in action, organization or sentiment. Some of what happened in the name of the struggle was authoritarian, conservative, anti-social, even a 'gross violation of human rights'. And the black resistance was far from being the only source in South African history of, for example, anti-colonial armed struggle or insurrectionary threats to the (white) state. The reading of South African history as characterized centrally by contention between black and white is a retrospective one. Before the end of the nineteenth century black–white struggle was one amongst many overlapping conflicts in the region; and before the later 1920s whites had not yet accorded the black–white question priority over the English–Afrikaner one. It is these complexities that this chapter will explore.

'Primary' resistance

Black resistance to white domination up to the end of the nineteenth century consisted mainly in the efforts of Khoi and later African chiefdoms and states to defend themselves against external attack. The first war between white settlers and blacks pitted Dutch settlers against the Penninsular Khoi ('Hottentots') in 1659. Although the Khoi societies were in full retreat by the time they were devastated by the smallpox epidemic of 1713, occasional settler warfare with either the Khoi or San (Bushmen) or their coloured descendants continued into the nineteenth century, arguably until the suppression of the 1878 Griqua rebellion. Military hostilities between European settlers and Africans (Bantu-speaking mixed farmers) began on the eastern frontier of the Cape Colony in 1779 and erupted on many occasions before concluding in the far northern interior in 1898, with the defeat of the Venda by the South African Republic (*Zuid-Afrikaanse Republiek*). The histories of Khoisan and African resistance cannot be rigidly partitioned: the Khoisan (and later coloureds) and Africans on occasion co-operated against whites, most famously during the 1799-1803 and 1850-53 wars on the eastern Cape frontier.

White settlements and societies on the subcontinent exhibited a high propensity to expand into territories which black groups had lived upon, exploited or felt entitled to use before the arrival of whites. White expansion was accompanied and facilitated by a high degree of violence, both conventional and informal, and its end result was invariably oppressive white rule over blacks. 'Primary resistance' was the ultimately failed but drawn out attempt by black societies to contain this white advance, and preserve their own independence, by force of arms.

Black groups were not, however, territorially static or invariably defensive. Although exclusive ownership and use of land was largely alien to black societies, the latter were in some cases, as with the Xhosa on the eastern frontier (Peires 1981: 53, 1988: 480), aggressively expansionist. African groups were propelled into territories coveted by whites by the search for water and grazing land, the tendency of (especially Nguni) African societies to fragment politically and by flight from rival African groups. On the eastern Cape frontier the expansionism of African societies brought them into head-on collision with white societies expanding in the opposite direction.

Nor did black people in this 'primary' phase constitute a single united people battling with an external white enemy. Black polities competed with one other, well before the pressures of white advance were fully felt, for agricultural resources, control of trade routes and for followers. In the 1820s and 1830s warfare between African polities cleared the path for white expansion by depopulating parts of Natal and the interior. On numerous occasions blacks – both Khoi and African – allied themselves militarily with whites or joined white forces to fight fellow blacks. White polities too were heterogeneous, their histories punctuated by minor internal rebellions and a few major outbreaks of interstate warfare; and whites too occasionally sought or contemplated alliances with blacks against rival whites. Most dramatically, both the British and Boer sides armed blacks during the South African War or made use of black servants (Nasson 1999). But white solidarity against blacks generally held much more firmly then that of blacks against whites and – as in the aftermath of the South African War – was rapidly rebuilt after breaches.

Primary resistance was incapable of preventing the destruction of autonomous black polities and the drawing of the whole South African land surface under white jurisdiction. White conquest was facilitated by the fragility of Khoisan polities and Khoisan vulnerability to disease, rivalries between black polities and above all by white settler access in the nineteenth century to the military resources and technology of Imperial Britain. The wide scope of white conquest – the fact that it extended to effective control of so much territory – was assisted by the substantial size of southern Africa's white population. White numbers were boosted by a number of factors. Boer women exhibited a high level of fertility. The temperate climate of the Cape and Highveld and the plenitude of land available for conquest and occupation attracted prospective European settlers. Many more were drawn by the economic opportunities opened up by the modern exploitation of diamond and gold reserves from 1867 and 1886 respectively. Yet the extent of white conquest was limited by several factors.

First, the African population of the interior and east was much less vulnerable to depletion than that of the initially-encountered Khoisan. It not only benefited from a mixed farming economy able to support relatively dense populations but was less vulnerable to European diseases than some aboriginal peoples more remote from Europe and the Middle East. Whites, for their part, while numerous compared to their settler counterparts in other parts of Africa, were few in number compared to, say, those in America or Australia. South Africa was too distant, dry and bereft of natural harbours and navigable waterways to draw very large numbers of white settlers, and before development of mining its economic attractions were few (Frederickson 1981: xxii-xxiii). One result of white demographic weakness was that Africans remained in the majority throughout South African history, and had greater potential to defend their territorial heartlands against complete dispossession than did Khoisan.

A second factor limiting the scope of white conquest was the colonial overlordship of the British. British military intervention was decisive in tipping the balance of forces in whites' favour in the nineteenth century (Atmore and Marks 1974). At the same time British governments were reluctant to entertain the financial expenses involved in conquering and ruling Africans by force, and were exposed to the agitation of a metropolitan humanitarian lobby sharply critical of settler conquest and exploitation of blacks. They thus refused to sanction the complete territorial dispossession of indigenes, and ensured that land was left or set aside for Africans. In the case of Natal's African-occupied areas the British left intact elements of traditional chiefly government, hoping thereby to control black subjects at minimum cost to the colonial treasury. The dilemma for European settlers was that they needed the British to ensure that whites could dominate Southern Africa, but had in Britain an ally keener on securing broad Imperial hegemony than on facilitating untrammelled settler dominion. They thus never acquired the freedom of action enjoyed by white settlers in America who were able to break decisively from British rule and dominate indigenes without external help (or restraint).

Thirdly, white labour requirements in many instances meshed with the African desire for land, especially from the late nineteenth century. Undercapitalized white farmers hungry for black labour but unable to pay wages had little incentive to either proletarianize or evict Africans. The same was true of speculative and absentee owners wanting to profit from unfarmed land. For transition periods of variable length, extending in some cases to the later twentieth century, groups of Africans in Natal and the interior were (in consequence) able to maintain a degree of semi-independent access to white-owned land as sharecroppers and rent tenants. As the twentieth century progressed this independent existence was drastically curtailed. White farmers in the interior and Natal were mostly able to reduce Africans on their land to dependent labour tenants and wage labourers. In the 1960s and 1970s they began to evict Africans from the *platteland* as mechanization diminished agricultural labour requirements.

The story on the reserves was different. Africans held on to land in the reserves officially set aside for them from 1913. The extent of this land was in fact modestly expanded from 1936. Whites had good reasons to maintain the reserves and few reasons to break them up. Through oscillating migrancy mines and other employers could obtain cheap African labour from reserves without depriving their employees of access to land (in fact they subsidized Africans to stay on it). In the twentieth century whites discovered additional political reasons freezing African land loss. Territorial segregation helped white rulers to contain African urbanization and to legitimate the disenfranchisement of blacks in the central polity.

Primary resistance did not exhaust the meaning or scope of black resistance before the end of the nineteenth century. It belongs to the period when black society was still largely, and attempting to remain, outside or external to white society; to a period when black–white conflict was still akin in important ways to interstate or border warfare. Nevertheless there were black individuals and groups who were 'inside' white society – under the jurisdiction of its laws and/or economically dependent upon white masters – from an early stage in the history of white settlement in South Africa. The slaves, imported from 1658, were from the beginning in this position. The Khoisan were initially considered, and dealt with economically and militarily, as a party external to the white colony at the Cape; but Khoisan individuals gradually came under its sway, as employees, clients, captives and semi-slaves. Africans began to enter the Cape from the 1820s as refugees and labourers. Resistance to white domination was thus also, to an extent at least, internal from the beginning. How effective was this early internal black opposition?

Slave resistance in the Cape was very limited, especially when compared to its counterpart in the Caribbean or Brazil. The Cape colonial slaves were more likely to desert, or commit individual acts of arson and violence, than to stage acts of collective opposition. The only near-significant slave uprisings occurred in the Zwartland in 1808 and on the Koue Bokkeveld in 1825, both spurred by the heightened expectation of freedom engendered by British policies of amelioration. Collective slave resistance was contained in part by controls over slave movement (lock-ups, curfews, passes) and brutal punishment of slaves who attacked colonists' property or person or attempted escape. The cultural heterogeneity of the slave population, the wide dispersal of farm slaves in a non-plantation economy and the absence of secure routes of escape further hampered slave opposition (Ross 1983: chs 1, 8, 9; Armstrong and Worden 1988: 157-62). Slave-owner paternalism also played a role in inducing quiescence (Shell 1994).

Khoisan servants were by the later eighteenth century treated as badly as slaves, but their capacity to resist was greater. Unlike the imported slaves (to whom they rarely gave support), they were not cut off from a hinterland outside white society. They possessed local skills and information, and Khoisan servants could make contact with Khoi or San groupings outside zones of white settlement, or with Xhosa waging battles of primary resistance, as occurred in the years 1799-1803 (Newton King 1994: 242-5). In the case of the Khoisan it is thus not possible to draw a neat line between internal and external resistance in the colonial period.

It is also crucial to note there had emerged by the late 1870s in the Cape – even as primary warfare raged elsewhere – a Christianized and often literate coloured and African elite committed to peaceful reformist politics waged from within white-dominated polities. This black elite set up newspapers, formed associations and engaged in electoral politics. It articulated its oppositional sentiments in the idiom not of African traditionalism but of Cape liberalism. The periods of external and internal resistance thus also overlapped in time.

Internal resistance in the twentieth century

Notions of 'resistance' and 'opposition' to white domination have been required by commentators to cover a very wide range of dispositions and actions amongst the black oppressed in South Africa. They have been understood to embrace everything from episodes of open and consciously political collective opposition to the seemingly apolitical, even antisocial, coping strategies of individuals faced with local impositions and hardships. Radical historians developed their expanded definition of resistance partly to counterbalance top-down historical accounts focusing exclusively on heroic episodes and leaders, but also, at least arguably, to sidestep the uncomfortable facts of conservatism and quiescence in the black population. The over-energetic search for resistance has at times vested the history of black opposition with a greater scope, continuity and coherence than it actually possessed and exaggerated the importance of politics in black people's lives.

Even so it would be a mistake to confine the resistance story to openly political or public opposition. White domination has covered so many fields of life, political, economic and cultural, that many blacks themselves inevitably drew connections between its various manifestations and, as a corollary, between individual and localized, collective and widespread, resistance to it. The fact that white domination took such an open form ensured that South Africa was (still is) a relatively highly politicized society; that choices of political significance could not always be avoided even by 'ordinary' and 'apolitical' black people. Moreover small-scale and apolitical acts of defiance or evasion could cumulatively pose a substantial challenge to the institutional effectiveness of the racial order. Equally 'gestures of tacit refusal or iconoclasm' (Comaroff and Comaroff 1991: 31) frustrated the efforts of rulers to suborn blacks to white ideological hegemony.

Open political opposition

That the white-dominated South African state established in 1910 suffered from the very beginning a shortfall of legitimacy in the eyes of its black subjects is illustrated by the determined (if pacific) efforts of black leaders to scupper its founding constitution (Odendaal 1984: chs 7-9). As Anthony Marx notes, the formally racist character of the polity virtually guaranteed racialized opposition in a way that more informally racist polities like Brazil did not (Marx 1998). Once in place, the South African state did not however face continuously resolute and open opposition from the black majority. There were many blacks who accepted the new order with resignation. Amongst active opponents of the order there was much disagreement about what should replace it and what tactics and strategies would work best against it.

Those adopting radical goals or militant tactics were marginal in black South African politics before the 1940s (Rich 1996: 58-9). Gandhi's militant Satyagraha philosophy dominated Indian politics for a while before the First World War. Garveyites preaching African ascendancy achieved some influence in the 1920s and early 1930s in the Western Cape ANC and the Transkei, more superficially in the national ANC, Industrial and Commercial Workers' Union and independent churches (Hill and Pirio 1987). The Communist Party of South Africa adopted the black cause in the 1920s but was largely politically ineffectual before the 1940s. Trotskyism was a minor movement whose principal impact – ironical given its revolutionary pretensions – was in reformist trade unionism on the Rand in the 1930s. Radicals were involved in some episodes of popular mobilization and enjoyed interludes of real influence within black opposition leadership, but the expulsion of Communists from the ICU in 1926 and the conservative capture of the ANC in 1930 curbed their ambitions.

Most of the political running at national level was made by politicians attracted to constitutional protest, mainly through resolutions, petitions, delegations to Britain and newspaper journalism, supplemented by schemes of economic self-help. Through the interwar years black leaders mostly stopped short of demanding a universal franchise. Some were prepared to work within a framework of territorial segregation and indirect rule through chiefs provided certain conditions (such as adequate provision of land for Africans) were satisfied (Walshe 1987: chs V, VIII; Dubow 1989: ch. 6; Rich 1996: ch. 5). Well into the 1940s the most prominent black leaders looked to white patrons –

members of liberal organizations who had some influence in official circles, natives' representatives in parliament, and so on – to press their case, and eschewed mass mobilization (Rich 1996: 12-13).

The 1940s marked a turning point. Black leaders, especially those of an upcoming younger generation (and most notably those in the ANC Youth League founded in 1944), grew increasingly disillusioned with failed moderate tactics. The anti-fascist atmosphere stirred by the Second World War, the adoption of the idealistic Atlantic Charter by the Allies in 1941 and the beginning of European decolonization in Asia by 1947 substantially raised black hopes of change. These the prevaricating Smuts government had mostly dashed already before the firmly reactionary Reunited (or *Herenigde*) National Party came to power in 1948. Black elites committed themselves increasingly to majority rule and militant tactics, expressed in documents like the Non-European Unity Movement's Ten Point Programme (1943) and ANC's 1949 Programme of Action and 1955 Freedom Charter (Walshe 1987: chs XI, XIII). Subsequent decades witnessed, albeit not unbrokenly, a more radical black politics. In the 1950s and into the 1960s the ANC, from 1959 the Pan-Africanist Congress, led campaigns of mass defiance of new apartheid laws and institutions. After being banned in 1961, the ANC and PAC pursued a strategy of armed struggle and (in the PAC's case) insurrection. Following a decade of quiescence on the domestic front, tactics of militant mass mobilization were revived in the 1970s and 1980s by the Black Consciousness movement, ANC-allied 'Charterists' and a new generation of trade unions.

The decisiveness of the shift in the 1940s should not be overstated. There remained through the post-Second World War years black leaders of note committed to more moderate tactics and goals. The difference was that it was now they, rather than the radicals, who faced the threat of marginalization.

Opposition to white domination at black elite level was, in one or another form, endemic through the century. It was however only in certain periods and on certain occasions that resistance assumed the form of collective mass action – industrial and general strikes, bus, school, pass, rent and consumer boycotts, marches and rallies. There was a burst of militancy amongst urban Africans in 1919-20 and amongst farm-based blacks in the late 1920s. The period from the very early 1940s to early 1960s was punctuated by episodes of industrial militancy, non-violent civil disobedience and urban and rural unrest. In 1976-77 student-led protests, backed by occasional strikes, gripped African and coloured townships and schools. During 1984-86 African and coloured township unrest, general strikes and rent and consumer boycotts brought paralysis to black education and municipal government. The whole period from around 1972, when industrial and mine labour forces began to stir, through to the abolition of apartheid in the early 1990s, was characterized generally by a tendency to heightened mass action.

What accounts for periods of intensified mass militancy? And what for periods of mass quiescence? Four factors seem decisive. One is leadership tactics and styles. Militant leaders, ideologies and tactics contributed to mass protest even in the period before the 1940s, and their marginalization by mainstream black organizations was one reason why levels of militancy fell back in the 1930s. The leadership shift to militant tactics in the 1940s was a crucial contributor to the heightened collective action evident in the 1950s, even if from time to time mass action bubbled up semi-spontaneously from below, ran ahead of leaders or escalated beyond their control. The recession of mass activity in the 1960s was due at least in part to the decision of ANC and PAC leaders to opt respectively for elite guerrilla warfare and conspiratorial violence, directed in both cases from exile, in place of tactics of internally-led mass mobilization. The ANC's turn in 1979 to a strategy of mass-based politics formed a part of the backdrop to the rise of pro-ANC community organizations in the 1980s and, ultimately, to the uprising of 1984-85 (Barrell 1990; Mbeki 1996). The organizational condition of the opposition was also a crucial consideration. This is well illustrated by the circumstances of the 1930s, when the fragmentation and discrediting of the ICU, organizational decline of the ANC and factionalism and sectarianism of the CPSA reinforced the passivity of the masses.

A second factor was the presence or absence of a social base for mass action, especially for that led by urban-based elites. Before the 1960s the black working class was relatively small, dispersed and unskilled despite three decades of urbanization and industrialization, and there was little by way of state mass provision of school and further education for blacks. These circumstances were not propitious to sustained organization in workplaces, schools and townships. From the later 1960s and into the 1970s the black working class grew in size and economic power (both as producers and consumers) and state provision of secondary and higher education for blacks expanded dramatically. State township building of the 1950s and 1960s ensured that increasing numbers of urban blacks dealt with common landlords and service providers. These alterations of the urban ecology favoured collective black consciousness and action in townships, factories and schools. They explain less the ebbs and flows of popular resistance than the tendency for urban mass action to assume larger proportions in the period from the 1970s.

A third factor underlying periods of more intense mass action is economic. Increases in economic hardship could rouse or harden black hostility to white governments and their policies just as periods of relative economic prosperity could mitigate it. Thus black living standards were put under strain by inflation after the First World War (Bonner 1982: 273-4) and by declining or stagnant black real wages between 1946 and 1960 (Hofmeyr 1994: 28-9) – both periods associated with popular unrest. The still greater unrest of the 1970s and 1980s has been convincingly linked by a range of analysts (e.g. Marx 1992: 245) to economic pressures. Rising inflation in the early 1970s lay behind the first stirrings of labour militancy in that decade (Lodge 1983: 327). Rising unemployment, perhaps also inflation, contributed to the discontent that surfaced in 1976-77 (Lodge 1983: 330-1). Economic austerity policies initiated in 1984 by the government of P. W. Botha, coinciding as they did with rising municipal rent and service charges, fed the unrest of 1984-86 (Murray 1987: 247-52). By contrast the economic boom of the 1960s – when black incomes rose (albeit slowly) and unemployment was not yet a serious problem – was a period of relative quiescence. So was the expansionary period of the middle and later 1930s.

The economic stimulants to dissent could be localized in time or space. Attacks on the income of particular parts of the population – on Zulu peasants by the 1905 poll tax in Natal, on the cattle economy of rural households in the name of dipping or betterment, on the beer brewing income of township women – were also implicated in outbreaks of rioting and rebellion. These were typically of a parochial kind. 'Natural' events too had political consequences in an illegitimate state. Episodes of drought or cattle disease could sharpen discontent both in rural areas (as in the Transkei 1911-12) and amongst rural migrants in urban locations (for example during the late 1940s and the early 1950s in East London) (Lodge 1983: 56; Beinart and Bundy 1987: 21). Regional variations of wealth may also have been significant for stimulating opposition: the traditional militancy of the eastern Cape has been attributed in part to its extreme poverty (Lodge 1983: 55-6).

However, the link between economic distress and mass action is both complicated and imperfect. It is complicated because there are circumstances in which mass unemployment can reduce a propensity to industrial action on the part of the working class, while rapid expansion – with its effect of extending employee bargaining power – can extend it. Such considerations might help explain why the early Second World War years, with their rapid economic growth, witnessed a rising curve of industrial mass action alongside rising real wages in manufacturing (though declining rural incomes also played a part). It was the upward mobility of certain sectors of the African working class, and therefore its enhanced bargaining power, as much as its subsequent economic difficulties, which contributed to the resurgence of industrial unrest and trade unionism in the 1970s. It may be that some circumstances encourage industrial militancy (e.g. inflation and a more skilled workforce with rising expectations) and other conditions (especially rising unemployment) prompt discontent amongst school leavers and the politicization of trade union activity (see Marx 1992: 246). The correlation between unrest and economic decline or crisis is also imperfect. There was no great surge of popular unrest in the depression years of the early 1930s, and secondary school unrest in 1980 occurred against the background of a short-lived (albeit inflationary) boom.

The role of the state is the fourth consideration. The South African state before 1994 was not continuously ultra-repressive; much of the time a degree of extraparliamentary legal opposition was tolerated. At the same time episodes of intense and sustained unrest were usually followed after a while by crackdowns involving large numbers of arrests and banning orders, proscription of organizations and other repressive measures. This episodic, wave-like nature of repression affected the rhythms of mass struggle. A state crackdown at the end of the 1920s and the beginning of the 1930s, involving the use of internal exile provisions, accelerated the demise of an already fading ICU. Mass arrests and bans in the early 1960s helped to bring internal unrest and guerrilla opposition to an end. The ban on organizations in 1977 put a brake on the development of the Black Consciousness movement that spearheaded the Soweto uprising. The crackdown of the second half of the 1980s, accompanied in this case by an unprecedented degree of 'dirty war' tactics by anti-radical vigilantes and hit squads, effectively curtailed the rebellion of 1984-86. Crackdowns were often the more successful because of their conjunction with popular exhaustion and internecine division following periods of prolonged mass action, violence and counter-violence. By contrast periods of relatively light-touch policing, such as the early years of the second Smuts government, and particularly the years under the Presidency of F. W. De Klerk from 1989, had the effect of boosting the confidence and expectations of the black population, encouraging mass mobilization.

On the boundaries of opposition

Not all manifestations of open collective opposition to white power-holders and impositions can be said to constitute opposition to white power as such. Often struggles flared in response to immediate slights and hardships and focused on immediate objectives, such as halting betterment schemes. In a few instances they proceeded from largely or partly conservative premises, their leading actors seeking to preserve aspects of the existing order – such as traditional African patterns of landholding, or access to land generally – rather than wider systemic change (Beinart and Bundy 1987; Bradford 1987a; Delius 1996). Nevertheless these different kinds of struggle so far discussed all involved open, conscious, collective resistance to white power or its particular applications. Some other forms of 'struggle' waged by black people lacked this irreducibly political character.

On the outer boundaries of what can plausibly be construed as resistance to white domination lay such (overlapping) actions as withdrawal, evasion, informal resistance and political violence.

Withdrawal involved attempts to escape the effects of domination rather than directly confront it. It could be an individual or collective act. It was not a form of openly political resistance but it did present a challenge to the aspiration of dominant whites to exercise effective control over black activity and thought. One form of withdrawal involved creating subcommunities freed of white ideological and organizational direction: the carving out of spaces, within yet apart from civil society, where black people could largely govern themselves under a cosmology of their own (re)making. The classic instance of this was 'Ethiopianism', the name given to a movement of independent African Christian churches emerging from the 1880s. Though initially exhibiting a radical potential, Ethiopianism developed into a largely reformist force by the early twentieth century. Nevertheless some branches were connected to militant politics in the Transkei in the 1920s and Ethiopian ideas formed part of a wider Africanist discourse. The Ethiopians' autonomy successfully challenged a white-run (and increasingly racist) missionary movement, and it was for some time a considerable source of anxiety to whites more widely (Beinart and Bundy 1987: introduction, ch. 3; Frederickson 1995: ch. 2). A movement of the African Methodist Christian elite, it presaged a burgeoning of independent African churches, syncretic in character but mainly Zionist or Pentecostal, appealing to the poor and women, in the middle and later twentieth century. These latter churches, with their other-worldly outlook, tended to be radically distinctive in their cosmology but conservative in their dealings with the white state (Frederickson 1995: 90-1; Pretorius and Jafta 1997).

Collective withdrawal could take other forms too. The emergence from 1944 of organized African squatter settlements around Johannesburg, typically under the control of charismatic local African bosses, caused alarm to white officials. The state stepped up the building of formal townships partly to regain effective control of African urban populations from squatter leaders. Semi-autonomous settlements re-emerged in a visible way in the 1980s. The organized settlements of the 1940s and 1980s represented in part a survival strategy for the urban underhoused (mainly sub-tenants) and recently urbanized, and offered a certain freedom from government regulation (especially valuable to unlicensed traders, women engaged in illegal brewing and pass law evaders). Squatter camp leaders levied fees, policed residents and administered services. The most effective, according to Stadler, 'established virtually a state within a state' (1979: 19). Their administration could however be authoritarian, corrupt, ethnically divisive and politically introverted. On occasion they formed alliances with conservative or pro-state forces (Stadler 1979; Bonner 1990a; Sapire 1992).

A more individualized form of withdrawal that played a significant part in South Africa's economic history was desertion by African employees who were dissatisfied with their wages or conditions. Two factors above all facilitated desertion. One was competitive poaching of employees by rival agricultural and mining employers. The other was the presence of alternative sources of livelihood for African workers outside mining and white agriculture – whether in African reserve areas or in higher-wage urban economic sectors. African mineworker desertion constituted a major threat to gold mine profitability from the 1890s into the 1920s (Jeeves 1985: 165-77; Harries 1994: ch. 5). In the 1930s and 1940s white farmers complained bitterly about labour tenants deserting the farms for the industrializing towns and cities.

In the long run the tactic had its limits as a form of defiance. Although in its heyday desertion forced concessions from mine owners and farmers, it also resulted in the creation of employer monopsonies on the mines and the tightening of pass laws, measures designed to limit the bargaining power of African workers and confine them to white farming areas. The tactic anyway became more difficult to employ as Africans lost their independent means of livelihood and mine owners and farmers found ways to overcome labour shortages.

Evasion was ultimately more corrosive of the racial order than withdrawal. The term is used here to refer to the efforts of countless individuals, households and small groups to evade the racial state's web of laws and its bureaucratic regulation and surveillance. Particularly important in frustrating the designs of state policy-makers and planners was African evasion of labour movement controls (Posel 1991: chs 5, 6) and, especially from the 1980s, urban segregation provisions (Kane-Berman 1991: 31-42). Sometimes black evasion was made more effective by the shared interest of certain groups of whites – urban slumlords, employers of illegal African labour, farmers illegally employing sharecroppers – in dodging state legislation. Evasion was often self-interested and survivalist, and its short-term effect during the period of NP rule, at least before the 1980s, was usually to encourage the state to tighten up laws and their enforcement. In the longer run though it proved impossible for the state to control, and it did much to confound the ambitions of apartheid's social engineers.

Informal resistance is a form of opposition invoked by social historians reluctant to dismiss as passive and quiescent those subordinate groups and individuals who do not engage in openly political or collective action. In tightly controlled institutions like mine compounds, Van Onselen famously argued in relation to Rhodesian mine labour, 'resistance ... should in the first instance be sought in the nooks and crannies of the day-to-day situation' (Van Onselen 1980: 239). Its forms could (Van Onselen and others suggested) included desertion and evasion (again), absenteeism, go-slows, refusal to perform tasks, playing stupid, theft from employers, attacks on employers' property and forgery of documents required by the state and employers.

Some of these sorts of actions hint at another form of resistance, what Hobsbawm termed 'social banditry' – forms of criminality emanating from marginal sectors of society which also involved rebellion against the existing order and its oppressions. The lumpenproletarian Zulu Ninevites who attacked white property and migrant workers on the Rand before 1920 are an example of this phenomenon cited by Van Onselen (1982b). Urban South Africa's long history of ganglandism offers a number of other plausible candidates.

The temptation should be resisted, though, to assimilate such rebellion too straightforwardly into South Africa's narratives of resistance. Where criminal gangs stepped into the political realm they could be found on both sides of the political divide, their allegiances being typically unstable. Some of the gangs whose actions signified rebellion against the *status quo* were decidedly anti-social, preying on their fellow blacks and poor or employing brutal violence (Glaser 2000). South Africa's currently endemic criminal violence, threatening the new democratic order, has cast prior periods of supposedly social criminality in a less romantic light.

Political violence in pre-1994 South Africa was in some instances directed straightforwardly against white power. The classic examples were crowd attacks on police and armed guerrilla action. Such manifestations could be semi-spontaneous (as in the case of many riots) or organized (as typically with pre-planned armed actions by trained guerrillas). Described in these terms political violence represents simply a sub-category (or perhaps extension) of open political opposition as already discussed. Nevertheless there were forms of violence under the old regime, continuing into the democratic era, which were clearly political yet did not take the form of open opposition to white power. Examples included violence between rival black political organizations, political violence which merged into criminal violence (as in the hands of the notorious 'comtsotsis' of the 1980s), political violence used as a cover to settle scores between neighbours (as occurred in the mid-1980s 'people's courts'), violence directed by the politically zealous against the apolitical or politically non-compliant, and black ethnic violence.

This precise boundary between violent opposition to white power and other forms of political violence is obscured by two considerations. In the first place, some black-on-black violence was surreptitiously stirred or aggravated by 'third forces' connected to the state. In the second, many of the blacks attacked by other blacks were targeted because they were perceived to be either agents or enemies of the 'system'. There is thus a real sense in which internecine violence constituted a form of displaced violence between system-linked forces and anti-system blacks. Even so, attacks on blacks 'collaborating' with or opposing the system all too easily merged into attacks on rivals, bystanders, social outsiders and the ethnically or ideologically different. Violence against collaborators often involved acts of gratuitous cruelty and severely polarized black communities, eliciting the counter-violence of right-wing vigilantes.

Some writers interpret black political violence as evidence of a crisis in black, especially African masculinity. Faced by unemployment and challenges to patriarchal authority, they suggest, African men restore their sense of self-importance through violence, domestic as well as political (Campbell 1992; Morrell 1998: 625). Morris and Hindson (1992) argue that political rivalries in KwaZulu-Natal tag onto conflicts between local power centres, notably the shack warlords and youth, over scarce urban resources and social position. Analyses such as these reveal factors which make possible political (and indeed criminal) violence in South Africa but not its sufficient conditions, specific content or incidence in time and space. The evidence suggests, as Johnston (1997) notes, that party-political rivalry is an independently important factor underlying at least a good deal of the violence.

Currents and discourses

The ideological currents which in the twentieth century dominated the politics of open opposition to white power in South Africa could be roughly divided into three: liberalism, nationalism and socialism.

Liberalism

The diverse currents of South African liberalism before 1994 shared little apart from the conviction that formalized racial discrimination was unjust and that a future South Africa should protect individual freedoms. Liberals disagreed both about oppositional tactics and in their political and economic philosophies.

Most liberals were gradualist, committed to encouraging economic self-help amongst blacks, educating white power-holders, lobbying sympathetic state officials and standing for parliament. There were however radical liberals who participated in peaceful mass protests, trade union work and, in the 1960s, even joined armed opposition forces like the PAC and African Resistance Movement (Lodge 1983: 210-12; Rich 1984: sections 1, 2; Du Toit 1994). With respect to race, some liberals were assimilationist. Mid-Victorian Cape liberals were confident that blacks could attain the level of civilization necessary for participation in a shared polity. The historian W. M. Macmillan and many liberal economists in the twentieth century insisted on the irreversible economic interdependence of black and white. Other liberals were more attracted to ethnic and cultural pluralism. A few toyed with segregationist ideas before the later 1920s or sympathetically appropriated relativist cultural anthropology from the mid-1920s. Their counterparts in the 1980s closely studied consociational models of communal power sharing designed for ethnically divided societies. In terms of economic philosophy, some liberals were social democrats, influenced for example by Fabianism and radical Liberalism in Britain. Others (notably those associated with the Anglophone press) were hard-nosed free marketeers (Rich 1984: chs 2, 3; Smith 1988: ch. 4; Saunders 1988: chs 5, 6; Dubow 1989: ch. 1; Nattrass 1991: 657-61). There were, in all these cases, liberals who straddled boundaries, combining elements of different positions or shifting ground over time.

The first white liberals in the South African area were drawn from the ranks of Anglophone missionaries, merchants, professionals and parliamentarians in the nineteenth century Cape (see Chapter 1). The English-speaking upper middle class, based mainly in metropolitan centres, dominated the ranks of white liberalism in twentieth century South Africa. Literate and Christianized Africans, especially in the Cape with its history of a common franchise, were also drawn to liberalism, arguably the dominant current in black opposition politics before the 1940s. White and black liberals in the twentieth century co-operated in a number of forums and organizations, notably in the moderate interwar Joint Councils Movement (1921–late 1940s) and in the more radical Liberal Party (1953-68). However the 1936 abolition of the Cape African franchise, which black liberals defended passionately, deprived black liberals of a key reference point and contributed to their disillusionment. From the 1940s liberalism was increasingly forced to the margins of black opposition politics by nationalism and socialism (Rich 1984, 1996; Walshe 1987: chs V, VIII).

Nationalism

Nationalism formed the dominant trend amongst the forces ranged against the racial order. Nationalists articulated the grievances and fought for the political rights of disenfranchised racial and sub-racial ethnic groups. Most black nationalists fought for majority rule. Despite these commonalities the term covers a range of distinctive currents.

Multi-racial nationalism involved a coalition between leaders of separately identified ethnic groups to facilitate common action against the white minority state. In some cases its vision of a future South Africa combined majority rule and a shared state with some notion of special recognition and protection for the rights of ethnic minorities. The classic example of a multi-racial formation was the ANC-led Congress Alliance of the 1950s, which brought together separately organized Africans, Indians, coloureds and whites, and whose Freedom Charter envisaged 'equal rights' for all 'national groups'. Elements of multi-racialism could be found also in the organizational make-up of the United Democratic Front in the 1980s (since it controversially included clearly Indian and white organizations).

Non-racial nationalism denied organizational or ideological recognition to ethnic distinctions amongst blacks, or indeed amongst South Africans. It was nationalist in the sense of being committed to the construction of a South African nation-state transcending ethnic boundaries. It was *black* nationalist only insofar as it championed the political rights of those excluded from the state on 'racial' grounds, who were in practice black. Though non-racial nationalists favoured majority rule, this preference was (at least theoretically) a function of their commitment to universal franchise rather than indicating any preference for rule by a *blacks* as such. They supported (in other words) a form of civic nationalism. Elements of non-racial nationalism could be found in the ANC by the 1950s, though it was formalized only with the admission of non-Africans in 1969. It found expression also in the non-racial membership policies of the Communist Party, Liberal Party, the Trotskyist left and the open industrial unions, and in the UDF (within which it was the dominant current).

Ethnic nationalism identified itself specifically with one ethnically defined section of the population whose cause it championed. It attached itself sometimes to small ethnicities, such as Indian or Zulu (in the cases of Ghandhi's Natal Indian Congress and Inkatha respectively). In other cases ethnic nationalists pursued the claims of larger ethnic groups, such as Africans (in the case of the Garveyites of the 1920s and the PAC, founded in 1959) or blacks (in the case of the BC movement of the 1970s). The 'non-racial' ANC itself emphasized the special concerns of Africans, and in power today it is viewed by some as increasingly Africanist. Black ethnic nationalists, though ambivalent on the subject, did not invariably seek political domination by the ethnic group they championed. Most PAC and BC exponents appeared to accept that whites might be full participants in a future state, rejecting only their participation in the struggle against minority rule. They seemed to envisage a future psychological and cultural Africanization of whites.

Tribunes of smaller ethnicities for their part sometimes saw themselves as fighting simply for minority civil rights (as in the case of Gandhi's NIC) – in which case they were not strictly nationalist – or for devolution within, or secession from, a future majority ruled state (as in the case of Inkatha).

Socialism

Socialists, especially of Marxist inclination, were distinguished by their commitment to the emancipation of the working class and the overthrow of capitalism. They nevertheless had to grapple, like Marxists elsewhere in the colonial and ex-colonial world, with the 'national question': the question of how to relate the proletarian struggle against capitalism to the black 'national' struggle against white rule (No Sizwe 1979; van Diepen 1988). The dominant Marxist party in South Africa, the CPSA (later the South African Communist Party) initially organized mainly white workers, but began to organize black workers in the mid-1920s, and later acquired an increasingly black membership. It was only from 1928, under pressure from the Communist International, that it reconceptualized its immediate goal as the establishment of a majority-ruled state – initially referred to as a 'native republic' – rather than socialism. Thus was born a two-stage revolutionary theory envisaging a first phase of national-democratic struggle followed by a second stage struggle for socialism. This reorientation away from immediately socialist objectives opened the door to co-operation with nationalist forces, and by the 1950s the banned CPSA/SACP was informally allied to the ANC, an alliance formalized in exile in the 1960s. Though committed to a national-democratic struggle – understood by the 1960s as a struggle against white 'internal colonialism' and for 'national democracy' – the SACP position at times leaned leftwards to embrace the idea that the national-democratic and socialist struggles were in practice inseparable, and that the former could not be waged successfully except by successful prosecution of the latter (Slovo 1976). This inflection produced a permutation of the theory, sometimes associated with Trotskyism, of 'permanent revolution'.

The second, Trotskyist, current was small yet (as is the way with Trotskyists) internally diverse and often fractious (Nasson 1990, 1991; Hirson 1994a, b; Legassick 1994). Though it had active exponents from all ethnic backgrounds and in all regions, its heartland was amongst the English-speaking coloured intelligentsia of the Western Cape. The main body of Trotskyists, like the Communists, sought alliances with black nationalists, though typically with different black nationalists to the Communists: those in the All-African Convention (founded in 1935), NEUM (1943) and the National Forum (1983). Like the Communists in 1955, NEUM Trotskyists supported in 1943 an immediate programme composed of national-democratic rather than socialist demands, presumably on the understanding that their realization would inevitably trigger deeper social transformations. In the 1970s, however, the Trotskyists attached a clearer priority to role of the black proletariat and the struggle for socialism (No Sizwe 1979: ch. 7). The leftist Cape Action League allied itself with the black nationalists of the Azanian People's Organization, but on the basis of a programme calling for anti-capitalist struggle.

In the 1970s a third socialist current joined the fray which can be characterized roughly as workerist. Initially associated mainly with white university radicals, it was closely involved in the rebuilding of militant trade unions amongst black workers in the 1970s and 1980s. Workerists ranged in character from social-democratic to syndicalist. They insisted on the centrality of working class leadership and of a workplace-centred struggle for economic democracy and socialism. Suspicious of nationalist cross-class politics, they kept their distance from national-level and township-based anti-apartheid groups (MacShane et al. 1984: ch. 10; Friedman 1987: ch. 4; Maree 1987: chs 12-16). Workerism went into retreat in the 1980s as 'workerist' unions were sucked into political and community struggles and later united with 'nationalist' or 'populist' trade unions under the banner of the Congress of South African Trade Unions. Important workerist activists were recruited into the ranks of the ANC and SACP. A workerist rump did hold on in some individual unions.

Ideological debates and alliances

Proponents of liberalism, nationalism and socialism competed in many areas, both political and intellectual; but there were also points of overlap between them that allowed for a range of alliances.

The socialist left usually found itself at loggerheads with organized liberalism, which was strongly anti-communist, though radicals made common cause with a range of left-sympathetic liberals. Radicals accused mainstream liberals of helping to frame segregationist ideas and, after abandoning segregation, of dampening black militancy in opposing it in the 1920s and 1930s. They presented liberalism as it developed from the 1950s as either a creature of the Anglophone bourgeoisie promoting a pro-capitalist agenda (especially in the case of the Anglo-American supported Progressive Party and press) or as hobbled in its efforts to link up with black mass organizations by anti-communism (in the case of the Liberal Party) (Legassick 1973a, 1976; Glaser 1984; Rich 1984). Liberals defended their record of opposition to the racial order and in turn attacked their radical critics (and left-leaning liberal 'slideaways') for supporting political violence and authoritarian politics (Kane-Berman 1991; Wentzel 1995).

Multi-racial and non-racial nationalism overlapped with liberalism, matching up with, respectively, ethno-pluralistic and assimilationist liberalism. They also shared the universalism of Marxist socialism, enabling, as we have seen, Communists and Trotskyists to link arms with nationalists. Nevertheless liberals mostly kept a distance from nationalist organizations, rejecting their militant tactics, philosophical collectivism and alliances with Communist groups and states. A minority of 'left' Marxists for their part worried that the nationalist idea of the 'people' concealed class differences within the black population under a patina of common interest, providing a cover for the sectional interests of the black petit bourgeoisie.

Ethnic nationalism was for the most part rejected as chauvinist by both liberals and Marxists, not least because it celebrated even more than other nationalisms organically conceived peoples, in the case of Anton Lembede's Africanism exhibiting (like Afrikaner nationalism) an affinity with European romantic nationalism (Gerhart 1978: 54-65). The liberal and Marxist rejection of ethnic nationalism was generally reciprocated. Africanists in the 1950s attacked the influence of white Communists in the anti-apartheid struggle and Black Consciousness ideologues in the 1980s lambasted white liberals. Even so ethnic nationalism could link up with both liberalism and socialism in surprising ways. A few radical liberals supported the PAC because of its anti-communism or showed sympathy for the BC emphasis on cultural and psychological liberation. In the 1980s some liberals identified with Inkatha – notwithstanding its authoritarianism, ethnic chauvinism and militarism – because of its anti-revolutionary, anti-sanctions and pro-capitalist stance. Marxism also came within the orbit of ethnic nationalism. The PAC in exile dabbled with Maoism. In 1983 the BC group Azapo allied itself with Western Cape Trotskyists of the Cape Action League. Both the PAC and BC developed variants of Marxist class analysis which they eclectically (and incoherently) joined to discourses of African or black nationalism (Callinicos 1988: 117-20; Marx 1992: 85-8; Alexander 1994: 201).

It was the non-racial nationalist ANC, allied to the socialist SACP and Cosatu, that finally inherited political power in 1994. By then however both mainstream black nationalism and socialism had made a certain peace with liberalism. Radicals were right to criticize liberalism's timidity in the face of minority rule and its reluctance to address structural inequalities in South African society. Nevertheless liberals made points about the dangers of political authoritarianism, and the value of political pluralism and civil liberties, which most radicals came to recognize as right. That recognition has helped to spare South Africa an authoritarian post-apartheid order.

Much more open to criticism is the ANC's appeasement of *economic* liberalism. The movement's rightward drift on economic policy has become a focus of contention between the ANC and its socialist allies. The left-Marxist prediction, that a black elite would use a nationalist discourse of shared interests amongst the oppressed to legitimate their self-enrichment, has been fully vindicated. Nor has the ANC's formally liberal-democratic political commitment prevented it from imposing severe internal party discipline or occasionally attempting to intimidate its critics.

The social bases of resistance

The black population did not confront white power as a singular entity even in the twentieth century with the emergence of black nationalism. Differences within the black population that militated against uniform patterns of resistance and sometimes impeded black unity fell along a number of axes. The following are but the most prominent.

Firstly, there were what can broadly be called ethnic differences. Africans, coloureds and Indians achieved a degree of unity in political action at various points in their history, both at elite level and in mass actions such as the student rebellions of 1976-77, 1980-81 and 1985. In some instances – the Communist and Liberal Parties, the ANC from 1969 – elite unity extended to an ethnicity-blind knitting together of leaders from different ethnic groups; it more typically involved the co-operation of leaders mobilizing sectional organizational bases (as in the Congress Alliance). Often however political organizations pursued sectional ethnic interests in isolation from each other (Gandhi's passive resistance campaigns are a case in point). In a few instances the members or organizations of black ethnic groups openly fought each other (as with Indians and Zulus in 1949).

Sub-African ethnicity manifested itself as a factor in twentieth-century opposition politics in two ways. In the singular instance of Inkatha and the Zulus it provided the basis for large-scale and sustained mobilization, directed mainly against black nationalists. Sub-African ethnic affiliation also correlated with differential levels of involvement in pre-1994 opposition political leadership. Xhosas tended (for various reasons) to predominate in the leadership of the ANC and other nationalist organizations, whereas sub-African ethno-regionalism has been most successful amongst rural Zulus.

A second noteworthy differential was class-based. Black resistance leadership was provided disproportionately by the petit bourgeoisie or middle layers and notably (in the African case) teachers, clerics, interpreters, clerks, journalists and lawyers. Other elite strata with important exceptions maintained a cautious distance from the struggle, and on occasions played a 'counter-revolutionary' role. Businessmen, traditional leaders and black politicians in municipal and 'homeland' structures were prominent among them. The black working class entered the political stage at various points through trade unions and instances of mass mobilization (such as strikes and work 'stayaways'), but they were far from continuously active or militant. Some sections of the working class, for example migrant workers, were wary of urban nationalist politics. Many black elite politicians before the 1940s were reluctant to activate the proletarian masses, but mobilization of the black working class became in time the holy grail of struggle, and black elites engaged in sharp debate about whether they should be appealed to in class or nationalist terms.

A third significant differential followed lines of gender. Almost all black opposition organizations were male-dominated. Women did form their own organizations, such as the ANC Women's League (established in 1948) and the Federation of South African Women (1954), but these tended to play an auxiliary role within a larger (male-led) 'national-democratic' struggle which prioritized 'race' (and class) issues over those of gender. A good deal of militant youth politics in the 1980s carried a macho flavour, tending as it grew more militaristic to marginalize politically active women (Seekings 1993: 82-4) or confine them to mainly supportive roles (Sitas 1992: 633). Male domination in opposition politics was consistent with, and reflected, the patriarchal character of all of South Africa's ethnic communities (Bozzoli 1983b; Guy 1990). Black women themselves internalized patriarchal norms, and much women's protest had a conservative aspect, defending pre-capitalist gender relations and communities against state and capitalist intrusion (Bozzoli 1983b: 166-7; Guy 1990: 46-7). Marginalized within male society, African women frequently sought refuge and support in associations in which they could play a more prominent role, particularly female Christian prayer unions, or find protection, as in the case of organized urban squatter movements (Bozzoli 1983b: 165; Bradford 1987b: 307-10; Bonner 1990a: 95; Gaitskell 1990).

There were however struggles in which women played a leading role, notably those against oppressive policies which threatened female economic independence or sources of livelihood. Women fought vigorously against the extension of passes to African females in the Orange Free State in 1913, and nationally in 1956. They resisted (most dramatically in Natal in 1929 and 1959) enforcement of municipal beer monopolies that undermined domestic brewing. In the reserves African women struggled against proletarianization and influx control measures (Witzieshoek 1950, Bafarutshe reserve 1957-58). These struggles could be very intense, and even see women adopt stereotypically male warrior-type roles (Bradford 1987b: 310-12). The 1913 protest in the Free State was the only black anti-pass campaign to succeed in containing the extension of pass laws prior to the 1980s (Wells 1986). In some cases women directed their grievances and militancy against their own men (Bradford 1987b). In the 1980s the impact of feminist thought began to be registered, and by the 1990s a substantial network of voluntary associations had developed pressing women's issues with regard to, for example, constitutional reform and legislation on abortion.

A fourth major differential was generational. The arrival on the political scene of a younger generation of activists heightened radicalism in African and coloured elite politics in the 1940s. It was only from the end of the 1960s, however, that the youth emerged as a distinctive sociological group with its own generational consciousness (Bundy 1987b: 3-4) and spearheading (by the mid-1970s) a particularly militant form of classroom and street politics. The emergence of a politicized youth had to do with a variety of factors, including the demographic expansion of the urban youth population, the growing proportion of blacks in secondary and tertiary education from the early 1970s (a factor at work in rural areas too) and rising unemployment amongst urban blacks (Bundy 1994). In the 1980s the youth were accorded heroic status by some as the 'young lions' challenging the state education system and confronting armed police in the townships, and vilified by others as a 'lost generation' of ill-educated, unskilled and militaristic men given to violence, intimidatory behaviour and criminality. Both reputations were deserved, the youth being a diverse and shifting group. Many were not politicized let alone militant (Seekings 1993). It was in the 1980s certainly a cohort whose militant members made maximal demands and expected their immediate satisfaction, and which eschewed the patience of its elders, including those elders involved in politics (Bundy 1986: 29). In some cases the older generation responded to this militancy of the young by attempting to support and channel it, while in other cases it felt its authority (and material well-being) threatened by youthful activism. In the latter cases elders could be drawn into supporting right-wing vigilantism.

Any general explanation of divisions in the black population must begin by noting the differential way in which the blacks were incorporated into the system of domination. Some blacks experienced the racial order as more oppressive than others. Whereas coloureds benefited from apartheid-inspired coloured labour preference policies in the Western Cape, Africans in that region suffered the harshest influx controls in the country. Black capitalists and bureaucrats had more of a stake in private property and social order than the black petit bourgeoisie and proletariat. Traditional leaders derived more benefits from apartheid than township dwellers. In these instances the more oppressed of the groups proved (on the whole) the more militant.

At the same time degree of oppression could not always be correlated in simple fashion with availability for militant action. Access to education and bargaining power were also influential factors. Members of the educated black elite were more ready to engage in nationalist politics than the mass of less well educated blacks mired in everyday struggles for survival. Workers with reasonably good skills and secure jobs were often better placed to engage in militant unionism than unskilled or insecurely employed workers. Equally, the better-off oppressed were likely to lead struggles against oppressions that targeted them specifically. Thus it was Indian merchants who spearheaded resistance to restrictions on Indian commercial freedom.

As this last example shows, blacks experienced not only different degrees of oppression but different kinds. Pass laws in the twentieth century were an African problem, and their extension to African women a problem mainly for those women. African women suffered disproportionately from municipal policies to restrict home brewing of beer. Betterment schemes formed part of the experience only of reserve-based Africans. Racial restrictions on free trade disproportionately hit Indians. Coloureds were the principal victims of train segregation in Cape Town. The selectiveness of oppression made it likely that different sections of the black population would give priority to different grievances at different times and in different places and made collective action more difficult to engineer.

In any case many categories of blacks lived lives separated in time and space. Africans, coloureds, Indians and (amongst migrants or the newly urbanized) sub-African ethnic groups showed a predilection for sticking to their own which compulsory segregation reinforced. Migrant labour separated African men from women. (Traditionalist African women and men anyway spend less time together than is typical in nuclear families.) Youth associations and gangs kept generations as well as, often, genders apart. Spatial and temporal distance limited shared experiences and inhibited co-ordinated action.

There was, finally, a logic of powerlessness at work amongst blacks. Unable to dislodge minority rule, they at times turned on each other, currying selective favour with whites, asserting their superiority over ethnically different subcategories of the black population, criminally preying on fellow blacks or battling rival activists for political turf. Blacks engaged in second-order conflicts over the scarce goods – economic, cultural and other – that the racial and capitalist order permitted to fall within their reach.

While the notion that a black 'people' collectively resisted the racial order should be abandoned, it would be wrong to imagine that blacks were marked by a degree of heterogeneity sufficient to confound all collective purpose and action. Some of the divisions amongst blacks were more intractable than others. Ethnic, class, gender and generational divisions within the African population provided the basis for tensions which persist to the present, but did not invariably prevent collective action, shared political allegiance or non-parochial identification. While the racial system separated people out on ethnic grounds, it compressed or connected many who might otherwise have been much more distant from each other: blacks of different classes, Africans of different sub-racial ethnicities, sections of the working class and the peasantry. All categories of blacks suffered from votelessness, segregation and forced removal, and their leaders, and on occasion their lower ranks too, felt enough grievance in common to inspire them to engage from time to time in joint action and sacrifice. The notion of an oppositional 'black people' had enough real-world plausibility to allow it to function as a potent revolutionary myth.

Sites of resistance

One of the issues most keenly debated in the ranks of the South African opposition was the appropriate choice of site: the right natural terrain, built environment or institutional context from which to launch struggles against the racial order.

Town and countryside

South Africa is easily the most industrialized and urbanized country in sub-Saharan Africa. Yet a very substantial if diminishing proportion of Africans continue to work or reside in the countryside, or remain attached to it by ties of kin. The persistence of a large rural population and extensive rural ties reflects partly the intermediate stage of economic development in South Africa. It is the product also of an institutionalized system of oscillatíng migrant labour 'unequaled in scale and longevity' (Crush et al. 1991: xiii), the preservation of communal tenure in the countryside (which contained land loss by African peasants) and urban influx controls which remained in place until the mid-1980s.

Blacks in rural areas faced multiple pressures during the twentieth century. In the reserves, these came from declining agricultural output and growing landlessness, compounded by heavy-handed state intervention to secure African labour (mainly from the mid-1890s through to around the First World War), extract revenue to pay for indirect rule, limit the spread of cattle disease and, from the 1930s, to shore up reserve agriculture (through for example cattle culling and villagization schemes). In white-owned farming areas pressures on Africans arose from white efforts to undermine the independence of African sharecroppers and rent tenants and to convert them into ultra-exploited labour tenants and wage labourers, a process accompanied by much violence and racism. The countryside thus unsurprisingly provided a terrain for periodic eruptions of black militancy. African reserve residents fought taxes, state-imposed councils, cattle dipping, agricultural 'betterment' and 'rehabilitation' and passes (Marks 1970; Lodge 1983: ch. 11; Chaskalson 1987; Beinart and Bundy 1987). In the white countryside, especially in the Transvaal, OFS and Natal in the later 1920s, tenants and wage workers resisted deteriorating terms of service (Bradford 1987a).

National opposition movements gave some attention to the countryside. The ICU evolved from an urban proletarian into a largely rural farmworkers' and tenants' organization during the late 1920s (Bradford 1987a). The AAC and NEUM were heavily influenced by currents of Trotskyism which prioritized the agrarian question, and they succeeded in the later 1940s in linking up with resistance in the Transkei (Bundy 1987a: 255-6, 266-75). In the early 1960s the PAC was implicated in an abortive and isolated revolt at small-town Paarl, and forged links in the Transkei (Lodge 1983: ch. 10, 286-8). From 1928 the Communist Party paid attention to the organization of the countryside, largely due to the prodding of the Communist International (Bundy 1987a: 259-63). The Garveyite and Communist-influenced Western Cape wing of the ANC campaigned militantly amongst coloured and African farm workers and location dwellers in the Worcester district in 1929-30. After the Communists in the branch were purged in 1930 they led a breakaway Independent ANC which continued for some time to win support in the rural western and eastern Cape (Lewis 1987: 107-18). Recent research has uncovered considerable Communist influence in episodes of rural militancy in Sekukuniland and the Northern Transvaal in the 1950s (Delius 1993). In the 1950s and early 1960s the ANC, itself undergoing radicalization, was drawn towards an interest in rural politics by episodes of militancy in the reserves (Mbeki 1963). In the 1960s the ANC (inspired as much by African peasant revolts as by then internationally fashionable guerrilla-ism) envisaged its armed struggle in terms largely of rural guerrilla warfare (Slovo 1973: 331; Fine and Davis 1990: 230-1). During the 1980s the influence of the ANC-aligned United Democratic Front spread into country towns and 'homeland' villages (Murray 1987: 272-4; Delius 1996: ch. 6).

Nevertheless the main focus of twentieth-century opposition organization was urban. Rebellions in the reserves could be fierce, but they tended to be localized and sporadic. South Africa (unlike neighbouring Mozambique, Rhodesia and South West Africa) never experienced sustained rural guerrilla warfare, and opponents of the state did not establish liberated zones in the countryside. Farm workers were, and remain, under-organized.

There were several reasons for the rearguard position of the countryside. Some had to do with the structural limits of the countryside as a field of operation: the conservatism and parochialism of many chiefs and peasants, the dispersal and vulnerability of black farm workers, the unsuitability of much of the rural terrain for guerrilla war and the capacity of the South African state's administrative and repressive apparatus to reach deeply into the countryside – and into neighbouring states supporting guerrillas. Clearly however the biases and orientations of black leaders also played a part in the relative neglect of the countryside: the educated backgrounds and urban location of black leaders, the hegemony of modernist discourse in black nationalism, the Communist Party's residual doctrinal favouritism towards the urban working class even after 1928 and the belief of many on the left that the future lay with the expanding urban and industrial sector. Uneasy, sometimes hostile relations with traditional African leaders made it difficult for urban-based organizations to operate in parts of the countryside –

as the ANC learned to its cost in KwaZulu. The 1990s has seen the ANC attempting to mend bridges with rural traditional leaders.

Between town and country: the compound and hostel

South Africa's system of oscillating long-range migrant labour spanned rural households and compounds (or men's hostels) in mining and urban areas. The availability of part-peasant, part-proletarian migrants for collective action against employers and the state was much debated before 1994.

Militancy amongst migrant gold miners – the country's most strategically important labour force – flared only occasionally before the 1970s. There was a major strike in 1920. Another, in 1946, was brutally crushed. Migrant municipal and dock workers also occasionally struck, as in the Transvaal and Durban respectively in 1918. Migrants sometimes acted as conduits of radical ideas and allegiances between town and country (Beinart 1987; Delius 1993). But union organization was difficult both to establish and sustain amongst migrants. Migrants were concentrated in compounds where they were subject to surveillance by African indunas and white officials. Their living quarters were ethnically segregated. They were vulnerable to being deported to the impoverished reserves. Many were committed to a rural existence and to traditionalist institutions, and were wary of the more militant towns and cities. Migrants took some pride in performing waged work especially on the mines, and accepted a degree of privation as part of a 'moral economy' of mining, reacting militantly only when its rules were violated (Webster 1991; Moodie 1994: 85-8; Harries 1994: 223). The advance of unionization amongst black workers generally was hindered as long as manufacturers continued to employ mainly migrants, as was the case (despite growing demand for more semi-skilled operative labour) before the 1960s.

In the 1970s migrant militancy erupted both in industry and on the mines. Migrants provided a large part of the base for the industrial strike action that spread from Durban to the Reef and Cape in 1972-74 and were prominent in the initial membership base of new independent trade unions (Mamdani 1996: ch. 7). On the gold mines both internecine violence and anti-employer militancy ballooned, and were followed in their wake by the successful organizational efforts of the National Union of Mineworkers in the 1980s. These developments were interpreted by some as proof against claims of migrant conservatism, but they were linked to the changing composition and character of the migrant labour force. In essence, migrants were being proletarianized and South Africanized. Gold mines offered their workers more long-term re-employment and hired an increasing proportion of South African based workers who were more militant in defence of their interests than previous migrant cohorts from neighbouring countries. More generally, impoverishment and landlessness in the reserves weakened the ties binding migrants to rural traditionalism and magnified the importance of their urban wages (Moodie 1994; Mamdani 1996: 239).

While mineworker militancy surged through the 1980s, peaking in the great strike of 1987, the militancy of migrants outside the mines was short-lived. According to Mamdani, migrants were marginalized from opposition politics from the mid-1970s. In 1976 young township residents grabbed the mantle of militancy while trade unions, infused with veterans of township revolt and faced with the retrenchment of their migrant members, grew more urban-centred (Mamdani 1996). Zulus in urban hostels, suspicious of settled urban residents and especially militant urban youth, clashed violently with township-dwellers in 1976 and from the later 1980s through to the early 1990s. Thus while some migrants became a part of the trend to rising militancy, in other cases burgeoning urban militancy polarized migrants and non-migrants. In both types of scenario it became evident that migrant compounds and hostels could metamorphose, in the appropriate circumstances, from employer- or state-dominated 'total institutions' into bastions of collective organization, whether by militant gold miners (James 1992: 111-12) or pro-Inkatha impis ravaging nearby townships and squatter settlements.

Educational institutions

The introduction of an inferior state-run 'Bantu Education' for Africans in 1953 was followed in 1955 by a brief, largely ineffectual boycott by parents and pupils (Lodge 1983: ch. 5), followed in turn by long years of quiescence in the classroom and lecture theatre. In the mid-1970s however the expanding network of schools and universities allocated to African, coloured and Indian people emerged as major flashpoints of militant anti-system struggle. Bantu Education corralled large numbers of young people across the country, in both urban and rural areas, within an under-resourced and authoritarian education system. Of particular significance was the expansion of secondary school enrolment from the very early 1970s (Hyslop 1988b). From the mid-1970s this expansion ran in parallel with a slowing economy, leaving a growing army of school leavers confronted with diminishing job prospects. Many discontented students were drawn to militant Black Consciousness and (in the 1980s) Charterist ideologies (Hyslop 1988a, b; Bundy 1994). School and university student boycotts shattered the state schooling system in 1976-77, 1980-81 and from 1984 onwards, especially in African areas, but also in some coloured ones. They thus posed a significant challenge to state efforts to expand the black skill base and win black hearts and minds to the merits of separate development (Hyslop 1989b: 201).

The disruption of schools carried a price for blacks. It was often difficult to bridge the gap between educational struggles and the concerns of an older generation of teachers, parents and workers. The school boycott tactic alienated parents concerned to obtain education for their children and was divisive amongst pupils. It effectively deprived tens of thousands of young Africans of even the rudimentary education offered by the state system at a time when demand for unskilled labour was in decline. Parents attempted in the mid-1980s to regain control of the education system, organizing a National Education Crisis Committee in 1985 to establish an alternative education system while simultaneously shepherding students back into the classrooms. They and later black leaders achieved only limited success: students had become conscious of their power and viewed all adult authority with suspicion (Hyslop 1988a: 199-204). The legacy of educational disruption lives on. Secondary and tertiary institutions remain restless, while cohorts of the young have entered post-apartheid South Africa bereft of appropriate skills.

Black school and university students intervened and, together with the black youth more widely, often attempted to give a lead to struggles outside the educational arena as well. Students were better than non-schoolgoing youth at linking up with the struggles of other sectors of society (Glaser 1998), but the interventions of the young generally were often coercive and clumsy. While the BC youth leaders of 1976-77 appealed for workers to support stayaways with some success, they did not link up effectively with then nascent labour organizations and (as we have seen) came into conflict with Zulu migrant workers (Hirson 1979: 244-58). From 1980 students pursued a more structured alliance with the organized working class but they, along with other youth, continued on occasion to be at odds with unionized workers and migrants (Hyslop 1988a: 194-8).

The workplace and the community

The capitalist-industrial separation of waged work and home opened within the urban setting two discrete arenas of struggle against the racial order: the workplace and the 'community' or residential area. In the 1980s anti-apartheid groups hotly debated the proper relationship between workplace and community action.

In both workplaces and townships blacks fought for short-term objectives (such as higher wages or lower rents) and the long-term goal of black liberation. In important respects though they offered distinctive terrains of action. Distinguishing features of the workplace as a site of struggle included its largely working-class character, the functional interdependence and spatial proximity of workers which facilitated organization and leadership accountability and the immediacy of capital (and its agents) as the enemy. The principal resource of blacks at work was their strategic power within production, which grew substantially from the 1960s. The residential community, by contrast, brought together blacks of different and sometimes antagonistic classes, was less easy to organize systematically and confronted as its immediate adversary the local state. The chief political resource of residents was their capacity to withhold payment for 'collective consumption' goods supplied by the municipality, province or various utilities, as well as to boycott goods sold by nearby white businessmen. They could also organize to stop people leaving for work. In the workplace the principal organization of black collective action was the trade union. Township residential areas threw up a range of organizations, most importantly civic and youth associations.

It was the 'workerists' associated with the Federation of South African Trade Unions (1979-85) who most vigorously championed workplace struggle. They insisted that the workplace provided the best platform for advancing the specific interests of the working class and for fostering a democratic organizational and political culture based on high levels of accountability. They worried that 'community' organization would subsume working-class interests under those of other classes, especially the black petit bourgeoisie. Workerists believed that community organizations were poorly organized, under top-down leadership and given to coercing workers into supporting militant actions. Defenders of community struggle tended to emphasize the limits of economism, in particular its failure to confront the central challenge of state power, as well as of workerism, with its neglect of non-workplace issues relevant to all classes. They tended to favour a linking of the two arenas, in practice usually favouring a leading role for organizations operating in the townships and on a national stage such as, in the 1980s, the UDF (Maree 1987: part V).

During the course of the 1980s this debate was largely superseded as 'economistic' unions entered tactical alliances with 'community' organizations in support of consumer boycotts and stayaways, and joined 'populist' unions inside Cosatu in 1985 (Fine and Webster 1990). Some saw these developments as heralding a new style of 'political' or 'social movement' unionism that combined economic and political concerns and represented the unemployed as well as those at work (Lambert and Webster 1988; Webster 1988). The 'people's power' movement of 1984-86 and the resurgence of urban civics after 1989 meanwhile suggested that bottom-up democracy could take root in the 'community' too. Sometimes as in Alexandra it was established under the guidance of union activists.

Workplace-centrism can be defended retrospectively as a necessary 'phase' in building up of trade unions sufficiently strong to withstand state repression and provide a durable platform for political action. At the same time many workerists in the 1970s and early 1980s clearly underestimated the magnetic pull of township-based, cross-class black politics in a society oppressed by a racist white state and in which economic and racial hierarchies massively overlapped. The workerist faith in the possibility of establishing workplace democracy as a foundation for a larger democratic polity also seems retrospectively naive, as does its township counterpart, the struggle for 'people's power' in the streets and neighbourhoods. The rhetoric of conciliar democracy precluded recognition of the limits of unions and civics as democratic representatives and failed to grasp the value of more inclusive forms of representative democracy.

Today in post-apartheid South Africa the workplace-community divide throws up a different, still unresolved question: whether unions are bearers of a wider project of egalitarian transformation that embraces the unemployed and rural poor, or sectional defenders of those relatively privileged workers with access to urban employment.

The state as a site of struggle

A key area of contestation in opposition ranks was how to relate to the white minority state and its black-staffed offshoots. Should opponents of the racial order stand for election to state bodies? Should trade unions register under industrial relations legislation? Should opponents of the system advise whites on how to vote in elections and referendums? These questions raised the issues of the nature of the state, reform versus revolution and tactics versus principle. Was the state an impregnable white fortress that could only be stormed from without, or a complex terrain of struggle? Could it be reformed from within, or at least offer tactical and strategic platforms for revolutionary oppositionists? Was it perhaps so evil that participation in it represented an unacceptable moral compromise?

For most liberals the state was a potential instrument of the common good, perverted for Afrikaner nationalist ends but reformable in principle. Liberals thus had few qualms about standing for election to statutory bodies. White liberals stood for parliament (both as ordinary Members of Parliament and as 'Native Representatives' in the House of Assembly and Senate) and for local councils (Lewsen 1987). African and coloured liberals participated vigorously in electoral politics (especially in the Cape) in support of their preferred white parties and candidates and in elections to black advisory or self-governing bodies (Trapido 1968, 1980a; Roth 1986; Lewis 1987; Rich 1996: chs 4, 8).

Radicals were divided on the issue of participation in the state, and their positions in many cases shifted over time. The SACP and, by the later 1940s, the ANC considered the existing state fundamentally illegitimate, an instrument of white power rather than (even potentially) of the common good. They did not, however, initially adopt an abstentionist position; until the late 1940s at least they saw tactical and strategic advantage in exploiting openings within the state while also acting in other arenas. Following the participationist precedent set by the International Socialist League, the CPSA put up candidates in a variety of municipal, provincial and parliamentary elections between the 1920s and 1940s (Lodge 1985: 6-7; Johns 1995: 56-8). A former CPSA member Solly Sachs' Independent Labour Party contested three (white) seats in the 1943 general election (Witz 1987). Although their electoral victories were few, Communists succeeded in winning a seat in the Senate (in 1942) and another in the House of Assembly (in 1948) as Natives' Representatives (Roth 1986). ANC members in the 1940s won places in the Natives' Representative Council (set up in 1936) and the movement directly involved itself in the internal politics of the body. The ANC also had supporters in the township-level Location Advisory Boards set up under 1920 legislation.

The interest of the CPSA/SACP and ANC in participation was overtaken by the militant turn of the late 1940s and the Congress Alliance's concentration on mass civil disobedience in the 1950s. In 1946 the ANC acted to suspend the NRC and three years later the organization's Programme of Action called for a boycott of racially differential institutions. In the 1950s the ANC opposed participation in school committees and boards set up under the Bantu Education Act (Hyslop 1989b: 205-7). Even so, the ANC participated in urban Advisory Board elections on the Witwatersrand throughout the 1950s and in 1958 the ANC gave whites advice on how to vote in general elections (Lodge 1983: 78, ch. 8). The turn to armed struggle in the 1960s marked an abandonment of above-ground politics generally, but during the 1970s an exiled ANC desperate for some leverage inside South Africa supported Buthelezi's participation in the KwaZulu 'homeland' government and participation by anti-independence candidates in Lebowa's legislative elections (Delius 1996: 173). Despite these dalliances the ANC-allied Charterists active inside the country in the 1980s were resolutely opposed to participation in 'homeland' structures or municipal, advisory, parliamentary and other bodies set up for coloureds, Indians or Africans.

Predominantly black trade unions for their part confronted the issue of whether or not to co-operate with state industrial relations machinery. Many chose to do so in the interwar period, appealing to Wage Boards for example (Hirson 1989: chs 3, 4). Some unions affiliated to the South African Congress of Trade Unions remained registered under state industrial relations law even after the NP in 1953 banned racially mixed unions, despite deregistration pressure from Sactu leaders and Communists (Fine and Davis 1990: 166-8). At the end of the 1970s and beginning of the 1980s re-emergent 'independent' black trade unions briefly but vigorously debated the issue of participation in the post-Wiehahn industrial relations machinery. The syndicalist General Workers Union and ANC-aligned unions voiced the view that registration would lead to bureaucratic and economistic unionism. Fosatu insisted that it would offer legal protection and new sites of struggle (Maree 1987: part IV).

The most vigorous opposition to participation in state bodies came from the coloured Trotskyists of the western Cape gathered in the NEUM (founded in 1943). For them non-collaboration, a policy first adopted in opposition to participation in the Coloured Advisory Council set up in 1943, had become by 1946 an untouchable creed. They vilified the Communists and ANC-aligned political organizations for participating in elections to bodies associated with a 'fascist' state (Lewis 1987: ch. 8; Alexander 1989). Exponents of Africanism in the 1940s and 1950s and Black Consciousness in the 1970s and 1980s also opposed participation in state bodies. They were, as we have seen, joined in their boycottist stance by the ANC and its allies, though the latter never made it the centrepiece of political doctrine that it was for the NEUM.

Boycottist politics could serve as an effective rallying point. It contributed to the revival and flourishing of Charterist politics in the first half of the 1980s. It was directly responsible for the collapse of Black Local Authorities and the subsequent restructuring of municipal government in a more democratic direction from the late 1980s. It may even have hastened the negotiated transition to a democratic order nationally by effectively delegitimating all that a reformist NP could offer by way of concessions to the black majority. By contrast participation, as in the Natives' Representative Council 1937-51, often yielded scanty results.

Nevertheless boycottism had its drawbacks. It was the main reason for the isolation and impotence suffered by western Cape Trotskyists, though it was debilitating in their case mainly because they extended the boycottist principle to include a refusal to join forces with 'collaborators' of any kind or to participate in 'reformist' struggles (Alexander 1989: 187-90). Boycottism at its extremes encouraged a politics effectively of anti-politics: of posturing rather than active struggle in the case of the NEUM, of 'dual power' insurrectionism rather than bargaining from a position of strength in the case of ANC-allied groups. Proceeding from a simplistic view of the South African state as fascist and internally homogeneous, boycottism may have led to the forfeiture of opportunities to use legal spaces and mechanisms to win concessions, block state policies from within and secure a degree of protection from state power (Wolpe 1980; Morris and Padayachee 1989). Boycottism also led opponents of the system to overestimate their active support – for example to equate coloured and Indian abstention from voting with active support for radical causes – and to engage in coercive forms of militancy which prepared the ground for repressive counter-violence.

There were occasions when participators won concessions or frustrated government plans. Inkatha's refusal to accept independence for KwaZulu contributed to the failure of 'homeland' policy. In 1987-88 white, coloured and

Indian parliamentarians helped stymie government plans for revamping urban segregation. While Inkatha and tricameral parliamentary MPs might be viewed as exemplifying co-opted participators, the experience of the more militant registered trade unions suggests that engagement with the state did not invariably preclude radical action. Nor did local-level negotiations with municipalities and businessmen in the late 1980s and early 1990s suffocate grassroots civic bodies. Whether or not participators could make gains depended on their resoluteness, the extent of their political clout outside state structures and on the wider political and economic climate. Again, whether or not participating organizations retained their autonomy depended on a range of factors, including the depth of their democratic organization. The issue of participation was always best addressed tactically rather than as a matter of principle.

Narratives of resistance

The history of resistance to the racial order in South Africa can be read as a story that passes through a series of logically sequential and necessary stages, marked by the trying out of progressively more militant methods of struggle, unavoidable defeats, temporary setbacks, lessons learned, leading to a heroic climax and inevitable ending. This is black struggle conceived as the rational unfolding of an historical Idea of Liberation through various stages of self-realization. Resistance history can also be read in a way that gives it a single central heroic character, the ANC, which, though it has its ups and downs, finally fulfils its destiny to lead the black majority in South Africa to victory. Stories of this kind, though often told to inductees into the ANC political tradition (Lodge 1990: 180), misleadingly weave an ineluctable logic into contested tactical and strategic shifts, and they read back into the ANC's entire historical course the importance it acquired at specific times.

The ANC, founded in 1912, is the oldest still-existing liberation movement in Africa. Its 'long walk' to power in 1994 passed through gentlemanly protest before the 1940s, peaceful mass mobilization in the 1950s, armed struggle from the 1960s and mass insurrection in the mid-1980s. Each of the steps along the road can be or have been presented as 'tragic, although historically inevitable and necessary', in a narrative illustrating either the ANC's essential reasonableness or its lack of choice but to progressively escalate the struggle, or both (see e.g. ANC 1969; Mandela 1994: 259).

Critics have, however, shown convincingly that the leadership of the ANC and its allies took these various steps as a result of specific choices. Though these were shaped in part by structural factors such as state repression and the size and militancy of the movement's constituencies, they were also based on quite particular analyses of historical conjunctures which were rarely the only ones possible. These analyses were influenced by amongst other things leadership self-interest and prevailing ideological and strategic fashions.

Two of the ANC's turns have been subject to particularly intense debate. One was the decision to pursue an elitist form of military action at the expense of building up mass-based organizations inside the country. This has rightly been called into question. Critics of the armed turn argue that the expansion of the urban working class in the 1960s afforded new opportunities for an effective challenge from below and insist that the ANC/SACP analysis of the political system as fascist and closed to all non-armed or legal action was mistaken (Fine and Davis 1990: 239-46). The ANC-supported shift from non-violent mass mobilization to an openly insurrectionary strategy in the mid-1980s has for its part been criticized, again with justification, as adventurist and premature. On this occasion the ANC and its domestic allies clearly underestimated the power and coherence of the state, exposing carefully nurtured organizations to massive reprisals (Callinicos 1988: 74-5; Jochelson 1990: 13) and missing opportunities for a more calibrated engagement with a divided white establishment (Morris and Padayachee 1989).

The point also needs making, in light of the movement's currently overwhelming political dominance, that the ANC's organizational ascendancy was not always guaranteed. The movement came remarkably close to being eclipsed four times in its history: by the more militant and populist ICU of the 1920s; by the initially broader alliance represented by the AAC from 1935; by the rise of the Africanist PAC in 1959; and by the Black Consciousness movement which in the 1970s filled a gap created by the ANC's relative absence from above-ground domestic politics. The ANC ultimately outlasted the ICU which retreated and fragmented towards the end of the 1920s under a weight of mercurial and corrupt leadership, internal division, ephemeral organization and the union's inability to meet the often wild expectations of its supporters (Bonner 1978). The AAC's relative passivity in the face of the segregationist advance meant that it failed to outflank even a languid ANC. The ANC anyway weakened the AAC by withdrawing from its work and was in turn able to stage a revival under A. B. Xuma's more effective leadership in the 1940s (Walshe 1987: ch. 10). The PAC, which flared into vigorous life during the 1960 anti-pass protests, succumbed in exile to chronic factionalism, poor leadership and ideological opportunism. It also alienated host African governments. The ANC experienced internal dissent and factionalism of its own, but benefited from more effective diplomacy in the West and Africa and from connections through the SACP to East Bloc arms sources (Lodge 1983: ch. 12). Finally, the ANC saw off the Black Consciousness challenge in the 1970s because it had the military and educational infrastructure to receive the large numbers of young people who fled the country in 1976-77. It made effective underground connections with the South African Student Movement leadership and its older long-serving prisoners won over BC converts in prison. BC broke up under the impact of state repression (especially in 1977) and the leadership rivalries which led to the Azanian Students' Organization joining the ANC camp in the early 1980s (Diseko 1991: 60-2; Marx 1992: ch. 3). By then ANC-allied 'Charterist' organizations were well on the way to establishing an untrammelled ascendancy on the domestic political stage.

The significance of resistance

A range of Marxist analysts have been keen to stress the importance of black struggle in contributing to crises which resulted in state policy shifts, notably in the 1940s and the 1970s and 1980s (Wolpe 1972; O'Meara 1979; Saul and Gelb 1981; Fine and Davis 1990). Such approaches stand in contrast to liberal political histories explaining policy changes largely in intra-white electoral terms, and also those Marxist writings attaching a central importance to intra-capitalist conflict (Davies et al. 1976; for a critique, see Innes and Plaut 1978). A wide range of writers, and not only Marxist or radical, consider black mass opposition to the system to have been a crucial factor, albeit variously ranked in importance, in persuading the white regime to dismantle racial laws and negotiate its own demise. To what extent did black resistance influence the actions of the white minority state or threaten its existence, and what part did it play in apartheid's downfall?

The black majority before the 1990s never had anything more than a peripheral presence in the state apparatus itself. It is nevertheless clear that a great deal of white policy-making in the twentieth century was about blacks – including how to contain the threat they were assumed to represent, as an oppressed and numerous population, to white political and economic power. Black resistance was thus 'influential' at least in its impact on the white imagination; and because this was so it could causally affect white political behaviour. This cause–effect relationship should not, however, be confused with black power. The 'black peril' could, and often did, provide a pretext for subjecting blacks to still tighter controls, whether in the form of police repression or regulation of black movement and settlement. Black resistance might cause whites to do what they would not otherwise have done, but it did not necessarily provide a medium for realizing effects intended by black resisters or for satisfying black needs.

Black resistance (and fear of it) did not however incur only repression. The South African state ruled the black majority through attempts at self-legitimation as well as via the use and threat of force. Often in South Africa fresh oppressions ran parallel with fresh concessions: the abolition of the Cape African franchise with the granting of a NRC in 1936, for example, or police repression with township upgrading in the later 1980s. Sometimes concessions and repression were twinned in a divide-and-rule formula, as when in the 1950s and early 1980s the state granted concessions to settled urban Africans at the expense of their rural counterparts. Some of the concessions were informed by paternalistic considerations too, and not all were minor. The apartheid state in the 1950s launched a massive house building programme for those it permitted to remain in the towns and cities. Sometimes the state calculated that it could win black support through an emphasis on material upliftment, but in doing this made the mistake of treating blacks as bodies rather than thinking subjects: even meaningful concessions could not erase the desire for equality and equal dignity. Co-optive concessions thus in the end could not close the legitimacy deficit which attended the whole period of white rule.

Because the black majority had the 'power' to withhold legitimacy from the state, it could frustrate whole areas of state policy-making whose precise purpose was winning legitimacy. The municipal and constitutional reforms of the mid-1980s are a signal case of blacks frustrating the state's ability to realize its own intended effects, for these incited rather than dampened black mass opposition.

State policy could be frustrated in other, more insidious ways. Through resistance by evasion – notably of influx control laws – Africans as individuals and small groups frequently outwitted and undermined state policy initiatives. Though over long periods (such as the 1950s and 1960s) the principal effect of their 'success' was to induce the state to get still tougher, by the 1980s black evasion had got the better of those attempting to control black movement and settlement. For the liberal writer J. Kane-Berman, the 'silent' revolution unleashed by blacks' evasion of apartheid was ultimately more subversive of apartheid than high-profile opposition (Kane-Berman 1991). Such rankings are inevitably speculative, but the evasions of ordinary people, coupled to the eventual decline in the divided ruling bloc's will to further escalate its commitment to surveillance and control of its subjects, undoubtedly dissolved aspects of apartheid on the ground.

These are points about the limits of (state) power and (black) powerlessness. On the side of the majority they imply a defensive power. What capacity did blacks have to exercise offensive power against the state? The South African state had at its disposal formidable resources of self-defence, easily mobilized, which beat off attacks and dissuaded prospective attackers. The state apparatus was reasonably well supplied with revenue, could maintain security forces (significantly expanded from the 1960s) drawn mainly from loyal (white) sectors of society and enjoyed powers of communication, mobility and physical destruction which greatly exceeded those of its opponents. In an emergency black townships were easily sealed. As a last resort the state had the option of deploying nuclear and biological weapons. Of course blacks had their own weapons of resistance, above all numbers, and refusal to work or buy, and the yield of these weapons grew considerably in the 1970s as a result of urbanization, skill shortages and the expansion of the black consumer market. It was however always more difficult to mobilize large numbers of workers and consumers than to train the state's firepower. Black oppositionists benefited from the material support of the East Bloc, Scandinavia and independent African neighbouring states but this was counterbalanced by the backing given to the regime by the United States and Britain during the Cold War. South Africa's military and economic power overshadowed that of the regional states that backed the ANC.

Did the state ever come close to being physically overthrown? There is no evidence of it. Certainly in the 1980s the periphery of the state began to unravel, with black local government wiped out in many areas in the middle of the decade and subject to disintegrative pressures until the end of apartheid. The 'homeland' periphery too began to fray, beginning with the military coup in the Transkei by pro-ANC Bantu Holomisa in 1987. Greater reliance on black police and soldiers increased the state's vulnerability. But physical overthrow of the central state, or the bulk of regional or even local authority taken across society as a whole, did not occur despite inflated expectations that it might during the 1984-86 insurrection. The term 'crisis' in its full medical meaning thus never confronted the South African state exclusively as a result of black resistance; if it did so at all, it was as a result of the conjuncture of a series of challenges. Black resistance was but one of a cluster of factors that induced political reform and finally the end of minority rule.

Nevertheless resisters on three occasions demonstrated a capacity to impose a high price for system maintenance. The crisis around Sharpeville did not have the potential as some postulated to produce an overthrow of the system (on the debate see Lodge 1983: 224-5), but it did briefly impose a severe economic cost on the state and capital. That cost was contained by repression, the bolstering of the security forces and the consolidation of white unity. The white regime in the 1960s demonstrated a formidable capacity to 'modernize racial domination' (Adam 1971), and the implementation of grand apartheid advanced rather than receded post-Sharpeville. The second occasion was 1976-77 when student-led township unrest reignited capital flight, this time against a less (for the state) favourable regional and economic backdrop. It could be argued that from this point there set in a crisis, not yet akin to a life threatening emergency, but certainly to a chronic malady. It was 1984-86 however that of the three imposed by far the greatest cost economically and internationally and induced the greatest division in the ruling bloc. It did not overthrow the state but arguably brought closer (though not immediately) its negotiated reordering.

Subversive threats to the white state during the twentieth century did not issue exclusively from the black population. As Yudelman notes, for the first quarter of the century the state faced a bigger challenge from two forces in the white population, Afrikaner nationalism and organized white labour (Yudelman 1984).

The 'native question' did not become a key issue in white South African politics until the late 1920s, the 'black peril' election of 1929 perhaps being a turning point. By then Afrikaner nationalism, which flared violently in 1914, had been diverted successfully onto a constitutional path, while white labour, which had staged an armed uprising in 1922, was co-opted into a new system of institutionalized bargaining with employers. By the 1930s, as Lacey notes, the white political establishment could turn a more or less united face to its black subjects (Lacey 1981). By the time that unity came apart again in the 1940s, the 'native question' had become the central divisive issue in white politics and blacks were posing an increasingly serious challenge. The alliance of black nationalism and black labour, electorally triumphant in 1994, carries echoes of past alliances of Afrikaner nationalism and white labour. Black nationalism in power, like that of Afrikaners before it, is showing every sign of accommodating the capitalist economic system it opposed in opposition. And like white labour in the late 1920s and from the 1960s, the ANC's labour allies now face the prospect of marginalization by a rising nationalist elite.

Does the termination of apartheid mean the end also of resistance? It does mean, by definition, the end of resistance to white political power. Resistance to white *economic* and *social* power continues in the form of, for example, industrial action, which has been extensive since 1994, and in battles over the 'transformation' of white-dominated institutions like universities. There is, in addition, an overhang of the anti-apartheid struggle in the shape of political violence and a culture of struggle. This impact of this culture is felt in a range of institutions, although the picture is confused by signs of simultaneous depoliticization. The rise of a new black political elite, and growing inequality in the black population, may provide a context for new forms of struggle and opposition in the future – struggles for full social inclusion and deeper democracy. These will not be entirely discontinuous with struggles past, but they are better treated within a different kind of narrative, and on another occasion. In any case the story of post-apartheid opposition is only just beginning.

8

The Dynamics of Transition

Explaining a 'miracle'

During the first half of the 1990s South Africa witnessed what Nelson Mandela (cited in Lawrence 1994: 1) termed a 'small miracle' – the negotiated dismantling of a system of white racial domination that had lasted (depending on definition) anything between ninety and well over three hundred years. In the latter half of the 1990s a new, mainly black political leadership elected in April 1994 steered the country through its democratic infancy. South Africa has since experienced a second 'free', or at least open and inclusive, election in June 1999. This chapter explores the circumstances that made possible the demise of apartheid, the prognosis for democratic consolidation and the prospects for the deeper social transformation that must occur if South Africa is to address its inheritance of vast inequalities.

Terminal apartheid

President P. W. Botha had by the beginning of 1989 achieved relative political and economic stability in South Africa following a period of severe turbulence that began in 1984. Yet within a year Botha's successor, F. W. De Klerk, had begun to negotiate the dismantling of white political power with the government's formerly most bitter enemies. The abruptness of this shift from relatively stable dominance to negotiated transfer of power fed a myth that South Africa's Afrikaner minority 'gave it all away' in an act of 'peaceful capitulation' almost unique amongst ethnic oligarchies (Waldmeir 1997: 108; Adam et al. 1997: 51). The actual evidence does not support the view that power was transferred either in an entirely voluntary fashion or from a position where the regime had full control of events. By 1989 the internal and external pressures on the white government to negotiate an end to apartheid were very strong and the long-term prospects of white minority rule looked dim. Moreover, the decade after 1984 was marked by widespread and brutal violence, perpetrated by both forces linked to the regime and its black opponents. The physical overthrow of the state never occurred, but nor had it done so elsewhere in Africa; South Africa's 'decolonization' was actually amongst the more violent on the continent.

What *was* noteworthy about South Africa, relative to Europe's African colonies, was that the dismantling of the old order was largely internally initiated and steered. This reflected in part the difference that South Africa had already decolonized long before handing power to the indigenous majority; there was no external colonial overlord to manage the handover, and no metropolitan redoubt to which the 'settlers' could flee rather than deal. The enfranchisement of the South African black majority had more in common with the extension of the vote to the middle and working classes in Britain than to processes of decolonization. It involved a surrender of exclusive political power by a domestic ruling class to its social subordinates, accompanied by an effort to protect social and economic privilege from the newly enfranchised.

The white minority's surrender of political control may not have constituted a unique concession to social groups demanding political inclusion, but it was dramatic for other reasons. Though the passage of power from white to black elites was not rapid – the negotiations stretched over four years – it was largely unforeseen and it was, in the end, unexpectedly complete. In these latter respects if not in terms of timescale, South Africa's political change paralleled (not unconnected) developments unfolding more or less simultaneously in the Soviet Union and East-Central Europe.

Structure, agency and the negotiated demise of apartheid

Commentators attempting to explain the dynamics of the South African transfer of power have differed over the relative importance of structural factors – political and economic pressures from within and without the country – and agency factors such as the predispositions and calculations of black and white leaders. However, there are no intrinsically structural and agential factors in the field of human action. What is a structure and who is an agent depend on vantage point. Black struggle was an example of collective agency, yet it confronted white rulers as an external structural constraint. Individual reformers like Mikhael Gorbachev and De Klerk could initiate political change but not control its direction. Their interventions were important above all because they released deeper forces. Agents are themselves constituted by structural forces, such as economic interest, culture or psychology. They do not confront structures and choices bereft of prior history or socialization. How distinguishable is De Klerk from the Afrikaner political culture that helped shape his subjectivity? Is he the agent, or is the culture?

Bearing in mind this perspectival quality of the structure–agent distinction, it remains possible and useful to discuss separately the role of key actors, both individual and collective, and the structural terrain on which they operated. The structural context of the late 1980s did not in itself compel regime and anti-apartheid forces to negotiate. Structural factors framed the choices that white and black leaders had to make, determining the trade-offs, and influencing the perceptions of potential risk and gain, entailed in competing options. There is little doubt that for both sides the perceived costs of rejectionism – of refusing to talk with the enemy – rose substantially from the mid-1980s.

System actors: Afrikaner leaders, Afrikanerdom and the state

The white 'agents' responsible for initiating the transfer of power can be conceptualized in different ways: as a group of key politicians, officials and influential people in white civil society; as 'Afrikanerdom' (and within it the NP); and as the state.

It was a small and identifiable group of individuals who were responsible for making the choices that (indirectly or directly) pointed the NP down the negotiation route. They included top people in the cabinet, National Intelligence Service, the Afrikaner Broederbond, and the Afrikaner press and journalistic world (Sparks 1996; Waldmeir 1997). Easily the most important figure on the side of the white regime was De Klerk, who became NP party leader in early 1989 and President in September of that year.

De Klerk was an improbable dismantler of neo-apartheid. He had a conservative reputation in the NP, and the rivals he beat in the party leadership race were all to his left. He was not party to secret talks with the then-illegal African National Congress that had begun around 1985, and he fought, according to Sparks, a 'reactionary' election campaign in September 1989 (Sparks 1996: 94). Within a month of that election however he had begun releasing ANC leaders and unofficially unbanning the ANC. On 2 February 1990 he dazzled the international public by announcing the official unbanning of the ANC, South African Communist Party and other anti-apartheid organizations and the release of long-term political prisoners including Nelson Mandela.

Historians of the period have still not offered a satisfactory explanation of what turned De Klerk into a political reformer. That De Klerk was not compelled by structural pressures to make the move is attested to by the fact other leading executive actors privy to much the same knowledge as he resisted it (and especially the unbanning of the SACP). De Klerk denies that he underwent a sudden conversion in 1989, but claims to have followed the NP down its reformist road after the party in 1986 accepted the case for universal franchise in a unitary South Africa. His earlier conservative politics may have been – as he insists – partly related to the tactical requirements of his role as Transvaal leader defending the NP's right flank against the breakaway Conservative Party. De Klerk can be viewed with hindsight as pragmatic conservative, willing to adjust his political line to ensure the survival of the NP, protect Afrikaner and white interests and preserve capitalism (Sparks 1996: 91, 94-5; Waldmeir 1997: 111-16; De Klerk 2000). Moreover, he had, much more than his belligerent and autocratic predecessor, the instincts of a 'reconciliator' and a team-builder (Giliomee 1994b: 46; O'Meara 1996: 396).

All the same at least some sort of change-of-heart must have occurred in 1989, and not all of it can be put down to the tipping effect of new conjunctural circumstances. A few have argued that his *Dopper* (Reformed Church) religious beliefs inspired him with a sense of calling, activated in his case by his presidential inauguration (Sparks 1996: 99), though others without denying his religiosity are sceptical about this (Waldmeir 1997: 111). O'Meara more plausibly suggests that De Klerk in 1989 felt a need to make a dramatic impression in order to still *verligte* (reformist) rivals whom he had beaten only narrowly to the NP leadership (O'Meara 1996: 399). Additional factors cited to explain De Klerk's unexpected reformism include his distrust of the securocrats who made the running with government policy-making in the later 1980s, his self-educative participation in a policy think-tank in the late 1980s and his desire to please a growing band of overseas friends (O'Meara 1996: 398; Sparks 1996: 95-7; Waldmeir 1997: 135).

If De Klerk and other Afrikaner leaders were the decisive individual actors on the white side, they in turn occupied key roles within a larger political and cultural collectivity (Afrikanerdom) and an institutional matrix (the state).

There is only a limited sense in which 'Afrikanerdom' was the active subject initiating the historic power transfer of 1990-94. It was, to be sure, Afrikaner leaders of a still largely Afrikaner party who made the decision to go down the negotiation route. It is clear that many Afrikaners were torn by uncertainty about apartheid's viability, and that their self-doubt was shared by most NP leaders. At the vanguard of self-questioning were young Afrikaner cultural dissidents, leading figures in the Afrikaner press, strategic planners in the Afrikaner Broederbond and a cohort of younger reformist NP politicians increasingly prominent in parliamentary standing committees and in deputy-ministerial positions after the 1987 general election.

The growth of a reformist wing of Afrikaner political society stimulated the negotiating process in several ways. Firstly, Afrikaner reformers could apply pressure on NP leaders by threatening to defect to the left unless the ruling party made decisive reformist moves. The NP was shaken by the challenge mounted against it in the 1987 election by three reformist defectors, two of them Afrikaners, who subsequently joined forces with the NP's principal liberal parliamentary opponents (O'Meara 1996: 372-5). Secondly, reformers generated new strategic reformist visions (such as the Broederbond's 1989 'conceptual guidelines', which informed the NP's election manifesto that year and its initial negotiating stance in the 1990s) (O'Meara 1996: 400, 404-5). Thirdly, the strengthening of Afrikaner reformist ranks ensured that Afrikaner political negotiators could depend upon a committed core of support within their otherwise unreliable traditional ethnic constituency.

Nevertheless Afrikaners were anything but united behind reformist moves either before 1989 or after. Though remarkably passive in the face of De Klerk's efforts to reach a deal with the ANC, the NP was by no means universally well disposed to far-reaching political change. The parliamentary NP selected De Klerk to replace Botha as NP leader because of his conservatism rather than his reformist zeal. More than once during the early 1990s deep divisions emerged in the cabinet over the extent of concessions that should be made to the ANC (Mattes 1994: 17). Key Afrikaner institutions, like the Broederbond and Church, fractured in the 1980s in a backlash against reformism. Opinion survey suggested that young Afrikaners were as fearful of change than their elders (Giliomee 1992: 356). The breakaway rightist Conservative Party captured large swathes of the Afrikaner vote from the NP in the general elections of 1987 (when the CP became the Official Opposition) and 1989. Afrikaner votes were split for and against negotiations in the whites-only referendum of March 1992.

Yet while the far right electoral threat supplied a strong incentive for the NP to proceed at best cautiously down the reformist road prior to 1989-90, it was in the end also a powerful (if paradoxical) reason for De Klerk rapidly to shift into negotiating mode. With the NP increasingly squeezed between left and right, the party had to choose either to seek vigorously to reclaim its lost Afrikaner heartland or to act decisively to staunch the loss of votes to the left, establish a new cross-racial reformist coalition and avoid a future whites-only election that the NP might lose.

The state too was in one sense an 'actor', even initiator, in the transition process. However, the state is not a unitary subject but a field of individual and institutional interests more or less effectively subject to law and executive command. It was not the state as such that initiated negotiations but elements of the executive, ruling party and intelligence services. The majority of senior and middle-level state personnel at the end of the 1980s were conservative whites willing to continue administering neo-apartheid. Their principal 'contribution' to the negotiated settlement after 1989 was to not stage an outright rebellion against it. Why did they accept or participate in the dismantling of a white-run political order?

One reason was that De Klerk acted fairly quickly after becoming president to tighten his grip on the state, most dramatically by dismantling the National Security Management System – the lair of the militaristic 'securocrats' – in November 1989. On top of that, recalcitrant police generals and South African Defence Force officers were purged in 1992. However, official quiescence was more importantly due to a residual culture of bureaucratic professionalism – notably present in the military – and to habits of obedience to the law and NP leadership acquired by Afrikaners over decades. Perhaps most importantly, many white state personnel, demoralized by the demise of apartheid, refocused their attention on protecting their material self-interest. Corruption amongst state personnel had already become fairly widespread by the time the transition process commenced (Lodge 1998: 164-71), and many bureaucrats were reconciled to far-reaching political change only by guarantees of their jobs and pensions under majority rule. Many white state personnel, used to a range of perks and a comfortable lifestyle, chose to give priority to their private material concerns over their (increasingly depleted) sense of ideological purpose.

Some parts of the state, however, did not co-operate with the political handover. Personnel associated with Military Intelligence, the SADF Special Forces, the security police and KwaZulu 'homeland' administration embarked on a covert dirty war against radical anti-apartheid groups in the mid-1980s. Some of these 'third force' elements actively attempted to destabilize South Africa politically during the 1990-94 transition period (TRC 1998). Their murderous efforts came close on several occasions to throttling negotiations, but the reactionaries lacked the leadership, numbers, resources, perhaps even the necessary spirit of self-sacrifice, to stop the transition in its tracks (or to destroy the ANC). Moreover while some state personnel tried to sabotage negotiations, other parts of state actively favoured a transfer of political power. Black policemen were increasingly radicalized from 1989 (Murray 1994: 191-2) and in 1990 some black local councillors switched allegiance to the ANC. The 'homeland' state apparatuses were largely African-controlled and staffed, and while some homeland elites remained loyal to the 'separate development' policy that sustained their power, others identified themselves with the goal of majority rule in a unitary state. This was true of the military government that seized power in Transkei in 1987 and of state employees and security personnel who helped overthrow the regime of Lucas Mangope in Bophutatswana in March 1994.

Opposition agents: black leaders, the ANC-led alliance

Nelson Rolihlahla Mandela's personal role in setting the negotiating process in motion was impressively large. To be sure, Mandela's authority and importance derived from his leadership of the ANC, and he had to keep on board both other ANC leaders as well as grassroots supporters in order to sustain his authority. Yet while as a prisoner Mandela communicated with the ANC, seeking its support and reassuring it of his intentions, he also acted on his own initiative on crucial occasions, helping to establish a bridge to white elites seeking a way out of the country's difficulties. After his 1990 release Mandela as ANC leader continued to exercise a commanding influence over opposition politics, with important supplementary roles played by other figures, notably the SACP leader Joe Slovo and the ANC's Secretary General and (from 1991) chief negotiator Cyril Ramaphosa.

What gave Mandela the will and self-confidence to take the initiatives that he did from 1985 in establishing contacts with government officials and exploring potential ground for negotiation? The answer has something to do with the sense of his own importance Mandela acquired from his connection to the Thembu royal house (Mandela 1994: part one), bolstered by his later role as an ANC leader in the 1950s and early 1960s and, subsequently, his legendary status as a long-term political prisoner; an imperious and autocratic personality; an openness to political accommodation typical of an older mission-schooled generation, doubtlessly reinforced by his ageing and long imprisonment; and the atmosphere of urgency and opportunity created by the nation-wide uprising of 1984-86. It was this same self-assurance that enabled Mandela to steer the ANC towards less radical economic policies around 1992, and to adopt the role of racial conciliator throughout the 1990s, often in the face of dissent from the ANC rank-and-file and the organization's allies.

Although Mandela as prisoner necessarily operated in a degree of isolation from the ANC headquartered in Lusaka, the organization began itself in the mid-

1980s to develop contacts in the white political establishment. The public face of this strategy involved an effort, in the wake of the 1984-86 uprising, to project itself symbolically as a government-in-waiting and to divide the white ruling bloc. For four years from 1985 the ANC received high profile delegations of white (in some cases Afrikaner) South African businessmen, journalists, clergymen, academics, politicians and students. The secret face of the strategy involved making indirect, later direct contacts with sections of the Afrikaner elite, and eventually with the the state's intelligence services (Sparks 1996: chs 1-9; Waldmeir 1997: chs 1-6). Although the ANC threw its weight behind the insurrection of the mid-1980s, it sought simultaneously, as part of its effort to present itself as a credible future government, to reassure whites about their well-being under ANC rule. While its noises on economic policy looked radical to visiting capitalists, the organization made clear that it envisaged a mixed rather than socialist economy. In 1988 it presented 'constitutional guidelines' which suggested that it accepted an essentially liberal-democratic model of state, and in 1989 in Harare the organization offered terms for negotiations.

The organization cannot be said to have participated as a whole in the negotiation process after 1990. The ANC camp's negotiation strategy in the early 1990s was directed by a few people at the top of the organization and of the SACP. It was viewed with suspicion by party members and supporters who feared their leaders were giving too much away. At leadership level a militant faction tried to maintain a secret revolutionary underground as a fallback strategy, but 'Operation Vula' was exposed by the police and dismantled in mid-1990. At the same time the more radical party rank-and-file were not silent or without symbolic power or political leverage. At the organization's July 1991 national conference they excoriated the leadership and elected a more youthful and radical National Executive Committee. The ANC leadership had to appease the militancy of ordinary party members, most obviously by supporting popular protest action in mid-1992. Rank-and-file ANC militancy in turn strengthened the bargaining position of ANC leaders. It reminded the party's opponents that the organization retained access to a substantial political resource in black numbers, and signalled to all contending parties the limits of the ANC's room for making concessions to white power-holders.

The domestic impasse

The shift to negotiation mode occurred against the backdrop of three long-term domestic trends that had a direct bearing on the calculations of political actors in 1989-90. The first was what commentators have referred to as a political 'impasse' or 'stalemate'. The rebellion of 1984-86 inflicted lasting damage on black municipal government, but it was largely contained by 1988 via state repression pursued under a State of Emergency. The prospect of overthrowing the state, real enough in the imagination of some of the street rebels and revolutionaries of 1985-86, vanished in the later 1980s. The state, however, was not able to conquer the black opposition. It could limit the extent of unrest, but only by repression, and even repression did not prevent successful general strikes year on year and other outbreaks of unrest. More seriously, South Africa's ruling groups had little desire, certainly by the 1980s, to rule by repression alone. They had throughout the post-1910 history of white rule seen the value of winning black consent, whether for segregation or 'separate development'; but the search for legitimacy grew more urgent in the 1980s as black opposition became more threatening to South Africa's political and economic stability. In the 1980s the opposition demonstrated an impressive capacity to confound all of the state's legitimacy-building initiatives, whether these took the form of creating independent black states, strengthening black municipal government or incorporating coloureds and Indians into the tricameral parliamentary system. Regime opponents could prevent the rulers from imposing their will on society, signalling a potentially permanent crisis of governance.

This crisis seemed all the more likely to be intractable in the light of demographic trends in South Africa. The most disaffected section of the population, Africans, was expanding fastest, while whites (at 13.2% of the population according to the 1991 census) looked set to shrink into an ever-smaller minority. The contracting white population seemed likely to become increasingly dependent on black auxiliaries to police the black majority, and (white) capitalists more and more dependent on Africans for skilled labourers and consumers. Meanwhile the boundaries of residential segregation were being breached as the government lost the will to keep in check a rising tide of black people determined to find jobs and adequate shelter in urban settings. As this tide advanced it raised the threshold of repression that would be needed to dam it.

The third trend was economic. After a long expansion between the early 1930s and early 1970s, the South African economy ran into serious and persistent trouble in the mid-1970s. Expansion of real gross domestic product slowed from 4.9% per annum for the period 1946-74 to only 1.5% per annum in the 1980s. The slowdown was initially in line with global trends, but it was deepened and prolonged by at least two local circumstances. The one was apartheid's legacy of an under-trained black workforce and a constricted internal market. The other was capital flight and increasing isolation from overseas capital markets, the price of apartheid's international unpopularity and tendency to generate internal unrest. Capital shortages were especially serious for an economy that – due to its dependence on imported capital goods, poor manufacturing export performance and the volatility of gold export revenues – had a tendency to bump up against balance of payment constraints as soon as it expanded. Labour market and educational reforms beginning in the 1970s could only partially address these difficulties, and persistent black opposition meant that shortages of foreign investment had grown rather than receded by the late 1980s (Gelb 1991b).

Economic stagnation carried real dangers for the country's rulers. It undercut government revenue and fuelled black discontent, threatening the effectiveness and stability of the state. Perhaps more immediately it threatened the tenure of a ruling party fending off right-wing electoral competition. Since the 1970s white real incomes had stagnated in the face of accelerating inflation while the real incomes of (employed) blacks had risen in spite of it. Less well off white voters resented this effective redistribution of income to blacks. Even middle-class whites worried that stagflation and a weakening currency would erode their living standards. Whereas poorer whites saw apartheid as a form of economic and status protection, many better-off whites came to view it as an obstacle to their continued prosperity. The ruling groups thus faced (in class terms) a choice between settling with blacks on terms acceptable to more affluent whites (who could reasonably hope to survive economically without the protection of apartheid) and seeking, by a shift to the right, to regain the support of working class whites fearful of black economic advance. The latter option appealed increasingly little to the politically dominant Afrikaner elites (themselves typically very materially comfortable) by the later 1980s.

Regional trends

By the mid-1980s the South African state had achieved considerable success in its efforts to reverse the gains which had accrued to radical black nationalism in Southern Africa following the Portuguese withdrawal from Angola and Mozambique in 1975. The SADF had pushed the guerrillas of the South West African People's Organization out of South West Africa/Namibia (which Swapo sought to liberate from Pretoria's colonial rule) back over the border into Angola. Angola itself was wracked by civil war, fuelled by Pretoria's active support for the armed campaign of the Union for the Total Independence of Angola (Unita) against the government of the Marxist-oriented Popular Movement for the Liberation of Angola in Luanda. Mozambique was close to collapse as a result of the Pretoria-backed armed struggle of the Mozambique National Resistance (Renamo). South African troops launched armed raids at will against ANC bases in Mozambique, Lesotho, Botswana, Zimbabwe and Zambia, and the ANC was forced to scale down its presence in countries adjacent to South Africa.

By the late 1980s however South Africa's regional imperium was under strain for two reasons. Firstly, Pretoria's military hegemony in Southern Africa appeared more brittle after a setback suffered by South African forces at Cuito Cuanavale in Angola in 1987. The battle, in which Cuban and Angolan forces successfully checked an SADF advance, suggested that Pretoria was overstretched and that the 1977 arms embargo was beginning to take its toll on South African military superiority, despite South Africa's flourishing domestic military-industrial complex. Secondly, and more crucially, the United States and the Soviet Union were working from the mid-1980s to secure an overall settlement for Angola and SWA/Namibia that included the withdrawal of Cuban troops (which supported the MPLA government) from Angola alongside South Africa's granting of independence to Namibia. By December 1988 a deal had been brokered in New York that would secure both ends. Namibia's first free election in November 1989 brought Swapo to power, and in March 1990 Namibia gained its formal independence from South Africa.

The partial retreat of Pretoria from the wider region need not itself have lessened its determination to defend South Africa as a last bastion of white rule, but it did add to the momentum behind a negotiated settlement with the ANC in two ways. Firstly, the decolonization of Namibia redirected the attention of the international community to its unfinished business in South Africa. Secondly, the South African occupiers brought home lessons from Namibia about how to secure a settlement with black nationalism on favourable terms. Swapo had agreed to a constitution which limited majoritarian powers, while South African counterinsurgency efforts to win the 'hearts and minds' of Namibian blacks had confined Swapo to a narrower than expected electoral majority.

Global developments

Co-ordinated action between the Soviet Union and the US over Namibia and Angola reflected a wider set of international developments impinging on the calculations of political actors in Southern Africa. One was Gorbachev's rise to power and his launch of a new Soviet foreign policy premised on co-operation with the capitalist world. This co-operation extended to resolving long-running regional conflicts, especially those that pitted superpower clients against each other. In the case of Southern Africa Gorbachev's approach found expression in a reorientation of the Soviet Union away from unconditional backing for the ANC's armed struggle and towards supporting a reformist rather than revolutionary dismantling of apartheid. Improved East–West relations in turn encouraged in the US a more conditional and critical support for its own Cold War clients and allies, notably the Pretoria government. As the Cold War wound down the US (together with other powerful Western states such as Britain and Germany) and the Soviet Union intensified their efforts to bring the South African government and the ANC respectively to the negotiating table. In doing so they removed important props to both the survival of South Africa's racial order in the decades after The Second World War and to the guerrilla strategy followed by the ANC and its allies since the early 1960s.

Moscow's foreign policy shift was bound up with a second important trend relevant to South Africa: the protracted decline in 'real socialist' economies evident by the later 1970s and openly acknowledged by Gorbachev in the mid-1980s. By diminishing the appeal of socialism as an alternative form of economy and society, the East Bloc's economic malaise reduced the fear on the part of white rulers that a post-apartheid government would risk dismantling South Africa's working capitalist economy. On the part of the ANC and especially the SACP the discrediting of socialist economics weakened the rationale for a maximalist strategy aimed at a revolutionary overthrow of South Africa's political and economic order.

Turning points

The 1989-90 conjuncture

A description of broad trends and forces leaves unanswered the question of why the regime and its main opponents decided to negotiate precisely in 1989-90. Clearly De Klerk's accession to power in 1989 was a key new development, but there were also alterations at this time to the political environment in which contending groups operated. These mainly involved broader trends coming to a head in a particular way.

To be sure, the risks associated with not negotiating increased slightly rather than massively for both sides in 1989-90. For white rulers the collapse of the East Bloc in 1989 suggested a likelihood of mounting superpower pressure to settle with black leaders, and of deepening isolation for South Africa in the event of a failure to do so. South Africa's debts were up for renegotiation in 1989, and agreement had to be reached on rolling them over if the country's capital shortage was to be addressed. It became clear from early in 1989 that late-1980s state repression and township upgrading had neither lastingly isolated black radicals nor won black hearts and minds. During the year a new Mass Democratic Movement staged a successful hunger strike, defiance campaign and stayaway. Black Local Authorities, stymied by a 1988 election boycott and an ongoing rent boycott, were by 1989 being propped up by the emergency financial intervention of provincial authorities. Urban segregation policy was in open flux. For the ANC and SACP the headlong retreat of the German Democratic Republic following the fall of the Berlin wall in November 1989, together with the loss of a guerrilla bases in Angola, spelt increasing logistical difficulty for a continued armed campaign.

By contrast the opportunities open to the major players suddenly expanded in 1989-90. To De Klerk the 1989 general election results suggested the existence of a reformist constituency amongst white voters. At the same time the 1989 implosion of East-Central European Communism offered NP propagandists the opportunity to outmanoeuvre the ANC by linking it (via its alliance with the SACP) to a spent and discredited ideology. De Klerk began to believe he could beat or contain the ANC electorally, dissipating its *élan* by forcing the movement to engage in conventional party politics, exposing its leaders, including the charismatic Mandela, to public scrutiny, and playing to the fears of whites, coloureds, Indians and conservative Africans about their fate under ANC rule. Prior to mid-1990 opinion surveys were suggesting that the ANC would be unable to win majority support (Mattes 1994: 6). For the alliance headed by the ANC the conjuncture offered more straightforward possibilities: an unexpected opportunity to secure a level of political influence in the short- to medium-term future that could not be won by physical force, as well as for exiles to return to their homeland and prisoners to gain freedom.

These sets of opportunities carried with them a common downside risk for both the government and ANC: of being forced to settle on unfavourable terms, retaining or gaining too little by way of political and economic influence, and alienating core supporters. Clearly in 1989-90 the major political players concluded that opportunities had come to outweigh risks.

The conjuncture of 1992-93

When De Klerk decided to negotiate in 1989-90 it was not, commentators agree, his intention to establish a majoritarian liberal democracy. While the NP early on abandoned hopes of an explicitly ethnic division of power, the party leadership initially envisaged a constitutional scheme which would level up minority and majority party powers in a multi-party cabinet under a presidential troika (Giliomee 1994b: 47). Strategically the NP seemed (despite vacillation) inclined to build an anti-ANC alliance with the Zulu-based Inkatha Freedom Party. With or without De Klerk's sanction elements in the state worked clandestinely with Inkatha to undermine the ANC.

The period between 1990 and late 1992 was largely unproductive of constitutional agreement, partly because of De Klerk's constitutional caution and inability (or reluctance) to rein in rightist subversives. Certain ground rules were forged in 1990-91, with the government agreeing to release prisoners and the ANC to suspend its armed struggle, but mutual suspicion and escalating political violence delayed the formal commencement of negotiations until December 1991, when the Convention for a Democratic South Africa sat for the first time. After his March 1992 whites-only referendum victory De Klerk hardened his negotiating stance. In May 1992 Codesa collapsed amidst disagreements about constitution-change mechanisms and negotiations were broken off in June by an ANC leadership furious about Inkatha's massacre of ANC supporters at Boipatong.

Yet by September 1992, when the NP and ANC signed a 'Record of Understanding', the NP had abandoned its strategy of alliance with Inkatha (amidst considerable top-level NP wrangling) in favour of bilateral deal-making with the ANC. By early 1993 it had come to accept the inevitability of some form of democratic majority rule in place of its cumbersome model of consociationalism. The shift in the NP's position from late 1992 into early 1993 represented a decisive second turning point in the negotiated transition that paved the way to open elections in April 1994.

The explanation for it appears to lie in several factors. One was the patent international unacceptability of the NP's group power-sharing scheme. A second was the unreliability of Inkatha as a negotiating partner – it had boycotted Codesa for failing to acknowledge its demand for a strong form of federalism – and the embarrassment caused to the NP by its association with an organization that seemed increasingly aggressive and mercurial. (Inkatha duly withdrew from negotiations altogether after the Record of Understanding.) A third factor was the increasingly evident moderation of the ANC leadership, which had begun to steer in a pro-capitalist direction following Mandela's visit to the World Economic Forum at Davos in January 1992. Shortly after the Record of Understanding SACP leader Joe Slovo proposed his famous 'sunset clauses' guaranteeing economic security to white civil servants. These were endorsed by the ANC in November. A final factor was the ANC's campaign of 'rolling mass action' waged during July and August 1992. On the one hand this campaign, which had as its high point a general strike on 3-4 August, demonstrated the force of the ANC's main bargaining weapon, its mass support. On the other hand the violence inadvertently unleashed by the campaign – and in particular the Bisho massacre of ANC supporters by Ciskei police on 7 September – suggested to both the ANC leadership and the government that the negotiating impasse could not be resolved by force, and that unless negotiations resumed and accelerated a post-apartheid government would inherit a collapsed economy and society. While the mass action unleashed the radicals, it ended up weakening the hard-liners on both sides and strengthening the tendency towards 'pacting' by black and white moderate elites.

Within a few months the ANC and NP had agreed to the creation of a parallel government, or Transitional Executive Council, to oversee a transition to free elections. The TEC was set up in late December 1993. By June an election date was set and by November an interim constitution was endorsed by the multi-party negotiating forum that had succeeded Codesa. The pace of events thus accelerated dramatically, proceeding rapidly to an outcome well beyond what most whites had thought they mandated in the 1992 referendum. The momentum of events, fed by the close co-operation of the NP and ANC, was sufficient to ensure that the election occurred on time despite the resistance of the Ciskei and Bophutatswana governments to reintegration into a unitary state and the fierce opposition of Inkatha and white far right. The spectacular failure of the white paramilitary intervention to prop up the Bophutatswana state accelerated splintering of the far right (with the new Freedom Front breaking ranks by deciding to contest elections) and heightened the isolation of the recalcitrant IFP leader Mangosuthu Buthelezi. The latter agreed at the eleventh hour to participate in elections.

While the ANC went on to win the 1994 election overwhelmingly, it should not be supposed that the 1992-93 turning point tipped the balance of advantage completely towards the ANC. The price which the ANC had to agree in exchange for a settlement approximating to liberal-democratic majority rule included constraints on bureaucratic reform, a pro-market economic policy reorientation and interim power-sharing arrangements. The 1992 turning point was decisive for enabling the black majority's representatives to win real governmental power, but did not place in their hands the instruments of fundamental social change.

The prognosis for liberal democracy

The liberal democratic consensus

During the course of the early 1990s all major political contenders in South Africa converged on the view that the country should become a liberal democracy. The NP, a party long geared to competitive parliamentary politics, from the late 1970s supported the extension of the franchise to coloureds and Indians (this occurred in 1984) and from 1986 envisaged its extension to Africans. Until 1992, however, the NP insisted that a universal franchise should be introduced in a context of constitutional arrangements that prevented anything recognizable as liberal-democratic majority rule. As we have seen, however, in 1993 it signed up to an interim constitution envisaging majority rule subject to more classically liberal types of limitation.

The ANC began explicitly to picture a liberal-democratic political system for South Africa from the middle to later 1980s. Until then the organization had appeared to envisage something much closer to a classic radical nationalist state in which a ruling party embodying the popular will would seek to build a unified nation out of ethnic fragments and address its centralized power to urgent developmental tasks. The ANC's crucial partner, the SACP, was one of the world's most notoriously Stalinist Communist parties, consistently defending the totalitarian systems of the Soviet Bloc. The ANC–SACP's conversion to liberal democracy was prodded in part by the example of liberalization in the Soviet Union and the discrediting of one-party states in Africa. The eventual collapse of East-Central European Leninist regimes strengthened rather than caused this shift. The ANC's reorientation was also a product of a practical concern to assuage white fears of oppressive black rule and accommodate a robust 'civil society' of independent-minded black trade unions, civic associations and other bodies forged in the domestic struggle against apartheid. That struggle also threw up a progressive clerical and legal elite steeped in human rights concerns and carrying influence in the ANC camp.

If it is liberals who might have been thought to be the natural custodians of liberal democracy in South Africa, the reality of their record is more complicated. Always committed to defending civil freedoms such as those of the press, South African liberals carried with them into the later twentieth century an old-fashioned liberal fear of majority rule. Before the 1960s most liberals supported a qualified rather than universal franchise, with the Liberal Party becoming, by 1960, the first major liberal formation unambiguously to support one person, one vote (Van der Westhuizen 1994: 89). The more important Progressive Federal Party only signed up to universal franchise in 1978. Some prominent liberal intellectuals continued to cast doubt on the suitability of liberal democracy for South Africa right up to the advent of a negotiated settlement, fearing that it would produce a new form of ethnic domination to replace the old (Giliomee and Schlemmer 1989: ch. 7). In the 1960s and 1970s, however, most liberals came round to accepting that the qualified franchise was antiquated and unacceptable to blacks (whose leaders had been demanding universal franchise since the 1940s) and Western opinion (which they valued). By the 1990s liberals were very largely joined to the consensus in favour of a liberalism that was also democratic.

The momentum behind the advance of liberal-democratic discourse was such that it took in also most players beside these main ones, from the mainstream of the Far Right to the Pan-Africanist Congress on the left. The early 1990s were a culminating moment of the global 'third wave' of democratization described by Huntington, and its impact could not but be felt by South Africans (Huntington 1991). The near-consensus around liberal-democratic principles and institutional designs (Van Zyl Slabbert 1992: ch. 1) effectively isolated advocates of authoritarian and totalitarian models of government. It did not however guarantee that liberal democracy in South Africa would be consolidated and durable. What are the longer-term prospects for liberal-democratic consolidation in South Africa?

The conditions of democratic consolidation

Political commentators attempting to calculate the chances of democratic consolidation in South Africa could draw upon the large literature that gathered in the wake of earlier 'third wave' democratization experiments, especially those of Southern Europe in the 1970s and Latin America in the 1980s. The thrust of much of this literature was to downplay the sorts of socio-structural conditions of democracy emphasized by theorists like Lipset between the 1950s and 1970s (Lipset 1960) and to amplify the importance to successful democratic consolidation of high calibre political leaders (e.g. Linz and Stepan 1978), suitable modes of democratic transition (O'Donnell and Schmitter 1986), appropriate democratic constitutional designs (Horowitz 1991) and other factors involved in the 'crafting of democracies' (Di Palma 1990). This revision offered a necessary counter to deterministic pessimism in assessing the democratic potential of less developed non-western societies, and restored a proper respect for the political moment of the transition process. The revisionists nevertheless overplayed their voluntarist hand. There is nothing predetermined, still less predictable about the fate of any democratic transition, but historical evidence suggests that there are inherited contextual circumstances which tend to either help or hinder democracy (Huntington 1991: ch. 2). These circumstances can be altered or bypassed by political will, but they are not limitlessly pliable. It is important to consider them in assessing the nature of the terrain upon which democratizers in South Africa operate.

The structural conditions of democratic consolidation commonly identified in literature on the subject can be divided into those of a socio-economic kind and those to do with political culture. Socio-economic conditions conducive to democratization include higher inherited levels of economic 'development' and the emergence, with economic growth and urbanization, of educated middle and organized working classes aspiring to greater political influence and capable of sustaining autonomous civil institutions. Cultural conditions often cited as propitious for democratic consolidation include democratic experience, widely shared values and identities, relatively low levels of interest in politics, cross-cutting rather than superimposed social cleavages and an alterable public opinion.

Such lists highlight considerations of real significance for democratic consolidation on any plausible definition of democracy. South Africa's prognosis, judged against them, is mixed. The country certainly inherits a democratic tradition of sorts. As in other formerly British settler colonies, whites are well versed in the rules of parliamentary politics. Peaceful transfers of power between political parties followed elections in the late Colonial Cape (in 1898, 1904 and 1908) and nationally in 1924 and 1948. White settlers in the Cape won press and religious freedoms in the nineteenth-century Cape (Davenport 1969), and Anglophone newspapers, universities and churches fought to defend their autonomy against the encroachment of Afrikaner-dominated governments after 1948. There is also an established tradition of rule of law going back to the 1820s in the case of the Cape. On the other hand successive white oligarchies subjected blacks to forms of domination ranging in character from paternalistically authoritarian to outrightly totalitarian. Governments in the twentieth century, especially those after 1948, presided over the aggrandizement of executive power, the elaboration of repressive laws and institutions and the subordination of the state apparatus to particularistic (Afrikaner) ethnic ends.

Black society too presents a mixed picture. It has, on the one hand, always automatically occupied the moral high ground that was its privilege as a voteless majority, supporting universal franchise and government by consent and condemning the injustices of minority rule. Black leaders have readily spoken a language of democracy, borrowing from discourses ranging from pre-capitalist African communalism through liberalism to various radical and populist ideologies of rule by the people. Some mainly black organizations, notably in the trade union movement, have moreover taken internal democracy fairly seriously. Nevertheless much of the actual practice of black elites and their followers has been anything but democratic, at least in the liberal sense. As we have seen, the ANC did not embrace a liberal-democratic model until the later 1980s. Those who ran its camps in exile have been accused by the Truth and Reconciliation Commission of 'gross human rights violations' including arbitrary arrest and torture. United Democratic Front sympathizers callously intimidated and murdered collaborators and suspected spies in the mid-1980s.

Given that the principal political actors since 1990 – the NP and ANC – are heirs to the legacies of Afrikaner and black nationalist authoritarianism, as well as of, in Inkatha's case, one-party statism and a belligerent ethnic chauvinism, the auguries for democracy in South Africa might (on this measure) be considered poor. Here, however, the more optimistic note of the process-centred rather than structuralist theorists is appropriate. Political cultures are not immutable, and at elite level at least there has been, as we have seen, a convergence around the necessity and desirability of liberal democracy. The evidence suggests that this consensus is both rationally self-interested and philosophically sincere. This (incomplete, to be sure) ideological conversion of previously authoritarian elites, when coupled to the country's more democratic legacies, offers a relatively promising basis for at least the formal observance of democratic rules.

Other conditions of a democratic political culture are at best uncertainly fulfilled. The hierarchical ordering of South Africa on the basis of substantially coincident categories of race and class has bequeathed a strong tendency for the white minority and African majority to identify with opposed political camps. Issues that generate divisions cutting across party-political, ethnic and class lines

– capital punishment and abortion for examples – are insufficiently central in popular consciousness to disturb primary political allegiances. There *are* counter-tendencies which could have significant effects in the future. The coincidence of racialized ethnicity and socio-economic class is breaking down as a result of social differentiation within ethnic groups. This raises at least the theoretical possibility of a future working class-based politics, either of a socialist or populist kind, able to challenge the predominance of nationalist and ethnic politics.

There is also a sense in which South Africa's political culture is overpoliticized. Certainly the contention that democratic consolidation requires low levels of political interest amongst the populace is deeply problematic, not least because it begs questions about what kind of democracy it is that one is seeking to consolidate. From the point of view of those building a participatory democratic culture, the plethora of trade unions, civics and non-governmental organizations that make up South Africa's 'civil society' constitutes a distinctly advantageous inheritance. Even some writers suspicious of mass activity recognize the value of voluntary organizations that can check state power, aggregate and articulate competing societal interests in a peaceful way, train up new political leaders, disseminate information and promote a culture of self-organization and self-help (Diamond 1994).

Nevertheless there are *senses* in which societies can be too political. The high levels of political violence that have scarred South Africa since the late 1980s are an indication that too many people in the country take their political causes too seriously. Their violence is at one level about leaders and followers competing for turf and influence, but it is given its lethal edge by the self-sustaining culture of 'struggle' engendered by apartheid oppression and the intensities of partisan loyalty associated with superimposed grievances. The containment of violence is not helped by the naive theory of participatory democracy held by some civic and union activists which favours the expression of popular power through continuous direct action in civil society. In South Africa mass action all too easily escapes disciplined democratic control. Its prevalence attests more to the mobilizational capacities of competing leaderships than to a culture of informed and deliberative citizen participation. What South Africa lacks is a *civil* society, if by that is meant a space in which political competition and negotiation can proceed in a climate free of violence and intimidation. This deficit is a potent obstacle to democratic consolidation.

Its presence places an additional obligation on political leaders to discipline violent supporters and channel their political expression into institutional channels. Their willingness to do so in South Africa is not always self-evident. To be sure, much of the impetus to political violence comes from local warlords rather than top-level political leaders, and if there is a positive side to the ANC's wide and durable support base it is that it acts as a counterweight to localism and sectionalism. By aggregating and trading off the concerns of constituents the organization dampens some potential sources of conflict. This is notably true of sub-African ethnic conflicts, partly contained by the ANC's demonstrated ability to win support in every African ethnic group. Insofar as this mechanism operates however it carries the price that much of democratic politics is displaced into the inner workings of the ANC. Whatever a movement's level of commitment to internal democracy, the absorption of the political process into a dominant party leaves politics too vulnerable to the strictures of party discipline and too insulated from the open clash of interests.

South Africa does possess elements of a shared cultural practice that simplify the task of constructing common institutions, and which are not dependent on the unifying power of the ANC. Linguistically English is a widely accepted medium at least amongst non-Afrikaans speakers. Although Anglophones constitute just 9% of the population and are almost entirely non-African, the routine public use of English keeps in check linguistic rivalries between sub-African ethnic groups. (Afrikaners, by contrast, resent the new prominence of English.)

Whether Christianity is similarly unifying is debatable. It has not always united: South African Christianity is culturally compartmentalized and most multiracial churches practised internal racial segregation in the past (Davenport 1997: 65-7). At the same time those claiming to be Christian make up a large majority of the population (72%) including 92% of whites, 86% of coloureds and 76% of Africans. The non-coincidence of religious and racial boundaries removes a potential additional stimulant to the politicization of ethnicity, while the proportional fewness of non-Christians weakens the basis for any religiously-based challenge to the *status quo*. Thus while Islam is a major rival to Christianity further north in Africa and has recently been radicalized in the Western Cape, its destabilizing potential in South Africa is limited by the fact that Muslims make up only 2% of the country's population. The conflicts associated with Muslim radicalism are, moreover, largely internal to the coloured population.

A third possible unifier is the western-style consumerism that pervades white and (urban) black society alike, with American influence in particular prominent in everything from suburban shopping malls to township music. (American cultural imperialism is now vividly symbolized by a gargantuan *Coca-Cola* sign glaring across inner-city Johannesburg from atop a tower block). Consumerism aggravates social atomization and anti-social behaviour yet paradoxically generates a sense of mutual recognition across ethnic boundaries.

Finally, international sporting competition has exhibited some nation-building potential, as exemplified by Mandela's close identification with South Africa's largely white rugby team in the 1995 World Cup. This remains so notwithstanding the ethnic differentiation of sporting preference in the country and racialized rows about the personnel and policies of sporting bodies.

In socio-economic terms South Africa's inheritance is conducive to democratization in some respects, hostile to it in others. As a middle-income industrialized country South Africa is better able to finance democratic consolidation than many poor (and all other Sub-Saharan African) countries. It also has a sizeable middle class which, though largely white, is in the process of being multiracialized. This is a sociological fact favourable for the autonomy of civil society and maintenance of democratic institutions as is the presence of a large organized urban working class. On the other hand post-apartheid South Africa inherits some of the world's most glaring social inequalities as well as very high unemployment – circumstances making for social division and conflict.

A list of the structural 'conditions' of democratic consolidation, and the question of whether or not they are satisfied in South Africa, cannot tell us anything definite about the fate of the country's transition process. The political values, tactics, strategies and institutional models of actors all crucially shape the prospects for democratic success. It is to these that we now turn.

There is a strong current in the democratization literature which argues that democratic consolidation is most likely to occur where moderate elites in opposing camps negotiate pacts based on their shared interests. Elite pacting is, on this view, more likely to succeed than either democratization from above or change driven by mass action from below. Whereas the former is vulnerable to delegitimation by radicals, the latter is likely to elicit authoritarian reaction if it fails and generate revolutionary dictatorship if it succeeds (O'Donnell and Schmitter 1986; Karl and Schmitter 1991; Przeworski 1991; Van Zyl Slabbert 1992). This sort of formulation is open to various lines of criticism which will be developed later. It does however contain some prescriptive insights valuable for democratization, as well as appear, descriptively, to account reasonably well for South Africa's own so far successful democratic transition.

The literature is right to recognize that successful democratization involves some negotiation and trade-off. These may be the only way to secure democratic concessions where (as was true of pre-1994 South Africa) democratizers are not strong enough to impose their will on outgoing authoritarian regimes. They expose areas of shared interest and value while helping to establish commonly accepted game rules for regulating deeper interest and value conflicts.

In the early 1990s contending elites in South Africa succeeded in establishing – far beyond expectations – a culture of negotiation. Negotiating forums proliferated, involving the government, organized capital and labour at national level and white councils, black civics, development agencies and civics in the municipalities. This multi-layered negotiation process developed because its protagonists shared an interest in avoiding all-out war and restoring a functioning economy and state, and was sustained in good measure by personal relationships forged in the thick of negotiating. It suggested that there existed, and helped to reinforce, the minimum of common ground needed to sustain a liberal-democratic order.

The obverse of this negotiating style was, however, a growing distance between negotiators and their rank-and-file constituents who were largely shut out of key decisions. The most crucial political changes were negotiated by a small group of people from the NP, ANC and SACP. The representatives of trade unions and civics could find themselves engaged with technical questions that ordinary members and supporters knew little about and had neither the time nor inclination to discuss. Many activists on the ground perceived the process to be undemocratic and excessively accommodationist.

Of course in these respects the negotiations corresponded closely to the elitist model of democratization. To be sure, the 'masses' were not entirely outside the negotiating process. If the term refers to either grassroots activists or large mobilized numbers, then clearly their pressure was felt in party congresses, in direct mass action (such as the 1991 strike against Value Added Tax) and in visible and intense agitation over policies. It was felt also in, for example, debates about the future of women in post-apartheid South Africa, in which organizations like the Women's National Coalition played an active part. The South African transition is thus not easily allocated to either an 'elitist' or 'mass-driven' typological pigeon-hole.

Even so, democratization in South Africa was certainly elitist in crucial ways. Mass assertions were often pacified through the creation of corporatist structures, in other cases they were ignored, and in still others they reinforced elite co-operation. Was this elitism a good or bad thing for democratic consolidation? In one sense the question is impossible to answer except by reference to the sorts of goods democratizers value. An elitist transition mode must be at least *problematic* for those who place a premium on participatory and accountable government or on the building of an egalitarian social order. Only naive participatory democrats will fail to recognize that mass action is not an unalloyed good: it can serve as an instrument of populist mobilizers, yield to the tyranny of the crowd and trigger violence. Equally, however, all liberal democrats but the most elitist would register some obvious downsides of top-down pacting. Amongst the elites it is liable to encourage self-serving behaviour and authoritarian habits of decision-making. On the side of the population it stands to weaken or demobilize organized civil society, the public associational sphere which liberals and radicals alike recognize as a potential democratic good. These downside symptoms were clearly visible in the South African transition period.

Another area where agency mattered for the future of liberal democracy was in respect of constitutional design. Theorists of democratic consolidation typically attach a premium to constitutions that encourage less adversarial forms of politics, minimize the political and material losses suffered by outgoing ruling groups and prevent incoming majority representatives from dominating individuals and minorities. Up to a point the reasoning here is sound: there is neither moral nor practical sense in constitutions that encourage gratuitous confrontation, sanction arbitrary confiscations and punishments or entrench majority tyranny. The danger is that such strictures might become a pretext for straitjacketing future governments seeking to introduce changes necessary in terms of both social justice and system stability. How well have South Africa's constitutional designers balanced the competing imperatives of liberal-democratic stability and urgently needed political and social changes?

The interim constitution agreed for South Africa in late 1993 was the outcome of a trade-off between the ANC's interest in effective majority rule, the NP's concern to entrench power-sharing and the IFP's demand for regional powers. Its designers also took account of demands emanating from a range of civil society interests, from progressive women's and labour organizations to movements of conservative traditional chiefs. In brief the interim constitution provided for a president elected by parliament, a multi-party power-sharing executive, a bicameral legislature (with a proportionately elected lower house) and an independent Constitutional Court. It designated nine new provinces, each with its own parliament and parliament-elected premier. It mandated independent offices, councils and commissions to monitor corruption, gender issues and human rights and to advise on traditional law.

The interim constitution was the object of the complaints of those who got too little of what they sought. The IFP attacked the weakness of the devolution arrangements, which granted the provinces a wide range of competencies but no exclusive powers. Women's advocates cogently drew attention to the contradiction between the constitution's equality commitments and its genuflection to patriarchal African customary law (Kaganas and Murray 1994; Walker 1996). Advocates of constituency-representative links disparaged the list-based form of proportional representation. Socialists disliked the (qualified) constitutional protection of private property and provision for an independent central bank. The 1996 final constitution (operative since 1997) retained most elements of the interim document, but added to the displeasure of advocates of federalism and consociationalism by dispensing with executive power sharing and reining in the provinces (see below). Despite their limitations, however, the 1993-94 and 1996-97 constitutions have done a reasonable job of meeting both liberal and social-democratic normative standards while addressing the needs of democratic consolidation.

The constitutions satisfied liberal-democratic standards by providing for government by freely given majority consent, constrained by a wide range of court-guarded individual rights to, for example, freedoms of expression and association. Constitutional designers responded to the concerns of the left and progressive human rights community by prohibiting unfair discrimination on grounds of ethnicity, gender and sexual orientation while permitting affirmative action, safeguarding the right of workers to strike and entrenching entitlements to a reasonable minimum of housing, education, health care, water and social security.

At the same time the interim and final constitutional documents addressed the inclusiveness requirements of democratic consolidation. Most notably, both offered opposition groups and minorities openings to establish provincial power bases as well as higher levels of parliamentary representation than they would achieve under less proportional voting systems.

The career of liberal democracy 1994-99

South Africa held its first ever open and inclusive national and provincial elections on 27 April 1994. The first democratic local government elections were conducted in 1995 and (in the Western Cape and KwaZulu-Natal) in 1996. A second national election was held on 2 June 1999.

The ANC captured 62.65% of the vote in the first 1994 National Assembly election, short of the two-thirds majority it needed unilaterally to approve a final constitution. In the 1999 election it came within a fraction of winning the two-thirds it needed to amend the final constitution. The reformed one-time party of apartheid, the NP, won 20.39% in 1994 but its successor, the New National Party, collapsed to under 7% in 1999. It was eclipsed in the latter election by the Democratic Party, successor to the white liberal parliamentary opposition. The DP boosted its vote from a meager 1.73% in 1994 to 9.55% in 1999, ironically by positioning itself to the NNP's right. The Zulu nationalist IFP secured 10.54% nationally in 1994 and 8.58% in 1999. The far right, at one point a worrying extraparliamentary menace, proved insignificant as an electoral force in both polls. The Freedom Front garnered 2.17% of the vote in 1994 and less than 1% in 1999.

In 1994 the ANC won a majority or plurality in seven, and in 1999 in eight, out of nine provincial assembly elections. The IFP won a tiny majority in KwaZulu-Natal in 1994; in 1999 the party held on to a narrow plurality. The NP rode to victory in the Western Cape in 1994 on the back of whites and coloured support, but came second to the ANC in provincial vote share in 1999 (forcing it to govern the province in coalition with the DP). Women received 22% of the seats in 1994 and (in world terms) an impressive 30% in 1999. Whites, coloureds and Indians all achieved better than proportional representation in both National Assembly elections.

Controversy surrounds whether South Africa's elections have been 'free and fair'. The Independent Electoral Commission and foreign observers maintained that the 1994 election was 'substantially free and fair'. It was certainly not fully so, and critics insisted with some justification that its flaws were ignored in order to sustain the myth of a 'miracle' election. Local political violence and intimidation marred much of the campaign. During the election ANC militants prevented the NP and DP from campaigning in many African townships. Parts of KwaZulu-Natal and the white-owned countryside were off-limits to the ANC while ANC-supporting townships were in turn closed to the IFP. The election campaign itself was administratively chaotic. The basic election machinery was only set in place a few months before the poll, and much of it was inadequate; difficulties were compounded by the IFP's decision to join the race at the last minute. There were numerous allegations of irregularities, especially in KwaZulu-Natal, and even of a negotiated result (Friedman and Stack 1994; Johnson 1996a).

On the plus side, public television provided reasonably balanced coverage and newspapers represented a range of preferences. Polling day witnessed a huge and enthusiastic turnout of voters in an atmosphere that was largely peaceful despite a right-wing bombing campaign. The close correspondence between election results and pre-election opinion surveys suggested that irregularities did not influence the outcomes nationally or in at least eight out of nine provinces. Only in KwaZulu-Natal, where the result contradicted polls predicting an ANC victory, was it credibly alleged by some (especially disgruntled ANC members in the province) that the IFP won by negotiating its vote share rather than on the basis of popular support. This interpretation was disputable, and the subsequent local and national elections in KZN confirmed that the IFP commanded a genuine plurality of support in the province (Johnson 1996b: 336-48, 1996c).

The 1999 election was, like its predecessor, an imperfect exhibition of democracy. On the plus side, it was more efficiently administered than the 1994 poll. The high turnout confirmed that the electoral process retained legitimacy. As in 1994, the results roughly reflected the popular will as far as it could be gauged. The second election nevertheless reproduced many of the questionable features of the first, with the added twist of a controversy about the legitimacy of requiring voters to carry bar-coded identity documents. Critics argued that this provision disenfranchised potential ANC opponents, since those not yet in possession of the document were disproportionately non-African. Even so, the 1999 election confirmed that the 1994 poll was not the one-off 'liberation election' that many white critics of African rule predicted. South Africa had become a working liberal democracy of sorts.

The huge scale of the ANC's victories in 1994 and 1999 nevertheless brought in its wake legitimate anxieties that South Africa might become a 'dominant party state' akin, say, to Mexico or Malaysia, with all of the corruption and political non-accountability which attend such regimes. Two factors point to continued overwhelming ANC dominance. One is the ANC's dual character as a liberation movement and political party. It is not merely a party that happened to win the first election; it was a longstanding opponent of white minority rule, a virtual government-in-exile between 1960 and 1990 and a key actor in the founding of a legitimate state. This *curriculum vitae* gives it the prestige to withstand political setbacks that would endanger a ruling party's future election prospects in more effectively multi-party systems.

Secondly, the ANC benefits from its symbolic association with the interests of the African majority. The 1994 and 1999 elections were not simple 'ethnic censuses' (see Chapter 6). Parties won votes across ethnic boundaries. The ANC commanded a majority of votes in all sub-African ethnic groups bar the Zulus and sizeable minorities of Zulu, coloured and Indians votes. Between them the NP/NNP and DP won majorities of coloured, Indian and white votes in both elections. It is however the African vote that grounds ANC dominance. The ANC won around 90% of African votes in 1994. While in 1999 it faced inroads into its African core vote in the territories of two ex-'homelands', Transkei and Bophutatswana, the party's overwhelming hold on the African electorate is not yet seriously threatened. The ANC is keen to garner support from all ethnic groups but it does not depend upon succeeding in doing so. If a sometimes talked-about ANC–IFP merger comes about the outcome will be a further extension of the ruling party's electoral hegemony.

Some of the external checks on the ANC's dominance have weakened since 1994 (Southall 1998). Under the interim constitution's rules the NP was entitled to a deputy presidency, the IFP to a cabinet seat, on the basis of their electoral performances. In June 1996 however the NP withdrew from the interim government of national unity, leaving the ANC sharing power at cabinet level only with the IFP. As noted earlier, the 1996-97 final constitution scrapped enforced coalition government. (Since the 1999 election the ANC and IFP coalition has continued on a voluntary basis.)

Provincial checks on the centre have also slackened. The 1996-97 constitution entrenched (and even extended) the powers and competencies of provincial governments, but it weakened the capacity of the upper house, representing the provinces, to challenge the government at national level. Recent years have seen the central government, which controls all financial purse-strings, move to impose tighter administrative and financial discipline on the provinces. In addition the ANC's provincial-level dominance and its control of a largesse of elective offices has enabled its national leadership to remove several provincial premiers, some of whom enjoyed wide local support, and to 'redeploy' them to other posts. This ability and willingness of ANC leaders to transfer elected politicians from one state job to another, and largely for internal party reasons, suggests an increasing fusion between party and state and subordination of the latter to the former (Southall 1998: 451-3).

The period since 1994 has, finally, witnessed a growing concentration of power in the executive branch relative to the legislative. In 1994 parliamentary committees were thrown open to the public, and showed an early vigour in challenging the executive. In more recent times ANC Members of Parliament have shown a reluctance to embarrass the government. Southall attributes this caution to a loss of able Members of Parliament and to ANC MPs' fear of expulsion from the party which (under South Africa's party-list electoral system) would mean ejection from parliament (Southall 1998: 453-4). Many commentators interpret the presidency of Thabo Mbeki, which began in 1999, as heralding a further concentration of power in the executive. Since taking over Mbeki has hugely augmented and centralized the office of the presidency in ways that may well insulate it further from parliamentary accountability.

These developments do not constitute evidence that South Africa has ceased to be liberal-democratic: only a minority of liberal democracies are either consociational or federal, and many are characterized by strong executives. It is their conjunction with the ANC's electoral dominance – much greater than that of ruling parties in established liberal democracies – which worries democrats. The ANC cannot be 'blamed' for winning as many votes as it does, but its dominance means that the fate of South Africa's young democracy depends to an alarming extent on the party's own democratic good behaviour.

There are two axes along which its behaviour can be assessed. One is in terms of the outward face the party presents to society: the degree to which as a ruling party it respects the constitution and the democratic rights and liberties of (non-ANC) others. The ANC's record in this regard has so far been reasonably good. The South Africa over which it presides has been characterized by freedom of expression and association, and by a commitment, thus far observed, to holding regular free elections. Opposition MPs, some sections of the media and a range of organizations in civil society freely criticize aspects of ANC rule. The Constitutional Court, though vulnerable to the charge of pro-ANC bias in its composition, has shown itself willing to disagree with the ruling party and has adopted rights-protective positions (for example on homosexuality). The ANC has defended aspects of the new human rights culture, in particular the constitutional prohibition of the death penalty, against a range of critics.

Some of the ANC government's human rights policies have been unfairly criticized. One object of controversy has been the TRC, set up in 1995 to unearth the 'truth' about 'gross violations of human rights' perpetrated by all sides in South Africa between 1960 and 1994. The Commission was given both investigative powers and the quasi-judicial authority to grant amnesties to perpetrators in return for their full disclosure of past deeds. Despite being accused of pro-ANC leanings the TRC produced a provisional report in 1998 which savaged the human rights record of the ANC and ANC-linked political figures even as it exposed the far graver crimes of the apartheid regime and its agents. The report has its critics. The TRC could not address the demands of thousands of victims of human rights abuses for retributive justice. Its focus on the worst human rights violations – torture, killings and so on – left it unable to reckon with the countless day-to-day injustices afflicted by racial rule (Mamdani 1998). Nor could a commission of such scope hope to satisfy the strictest judicial standards of proof in all of its findings (Jeffrey 1999). Even so, the TRC steered an impressively careful course between a democracy-threatening pursuit of justice at all costs and the blanket amnesty and amnesia that have marked democratic transitions in many other countries. It also excavated a wealth of information that might otherwise never have come to light.

Other controversies surround the methods used by the government to achieve greater equality. In 1998 parliament passed an Employment Equity Act to promote affirmative action employment of blacks, women, the disabled and other historically disadvantaged groups. In 2000 a Promotion of Equality and Prevention of Unfair Discrimination Act outlawed hate speech and unfair discrimination in various spheres of life. Liberal opponents of these measures argue that they are re-racializing South African society and, in the case of speech prohibitions, licensing Orwellian thought control. For the most part these sorts of criticisms are exaggerated. There are legitimate arguments for and against affirmative action, but the idea that it amounts to a back-door reintroduction of apartheid cannot be taken seriously. Nor can the legal suppression of racial abuse and harassment be considered illiberal in principle or a harbinger of certain authoritarianism. There is a vast problem of racism to be tackled in South Africa and straightforward liberal colour blindness on the part of the ANC is neither desirable nor realistically to be expected.

At the same time there are real grounds for worrying that the ANC, and the rising black elite generally, is using the accusation of racism to smear opponents and intimidate critics. The most immediate threat to political liberty emanates from the Human Rights Commission, a standing investigative body mandated by the constitution. The HRC chose a while back to investigate the human rights performance of the independent media, including at least one newspaper with a record of strong opposition to apartheid. In late 1999 the Commission released a report attributing media criticism of political corruption to subliminal racism and it has since subpoenaed newspaper editors to explain their editorial decision-making. At the time of writing it is still too early to say whether the HRC's reckless behaviour marks the beginning of a repressive press regime in South Africa.

The ANC itself has made clear its displeasure at public criticism. It has defended the HRC investigation and placed moral pressure on black journalists to support government policies and actions. In 1998 it aroused widespread opposition by attempting – fortunately without success – to stop the TRC from publishing criticisms of the ANC's past human rights record. Even the party's political allies, the SACP and Congress of South African Trade Unions, have felt the lash of ANC criticism for questioning government economic policy.

So far the starkest instances of human rights violations by the post-1994 state have resulted from the unsanctioned behaviour of police – many inherited from the previous regime – who have continued to kill and batter suspects in their pursuit of criminals. The nearest thing to an outright human rights violation sanctioned by top-level leaders is the harsh treatment of illegal African immigrants, hundreds of thousands of whom are deported annually. The ANC's warm relations with corrupt dictators abroad has further tarnished its human rights record in office.

It is in respect of internal party democracy, however, that the ANC's record so far is most open to criticism. In 1996 the leadership forced the internally popular dissident Bantu Holomisa from both party and parliament for raising public questions about the past behaviour of a minister; and the national leadership has interfered freely in the affairs of the provincial-level parties. Centralized parties are not unusual in liberal democracies and inner-party democracy is less important to their operation than effective inter-party competition. Even so it matters in South Africa how internally democratic the ANC is, since the party has, by virtue of its enormous size and dominance, absorbed a wide swathe of civil and political society.

Important as the ANC is, there are other groups that also have a direct bearing on the prospects of liberal democracy in South Africa. Some of what looked in the early 1990s like potentially urgent counter-revolutionary threats to democratic consolidation have, for now, receded. The white far right remains partially incorporated into the new parliamentary politics (within which it constitutes a tiny force) and otherwise fragmented, its militants subdued. The IFP, whose regional hegemonism spurred on political violence in the past and which periodically threatened to push for the secession of KwaZulu-Natal from South Africa, is part of a coalition with the ANC and seems set to remain so. Political violence is chronic, but less acute than before 1994. The inherited civil service has been blamed for slowing up policy implementation in some areas, but it is being streamlined and placed rapidly under black departmental leadership. The military has mostly co-operated with the transition process since 1990, including the integration of former guerrillas. Rightist elements accused of seeking to destabilize the government by planting rumours of a leftist coup have been purged.

The state machine's descent into corruption poses a more immediate danger to democratic consolidation than any putative counter-revolutionary threat. The corruption is a compound of two elements. One is the venality of the later apartheid years – especially that found in the 'homeland' statelets and central government departments dealing with blacks. The other is the self-seeking behaviour of the new black elite taking advantage of the patronage opportunities opened up by affirmative action in recruitment and tendering. For blacks still weakly placed in the private sector the state offers a valuable route to accumulation. Corrupt behaviour is especially concentrated in provincial governments (most notoriously the Eastern Cape and Mpumalanga) which have been required by the ANC to absorb former 'homeland' bureaucracies, but it is entrenched also in some central government departments (Lodge 1998: 172-183). The top ANC leadership has not been directly implicated in large-scale corruption and in 1995 it set up the highly effective Heath Commission to seek out corrupt practice. It also appointed, in accordance with the constitution, an investigative watchdog called the Public Protector tasked with watching over state administration. The government's behaviour is, however, inconsistent. It seems reluctant to punish the corrupt, who often simply get reallocated to new posts, while the Public Protector has been left underfunded.

Corruption is linked to a wider problem of escalating crime. Criminality has ballooned since the early 1990s. Many countries undergoing democratization in Eastern Europe, Latin America and elsewhere have faced escalating crime, but South Africa may well have the highest levels of murder and rape in the world. Armed robberies, 'carjackings', gang warfare and shoot-outs between rival taxi operators testify to a deep social pathology. The causes of the crime wave include massive inequality, rising black youth unemployment, the breakdown of social authority structures in the townships, penetration by foreign drug syndicates and an influx of guns from war-ravaged nearby African states. A demoralized and under-resourced criminal justice system is unable to cope and police are often implicated in crime. Though blacks remain the main victims of crime, white suburbs and farms have increasingly fortified themselves against the black poor.

Corruption and crime pose an immediate threat to human welfare and social development, but they also impede democratic consolidation. Corruption corrodes the rule of law, confounding citizen expectations of uniform and predictable treatment by state officials. Widespread criminality undermines citizens' confidence in the democratic state's capacity to perform basic order-keeping functions. In South Africa it has generated pressures for repressive policing, spawned overcrowded prisons and encouraged unaccountable extra-state law enforcement in the shape of vigilante gangs and private security firms (Shaw 1997). In the longer run the atmosphere of crisis around crime and corruption could provide openings for would-be dictators promising salvation from the 'anarchy' of democracy.

The prospects of democratic consolidation are affected not only by the inherited strengths and weaknesses of the economy but also by the performance of the democrats in office. South Africa has not performed especially well economically since 1994. Growth initially rose on the preceding period, but the economy has since been through a fresh recession; it may now be about to grow again modestly. The hoped-for influx of direct foreign investment never materialized. Most incoming capital has been short-term investment vulnerable to speculative shifts. Unemployment has shot up, on some measures, from around 30% in 1994 to 40% in 2000 (Horton et al. 1998: 17; Anonymous 2000: Political Briefing). Inequality has deepened amongst blacks, per capita income has eroded for the poorest and welfare gains have been uncertain. If a growing and equitable economy is necessary for democratic consolidation, the prognosis for democracy in South Africa must be considered less than rosy thus far. Fortunately for the state's democratic legitimacy, post-1994 Finance Ministers and Reserve Bank governors have succeeded in projecting an aura of competence; and given the ANC's prestige the legitimacy of the post-apartheid state is anyway not straightforwardly dependent on its economic and social policy performance. This is however small consolation to the socially excluded.

Deeper democracy?

For many of those who fought white domination the struggle against it was always about more than establishing a minimalistic form of non-racial liberal democracy accompanied by business-as-usual capitalism. Its objective was a participatory democracy and egalitarian society. On the left there was for long the belief that liberal democracy was essentially elitist and bourgeois and thus inadequate to the task of political and economic emancipation. For very good reasons most on the left now accept that liberal-democratic rights are as essential to working and poor people as to other citizens. The 'substantive freedoms' entailed in economic equality and social security are best defended within a framework of liberal-democratic rights, which include those of workers to form unions and parties. And freedom is truncated where it enables the poor to escape the lower realm of material necessity only to deny them entry to a higher realm of political and cultural freedom. It is patronizing to assume that elites alone can engage in the independent thought and creativity which liberal freedoms permit.

Even so there is more than one kind of liberal democracy. Not only is there a variety of operative liberal-democratic models of government in the world, but there is no reason to believe that actually existing models exhaust the field of possible ones. Moreover liberal-democratic institutions are compatible with a range of social systems (albeit not with a limitless range). The hope of radicals converted to liberal democracy is that (precisely because it is not after all essentially 'bourgeois' or elitist) liberal democracy can accommodate a participatory and egalitarian socio-political order. In expressing and seeking to realize this hope radical liberal democrats face opposition from two quarters (leaving aside the neo-Stalinist left): democratization theorists who argue that the consolidation of liberal democracy in a polarized and previously authoritarian society depends upon the co-option or marginalization of radical forces; and proponents of the new orthodoxy that links liberal-democratization to market-based economic reform and even to economic liberalization (Przeworski 1991; Van Zyl Slabbert 1992; Huntington 1994).

While it has its strengths (acknowledged earlier) the more elitist democratization literature is open to four types of criticism, the first two of a normative or philosophical kind. Firstly, it proceeds from a narrow and question-begging vision of democracy. Its vision is narrow in that it so actively distances itself from the classical democratic standard of rule by the people and because it requires citizens to forgo a legitimate right to choose something other than ideological centrism. It thus sidelines the issue of what democratic transition is *for*.

A second normative criticism of elitist democratization literature is that it engages in victim blaming. Radical forces that seek seriously to challenge the *status quo* are held (in effect) responsible for any suppression of democracy designed to stop them from obtaining power – even where the radicals are committed to democratic game-rules. The radicals as chief objects of reactionary repression become co-responsible for their own victimization. The precondition of democratization comes to be seen as the marginalization of radical forces rather than the typically more challenging one of thwarting forces of anti-democratic reaction.

A third flaw in the elitist democratization literature is that it homogenizes radical forces, stigmatizing them collectively as threatening to democracy irrespective of their specific histories, organizational cultures and programmes. There are radical forces of both the right and left which are anti-democratic, but there are others committed to constitutional politics, observance of democratic rules and (within these constraints) to the deepening of democratic politics through, say, encouraging workplace or neighbourhood self-organization. In some cases, as with trade unions and civics, social movements have played a direct role in the creation of a culture of negotiation (Adler and Webster 1995). It seems improbable that these sorts of differences would not affect the extent to which radical forces are democracy-threatening or otherwise.

Fourthly, formulaic versions of elitist democratization theory invite premature and unnecessary moderation on the part of democrats. The extent to which conservative authoritarians will make concessions to radical democrats depends not only, or above all, on how 'radical' the democratizers are. The South African evidence suggests that it depends also on the interest profile of the conservative social base, the balance of forces in society, perceptions about the tide of history, the dynamics of negotiation and the relative ideological self-confidence of contending parties. While conservatives doubtlessly are influenced by the behaviour of their opponents, radicals can persuade conservative authoritarians to make concessions by militant action as well as by moderating their demands (Adler and Webster 1995). The very definition of what is radical can change in the course of a democratic transition. As has been shown, the creation of a genuine majoritarian liberal democracy in South Africa was initially ruled out by representatives of the old regime, but was conceded by them, contrary to the expectations of many, in 1993.

If democratic transition does not depend on the evisceration of radical forces, the story of the 1990s has nevertheless been one of continuous pressure on radicals to moderate their programmes as a condition of obtaining power or retaining influence.

At the outset of the 1990s trade union, civic and other popular formations were called upon to shift from an oppositional to developmental or reconstructive mode as the prospect opened of a democratic government. This imperative was felt especially by ANC-aligned groups given the ANC's always probable dominance in a post-apartheid government. Debates sprung up about the role of civil society organizations in the transition period and under a future ANC government. Some saw new opportunities for extending the influence of grassroots organizations, setting them up as proxy local governments, intermediaries between citizens and state or vigilant watchdogs and pressure groups. Others saw dangers of co-option into corporatist arrangements. A utopian discourse of 'civil society' predominated in opposition ranks alongside intense debates about what civil society was and could be (Mayekiso 1992; Seekings 1992; Swilling 1992; Glaser 1997).

From 1994 many civil society organizations were under pressure. Their legitimacy as popular representatives was weakened by the advent of elected national and later local governments. Increasing proportions of donor funds that once went the way of anti-apartheid non-governmental organizations were redirected towards state development projects. Many of the most experienced personnel in the trade unions, civics and other grassroots formations were drawn to more lucrative and influential positions in the state and private sector. Organized workers have access to a range of new corporatist channels from the workplace to the national level, but union representatives have been outmanoeuvred in many of them. Some of the more durable civil society groups, notably trade unions, have meanwhile grown increasingly professionalized and bureaucratic as they expand in size and coverage (Ray 1988a, b). Civil organizations have not been entirely stilled either as critics or mobilizers, and a very substantial voluntary associational sector remains one of the more promising features of the post-apartheid order. Expectations that the diverse and struggling civil sector might form the basis of a new kind of libertarian socialism have, however, dissipated. They were probably never very realistic.

Radical possibilities have evaporated also in the sphere of economic policy. Though it started out the decade with a fairly ambitious left social-democratic agenda, by the late 1990s the ANC in power was implementing neo-liberal policies. After 1992 the recommendations of radical think-tanks were increasingly shoved aside as the ANC's economic policy-makers proceeded to the right. In that year the ANC backed away from its rhetoric of nationalizing some economic sectors. By late 1993 it had agreed to constitutional safeguards for private property and an independent central bank. The ANC began in government in 1994 with a Cosatu-influenced Reconstruction and Development Programme that still bore hallmarks of radical thinking, and which rapidly acquired iconic status (Munslow and FitzGerald 1997: 42). In 1996, however, the government abolished the RDP office and reallocated the RDP minister. The RDP was effectively superseded by a more conservative Growth, Employment and Redistribution strategy. The government and the South African Reserve Bank have held to a conservative fiscal and monetary stance that gives priority to low budget deficits and inflation. The ANC is signed up for the privatization of the state's electricity, telecommunication and transport networks. It has also embarked on a path of trade liberalization, despite the vulnerability of the country's long-protected industrial base to foreign competitive attack and more recent evidence that the European Union is less than eager to lower its own protectionist barriers to South African goods. President Mbeki seems even more firmly committed to neo-liberalism than his predecessor. The irony, as Munslow and FitzGerald note, is that a party with an historical commitment to economic interventionism is now moving to liberalize the economy in ways that the NP, a fount of free market rhetoric in its final decades of office, never managed to do (Munslow and FitzGerald 1997: 43-4).

The ANC in government has not abandoned its socially progressive concerns. It has redirected state spending more fully towards the poor. Workers have seen a range of rights entrenched in bargaining and fair employment legislation. Women have benefited from enlightened legislation on abortion. There has been an impressive increase in the number of households connected to electricity and potable water and, after a long delay, the delivery of low cost housing has accelerated. The machinery of land reform has begun to grind slowly into action. Clinics have been built, free medical care has been offered to pregnant mothers and children and a school-feeding programme has improved child nutrition. These gains are, however, brittle. Some social welfare schemes were badly thought-out or damaged by corruption. President Mbeki is talking of scaling back labour reforms. A rapidly multiplying incidence of HIV/Aids, part of a wider African pandemic but ineptly addressed by the government in Pretoria, is set to reduce South Africans' average life expectancy down to somewhere in the 40s. Punitive monetary policies and (in the cases of clothing, textiles and car production) rapid tariff reductions have contributed to relentlessly rising unemployment.

It is not difficult to discern the forces that drove economic policy-making to the right. The collapse of Communism and setbacks of European social democracy left the ANC without an ideological compass. Threats and inducements emanating from foreign governments and lending agencies (in particular the International Monetary Fund) and a concern to attract overseas investors left ANC policy-makers feeling that they had little choice but to adopt business-friendly economic policies. In doing so they followed a nearly universal international pattern.

The rhetoric of the powerful in the West, and that of not a few democratization theorists, presents the process of democratic transition as either synonymous with marketization or dependent on it. It celebrates the market-oriented policy as a way of reducing unreasonable expectations of the transitional state, lowering the stakes involved in holding political power and providing the basis, through private property and voluntary exchange, for an autonomous civil realm. Economic liberalization, however, also carries risks for democratic consolidation. The pain associated with neo-liberal policies, though supposed to be short to medium term, can inflict lasting damage on the reputation of democracy, providing ground for the growth of anti-democratic forces on the populist left and right. It is unsurprising that some right-wing theorists, recognizing a potential contradiction between democratization and economic liberalism, view with sympathy the option of economically liberalizing first and democratizing later. For those who rule out this Chilean or Hungarian option on principle the challenge is to find a way of decoupling democracy from economic pain. There is decreasing evidence that this can be done while neo-liberal fashions prevail. The ANC's prestige provides a buffer against authoritarian populist forces, the tribunes of which are visible on the South African scene. But the party's popularity is not inexhaustible, and may not survive another decade of economic hardship.

Nor should the ANC's right-turn economically be attributed entirely to the inescapable pressures of 'globalization'. As writers like Bell and others have noted, in certain respects South Africa has used the economic policy manoeuvring room available to it to push even further down the liberalization road than organizations like the World Trade Organization have demanded (Bell 1997: 76). And the structural forces impinging on ANC economic policy-making come not only from external agencies but also from the changing sociological profile of the anti-apartheid political elite. The ANC in power has becoming a self-conscious vehicle for the creation and expansion of a black middle class. The black bourgeoisie remains tiny compared to the white and has suffered large recent setbacks on the Johannesburg Stock Exchange (after some impressive gains before 1997), but the government remains determined to strengthen it. A culture of acquisitive individualism has mushroomed in the ranks of black politicos (Adam et al. 1997: chs 9, 11). The ANC is mutating into a bourgeois party.

This metamorphosis is far from complete. Sections of the ANC alliance, notably in Cosatu and on the left of the SACP, continue to resist the rightward drift and suggest policy alternatives. Industrial militancy has not disappeared, despite new strike resolution mechanisms (Baskin and Grawitsky 1998). A question that must remain for the future is whether there is space for the emergence of an effective labour party to the ANC's left. A vigorous opposition party of democratic constitutional socialism would have much to commend it. It could, in addition to countering the drift towards neo-liberalism, offer a form of politics that is non-ethnic and committedly democratic. It could provide an outlet for popular discontent on the terrain of high politics, moving beyond the necessarily limited vision of civil society as the principal source of radical opposition to a dominant party. There are however huge obstacles to the emergence of such a formation, beginning with the ANC's hold on African support. Perhaps more seriously, the ideological function of a successful democratic left party will necessarily be limited for as long as radicals lack a believable vision of socialism. There are good reasons, all the same, to keep alive more radically egalitarian and democratic hopes.

References

Adam, H. 1971, *Modernizing Racial Domination: The Dynamics of South African Politics*, University of California Press, Berkeley and London.

Adam, H. and Giliomee, H. 1979, *Ethnic Power Mobilized: Can South Africa Change?*, Yale University Press, New Haven, CT and London.

Adam, H., Slabbert, F. and Moodley, K. 1997, *Comrades in Business: Post-Liberation Politics in South Africa*, Tafelberg, Cape Town.

Adler, G. c.1987, '"Trying Not to be Cruel": Local Government Resistance to Application of the Group Areas Act in Uitenhage, 1945-1962', *The Societies of Southern Africa in the 19th and 20th Centuries*, seminar paper, Institute of Commonwealth Studies.

Adler, G. and Webster, E. 1995, 'Challenging Transition Theory: The Labour Movement, Radical Reform, and the Transition to Democracy in South Africa', *Politics and Society*, 23, 1, 75-106.

Adorno, T. and Horkheimer, M. 1972, *Dialectic of Enlightenment*, Herder and Herder, New York.

African National Congress 1969, *Strategy and Tactics of the ANC*, adopted by Morogoro Conference, Tanzania.

Alden, A. 1996, *Apartheid's Last Stand: The Rise and Fall of the South African Security State*, Macmillan Press, Basingstoke and London.

Alexander, N. 1989, 'Non-Collaboration in the Western Cape', in James, W. G. and Simons, M. (eds), *The Angry Divide: Social and Economic History of the Western Cape*, David Philip, Cape Town and Johannesburg.

Alexander, N. 1994, 'The National Forum', in Liebenberg, I., Lortan, F., Nel, B. and van der Westhuizen, G. (eds), *The Long March: The Story of the Struggle for Liberation in South Africa*, Haum, Pretoria.

Anderson, P. 1983, *Imagined Communities: Reflections on the Origin and Spread of Nationalism*, Verso, London.

Anonymous, 'Political Briefing: Where is Thabo Mbeki Taking South Africa?' and 'Issue Briefing. The Reformed Presidency: Too Powerful or Better for Joined-up Government?', *ePolitics* 2000, 9.

Armstrong, J. C. and Worden, N. A. 1988, *The Slaves, 1652-1834*, in Elphick, R. and Giliomee, H. (eds), *The Shaping of South African Society, 1652-1840*, Wesleyan University Press, Middletown, CT.

Ashforth, A. 1990, *The Politics of Official Discourse in Twentieth-Century South Africa*, Clarendon Press, Oxford.

Atmore, A. and Marks, S. 1974, 'The Imperial Factor in South Africa in the Nineteenth Century: Towards a Reassessment', *Journal of Imperial and Commonwealth History*, 3, 2, 105-39.

Bank, L. 1995, 'The Failure of Ethnic Nationalism: Land, Power and the Politics of Clanship on the South African Highveld 1860-1990', *Africa*, 65, 4, 565-91.

Barrell, H. 1990, *MK: The ANC's Armed Struggle*, Penguin, Harmondsworth.

Baskin, J. and Grawitsky, R. 1998, 'Year of Fire: Industrial Action in 1998', *South African Labour Bulletin*, 22, 6, 6-13.

Beall, J. 1990, 'Women Under Indentured Labour in Colonial Natal, 1860-1811', in Walker, C. (ed.), *Women and Gender in Southern Africa to 1945*, David Philip, Cape Town and James Currey, London.

Beck, R. E. 1997, 'Monarchs and Missionaries among the Tswana and Sotho', in Elphick, R. and Davenport, R. (eds), *Christianity in South Africa: A Political, Social, and Cultural History*, University of California Press, Berkeley.

Beinart, W. 1982, *The Political Economy of Pondoland 1860-1930*, Cambridge University Press, Cambridge, London and New York.

Beinart, W. 1986, 'Settler Accumulation in East Griqualand from the Demise of the Griqua to the Natives Land Act', in Beinart, W., Delius, P. and Trapido, S. (eds), *Putting a Plough to the Ground: Accumulation and Dispossession in Rural South Africa 1850-1930*, Ravan Press, Johannesburg.

Beinart, W. 1987, 'Worker Consciousness, Ethnic Particularism and Nationalism: The Experiences of a South African Migrant, 1930-1960', in Marks, S. and Trapido, S. (eds), *The Politics of Race, Class and Nationalism in Twentieth-Century South Africa*, Longman, London and New York.

Beinart, W. 1994, *Twentieth-Century South Africa*, Oxford University Press, Cape Town and Oxford.

Beinart, W. and Bundy, C. 1987, *Hidden Struggles in Rural South Africa: Politics and Popular Movements in the Transkei and Eastern Cape 1890-1930*, James Currey, London, University of California Press, Berkeley, and Ravan Press, Johannesburg.

Beinart, W. and Delius, P. 1986, 'Introduction', in Beinart, W., Delius, P. and Trapido, S. (eds), *Putting a Plough to the Ground: Accumulation and Dispossession in Rural South Africa 1850-1930*, Ravan Press, Johannesburg

Bekker, S. 1993, *Ethnicity in Focus: The South African Case*, Indicator South Africa Issue Focus, Centre for Social and Development Studies, University of Natal, Durban.

Bekker, S. and Humphries, R. 1985, *From Control to Confusion: The Changing Role of the Administration Boards in South Africa, 1971-1983*, Shuter and Shooter, Pietermaritzburg and Institute of Social and Economic Research, Rhodes University.

Bell, T. 1987, 'Is Industrial Decentralisation a Thing of the Past?', in Tomlinson, R. and Addleson, M. (eds), *Regional Restructuring Under Apartheid: Urban and Regional Policies in Contemporary South Africa*, Ravan Press, Johannesburg.

Bell, T. 1997, 'Trade Policy', in Mitchie, J. and Padayachee, V. (eds), *The Political Economy of South Africa's Transition: Policy Perspectives in the Late 1990s*, The Dryden Press, London.

Berger, I. 1992, *Threads of Solidarity: Women in South African Industry, 1900-1980*, Indiana University Press, Bloomington and Indianapolis and James Currey, London.

Bhana, S. 1985, 'Indian Trade and Trader in Colonial Natal', in Guest, G. and Sellers, J. M. (eds), *Enterprise and Exploitation in a Victorian Colony: Aspects of the Economic and Social History of Colonial Natal*, University of Natal Press, Pietermaritzburg.

Bickford-Smith, V. 1989, 'A "Special tradition of Multi-Racialism?" Segregation in Cape Town in the Late Nineteenth and early Twentieth Centuries', in James, W. G. and Simons, M. (eds), *The Angry Divide: Social and Economic History of the Western Cape*, David Philip, Cape Town and Johannesburg.

Bickford-Smith, V. 1995, *Ethnic Pride and Racial Prejudice in Victorian Cape Town*, Cambridge University Press, Cambridge.

Black, A. 1991, 'Manufacturing Development and the Economic Crisis: A Reversion to Primary Production?', in Gelb, S. (ed.), *South Africa's Economic Crisis*, David Philip, Cape Town and Zed books, London and New Jersey.

Bloch, R. 1984, 'Sounds in the Silence: Painting a Picture of the 1960s', *Africa Perspective*, 25, 3-20.

Block, F. 1980, 'Beyond Relative Autonomy: State Managers as Historical Subjects', in Miliband, R. and Saville, J. (eds), *Socialist Register*, Merlin Press, London.

Bonner, P. 1978, 'The Decline and Fall of the I.C.U. – A Case of Self-Destruction?', in Webster, E. (ed.), *Essays in Southern African Labour History*, Ravan Press, Johannesburg.

Bonner, P. 1980, 'Classes, the Mode of Production and the State in Pre-Colonial Swaziland', in Marks, S. and Atmore, A. (eds), *Economy and Society in Pre-Industrial South Africa*, Longman, London.

Bonner, P. 1982, 'The Transvaal Native Congress 1917-1920: The Radicalisation of the Black Petty Bourgeoisie on the Rand', in Marks, S.

and Rathbone, B. (eds), *Industrialisation and Social Change in South Africa: African Class Formation, Culture, and Consciousness, 1870-1930*, Longman, London and New York.

Bonner, P. 1983, *Kings, Commoners and Concessionaires: The Evolution and Dissolution of the Nineteenth-Century Swazi State*, Ravan Press, Johannesburg.

Bonner, P. 1990a, 'The Politics of Black Squatter Movements on the Rand, 1944-1952', *Radical History Review*, 46/7, 89-115.

Bonner, P. 1990b, '"Desirable or Undesirable Basotho Women?" Liquor, Prostitution and the Migration of Basotho Women to the Rand, 1920-1945', in Walker, C. (ed.), *Women and Gender in Southern Africa to 1945*, David Philip, Cape Town and James Currey, London.

Bonner, P. 1993, 'The Russians on the Reef, 1947-1957: Urbanisation, Gang Warfare and Ethnic Mobilisation', in Bonner, P., Delius, P. and Posel, D. (eds), *Apartheid's Genesis 1935-1962*, Ravan Press and Witwatersrand University Press, Johannesburg.

Bozzoli, B. 1978, 'Class Struggle and the State', *Review of African Political Economy*, 11, 40-50.

Bozzoli, B. 1981, *The Political Nature of a Ruling Class: Capital and Ideology in South Africa 1890-1933*, Routledge and Kegan Paul, London, Boston and Henley.

Bozzoli, B. 1983a, 'Introduction: History, Experience and Culture', in Bozzoli, B. (ed.), *Town and Countryside in the Transvaal: Capitalist Penetration and Popular Response*, Ravan Press, Johannesburg.

Bozzoli, B. 1983b, 'Marxism, Feminism and South African Studies', *Journal of Southern African Studies*, 9, 2, 139-71.

Bozzoli, B. 1987, 'Class, Community and Ideology in the Evolution of South African Society', in Bozzoli, B. (ed.), *Class, Community and Conflict: South African Perspectives*, Ravan Press, Johannesburg.

Bozzoli, B. and Delius, P. 1990, 'Radical History and South African Society', *Radical History Review*, 46, 7, 13-45.

Bradford, H. 1986, 'Class Contradictions and Class Alliances: The Social Nature of the ICU Leadership, 1924-1929', in Lodge, T. (ed.), *Resistance and Ideology in Settler Societies*, Ravan Press, Johannesburg.

Bradford, H. 1987a, *A Taste of Freedom: The ICU in Rural South Africa 1924-1930*, Yale University Press, New Haven, CT and London.

Bradford, H. 1987b, '"We are Now the Men": Women's Beer Protests in the Natal Countryside, 1929', in Bozzoli, B. (ed.), *Class, Community and Conflict: South African Perspectives*, Ravan Press, Johannesburg.

Bradford, H. 1990, 'Highways, Byways and Cul-de-Sacs: The Transition to Agrarian Capitalism in Revisionist South African History', *Radical History Review*, 46/7, 59-88.

Bradford, H. 1993, 'Getting Away With Murder: "Mealie Kings", the State and Foreigners in the Eastern Transvaal, c.1918-1950', in Bonner, P., Delius, P. and Posel, D. (eds), *Apartheid's Genesis 1935-1962*, Ravan Press and Witwatersrand University Press, Johannesburg.

Brain, J. 1989, 'Natal's Indians, 1860-1910: From Co-operation, Through Competition, to Conflict', in Duminy, A. and Guest, B. (eds), *Natal and Zululand from Earliest Times to 1910*, Shuter and Shooter/University of Natal Press, Pietermaritzburg.

Brink, E. 1987, '"Maar 'n Klomp 'Factory' Meide": Afrikaner Family and Community on the Witwatersrand During the 1920s', in Bozzoli, B. (ed.), *Class, Community and Conflict: South African Perspectives*, Ravan Press, Johannesburg.

Brink, E. 1990, 'Man-Made Women: Gender, Class and the Ideology of the *Volksmoeder*', in Walker, C. (ed.), *Women and Gender in Southern Africa to 1945*, David Philip, Cape Town and James Currey, London.

Bundy, C. 1986, 'Vagabond Hollanders and Runaway Englishmen: White Poverty in the Cape Before Poor Whiteism', in Beinart, W., Delius, P. and Trapido, S. (eds), *Putting a Plough to the Ground: Accumulation and Dispossession in Rural South Africa 1850-1930*, Ravan Press, Johannesburg.

Bundy, C. 1987a, 'Land and Liberation: Popular Rural Protest and the National Liberation Movements in South Africa 1920-1960', in Marks, S. and Trapido, S. (eds), *The Politics of Race, Class and Nationalism in Twentieth-Century South Africa*, Longman, London and New York.

Bundy, C. 1987b, 'Street Sociology and Pavement Politics: Aspects of Youth/Student Resistance in Cape Town, 1985', History Workshop, University of Witwatersrand, Johannesburg.

Bundy, C. 1988, *The Rise and Fall of The South African Peasantry* (second edition: first edition 1979), David Philip, Cape Town and Johannesburg and James Currey, London.

Bundy, C. 1994, 'At War with the Future? Black South African Youth in the 1990s', in Stedman, S. J. (ed.), *South Africa: The Political Economy of Transformation*, Lynne Rennier Publishers, Boulder, CO and London.

Bunting, B. 1964, *The Rise of the South African Reich*, Penguin, Harmondsworth.

Callinicos, L. 1987, 'The "People's Past": Towards Transforming the Present', in Bozzoli, B. (ed.), *Class, Community and Conflict: South African Perspectives*, Ravan Press, Johannesburg.

Callinicos, A. 1988, *South Africa Between Reform and Revolution*, Bookmarks, London, Chicago and Melbourne.

Campbell, C. 1992, 'Learning to Kill? Masculinity, the Family and Violence in Natal', *Journal of Southern African Studies*, 18, 3, 614-28.

Cell, J. W. 1982, *The Highest Stage of White Supremacy: The Origins of Segregation in South Africa and the American South*, Cambridge University Press, Cambridge, London and New York.

Charney, C. 1984, 'Class Conflict and the National Party Split', *Journal of Southern African Studies*, 10, 2, 269-82.

Charney, C. 1987, 'The National Party, 1982-1985', in James, W. (ed.), *The State of Apartheid*, Lynne Rennier Publishers, Boulder, CO.

Charney, C. 1988, 'Janus in Blackface? The African Petite Bourgeoisie in South Africa', *Con-Text*, 1, 5-44.

Chaskalson, M. 1987, 'Rural Resistance in the 1940s and 1950s', *Africa Perspective*, 1, 5-6 (new series), 47-59.

Chaskalson, M. 1988, 'Apartheid with a Human Face: Punt Janson and the Origins of Reform in Township Administration, 1972-1976', seminar paper, African Studies Institute, University of Witwatersrand.

Christie, R. 1984, *Electricity, Industry and Class in South Africa*, Macmillan, London and New York.

Christie, R. 1991: 'Antiquated Industrialization: A Comment on William Martin's "The Making of an Industrial South Africa"', *The International Journal of African Historical Studies*, 24, 3, 589-608.

Clark, N. 1987, 'South African State Corporations: "The Death Knell of Economic Colonialism"?', *Journal of Southern African Studies*, 14, 1, 99-122.

Clark, N. 1993, 'The Limits of Industrialisation Under Apartheid', in Bonner, P., Delius, P. and Posel, D. (eds), *Apartheid's Genesis 1935-1962*, Ravan Press and Witwatersrand University Press, Johannesburg.

Clark, N. 1994, *Manufacturing Apartheid: State Corporations in South Africa*, Yale University Press, New Haven, CT and London.

Clarke, S. 1978, 'Capital, Fractions of Capital and the State: "Neo-Marxist" Analysis of the South African State', *Capital and Class*, 5, 32-77.

Cobbett, W., Glaser, D., Hindson, D. and Swilling, M. 1988, 'A Critical Analysis of the South African State's Reform Strategy in the 1980s', in Frankel, P., Pines, N. and Swilling, M. (eds), *State, Resistance and Change in South Africa*, Croom Helm, London, New York and Sydney.

Cobbing, J. 1988, 'The Mfecane as Alibi: Thoughts on Dithakong and Mbolompo', *Journal of African History*, 29, 487-519.

Cock, J. and Nathan, L. (eds) 1989, *Society at War: The Militarisation of South Africa*, St. Martin's Press, New York.

Coleman, F. J. (ed.) 1983, *Economic History of South Africa*, Haum, Pretoria.

Comaroff, J. and Comaroff, J. 1991, *Of Revelation and Revolution: Christianity, Colonialism, and Consciousness in South Africa: Volume One*, University of Chicago Press, Chicago and London.

Connor, W. 1994, *Ethnonationalism: The Quest for Understanding*, Princeton University Press, Princeton, NJ.

Cooper, D. 1988, 'Ownership and Control of Agriculture in South Africa', in Suckling, J. and White, L. (eds), *After Apartheid: Renewal of the South African Economy*, Centre for Southern African Studies, York, James Currey, London and World Africa Press, Trenton, NJ.

Cope, N. 1993, *To Bind the Nation: Solomon kaDinizulu and Zulu Nationalism 1913-1933*, University of Natal Press, Pietermaritzburg.

Crais, C C. 1986, 'Gentry and Labour in Three Eastern Cape Districts: 1820-1865', *South African Historical Journal*, 18, 125-46.

Crais, C. 1992, *The Making of the Colonial Order: White Supremacy and Black Resistance in the Eastern Cape, 1770-1865*, Witwatersrand University Press, Johannesburg.

Crankshaw, O. 1997, *Race, Class and the Changing Division of Labour under Apartheid*, Routledge, London and New York.

Crush, J., Jeeves, A. and Yudelman, D. 1991, *South Africa's Labour Empire: A History of Black Migrancy to the Gold Mines*, Westview Press, Boulder, CO San Francisco and Oxford and David Philip, Cape Town.

Davenport, R. 1966, *The Afrikaner Bond, 1880-1911*, Oxford University Press, Cape Town and London.

Davenport, R. 1997, 'Settlement, Conquest, and Theological Controversy: The Churches of Nineteenth-Century European Immigrants', in Elphick, R. and Davenport, R. (eds), *Christianity in South Africa: A Political, Social, and Cultural History*, University of California Press, Berkeley.

Davenport, T. R. H. 1969, 'The Consolidation of a New Society: The Cape Colony', in Wilson, M. and Thompson, L. (eds), *The Oxford History of South Africa*, vol. 1: *South Africa to 1870*, Clarendon Press, Oxford.

Davies, R., Kaplan, D., Morris, M. and O'Meara, D. 1976, 'Class Struggle and the Periodisation of the South African State', *Review Of African Political Economy*, 7, 4-30.

Davies, R. 1979, *Capital, State and White Labour in South Africa 1900-1960: An Historical Materialist Analysis of Class Formation and Class Relations*, The Harvester Press, Brighton, 1979.

De Klerk, M. 1991, 'The Accumulation Crisis in Agriculture', in Gelb, S. (ed.), *South Africa's Economic Crisis*, David Philip, Cape Town and Zed books, London and New Jersey.

De Klerk, F. W. 2000, *The Last Trek – A New Beginning: The Autobiography*, Pan, London.

Delius, P. 1983, *The Land Belongs To Us: The Pedi Polity, the Boers and the British in the Nineteenth-Century Transvaal*, Ravan Press, Johannesburg.

Delius, P. 1989, 'The Ndzundza Ndebele: Indenture and the Making of Ethnic Identity, 1883-1914', in Bonner, P., Hofmeyr, I., James, D. and Lodge, T.

(eds), *Holding Their Ground: Class, Locality and Culture in 19th and 20th Century South Africa*, Witwatersrand University Press and Ravan Press, Johannesburg.

Delius, P. 1993, 'Migrant Organisation, the Communist Party, the ANC and the Sekhukhuneland Revolt, 1940-1958', in Bonner, P., Delius, P. and Posel, D. (eds), *Apartheid's Genesis 1935-1962*, Ravan Press and Witwatersrand University Press, Johannesburg.

Delius, P. 1996, *A Lion Amongst the Cattle: Reconstruction and Resistance in the Northern Transvaal*, Heinemann, Portsmouth, NH, Ravan Press, Johannesburg and James Currey, London.

Denoon, D. 1980, 'Capital and the Capitalists in the Transvaal in the 1890s and 1900s', *The Historical Journal*, 23, 1, 111-32.

De V. Graaff, J. F. 1990, 'Theorising the Bantustan State in South Africa: Breaking Bonds and Boundaries', in Swilling, M. (ed.), *Views on the South African State*, Human sciences Research Council, Pretoria.

Diamond, L. 1994, 'Civil Society and Democratic Consolidation: Building a Culture of Democracy in a New South Africa', in Giliomee, H., Schlemmer, L. and Hauptfleisch, S. (eds), *The Bold Experiment: South Africa's New Democracy*, Southern Book Publishers, Halfway House, South Africa.

Di Palma, G. 1990, *To Craft Democracies: An Essay on Democratic Transitions*, University of California Press, Berkeley and Oxford.

Diseko, N. 1991, 'The Origins and Development of the South African Student's Movement (SASM): 1968-1976', *Journal of Southern African Studies*, 18, 1, 40-62.

Dubow, S. 1989, *Racial Segregation and the Origins of Apartheid in South Africa, 1919-36*, Macmillan, Basingstoke.

Dubow, S. 1995, *Scientific Racism in Modern South Africa*, Cambridge University Press, Cambridge.

Duncan, D. 1995, *The Mills of God: The State and African Labour in South Africa 1918-1948*, Witwatersrand University Press, Johannesburg.

Du Toit, A. 1983, 'No Chosen People: The Myth of the Calvinist Origins of Afrikaner Nationalism and Racial Ideology', *American Historical Review*, 88, 2, 920-52.

Du Toit, A. 1985, 'Puritans in Africa? Afrikaner "Calvinism" and Kuyperian Neo-Calvinism in Late Nineteenth Century South Africa', *Comparative Studies in Society and History*, 27, 209-40.

Du Toit, A. 1994, 'Fragile Defiance: The African Resistance Movement', in Liebenberg, I., Lortan, F., Nel, B. and van der Westhuizen, G. (eds), *The Long March: The Story of the Struggle for Liberation in South Africa*, Haum, Pretoria.

Elbourne, E. and Ross, R. 1997, 'Combating Spiritual and Social Bondage: Early Missions in the Cape Colony', in Elphick, R. and Davenport, R. (eds),

Christianity in South Africa: A Political, Social, and Cultural History, University of California Press, Berkeley.

Eldredge, E. A. 1993, *A South African Kingdom: The Pursuit of Security in Nineteenth-Century Lesotho*, Cambridge University Press, Cambridge.

Eldredge, E. A. 1994, 'Slave Raiding Across the Cape Frontier', in Eldredge, E. A. and Morton, F. (eds), *Slavery in South Africa: Captive Labour on the Dutch Frontier*, Westview Press, Boulder, CO, San Francisco and Oxford and Natal University Press, Pietermaritzburg.

Eldredge, E. A. and Morton, F. (eds) 1994, *Slavery in South Africa: Captive Labour on the Dutch Frontier*, Westview Press, Boulder, CO, San Francisco and Oxford and Natal University Press, Pietermaritzburg.

Eldredge, E. A. 1995, 'Sources of Conflict in Southern Africa c.1800-1830: The "Mfecane" Reconsidered', in Hamilton, C. (ed.), *The Mfecane Aftermath: Reconstructive Debates in Southern African History*, Witwatersrand University Press, Johannesburg.

Elphick, R. 1981, 'Africans and the Christian Campaign in Southern Africa', in Lamar, H. and Thompson, L. (eds), *The Frontier in History: North America and Southern Africa Compared*, Yale University Press, New Haven, CT and London.

Elphick, R. 1985, *Khoikhoi and the Founding of White South Africa*, Ravan Press, Johannesburg.

Elphick, R. 1988, 'The Khoisan to 1828', in Elphick, R. and Giliomee, H. (eds), *The Shaping of South African Society, 1652-1840*, Wesleyan University Press, Middletown, CT.

Elphick, R. 1997, 'Introduction: Christianity in South African History', in Elphick, R. and Davenport, R. (eds), *Christianity in South Africa: A Political, Social, and Cultural History*, University of California Press, Berkeley.

Elphick, R. and Giliomee, H., 1988, 'The Origins and Entrenchment of European Dominance at the Cape, 1652-c.1840', in Elphick, R. and Giliomee, H. (eds), *The Shaping of South African Society, 1652-1840*, Wesleyan University Press, Middletown, CT.

Elphick, R. and Shell, R., 1979/80, 'Intergroup Relations: Khoikhoi, Settlers, Slaves and Free Blacks, 1652-1795', in Elphick, R. and Giliomee, H. (eds) *The Shaping of South African Society, 1652-1820*, Longman, Cape Town and London.

Etherington, N. 1978, *Preachers Peasants and Politics in Southeast Africa, 1835-1880: African Christian Communities in Natal, Pondoland and Zululand*, Royal Historical Society, London.

Etherington, N. 1985, 'African Economic Experiments in Colonial Natal, 1845-1880', in Guest, G. and Sellers, J. M. (eds), *Enterprise and Exploitation in a*

Victorian Colony: Aspects of the Economic and Social History of Colonial Natal, University of Natal Press, Pietermaritzburg.

Feit, E. 1975, *Workers Without Weapons: Sactu and the Organisation of African Workers*, Archon Books, Hamden.

Fine, A. and Webster, E. 1990, 'Transcending Traditions: Trade Unions and Political Unity', in Moss, G. and Obery, I. (eds), *South African Review*, 5, Hans Zell Publishers, London, Munich and New York.

Fine, B. and Rustomjee, Z. 1996, *The Political Economy of South Africa: From Minerals-Energy Complex to Complex Industrialisation*, Westview Press, Boulder, CO.

Fine, R. and Davis, D. 1990, *Beyond Apartheid: Labour and Liberation in South Africa*, Pluto Press, London and Concord, NH.

Foucault, M. 1977, *Discipline and Punish: The Birth of the Prison*, Allen Lane, London.

Frankel, P. 1984, *Pretoria's Praetorians: Civil–Military Relations in South Africa*, Cambridge University Press, Cambridge, London and New York.

Frederickson, G. M. 1981, *White Supremacy: A Comparative Study in American and South African History*, Oxford University Press, New York and Oxford.

Frederickson, G. M. 1995, *Black Liberation: A Comparative History of Black Ideologies in the United States and South Africa*, Oxford University Press, New York and Oxford.

Freund, W. 1976, 'Race in the Social Structure of South Africa, 1652-1836', *Race and Class*, 18, 1, 53-67.

Freund, W. 1979/80, 'The Cape Under the Transitional Governments', in Elphick, R. and Giliomee, H. (eds), *The Shaping of South African Society, 1652-1820*, Longman, Cape Town and London.

Freund, W. 1989, 'The Social Character of Secondary Industry in South Africa: 1915-1945', in Mabin, A. (ed.), *Organisation and Economic Change*, Ravan Press, Johannesburg.

Freund, W. 1995, *Insiders and Outsiders: The Indian Working Class of Durban, 1910-1990*, Heinemann, Portsmouth, N. H., University of Natal Press, Pietermaritzburg and James Currey, London.

Friedman, S. 1987, *Building Tomorrow Today: African Workers in Trade Unions, 1970-1984*, Ravan Press, Johannesburg.

Friedman, S. and Stack, L. 1994, 'The Magic Moment: The 1994 Election', in Friedman, S. and Atkinson, D. (eds), *The Small Miracle: South Africa's Negotiated Settlement/South African Review*, 7, Ravan Press, Johannesburg.

Furlong, P. J. 1991, *Between Crown and Swastika: The Impact of the Radical Right on the Afrikaner Nationalist Movement in the Fascist Era*, Wesleyan University Press/University Press of New England, Hanover and London, 1991.

Gaitskell, D. 1990, 'Devout Domesticity? A Century of African Women's Christianity in South Africa', in Walker, C. (ed.), *Women and Gender in Southern Africa to 1945*, David Philip, Cape Town and James Currey, London.

Garson, N. 1962, 'The Boer Rebellion of 1914', *History Today*, 12, 2.

Gelb, S. 1989, 'The Origins of the South African Reserve Bank, 1914-1920', in Mabin, A. (ed.), *Organisation and Economic Change*, Ravan Press, Johannesburg.

Gelb, S. 1991a, 'South Africa's Economic Crisis: An Overview', in Gelb, S. (ed.), *South Africa's Economic Crisis*, David Philip, Cape Town and Zed books, London and New Jersey.

Gelb, S. (ed.) 1991b, *South Africa's Economic Crisis*, David Philip, Cape Town and Zed books, London and New Jersey.

Gellner, E. 1983, *Nations and Nationalism*, Blackwell, Oxford.

Gerhart, G. 1978, *Black Power in South Africa: The Evolution of an Ideology*, University of California Press, Berkeley and London.

Gerstner, J. N. 1997, 'A Christian Monopoly: The Reformed Church and Colonial Society under Dutch Rule', in Elphick, R. and Davenport, R. (eds), *Christianity in South Africa: A Political, Social, and Cultural History*, University of California Press, Berkeley.

Giliomee, H. 1979/80, 'The Eastern Frontier', in Elphick, R. and Giliomee, H. (eds), *The Shaping of South African Society, 1652-1840*, Wesleyan University Press, Middletown, CT.

Giliomee, H. 1980, 'The National Party and the Afrikaner Broederbond', in Price, R. M. and Rotberg, C. G. (eds) *The Apartheid Regime: Political Power and Racial Domination*, Institute of International Studies, University of California, Berkeley.

Giliomee, H. 1981, 'Processes in Development of the Southern African Frontier', in Lamar, H. and Thompson, L. (eds), *The Frontier in History: North America and Southern Africa Compared*, Yale University Press, New Haven, CT and London.

Giliomee, H. 1983, 'Constructing Afrikaner Nationalism', *Journal of Asian and African Studies*, 18, 1-2, 83-98.

Giliomee, H. 1989a, 'The Communal Nature of the South African Conflict', in Giliomee, H. and Schlemmer, L. (eds), *Negotiating South Africa's Future*, Centre for Policy Studies, University of Witwatersrand and Macmillan, Basingstoke.

Giliomee, H. 1989b, 'Aspects of the Rise of Afrikaner Capital and Afrikaner Nationalism in the Western Cape, 1870-1915', in James, W. G. and Simons, M. (eds), *The Angry Divide: Social and Economic History of the Western Cape*, David Philip, Cape Town and Johannesburg.

Giliomee, H. 1989c, 'The Beginnings of Afrikaner Ethnic Consciousness, 1850-1915', in Vail, L. (ed.), *The Creation of Tribalism in Southern Africa*, James Currey, London and University of California Press, Berkeley.

Giliomee, H. 1989d, 'Afrikaner Politics 1977-1987: From Afrikaner Nationalist Rule to Central State Hegemony', in Brewer, J. D. (eds), *Can South Africa Survive? Five Minutes to Midnight*, Macmillan Press, Basingstoke and London.

Giliomee, H. 1992, '*Broedertwis*: Intra-Afrikaner Conflicts in the Transition From Apartheid', *African Affairs*, 91, 339-64.

Giliomee, H. 1994a, 'The Leader and the Citizenry', in Schrire, R. (ed.), *Leadership in the Apartheid State: From Malan to De Klerk*, Oxford University Press, Cape Town.

Giliomee, H. 1994b, 'The National Party's Campaign for a Liberation Election', in Reynolds, E. (ed.), *Election '94 South Africa: The Campaigns, Results and Future Prospects*, James Currey, London, David Philip, Cape Town and Johannesburg and St. Martin's Press, New York.

Giliomee, H. and Schlemmer, L. 1989, *From Apartheid to Nation-Building: Contemporary South African Debates*, Oxford University Press, Cape Town.

Glaser, C. 1993, '"When are they Going to Fight?" Tsotsis, Youth Politics and the PAC', in Bonner, P., Delius, P. and Posel, D. (eds), *Apartheid's Genesis 1935-1962*, Ravan Press and Witwatersrand University Press, Johannesburg.

Glaser, C. 1998, '"We Must Infiltrate the Tsotsis": School Politics and Youth Gangs in Soweto, 1968-1976', *Journal of Southern African Studies*, 24, 2, 301-24

Glaser, C. 2000 (forthcoming), *Bo-Tsotsi: The Youth Gangs of Soweto, 1935-1976*, Heinemann, London.

Glaser, D. J. 1984, 'Liberalism in the 1980s', *Work in Progress,* 30.

Glaser, D. J. 1988, *The State, Capital and Decentralisation Policy in South Africa, 1932-1985*, M.A. thesis, University of Witwatersrand, Johannesburg.

Glaser, D. J. 1997, 'South Africa and the Limits of Civil Society', *Journal of Southern African Studies*, 23, 1, 5-25.

Goldin, I. 1987, *Making Race: The Politics and Economics of Coloured Identity in South Africa*, Maskew Miller Longmans, Cape Town.

Greenberg, S. 1980, *Race and State in Capitalist Development: South Africa in Comparative Perspective*, Ravan Press, Johannesburg.

Greenberg, S. 1987a, 'Ideological Struggles within the South African State', in Marks, S. and Trapido, S. (eds), *The Politics of Race, Class and Nationalism in Twentieth-Century South Africa*, Longman, London and New York.

Greenberg, S. 1987b, *Legitimating the Illegitimate: State, Markets and Resistance in South Africa*, University of California Press, Berkeley and London.

Greenstein, R. 1993, 'Racial Formation: Towards a Comparative Study of Collective Identities in South Africa and the United States', *Social Dynamics*, 19, 2, 1-29.

Grundy, K. W. 1986, *The Militarization of South African Politics*, Indiana University Press, Bloomington.

Guelke, L. 1979/80, 'The White Settlers, 1652-1795', in Elphick, R. and Giliomee, H. (eds), *The Shaping of South African Society, 1652-1820*, Longman, Cape Town and London.

Guelke, L. 1988, 'Freehold Farmers and Frontier Settlers, 1657-1780', in Elphick, R. and Giliomee, H. (eds), *The Shaping of South African Society, 1652-1840*, Wesleyan University Press, Middletown, CT.

Guelke, L. and Shell, R. 1983, 'An Early Colonial Landed Gentry: Land and Wealth in the Cape Colony, 1682-1731', *Journal of Historical Geography*, 9, 265-86.

Guy, J. 1980, 'Ecological Factors in the Rise of Shaka and the Zulu Kingdom', in Marks, S. and Atmore, A. (eds), *Economy and Society in Pre-Industrial South Africa*, Longman, London.

Guy, J. 1990, 'Gender Oppression in Southern Africa's Precapitalist Societies', in Walker, C. (ed.), *Women and Gender in Southern Africa to 1945*, David Philip, Cape Town and James Currey, London.

Habermas, J. 1984, *The Theory of Communicative Action*, vol. 1: *Reason and the Rationalization of Society*, Heinemann, London.

Habermas, J. 1987, *The Theory of Communicative Action*, vol. 2: *Lifeworld and System: A Critique of Functionalist Reason*, Polity, Cambridge.

Hall, M. 1987, *The Changing Past: Farmers, Kings and Traders in Southern Africa, 200-1860*, David Philip, Cape Town.

Hamilton, C. (ed.) 1995, *The Mfecane Aftermath: Reconstructive Debates in Southern African History*, Witwatersrand University Press, Johannesburg.

Hamilton, C. 1998, *Terrific Majesty: The Powers of Shaka Zulu and the Limits of Historical Invention*, Harvard University Press, Cambridge, MA.

Harries, P. 1986, 'Capital, State, and Labour on the 19th Century Witwatersrand: A Reassessment', *South African Historical Journal*, 18, 25-45.

Harries, P. 1989, 'Exclusion, Classification and Internal Colonialism: The Emergence of Ethnicity among the Tsonga-speakers of South Africa', in Vail, L. (ed.), *The Creation of Tribalism in Southern Africa*, James Currey, London and University of California Press, Berkeley.

Harries, P. 1994, *Work, Culture, and Identity: Migrant Laborers in Mozambique and South Africa c.1860-1910*, Witwatersrand University

Press, Johannesburg, Heinemann, Portsmouth, NH and James Currey, London.

Hexham, I. 1981, *The Irony of Apartheid: The Struggle for National Independence of Afrikaner Calvinism Against British Imperialism*, Edwin Mellen Press, New York.

Hexham, I. And Poewe, K. 1997, 'The Spread of Christianity among Whites and Blacks in Transorangia', in Elphick, R. and Davenport, R. (eds), *Christianity in South Africa: A Political, Social, and Cultural History*, University of California Press, Berkeley.

Hill, R. A. and Pirio, G. A. 1987, '"Africa for the Africans": the Garvey Movement in South Africa, 1920-1940', in Marks, S. and Trapido, S. (eds), *The Politics of Race, Class and Nationalism in Twentieth-Century South Africa*, Longman, London and New York.

Hindson, D. 1987, *Pass Controls and the Urban African Proletariat in South Africa*, Ravan Press, Johannesburg.

Hirson, B. 1979, *Year of Fire, Year of Ash: The Soweto Revolt: Roots of a Revolution?*, Zed Press, London.

Hirson, B. 1989, *Yours For The Union: Class and Community Struggles in South Africa, 1930-1947*, Zed books, London and New Jersey and Witwatersrand University Press, Johannesburg.

Hirson, B. 1994a, 'The Trotskyist Groups in South Africa, 1932-1948', in Liebenberg, I., Lortan, F., Nel, B. and van der Westhuizen, G. (eds), *The Long March: The Story of the Struggle for Liberation in South Africa*, Haum, Pretoria.

Hirson, B. 1994b, 'The Trotskyists and the Trade Unions', in Liebenberg, I., Lortan, F., Nel, B. and van der Westhuizen, G. (eds), *The Long March: The Story of the Struggle for Liberation in South Africa*, Haum, Pretoria.

Hodgson, J. 1997, 'A Battle for Sacred Power: Christian Beginnings Amongst the Xhosa', in Elphick, R. and Davenport, R. (eds), *Christianity in South Africa: A Political, Social, and Cultural History*, University of California Press, Berkeley.

Hofmeyr, I. 1987, 'Building a Nation From Words: Afrikaans Language, Literature and Ethnic Identity, 1902-1924', in Marks, S. and Trapido, S. (eds), *The Politics of Race, Class and Nationalism in Twentieth-Century South Africa*, Longman, London and New York.

Hofmeyr, J. F. 1994, *An Analysis of African Wage Movements in South Africa*, Research Monograph 9, Economic Research Unit, University of Natal, Durban.

Horowitz, D. L. 1991, *A Democratic South Africa? Constitutional Engineering in a Divided Society*, University of California Press, Berkeley and Oxford.

Horton, C., Tregenna, F. and Ngqungwana, T. 1998, 'After GEAR: Changing Economic Policy', *South African Labour Bulletin*, 22, 6, 16-22.

Hudson, P. and Sarakinsky, M. 1986, 'Class Interests and Politics: The Case of the Urban African Bourgeoisie', in South African Research Service (ed.), *South African Review*, 3, Ravan Press, Johannesburg.

Humphries, R. 1989, 'Administrative Politics and the Coloured Labour Preference Policy', in James, W. G. and Simons, M. (eds), *The Angry Divide: Social and Economic History of the Western Cape*, David Philip, Cape Town and Johannesburg.

Humphries, R., Rapoo, T. and Friedman, S. 1994, 'The Shape of the Country: Negotiating Regional Government', in Friedman, S. and Atkinson, D. (eds), *The Small Miracle: South Africa's Negotiated Settlement/South African Review*, 7, Ravan Press, Johannesburg.

Huntington, S. P. 1991, *The Third Wave: Democratization in the Late Twentieth Century*, University of Oklahoma Press, Norman (Oklahoma) and London.

Huntington, S. P. 1994, 'Democracy and/or Economic Reform?', in Giliomee, H., Schlemmer, L. and Hauptfleisch, S. (eds), *The Bold Experiment: South Africa's New Democracy*, Southern Book Publishers, Halfway House, South Africa.

Hyslop, J. 1988a, 'School Student Movements and State Education Policy', in Cobbett, W. and Cohen, R. (eds), *Popular Struggles in South Africa*, Review of African Political Economy, Sheffield and James Currey, London.

Hyslop, J. 1988b, 'State Education Policy and the Reproduction of the Urban African Working Class: The Case of the Southern Transvaal, 1955-1976', *Journal of Southern African Studies*, 14, 3.

Hyslop, J. 1989a, 'Introduction', in Moss, G. and Obery, I. (eds), *South African Review*, 5, Hans Zell Publishers, London, Munich and New York.

Hyslop, J. 1989b, 'School Boards, School Committees and Educational Politics: Aspects of the Failure of Bantu Education as a Hegemonic Strategy, 1955-1976', in Bonner, P., Hofmeyr, I., James, D. and Lodge, T. (eds), *Holding Their Ground: Class, Locality and Culture in 19th and 20th Century South Africa*, Witwatersrand University Press and Ravan Press, Johannesburg.

Hyslop, J. 1993, '"A Destruction Coming In": Bantu Education as Response to Social Crisis', in Bonner, P., Delius, P. and Posel, D. (eds), *Apartheid's Genesis 1935-1962*, Ravan Press and Witwatersrand University Press, Johannesburg.

Innes, D. 1984, *Anglo: Anglo American and the Rise of Modern South Africa*, Ravan Press, Johannesburg.

Innes, D. and Plaut, M. 1978, 'Class Struggle and the State', *Review of African Political Economy*, 11.

James, W. 1992, *Our Precious Metal: African Labour in South Africa's Gold Industry, 1970-1990*, David Philip, Cape Town, James Currey, London and Indiana University Press, Bloomington and Indianapolis.

Jeeves, A. H. 1985, *Migrant Labour in South Africa's Mining Economy: The Struggle for the Gold Mines' Labour Supply 1890-1920*, McGill-Queens University Press, Kingston and Montreal and Witwatersrand University Press, Johannesburg.

Jeffrey, A. 1999, *The Truth About the Truth Commission*, Institute of Race Relations, Johannesburg.

Jessop, B. 1982, *The Capitalist State: Marxist Theories and Methods*, Martin Robinson, Oxford.

Jochelson, K. 1990, 'Reform, Repression and Resistance in South Africa: A Case Study of Alexandra Township, 1979-1989', *Journal of Southern African Studies*, 16, 1, 1-32.

Johns, S. 1995 *Raising the Red Flag: The International Socialist League and the Communist Party of South Africa 1914-1932*, Mayibuye Books, Bellville (SA).

Johnson, R. W. 1996a, 'The 1994 Election: Outcome and Analysis', in Johnson, R. W. and Schlemmer, L. (eds), *Launching Democracy in South Africa: The First Open Election, April 1994*, Yale University Press, New Haven, CT and London.

Johnson, R. W. 1996b, 'How Free? How Fair?', in Johnson, R. W. and Schlemmer, L. (eds), *Launching Democracy in South Africa: The First Open Election, April 1994*, Yale University Press, New Haven, CT and London.

Johnson, R. W. 1996c, 'Understanding the Elections', *KwaZulu-Natal Briefing*, 3, 11-20.

Johnston, A. 1997, 'Politics and Violence in KwaZulu-Natal', in Gutteridge, W. and Spence, J. E. (eds), *Violence in Southern Africa*, Frank Cass, London and Portland, OR.

Johnstone, F. A. 1970, 'White Prosperity and White Supremacy in South Africa Today', *African Affairs*, 69, 275, 124-40.

Johnstone, F.A. 1976, *Class, Race and Gold: A Study of Class Relations and Racial Discrimination in South Africa*, Routledge and Kegan Paul, London, Henley and Boston.

Jones, P. S. 1999, 'From "Nationhood" to Regionalism to the North West Province: "Bophutatswananess" and the Birth of the "New" South Africa', *African Affairs*, 98, 509-34.

Jones, S. (ed.) 1992, *Financial Enterprise in South Africa Since 1950*, Macmillan, Basingstoke.

Jones, S. and Müller, A. 1992, *The South African Economy, 1910-90*, Macmillan, Basingstoke.

Kaganas, F. and Murray, C. 1994, 'The Contest Between Culture and Gender Equality Under South Africa's Interim Constitution', *Journal of Law and Society*, 21, 4, 409-33.

Kahn, B. 1991, 'The Crisis and South Africa's Balance of Payments' in Gelb, S. (ed.), *South Africa's Economic Crisis*, David Philip, Cape Town and Zed books, London and New Jersey.

Kane-Berman, J. 1991, *South Africa's Silent Revolution*, South African Institute of Race Relations and Southern Book Publishers, Johannesburg and Halfway House.

Kaplan, D. 1980, 'The South African State: The Origins of a Racially Exclusive Democracy', *Insurgent Sociologist*, 10, 2, 85-96.

Kaplan, D. 1990, *The Crossed Line: Technological Change and Telecommunications in South Africa*, Witwatersrand University Press, Johannesburg.

Karl, T. L. and Schmitter, P. 1991, 'Modes of Transition in Latin America, Southern and Eastern Europe', *International Social Science Journal*, 43, 128.

Keegan, T. 1982, 'The Sharecropping Economy, African Class Formation and the 1913 Natives' Land Act in the Highveld Maize Belt', in Marks, S. and Rathbone, B. (eds), *Industrialisation and Social Change in South Africa: African Class Formation, Culture, and Consciousness, 1870-1930*, Longman, London and New York.

Keegan, T. 1986a, *Rural Transformations in Industrializing South Africa: The Southern Highveld to 1914*, Ravan Press, Johannesburg.

Keegan, T. 1986b, 'White Settlement and Black Subjugation on the South African Highveld: The Tlokoa Heartland in the North Eastern Orange Free State, ca. 1850-1914', in Beinart, W., Delius, P. and Trapido, S. (eds), *Putting a Plough to the Ground: Accumulation and Dispossession in Rural South Africa 1850-1930*, Ravan Press, Johannesburg.

Keegan, T. 1996, *Colonial South Africa and the Origins of the Racial Order*, Leicester University Press, London.

Kimble, J. 1982, 'Labour Migration in Basutoland c.1870-1885', in Marks, S. and Rathbone, B. (eds), *Industrialisation and Social Change in South Africa: African Class Formation, Culture, and Consciousness, 1870-1930*, Longman, London and New York.

Kinghorn, J. 1994, 'Social Cosmology, Religion and Afrikaner Ethnicity', in *Journal of Southern African Studies*, 20, 3, 393-404.

Koch, E. 1983, '"Without Visible Means of Subsistence": Slumyard Culture in Johannesburg 1918-1940', in Bozzoli, B. (ed.), *Town and Countryside in the Transvaal: Capitalist Penetration and Popular Response*, Ravan Press, Johannesburg.

Krikler, J. 1993, *Revolution from Above, Revolution from Below: The Agrarian Transvaal at the Turn of the Century*, Clarendon Press, Oxford.

La Hausse, P. 1993, 'So Who Was Elias Kuzwayo? Nationalism, Collaboration and the Picaresque in Natal', in Bonner, P., Delius, P. and Posel, D. (eds), *Apartheid's Genesis 1935-1962*, Ravan Press and Witwatersrand University Press, Johannesburg.

Lacey, M. 1981, *Working for Boroko: The Origins of a Coercive Labour System in South Africa*, Ravan Press, Johannesburg.

Lamar, H. and Thompson, L. 1981, 'Comparative Frontier History', in Lamar, H. and Thompson, L. (eds), *The Frontier in History: North America and Southern Africa Compared*, Yale University Press, New Haven, CT and London.

Lambert, R. and Webster, E. 1988, 'The Re-Emergence of Political Unionism in Contemporary South Africa?', in Cobbett, W. and Cohen, R. (eds), *Popular Struggles in South Africa*, Review of African Political Economy, Sheffield and James Currey, London.

Lawrence, R. 1994, 'Introduction: From Soweto to Codesa', in Friedman, S. and Atkinson, D. (eds), *The Small Miracle: South Africa's Negotiated Settlement/South African Review*, 7, Ravan Press, Johannesburg.

Lazar, J. 1987, *Conformity and Conflict: Afrikaner Nationalist Politics in South Africa, 1948-1961*, PhD thesis, Balliol College, Oxford.

Lazar, J. 1993, 'Verwoerd versus the "Visionaries": The South African Bureau of Racial Affairs (Sabra) and Apartheid, 1948-1961', in Bonner, P., Delius, P. and Posel, D. (eds), *Apartheid's Genesis 1935-1962*, Ravan Press and Witwatersrand University Press, Johannesburg.

Legassick, M. 1973a, 'The Rise of Modern South African Liberalism: Its Assumptions and its Social Base', seminar paper, Institute of Commonwealth Studies, University of London.

Legassick, M. 1973b, 'The Making of South African "Native Policy", 1903-1923: The Origins of "Segregation"', seminar paper, Institute of Commonwealth Studies, University of London.

Legassick, M. 1974a, 'Capital Accumulation and Violence', *Economy and Society*, 3, 253-291.

Legassick, M. 1974b, 'Legislation, Ideology and Economy in Post-1948 South Africa', *Journal of Southern African Studies*, 1, 1, 5-35.

Legassick, M. 1975, 'South Africa: Forced Labour, Industrialization, and Racial Differentiation', in Harris, R. (ed.), *The Political Economy of Africa*, John Wiley and Sons, New York, London, Sydney and Toronto.

Legassick, M. 1976, 'Race, Industrialization and Social Change in South Africa: The Case of R. F. A. Hoernlé', *African Affairs*, 75, 224-39.

Legassick, M. 1979/80, 'The Northern Frontier to 1820: The Emergence of the Griqua People', in Elphick, R. and Giliomee, H. (eds), *The Shaping of South African Society, 1652-1820*, Longman, Cape Town and London.

Legassick, M. 1980, 'The Frontier Tradition in South African Historiography', in Marks, S. and Atmore, A. (eds), in *Economy and Society in Pre-Industrial South Africa*, Longman, London.

Legassick, M. 1988, 'The Northern Frontier to c.1840: The Rise and Decline of the Griqua People', in Elphick, R. and Giliomee, H. (eds), *The Shaping of South African Society, 1652-1840*, Wesleyan University Press, Middletown, CT.

Legassick, M. 1994, 'The Past and Present Role of the Marxist Workers' Tendency of the ANC in the Liberation Struggle in South Africa', in Liebenberg, I., Lortan, F., Nel, B. and van der Westhuizen, G. (eds), *The Long March: The Story of the Struggle for Liberation in South Africa*, Haum, Pretoria.

Lewis, G. 1987, *Between the Wire and the Wall: A History of South African "Coloured" Politics*, David Philip, Cape Town and Johannesburg.

Lewis, J. 1984, *Industrialisation and Trade Union Organisation in South Africa, 1924-55: The Rise and Fall of the South African Trades and Labour Council*, Cambridge University Press, Cambridge, London and New York.

Lewsen, P. 1983, 'Cape Liberalism in its Terminal Phase', in Hindson, D. C. (ed.), *Working Papers in Southern African Studies*, vol. 3, Ravan Press, Johannesburg.

Lewsen, P. 1987, 'Liberals in Politics and Administration, 1936-1948', in Butler, J., Elphick, R. and Welsh, D. (eds), *Democratic Liberalism in South Africa: Its History and Prospect*, Wesleyan University Press, Middletown, CT and David Philip, Cape Town.

Linz, J. and Stepan, A. 1978, *The Breakdown of Democratic Regimes: Crisis, Breakdown and Re-Equilibriation*, Johns Hopkins University Press, Baltimore.

Lipset, S. M. 1960, *Political Man: The Social Bases of Politics*, Johns Hopkins University Press, Baltimore.

Lipton, M. 1979, 'The Debate About South Africa: Neo-Marxists and Neo-Liberals', *African Affairs*, 78, 310, 57-80.

Lipton, M. 1986, *Capitalism and Apartheid: South Africa, 1910-1986*, David Philip, Cape Town and Wildwood House, London.

Lodge, T. 1983, *Black Politics in South Africa Since 1945*, Ravan Press, Johannesburg.

Lodge, T. 1985, 'Class Conflict, Communal Struggle and Patriotic Unity: The Communist Party of South Africa during the Second World War', paper presented to the African Studies Institute, Johannesburg.

Lodge, 1990, 'Chapters from the Past: The African National Congress and its Historiographical Traditions', *Radical History Review*, 46/7, 161-188.

Lodge, T. 1998, 'Political Corruption in South Africa', *African Affairs*, 97, 157-87.

Mabin, A. 1986, 'Labour, Capital, Class Struggle and the Origins of Residential Segregation in Kimberley, 1880-1920', *Journal of Historical Geography*, 12, 1, 4-26.

Mabin, A. 1992, 'Comprehensive Segregation: The Origins of the Group Areas Act and its Planning Apparatuses', *Journal of Southern African Studies*, 18, 2, 405-29.

McAllister, P. A. 1991, 'Using Ritual to Resist Domination in the Transkei', in Spiegel, A. D. and McAllister, P. A. (eds), *Tradition and Transition in Southern Africa*, Transaction Publishers, New Brunswick, NY and London.

MacCrone, I. D. 1937, *Race Attitudes in South Africa*, Oxford University Press, London.

McKendrick, B. and Hoffman, W. (eds) 1990, *People and Violence in South Africa*, Oxford University Press, Cape Town.

Macroeconomic Research Group (MERG) 1993, *Making Democracy work: A Framework for Macroeconomic Policy in South Africa*, Centre for development Studies, University of Western Cape.

MacShane, D., Plaut, M. and Ward, D. 1984, *Power! Black Workers, their Unions and the Struggle for Freedom in South Africa*, Spokesman, Nottingham.

Magubane, B. 1979, *The Political Economy of Race and Class in South Africa*, Monthly Review Press, New York.

Maharaj, B. 1992, 'The "Spatial Impress" of the Central and Local States: the Group Areas Act in Durban', in Smith, D. M. (ed.), *The Apartheid City and Beyond: Urbanization and Social Change in South Africa*, Routledge, London and Witwatersrand University Press, Johannesburg.

Mamdani, M. 1996, *Citizen and Subject: Contemporary Africa and the Legacy of Late Colonialism*, Princeton University Press, Princeton.

Mamdani, M. 1998, 'A Diminished Truth', *Siyaya*, 3.

Mandela, N. 1994, *Long Walk to Freedom: The Autobiography of Nelson Mandela*, Little, Brown and Company, London.

Manganyi, N. C. and Du Toit, A. (eds.) 1990, *Political Violence and the Struggle in South Africa*, Southern Book Publishers, Johannesburg and Macmillan, London.

Manicom, L. 1992, 'Ruling Relations: Rethinking State and Gender in South African History', *Journal of African History*, 33, 441-65.

Mann, M. 1988, 'The Giant Stirs: South African Business in the Age of Reform', in Frankel, P., Pines, N. and Swilling, M. (eds), *State, Resistance and Change in South Africa*, Croom Helm, London, New York and Sydney.

Manson, A. 1995, 'Conflict in the Western Highveld/Southern Kalahari c.1750-1820', in Hamilton, C. (ed.), *The Mfecane Aftermath: Reconstructive Debates in Southern African History*, Witwatersrand University Press, Johannesburg.

Maré, G. 1993, *Ethnicity and Politics in South Africa*, Zed books, London and New Jersey.

Maré, G. and Hamilton, G. 1987, *An Appetite for Power: Buthelezi's Inkatha and the Politics of 'Loyal Resistance'*, Ravan Press, Johannesburg.

Maree, J. (ed.) 1987, *The Independent Trade Unions 1974-1984: Ten Years of the South African Labour Bulletin*, Ravan Press, Johannesburg.

Marks, S. 1970, *Reluctant Rebellion: The 1906-8 Disturbances in Natal*, Clarendon Press, Oxford.

Marks, S. 1986, *The Ambiguities of Dependence in South Africa: Class, Nationalism, and the State in Twentieth-Century Natal*, Johns Hopkins University Press, Baltimore and London.

Marks, S. and Rathbone, B. 1982, 'Introduction', in Marks, S. and Rathbone, B. (eds), *Industrialisation and Social Change in South Africa: African Class Formation, Culture, and Consciousness, 1870-1930*, Longman, London and New York.

Marks, S. and Trapido, S. 1981, 'Lord Milner and the South African State', in Bonner, P. (ed.) *Working Papers in Southern African Studies*, vol. 2, Ravan Press, Johannesburg.

Martin, W. G. 1990, 'The Making of an Industrial South Africa: Trade and Tariffs in the Interwar Period', *The International Journal of African Historical Studies*, 23, 2, 59-85.

Martin, W. G. 1991, 'Developmentalism: The Pernicious Illusion. A Response to Renfrew Christie's "Antiquated Industrialization"', *The International Journal of African Historical Studies*, 24, 3, 609-17.

Marx, A. W. 1992, *Lessons of Struggle: South African Internal Opposition, 1960-1990*, Oxford University Press, New York, Oxford.

Marx, A. W. 1998, *Making Race and Nation: A Comparison of South Africa, the United States and Brazil*, Cambridge University Press, Cambridge and New York.

Mattes, R., 1994, 'The Road to Democracy: From 2 February 1990 to 27 April 1994', in Reynolds, E. (ed.), *Election '94 South Africa: The Campaigns, Results and Future Prospects*, James Currey, London, David Philip, Cape Town and Johannesburg and St. Martin's Press, New York.

Mattes, R., Giliomee, H. and James, W. 1996, 'The Election in the Western Cape', in Johnson, R. W. and Schlemmer, L. (eds), *Launching Democracy in South Africa: The First Open Election, April 1994*, Yale University Press, New Haven, CT and London.

Mayekiso, M. 1992, 'Working Class Civil society: Why We Need It, and How To Get It', *African Communist*, second quarter, 33-40.

Mayer, P. and Mayer, I. 1971, *Townsmen or Tribesmen*, Oxford University Press, Cape Town (originally published 1961).

Maylam, P. 1986, *A History of The African People of South Africa: From the Early Iron Age to the 1970s*, Croom Helm, London and David Philip, Cape Town and Johannesburg.

Maylam, P. 1995, 'Explaining the Apartheid City: 20 Years of South African Urban Historiography', *Journal of Southern African Studies*, 21, 1, 19-38.

Mbeki, G. 1963, *The Peasants' Revolt*, Penguin, Harmondsworth.

Mbeki, G. 1996, *Sunset at Midday*, Nolwazi, Gauteng, South Africa.

Moll, T. 1990, 'From Booster to Brake? Apartheid and Economic Growth in Comparative Perspective', in Nattrass, N. and Ardington, E. (eds), *The Political Economy of South Africa*, Oxford University Press, Cape Town.

Moll, T. 1991, 'Did the Apartheid Economy "Fail"?', *Journal of Southern African Studies*, 17, 2, 271-91.

Molteno, F. 1977, 'The Historical Significance of the Bantustan Strategy', *Social Dynamics* 3, 2, 15-33.

Moodie, T. D. 1975, *The Rise of Afrikanerdom: Power, Apartheid and the Afrikaner Civil Religion*, University of California Press, Berkeley.

Moodie, T. D. (with Ndatshe, V.) 1994, *Going for Gold: Men, Mines, and Migration*, University of California Press, Berkeley and London.

Moore-Gilbert, B. 1997, *Postcolonial Theory*, Verso, London.

Morrell, R. 1986, 'Competition and Co-operation in Middelburg, 1900-1930', in Bonner, P., Delius, P. and Posel, D. (eds), *Apartheid's Genesis 1935-1962*, Ravan Press and Witwatersrand University Press, Johannesburg.

Morrell, R. 1988, 'The Disintegration of the Gold and Maize Alliance in South Africa in the 1920s', *The International Journal of African Historical Studies*, 21, 4, 619-635.

Morrell, R. (ed.) 1992, *White But Poor: Essays on the History of Poor Whites in Southern Africa 1880-1940*, University of South Africa, Pretoria and Pretoria/Sigma Press, Koedoespoort.

Morrell, R. 1998, 'Of Boys and Men: Masculinity and Gender in Southern African Studies', *Journal of Southern African Studies*, 24, 4, 605-30.

Morris, M. L. 1976, 'The Development of Capitalism in South African Agriculture: Class Struggle in the Countryside', *Economy and Society*, 5, 292-343.

Morris, M. L. 1977, 'State Intervention and the Agricultural Labour Supply Post-1948', in Wilson, F., Kooy, A. and Hendrie, D. (eds), *Farm Labour in South Africa*, David Philip, Cape Town.

Morris, M. 1991, 'State, Capital and Growth: The Political Economy of the National Question', in Gelb, S. (ed.), *South Africa's Economic Crisis*, David Philip, Cape Town and Zed books, London and New Jersey.

Morris, M. and Padayachee, V. 1989, 'Hegemonic Projects, Accumulation Strategies and State Reform Policy in South Africa', *Labour, Capital and Society*, 22, 1, 65-109.

Morris, M. and Hindson, D. 1992, 'South Africa: Political Violence, Reform and Reconstruction', *Review of African Political Economy*, 53, 43-59.

Morton, F. 1994a, 'Slavery and South African Historiography', in Eldredge, E. A. and Morton, F. (eds), *Slavery in South Africa: Captive Labour on the Dutch Frontier*, Westview Press, Boulder, CO, San Francisco and Oxford and Natal University Press, Pietermaritzburg.

Morton, F. 1994b, 'Captive Labour in the Western Transvaal After the Sand River Convention', in Eldredge, E. A. and Morton, F. (eds), *Slavery in South Africa: Captive Labour on the Dutch Frontier*, Westview Press, Boulder, CO, San Francisco and Oxford and Natal University Press, Pietermaritzburg.

Morton, F. 1994c, 'Slavery in South Africa', in Eldredge, E. A. and Morton, F. (eds), *Slavery in South Africa: Captive Labour on the Dutch Frontier*, Westview Press, Boulder, CO, San Francisco and Oxford and Natal University Press, Pietermaritzburg.

Moss, G. 1980, '"Total Strategy"', *Work in Progress* 11, 1-12.

Munslow, B. and FitzGerald, P. 1997, 'Search for a Development Strategy: The RDP and Beyond', in FitzGerald, P., Mc Lennan, A. and Munslow, B. (eds), *Managing Sustainable Development in South Africa*, Oxford University Press, Cape Town.

Murray, C. 1992, *Black Mountain: Land, Class and Power in the Eastern Orange Free State, 1880s to 1980s*, Edinburgh University Press, Edinburgh.

Murray, M. 1987, *South Africa: Time of Agony, Time of Destiny: The Upsurge of Popular Protest*, Verso, London.

Murray, M. 1994, *The Revolution Deferred: The Painful Birth of Post-Apartheid South Africa*, Verso, London and New York.

Nasson, B. 1990, 'The Unity Movement: Its Legacy in Historical Consciousness', *Radical History Review* 46/7, 189-211.

Nasson, B. 1991, 'Political Ideologies in the Western Cape', in Lodge, T. and Nasson, B., *All, Here and Now: Black Politics in South Africa in the 1980s*, Hurst and Company, London.

Nasson, B. 1999, *Uyadela wen'osulapho: Black Participation in the Anglo-Boer War*, Ravan Press, Randburg.

Nattrass, N. 1990, 'Economic Power and Profits in Post-war Manufacturing', in Nattrass, N. and Ardington, E. (eds), *The Political Economy of South Africa*, Oxford University Press, Cape Town.

Nattrass, N. 1991, 'Controversies About Capitalism and Apartheid in South Africa: An Economic Perspective', *Journal of Southern African Studies*, 17, 4, 654-77.

Nattrass, N. 1999, 'The Truth and Reconciliation Commission on Business and Apartheid: A Critical Evaluation', *African Affairs*, 98, 373-91.

Neumark, S. D. 1957, *Economic Influences on the South African Frontier: 1652-1836*, Stanford University Press, Stanford, CA.

Newbury, C. 1989, *The Diamond Ring: Business, Politics and Precious Stones in South Africa, 1867-1947*, Clarendon Press, Oxford.

Newton-King, S. 1994, 'The Enemy Within', in Worden, N. and Crais, C. (eds), *Breaking the Chains: Slavery and its Legacy in the Nineteenth-Century Cape Colony*, Witwatersrand University Press, Johannesburg.

Nolutshungu, S. 1983, *Changing South Africa: Political Considerations*, David Philip, Cape Town and Johannesburg.

Nordlinger, E. 1981, *On the Autonomy of the Democratic State*, Harvard University Press, Cambridge, MA.

Norval, A. 1996, *Deconstructing Apartheid Discourse*, Verso, London and New York.

No Sizwe (Neville Alexander) 1979, *One Azania, One Nation: The National Question in South Africa*, Zed Press, London.

Nzimande, B. 1986, 'Managers and the New Middle Class', *Transformation*, 1, 36-92.

Nzimande, B. 1990, 'Class, National Oppression and the African Petty Bourgeoisie: The Case of African Traders', in Cohen, R. (ed.), *Repression and Resistance: Insider Accounts of Apartheid*, Hans Zell, London.

Odendaal, A. 1984, *Vukani Bantu! The Beginnings of Black Protest Politics in South Africa to 1912*, David Philip, Cape Town and Johannesburg.

O'Donnell, G. and Schmitter, P. 1986, *Transitions from Authoritarian Rule: Tentative Conclusions About Uncertain Democracies*, Johns Hopkins University Press, Baltimore.

O'Dowd, M. C. 1978, 'The Stages of Economic Growth and the Future of South Africa', in Schlemmer, L. and Webster, D. (eds), *Change, Reform and Economic Growth in South Africa*, Ravan Press, Johannesburg.

O'Meara, D. 1979, 'The 1946 African Mine-Workers' Strike in the Political Economy of South Africa', in Bonner, P. L. (ed.), *Working Papers in Southern African Studies: Papers Presented in the A.S.I. African Studies Seminar, African Studies Institute*, University of the Witwatersrand, Johannesburg.

O'Meara, D. 1982, '"Muldergate" and the Politics of Afrikaner Nationalism', *Work in Progress* 22 (supplement).

O'Meara, D. 1983, *Volkskapitalisme: Class, Capital and Ideology in the Development of Afrikaner Nationalism, 1934-1948*, Ravan Press, Johannesburg.

O'Meara, D. 1996, *Forty Lost Years: The Apartheid State and the Politics of the National Party, 1948-1994*, Ravan Press, Johannesburg and Ohio University Press, Athens, OH.

Omer-Cooper, J. D. 1966/78, *The Zulu Aftermath: A Nineteenth-Century Revolution in Bantu Africa*, Longman, London.

Padayachee, V., Vawda, S. and Tichmann, P. 1985, *Indian Workers and Trade Unions in Durban: 1930-50*, Report 20, Institute for Social and Economic Research, University of Durban-Westville.

Parnell, S. and Mabin, A. 1995, 'Rethinking Urban South Africa', *Journal of Southern African Studies*, 21, 1, 39-61.

Parsons, N. 1995, 'Prelude to Difaquane in the Interior of Southern Africa c.1600-c.1822', in Hamilton, C. (ed.), *The Mfecane Aftermath: Reconstructive Debates in Southern African History*, Witwatersrand University Press, Johannesburg.

Peires, J. B. 1981, *The House of Phalo: A History of the Xhosa People in the Days of their Independence*, Ravan Press, Johannesburg.

Peires, J. B. 1988, 'The British and the Cape 1814-1834', in Elphick, R. and Giliomee, H. (eds), *The Shaping of South African Society, 1652-1840*, Wesleyan University Press, Middletown, CT.

Penn, N. 1989, 'Labour, Land and Livestock in the Western Cape in the Eighteenth Century: The Khoisan and the Colonists', in James, W. G. and Simons, M. (eds), *The Angry Divide: Social and Economic History of the Western Cape*, David Philip, Cape Town and Johannesburg.

Penn, N. 1999, *Rogues, Rebels and Runaways. Eighteenth-century Cape Characters*, David Philip, Cape Town.

Phillips, A. 1995, *The Politics of Presence*, Clarendon Press, Oxford.

Pinnock, D. 1987, 'Stone's Boys and the Making of a Cape Flats Mafia', in Bozzoli, B. (ed.), *Class, Community and Conflict: South African Perspectives*, Ravan Press, Johannesburg.

Posel, D. 1987, 'The Language of Domination, 1973-1983', in Marks, S. and Trapido, S. (eds), *The Politics of Race, Class and Nationalism in Twentieth-Century South Africa*, Longman, London and New York.

Posel, D. 1989, 'A "Battlefield of Perceptions": State Discourse on Political Violence, 1985-1998', in Cock, J. and Nathan, L. (eds), *Society at War: The Militarisation of South Africa*, St. Martin's Press, New York.

Posel, D. 1991, *The Making of Apartheid 1948-1961: Conflict and Compromise*, Clarendon Press, Oxford.

Posel, D. 1996, 'Modernity and Measurement: Further Thoughts on the Apartheid State', seminar paper (407), Institute for Advanced Social Research, University of Witwatersrand, Johannesburg.

Poulantzas, N. 1978, *Political Power and Social Classes*, Verso, London (originally published 1968).

Poulantzas, N. 1980, *State, Power, Socialism*, Verso, London (originally published 1978).

Pretorius, L. 1994, 'The Head of Government and Organised Business', in Schrire, R. (ed.), *Leadership in the Apartheid State: From Malan to De Klerk*, Oxford University Press, Cape Town.

Pretorius, H. and Jafta, L. 1997, '"A Branch Springs Out": African Initiated Churches', in Elphick, R. and Davenport, R. (eds), *Christianity in South Africa: A Political, Social, and Cultural History*, University of California Press, Berkeley.

Price, R. M. 1991, *The Apartheid State in Crisis: Political Transformation in South Africa*, Oxford University Press, New York and Oxford.

Przeworski, A. 1991, *Democracy and the Market: Political and Economic Reforms in Eastern Europe and Latin America*, Cambridge University Press, Cambridge.

Ray, M. 1998a, 'Chalk and Cheese? SASBO and COSATU', *South African Labour Bulletin*, 22, 1, 34-8.

Ray, M. 1998b, 'Will Bigger be Better? Forms of Union Organisation', *South African Labour Bulletin*, 22, 3, 65-70.

Rich, P. B. 1979, 'The Agrarian Counter-revolution in the Transvaal and the Origins of Segregation: 1902-1913', in Bonner, P. (ed.), *Working Papers in Southern African Studies*, African Studies Institute, University of the Witwatersrand, Johannesburg.

Rich, P. B. 1984, *White Power and the Liberal Conscience: Racial Segregation and South African Liberalism 1921-60*, Ravan Press, Johannesburg.

Rich, P. B. 1996, *State Power and Black Politics in South Africa, 1912-51*, Macmillan, Houndmills, Basingstoke.

Richardson, P. 1982, *Chinese Mine Labour in the Transvaal*, Macmillan, London and Basingstoke.

Richardson, P. 1986, 'The Natal Sugar Industry in the Nineteenth Century', in Beinart, W., Delius, P. and Trapido, S. (eds), *Putting a Plough to the Ground: Accumulation and Dispossession in Rural South Africa 1850-1930*, Ravan Press, Johannesburg.

Robinson, J. 1992, 'Power, Space and the City: Historical Reflections on Apartheid and Post-Apartheid Urban Orders', in Smith, D. M. (ed.), *The Apartheid City and Beyond: Urbanization and Social Change in South Africa*, Routledge, London and Witwatersrand University Press, Johannesburg.

Ross, R. 1983, *Cape of Torments: Slavery and Resistance in South Africa*, Routledge and Kegan Paul, London, Boston, Melbourne and Henley.

Ross, R. 1986, 'The Origins of Capitalist Agriculture in the Cape Colony: A Survey', in Beinart, W., Delius, P. and Trapido, S. (eds), *Putting a Plough to the Ground: Accumulation and Dispossession in Rural South Africa 1850-1930*, Ravan Press, Johannesburg.

Ross, R. 1989, 'Structure and Culture in Pre-Industrial Cape Town: A Survey of Knowledge and Ignorance', in James, W. G. and Simons, M. (eds), *The Angry Divide: Social and Economic History of the Western Cape*, David Philip, Cape Town and Johannesburg.

Ross, R. 1993, *Beyond the Pale: Essays on the History of Colonial South Africa*, Witwatersrand University Press, Johannesburg.

Ross, R. 1994, '"Rather Mental than Physical": Emancipations and the Cape Economy', in Worden, N. and Crais, C. (eds), *Breaking the Chains: Slavery and its Legacy in the Nineteenth-Century Cape Colony*, Witwatersrand University Press, Johannesburg.

Roth, M. 1986, 'Domination by Consent: Elections Under the Representation of Natives Act, 1937-1948', in Lodge, T. (ed.), *Resistance and Ideology in Settler Societies*, Ravan Press, Johannesburg.

Sapire, H. 1987, 'The Stay-Away of the Brakpan Location, 1944', in Bozzoli, B. (ed.), *Class, Community and Conflict: South African Perspectives*, Ravan Press, Johannesburg.

Sapire, H. 1992, 'Politics and Protest in Shack Settlements of the Pretoria-Witwatersrand-Vereeniging Region, South Africa, 1980-1990', *Journal of Southern African Studies*, 18, 3, 670-97.

Sapire, H. 1993, 'African Political Organisations in Brakpan in the 1950s', in Bonner, P., Delius, P. and Posel, D. (eds), *Apartheid's Genesis 1935-1962*, Ravan Press and Witwatersrand University Press, Johannesburg.

Sarakinsky, M. 1987, 'The Ideology and Politics of African Capitalists', *Africa Perspective*, 1, 3-4 (new series), 43-61.

Saul, J. S. and Gelb, S. 1981, *The Crisis in South Africa: Class Defense, Class Revolution*, Monthly Review Press, New York and London.

Saunders, C. 1981, 'Political Processes in the Southern African Frontier Zones', in Lamar, H. and Thompson, L. (eds), *The Frontier in History: North America and Southern Africa Compared*, Yale University Press, New Haven, CT and London.

Saunders, C. 1988, *The Making of the South African Past: Major Historians on Race and Class*, David Philip, Cape Town and Johannesburg.

Schutte, G. 1979/80, 'Rulers and Ruled in the Cape Colony', in Elphick, R. and Giliomee, H. (eds), *The Shaping of South African Society, 1652-1820*, Longman, Cape Town and London.

Seegers, A. 1994, 'The Head of Government and the Executive', in Schrire, R. (ed.), *Leadership in the Apartheid State: From Malan to De Klerk*, Oxford University Press, Cape Town.

Seekings, J. 1992, 'Civic Organisations in South African Townships', *South African Review*, 6, South African Research Service and Ravan Press, Johannesburg, 216-38.

Seekings, J. 1993, *Heroes or Villains? Youth Politics in the 1980s*, Ravan Press, Johannesburg.

Seidman, A. and Seidman, N. 1978, *South Africa and U.S. Multinational Corporations*, Lawrence Hill and Company, Westport, CT.

Shaw, M. 1997, 'South Africa: Crime in Transition', in Gutteridge, W. and Spence, J. E. (eds), *Violence in Southern Africa*, Frank Cass, London and Portland, OR.

Shell, R. 1994, *Children of Bondage: A Social History of the Slave Society at the Cape of Good Hope, 1652-1838*, Witwatersrand University Press, Johannesburg.

Shell, R. 1997, 'Between Christ and Mohammed: Conversion, Slavery and Gender in the Urban Western Cape', in Elphick, R. and Davenport, R. (eds), *Christianity in South Africa: A Political, Social, and Cultural History*, University of California Press, Berkeley.

Shillington, K. 1985, *The Colonisation of the Southern Tswana 1870-1900*, Ravan Press, Johannesburg.

Simson, H. 1973, 'Fascism in South Africa', *African Review*, 3, 3, 423-51.

Simson, H. 1974, 'The Myth of the White Working Class in South Africa', *African Affairs*, 4, 2, 189-203.

Sitas, A. 1992, 'The Making of the "Comrades" Movement in Natal, 1985-91', *Journal of Southern African Studies*, 18, 3, 629-41.

Skocpol, T. 1985, 'Bringing the State Back In: Strategies of Analysis in Current Research', in Evans, P. B., Rieschmeyer, D. and Skocpol, T., *Bringing the State Back In*, Cambridge University Press, Cambridge.

Slater, H. 1980, 'The Changing Pattern of Economic Relationships in Rural Natal, 1838-1914', in Marks, S. and Atmore, A. (eds), *Economy and Society in Pre-Industrial South Africa*, Longman, London.

Slovo, J. 1973, 'Southern Africa: Problems of Armed Struggle', *Socialist Register*, 319-40.

Slovo, J. 1976, 'South Africa – No Middle Road', in Davidson, B., Slovo, J. and Wilkinson, A. (eds), *Southern Africa: The New Politics of Revolution*, Penguin, London.

Smith, A. 1986, *The Ethnic Origins of Nations*, Blackwell, Oxford.

Smith, K. 1988, *The Changing Past: Trends in South African Historical Writing*, Ohio University Press, Athens, OH.

Southall, R. 1982, *South Africa's Transkei: The Political Economy of an 'Independent' Bantustan*, Heinemann, London.

Southall, R. 1998, 'The Centralization and Fragmentation of South Africa's Dominant Party System', *African Affairs*, 97, 443-69.

Sparks, A. 1996, *Tomorrow is Another Country: The Inside Story of South Africa's Negotiated Revolution*, Mandarin, London.

Stadler, A. 1979, 'Birds in the Cornfields: Squatter Movements in Johannesburg, 1944-1947', in Bozzoli, B. (ed.), *Labour, Townships and Protest: Studies in the Social History of the Witwatersrand*, Ravan Press, Johannesburg.

Streek, B. 1984, 'Disunity through the Bantustans', in South African Research Service (ed.), *South African Review*, 2, Ravan Press, Johannesburg.

Stultz, N. M. 1974, *Afrikaner Politics in South Africa*, University of California Press, Berkeley.

Swan, M. 1985, *Gandhi: The South African Experience*, Ravan Press, Johannesburg.

Swanson, M. W. 1976, '"The Durban System": Roots of Urban Apartheid in Colonial Natal', *African Studies*, 35, 3-4, 159-76.

Swanson, M. W. 1977, 'The Sanitation Syndrome: Bubonic Plague and Urban Native Policy in the Cape Colony, 1900-1909', *Journal of African History*, 18, 3, 387-410.

Swanson, M. W. 1983, '"The Asiatic Menace": Creating Segregation in Durban, 1870-1900', *International Journal of African Historical Studies*, 16, 3, 401-21.

Swilling, M. 1992, 'Socialism, Democracy and Civil Society: The Case for Associational Socialism', *Theoria*, 79, 75-82.

Swilling, M. and Phillips, M. 1989a, 'The Emergency State: Its Structure, Power and Limits', in Moss, G. and Obery, I. (eds), *South African Review*, 5, Hans Zell Publishers, London, Munich and New York.

Swilling, M. and Phillips, M. 1989b, 'State Power in the 1980s: From "Total Strategy" to "Counter-Revolutionary Warfare"', in Cock, J. and Nathan, L. (eds), *Society at War: The Militarisation of South Africa*, St. Martin's Press, New York.

Thompson, L. 1985, *The Political Mythology of* Apartheid, Yale University Press, New Haven, CT and London.

Thompson, L. 1995, *A History of South Africa: Revised Edition*, Yale University Press, New Haven and London.

Todes, A., Watson, V. and Wilkinson, P. 1989, 'Local Government Restructuring in Greater Cape Town', in James, W. G. and Simons, M. (eds), *The Angry Divide: Social and Economic History of the Western Cape*, David Philip, Cape Town and Johannesburg.

Trapido, S. 1968, 'African Divisional Politics in the Cape Colony, 1884 to 1910', *Journal of African History*, 9, 1, 79-98.

Trapido, S. 1971, 'South Africa in a Comparative Study of Industrialization', *The Journal of Development Studies*, 7, 3, 309-20.

Trapido, S. 1978, 'Landlord and Tenant in a Colonial Economy: The Transvaal 1880-1910', *Journal of Southern African Studies*, 5, 26-58.

Trapido, S. 1980a, '"The Friends of the Natives": Merchants, Peasants and the Political and Ideological Structure of Liberalism in the Cape, 1854-1910', in Marks, S. and Atmore, A. (eds), *Economy and Society in Pre-Industrial South Africa*, Longman, London.

Trapido, S. 1980b, 'Reflections on Land, Office and Wealth in the South African Republic, 1850-1900', in Marks, S. and Atmore, A. (eds), *Economy and Society in Pre-Industrial South Africa*, Longman, London.

Trapido, S. 1986, 'Putting a Plough to the Ground: A History of Tenant Production on the Vereeniging Estates, 1896-1920', in Beinart, W., Delius, P. and Trapido, S. (eds), *Putting a Plough to the Ground: Accumulation and Dispossession in Rural South Africa 1850-1930*, Ravan Press, Johannesburg.

Truth and Reconciliation Commission 1998, *Final Report*.

Turrell, R. C. 1987, *Capital and Labour on the Kimberley Diamond Fields 1871-1890*, Cambridge University Press, Cambridge, London and New York.

Vail, L. 1989, 'Introduction', in Vail, L. (ed.), *The Creation of Tribalism in Southern Africa*, James Currey, London and University of California Press, Berkeley.

Van der Vliet, V. 1991, 'Traditional Husbands, Modern Wives? Constructing Marriages in a South African Township', in Spiegel, A. D. and McAllister, P. A. (eds), *Tradition and Transition in Southern Africa*, Transaction Publishers, New Brunswick, NY and London.

Van der Westhuizen, G. 1994, 'The Liberal Party of South Africa, 1953-1968', in Liebenberg, I., Lortan, F., Nel, B. and Van der Westhuizen, G. (eds), *The Long March: The Story of the Struggle for Liberation in South Africa*, Haum, Pretoria.

Van Diepen, M. (ed.) 1988, *The National Question in South Africa*, Zed books, London.

Van Duin, P. 1989, 'Artisans and Trade Unions in the Cape Town Building Industry, 1900-1924', in James, W. G. and Simons, M. (eds), *The Angry Divide: Social and Economic History of the Western Cape*, David Philip, Cape Town and Johannesburg.

Van Helten, J.-J. 1982, 'Empire and High Finance: South Africa and the International Gold Standard 1890-1914', *Journal of African History*, 23, 529-48.

Van Onselen, C. 1980, *Chibaro: African Mine Labour in Southern Rhodesia 1900-1933*, Ravan Press, Johannesburg (originally published by Pluto Press, 1976).

Van Onselen, C. 1982a, *Studies in the Social and Economic History of the Witwatersrand 1886-1914: 1 New Babylon*, Ravan Press, Johannesburg.

Van Onselen, C. 1982b, *Studies in the Social and Economic History of the Witwatersrand 1886-1914: 2 New Nineveh*, Ravan Press, Johannesburg.

Van Onselen, C. 1990, 'Race and Class in the South African Countryside: Cultural Osmosis and Social Relations in the Sharecropping Economy of the South-Western Transvaal, 1900-1950', *The American Historical Review*, 95, 1, 99-123.

Van Onselen, C. 1996, *The Seed is Mine: The Life of Kas Maine, A South African Sharecropper 1894-1985*, David Philip, Cape Town.

Van Tonder, D. 1993, '"First Win the War, Then Clear the Slums": The Genesis of the Western Areas Removal Scheme, 1940-1949', in Bonner, P., Delius, P. and Posel, D. (eds), *Apartheid's Genesis 1935-1962*, Ravan Press and Witwatersrand University Press, Johannesburg.

Van Zyl Slabbert, F. 1992, *The Quest for Democracy: South Africa in Transition*, Penguin Books, London.

Waldmeir, P. 1997, *Anatomy of a Miracle: The End of Apartheid and the Birth of the New South Africa*, Penguin Books, London.

Walker, C. 1996, 'Reconstructing Tradition: Women and Land Reform', in Rich, P. B. (ed.), *Reaction and Renewal in South Africa*, Macmillan, Basingstoke and St. Martin's Press, New York.

Walshe, P. 1987, *The Rise of African Nationalism in South Africa*, A. D. Donker, Cape Town (originally published 1970).

Webster, D. 1991, 'Abafazi Bathonga Bafihlakala: Ethnicity and Gender in a KwaZulu Border Community', in Spiegel, A. D. and McAllister, P. A. (eds), *Tradition and Transition in Southern Africa*, Transaction Publishers, New Brunswick, NY and London.

Webster, E. (ed.) 1978, *Essays in Southern African Labour History*, Ravan Press, Johannesburg.

Webster, E. 1985, *Cast in a Racial Mould: Labour Process and Trade Unionism in the Foundries*, Ravan Press, Johannesburg.

Webster, E. 1988, 'The Rise of Social Movement Unionism: The Two Faces of the Black Trade Union Movement in South Africa', in Frankel, P., Pines, N. and Swilling, M. (eds), *State, Resistance and Change in South Africa*, Croom Helm, London, New York and Sydney.

Wells, J. 1983, '"The Day the Town Stood Still": Women in Resistance in Potchefstroom 1912-1930', in Bozzoli, B. (ed.), *Town and Countryside in the Transvaal: Capitalist Penetration and Popular Response*, Ravan Press, Johannesburg.

Wells, J. 1986, 'The War of Degradation: Black Women's Struggle against Orange Free State Pass Laws, 1913', in Crummey, D. (ed.), *Banditry, Rebellion and Social Protest in Africa*, James Currey, London.

Welsh, D. 1971, *The Roots of Segregation: Native Policy in Colonial Natal, 1845-1910*, Oxford University Press, Cape Town, London and New York.

Welsh, D. 1994, 'The Executive and the African Population: 1948 to the Present', in Schrire, R. (ed.), *Leadership in the Apartheid State: From Malan to De Klerk*, Oxford University Press, Cape Town.

Wentzel, J. 1995, *The Liberal Slideaway*, South African Institute of Race Relations, Johannesburg.

West, M. 1988, 'Confusing Categories: Population Groups, National States and Citizenship', in Boonzaier, E. and Sharp, J. (eds), *South African Keywords: The Uses and Abuses of Political Concepts*, David Philip, Cape Town and Johannesburg.

Whiteford, A. and van Seventer, D. E. 1999, *Winners and Losers: South Africa's Changing Income Distribution in the 1990s*, Wharton Economic Forecasting Associates, Menlo Park and Pretoria.

Wilkinson, P. 1983, 'Providing "Adequate Shelter": The South African State and the Resolution of the African Urban Housing Crisis, 1948-1954', in Hindson, D. C. (ed.), *Working Papers in Southern African Studies*, vol. 3, Ravan Press, Johannesburg.

Wilson, M. 1971/78, 'The Growth of Peasant Communities', in Wilson, M. and Thompson, L. (eds), *The Oxford History of South Africa*, vol. 2: *South Africa 1870-1960*, Clarendon Press, Oxford.

Witz, L. 1987, 'A Case of Schizophrenia: The Rise and Fall of the Independent Labour Party', in Bozzoli, B. (ed.), *Class, Community and Conflict: South African Perspectives*, Ravan Press, Johannesburg.

Wolpe, H. 1970, 'Industrialism and Race in South Africa', in Zubaida, S. (ed.), *Race and Racialism*, Tavistock, London.

Wolpe, H 1972, 'Capitalism and Cheap Labour in South Africa: From Segregation to Apartheid', in Wolpe, H. (ed.), *The Articulation of Modes of Production: Essays from* Economy and Society, Routledge and Kegan Paul, London, Boston and Henley.

Wolpe, H. 1977, 'The Changing Class Structure in South Africa: The African Petit Bourgeoisie', in Zarembka, P. (ed.), *Research in Political Economy*, vol. 1: *An Annual Compilation of Research*, JAI Press, Greenwich, CT.

Wolpe, H. 1980, 'Towards an Analysis of the South African State', *International Journal of the Sociology of Law*, 8, 339-421.

Wolpe, H. 1988, *Race, Class and the Apartheid State*, James Currey, London, OAU Inter-African Cultural Fund, Addis Ababa and Unesco Press, Paris.

Worger, W. 1987, *South Africa's City of Diamonds: Mine Workers and Monopoly Capitalism in Kimberley, 1867-1895*, Yale University Press, New Haven, CT and London.

Yudelman, D. 1984, *The Emergence of Modern South Africa: State, Capital, and the Incorporation of Organized Labour on the South African Gold Fields, 1902-1939*, David Philip, Cape Town and Johannesburg.

Yudelman, D. 1987, 'State and Capital in Contemporary South Africa', in Butler, J., Elphick, R. and Welsh, D. (eds), *Democratic Liberalism in South Africa: Its History and Prospect*, Wesleyan University Press, Middletown, CT and David Philip, Cape Town.

Index